# Shakespeare
*The Critical Complex*

Series Editors

**Stephen Orgel** and **Sean Keilen**
*Stanford University*

# A GARLAND SERIES

# Series Contents

# Shakespeare's Poems

Edited with an introduction by

**Stephen Orgel** and **Sean Keilen**
*Stanford University*

GARLAND PUBLISHING, INC.
A MEMBER OF THE TAYLOR & FRANCIS GROUP
*New York & London*
*1999*

**Library of Congress Cataloging-in-Publication Data**

Shakespeare's poems / edited with an introduction by Stephen Orgel,
Sean Keilen.
     p.   cm. — (Shakespeare, the critical complex ; 4)
     Includes bibliographical references.
     ISBN 0-8153-2964-4 (alk. paper)
     1. Shakespeare, William, 1564–1616—Poetic works. 2.
Shakespeare, William, 1564–1616. Rape of Lucrece. 3. Narrative
poetry, English—History and criticism. 4. Shakespeare, William,
1564–1616. Sonnets. 5. Sonnets, English—History and criticism. 6.
Lucretia—In literature. I. Orgel, Stephen. II. Keilen, Sean. III.
Series.

PR2984.S53 1999
821'.3—dc21                                99-049783

Printed on acid-free, 250-year-life paper
Manufactured in the United States of America

# Contents

# Introduction

The First Folio of Shakespeare's works includes only works for the theater. The poet's career, therefore, under the determining influence of that monumental volume, has been viewed primarily as a life in the theater. But Shakespeare was serious about being a narrative and lyric poet as well, and eagerly courted some of the most influential patrons of poetry in the age. The contexts discussed here range from questions of form to cultural and political issues, as well as to the surprisingly belated history and practice of editing Shakespeare's poems.

Colin Burrow poses the question directly, asking why we do not consider Shakespeare essentially and primarily as a poet, and treat the non-dramatic poems as central to his oeuvre. Jonathan Bate historicizes the question, locating the poetry in relation to the classical lyric tradition and to the reception of Shakespeare's poems in his own time. Bate turns to sixteenth-century theorists of the relation of poetry to its antecedents to revise and complicate modern notions of influence and literary paternity.

A group of essays on the sonnets place this perennially open-ended sequence in a variety of historical contexts. Thomas Greene, invoking Renaissance concepts of husbandry and domestic economy, finds a grand elegiac tone informing the lyric structuring of the poet's enterprise and career. Margreta de Grazia, Randall McLeod, Katherine Duncan-Jones and Peter Stallybrass interrogate the textual history of the sonnets. De Grazia and Stallybrass show how the cultural imperatives of later ages inform ostensibly historicized treatments of the text — John Benson's emendation, in the 1640 *Poems*, of masculine to feminine pronouns in the love sonnets, for example, or Wordsworth's much broader claim that in the sonnets Shakespeare unlocked his heart. Katherine Duncan-Jones deconstructs traditional views of the circumstances surrounding the publication of the 1609 sonnets, observing that assumptions about piracy or even unauthorized printing are unfounded, and have significantly affected the story we believe these poems tell. Randall McLeod shows how the very effort to establish a reliable text of the sonnets opens rather than forecloses interpretive possibility.

In a characteristically sweeping and provocative essay, Joel Fineman essentially credits Shakespeare's sonnets with the invention not only of modern subjectivity, but of modern notions of sexuality as well — the transition from the beloved but unobtainable youth to the unloved but passionately desired woman is a transition from past to present, Renaissance to modern. Heather Dubrow, in contrast, argues for an anti-narrative strategy in the sequence, observing that both the uncertain order of the poems and the radical indeterminacy of their addressees offer us instead a far less assured and closed body of poetry, not at all what is implied by calling it a sequence. Dubrow pursues the argument in a second essay that shows Shakespeare deliberately avoiding the narrative and dramatic modes in favor of a tentative and contingent structure of a kind that is, in fact, traditionally an emotional characteristic of the sonnet as a form. Thomas Greene and Edward Snow round out this section with two quite different readings of individual sonnets, one moving inward, the other outward. Greene argues against the modernization of sonnet 129, urging us to regard the remote text as genuinely remote, to respect and come to terms with its otherness. Snow reintegrates the sonnets with the plays by reading sonnet 138 as elucidating a characteristic moment of high emotion in Shakespearean drama, epitomized in *Othello* and *Antony and Cleopatra*.

Turning to the narrative poems, William Empson's classic essay invokes a broadly biographical matrix, viewing the poems through Shakespeare's social origins, education, professional career, relations with patrons and with other poets. Catherine Belsey reads *Venus and Adonis* in a social and sociological context, as marking a critical moment in the cultural history of love. Four essays on *The Rape of Lucrece* address the difficulties of finding an adequate critical stance from which to view the poem. Katharine Eisaman Maus argues for the centrality of elements that have traditionally been seen as marginal: the poem's tropes, extended ekphrases, rhetorical setpieces. Jane Newman addresses the question of poetic sources, showing how the Ovidian story of the rape of Philomel is both evoked and disavowed, and how at the margins of Shakespeare's narrative is found its ideological center. Richard Lanham is also concerned with Shakespeare's relation to the classics, but the relationship in this case is seen as primarily rhetorical, as a dialectic between the tragic Ovidian Philomel and the political exemplum as narrated by Livy. Nancy Vickers places the poem in the Renaissance blazon tradition, in which the woman becomes an ideal commodity; and the rape thereby becomes, in effect, the logical consequence of Shakespeare's rhetorical strategy.

As the essays in this volume present it, Shakespeare's poetry is not an adjunct to his drama, but a significant chapter in the history of English poetry, the work of a poet fully conversant with the lyric and epic tradition, and one with a unique lyric and narrative sensibility.

# Life and Work in Shakespeare's Poems

COLIN BURROW

*Gonville and Caius College, Cambridge*

IN BORGES'S HAUNTING TALE CALLED 'Shakespeare's Memory' a Shakespearean scholar meets a man called Thorpe (a name which we will meet again later on) who claims to possess Shakespeare's memory, and who offers to pass it on to our hero. The scholar, a thorough German, thinks this will enable him to write his master work: a biography of Shakespeare, written with true inside know-ledge, and so he accepts the offer of Shakespeare's memory. At first nothing happens; then odd sounds and half-glimpses of something almost forgotten begin to spring on him at unexpected moments. These sensual recollections become more frequent until they form a pervasive sense of guilt at some unremembered act. He finds, though, that Shakespeare's memory can tell him nothing specific about the content of Shakespeare's mental processes and nothing at all about Shakespeare's works. Despite this he is gradually dominated by his parasitic memory, until it begins to swamp his own recollec-tions. Eventually, fearing madness, he dials a telephone number at random, and passes on Shakespeare's memory to its next, anonymous, host.[1]

Surely this is a tale with a moral for anyone attempting to write about Shakespeare's life and works: it suggests that the experience of being Shakespeare is irretrievable even to someone who possesses his memory.

---

[1] Jorge Luis Borges, *Obras Completas 1975–1985* (Buenos Aires, 1989), pp. 393–9. The tale contains what is either a delicious typo or an engaging deliberate Borgesian error: the scholar writes an article to prove that Sonnet 117 was written in the Armada year of 1588, and then discovers that Samuel Butler had suggested the same date for the poem in 1899. This clearly must be a reference to Sonnet 107 rather than 117, and suggests that one model for Borges' hero was the indefatigable Leslie Hotson, who dates 107 to 1588 (as Butler had done) in 'The Mortall Moone', repr. in *Shakespeare's Sonnets Dated and Other Essays* (London, 1949), pp. 4–21.

*Proceedings of the British Academy*, **97** 15–50. © The British Academy 1998.
Read at the Academy 21 October 1997.

Few of us, if we were honest about it, would wish to re-enact Shakespeare's life — to inhabit the anxieties of a first performance, or the even greater anxiety of the desperate last-minute revisions which might have occupied the night before a first performance, to feel the chill of touring performances outside, or to relive the possible infidelities of his love life. Fortunately my aim is not to retrieve Shakespeare's life and mind from his works. I have slightly rearranged the brief of the Chatterton lecture, and have decided not to discuss 'the life and works of a dead English poet', as the lecturer is supposed to, but to talk about life and work *in* Shakespeare's poems instead. This may keep at bay the insanity suffered by Borges's hero, as well as the pandemic of madness which strikes those who have attempted in real life to consider Shakespeare's poems as the key to his mind. Poor Delia Bacon was the first to drive herself into madness and destitution in her attempts to prove that Francis Bacon wrote Shakespeare, but her life has its fictional parallel in the zealous efforts of the hero of Oscar Wilde's 'The Portrait of Mr W. H.' to prove that the Sonnets were addressed to a boy player called Willie Hughes.[2] One of the most entertaining pieces of biographical madness is G. W. Phillips's *Sunlight in Shakespeare's Sonnets*,[3] which proves (how could so many readers have missed it?) that the Sonnets tell how Shakespeare was seduced by an aristocratic woman, whose illegitimate son by Shakespeare then went on to cuckold his father with Anne Hathaway. With sunlight (and what a terrible pun it is) like that who needs darkness? But there are darker biographical productions: the ingenious Martin Green infers from the lines 'Why didst thou promise such a beauteous day, I And make me travel forth without my cloak' (34. 1–2)[4] that Shakespeare had forgotten to wear a condom, which his father, a glover, sold under the counter, and so had contracted venereal disease from the young man. Green is undeterred by the facts that condoms are not recorded in England before 1660 and were never called 'cloaks'.[5] The end of this lecture will make a case for keeping something like life in play while reading Shakespeare's Sonnets, but it will be a slightly less sickly version of life.

The chief aim of this lecture is to think about the Sonnets and the narrative poems as a group, and to relate them to some of the material realities from

---

[2] See S. Schoenbaum, *Shakespeare's Lives*, 2nd edn. (Oxford, 1991), pp. 385–94.
[3] (London, 1935).
[4] All quotations from the non-dramatic verse will be my own modernisations of the earliest quartos.
[5] Martin Green, *The Labyrinth of Shakespeare's Sonnets: An Examination of Sexual Elements in Shakespeare's Language* (London, 1974), pp. 16–24. Green speculates further (p. 24) that 'Conceivably, his observation as a child of the traffic in condoms which might have formed a significant portion of his father's business, and the resultant exposure to him of the horrors of venereal disease, may have imbued in Shakespeare both that fascination with, and revulsion over, sexual activities, which is so characteristic a feature of his works.' It is a great shame that 'conceivably' there is not a joke.

which they grew. I hope in the process to go some way towards explaining why scholars have worried for so long about the life that lies behind those enigmatic works, the Sonnets. This does not sound a radical aim. But actually Shakespeare's poems and Sonnets have rarely been considered together as a group and are even more rarely treated as a major part of Shakespeare's works. Indeed the poems and Sonnets tend to moulder at the back of collected editions of his work, and lurk unobtrusively in multiple volume editions: they are found in volume twenty of twenty one in the Boswell Variorum, in volume ten of ten in Malone, or, more remarkably, in volume seven of Rowe's six volume edition. The Sonnets first appeared in 1609, towards the end of Shakespeare's theatrical career, which might give some chronological basis to this positioning; but, if recent and rigorous stylometric tests are to be believed, several of the Sonnets are very likely to have been composed at the start of Shakespeare's career, and the whole sequence should be thought of as something approaching Shakespeare's life's work, receiving touches of the poet's pen until shortly before its publication.[6] The first printed work to bear Shakespeare's name was *Venus and Adonis* (1593). The second was *Lucrece* (1594). These facts give strong grounds for putting the poems at the front of our thinking about Shakespeare, and perhaps even at the front of collected editions of his works. It also should prompt us to ask why we do not think of Shakespeare as primarily a non-dramatic poet.

One reason for this is, of course, that he wrote quite a few pretty good plays. But there are other reasons. The narrative poems were extremely successful in their time. Eight editions of *Lucrece* and sixteen of *Venus and Adonis* survive from between 1593 and 1640 (and it is quite possible that other editions were printed and then eagerly read to pieces). *Venus and Adonis* was Shakespeare's most popular printed work. The very success of the narrative poems, oddly, made them peripheral to the Shakespearean canon: since they remained market-able commodities through the seventeenth century printers jealously guarded their right to reprint the copy. This may well explain why there was appar-ently no serious effort to include the poems in the first Folio of 1623. In the eighteenth-century editions which until very recently provided the models of editorial method and disposition the poems will very often be found in the supplementary volumes which contain *dubia* and *spuria*, somewhere among *Edward III* and *A Yorkshire Tragedy*. This is usually thought to be a conse-quence of the low critical esteem which the poems enjoyed. But it may be one of the more unlikely by-products of the copyright act of 1710. This act is chiefly famous for having granted, for the first time in English law, limited rights to authors to control and benefit from the printing of their works. But the same act also provided that printers who already owned the copyright on existing works

---

[6] See A. Kent Hieatt, Charles W. Hieatt, and Anne Lake Prescott, 'When did Shakespeare Write *Sonnets* 1609?', *Studies in Philology*, 88 (1991), 69–109.

would retain it for twenty-one years. This meant that if a printer could rapidly find and print old works to which no-one else had a valid claim, he might expect to enjoy the benefit of copyright for the majority of his working life.[7] This unique legal position may well have been the precipitating force behind a scramble for Shakespeare's poems at the end of the first decade of the eighteenth century. In 1709 Bernard Lintott produced a reprint of the narrative poems and the first quarto of Shakespeare's Sonnets; in 1710 Edmund Curll and E. Sanger printed a volume of the poems, edited by the shadowy George Gildon[8] which was designed to look like the seventh volume of Rowe's collected edition of the theatrical works. For copyright purposes it seems likely that Gildon's volume could count as a different work from Lintott's, since it presents a version of John Benson's re-ordered and partly bowdlerised version of the Sonnets, in which individual poems are combined together and given titles of a kind that makes them appear to resemble Cavalier epistles to a mistress. The dates at which Lintott's and Curll's volumes appeared are extremely significant, however, both for their proximity to each other and for their proximity to the 1710 copyright act.[9] It is not clear who, if anyone, owned the copyright to the Sonnets before this date, since their first publisher, Thomas Thorpe, is not known to have assigned it to anyone else; but it does appear from the subsequent printing history of the poems and Sonnets that Curll and Sanger's rights to the copy of Benson's reordered and re-titled version were respected.[10] There were two issues of

---

[7]  See Marjorie Plant, *The English Book Trade: An Economic History of the Making and Sale of Books* (London, 1965), pp. 117–18 and Terry Belanger, 'Tonson, Wellington and the Shakespeare Copyrights', in R. W. Hunt, I. G. Phillips, and R. J. Roberts (eds.), *Studies in the Book Trade in Honour of Graham Pollard*, Oxford Bibliographical Society Publications, NS 18 (Oxford, 1975), pp. 195–209. Also of note is Giles E. Dawson, 'The Copyright of Shakespeare's Dramatic Works', in Charles T. Prouty (ed.), *Studies in Honour of A. H. R. Fairchild*, University of Missouri Studies, 21 No. 1 (Columbia, 1946), pp. 12–35.

[8]  Gildon's name appears attached to the introduction in few extant copies (the remainder are signed 'S. N.'), but later editors attribute the work to him: so Thomas Evans, *Poems Written by Mr William Shakespeare* (London, n.d. [1775]), fol. ¶2[a] refers to 'Mr Gildon'. On Gildon see R. M. Alden, 'The 1710 and 1714 Texts of Shakespeare's Poems', *Modern Language Notes*, 31 (1916), 268–74. It is unclear whether or not Gildon was responsible for the significant revisions to the 1714 edition: Tonson paid £28 7s. to John Hughes, the editor of Spenser, in connection with the 1714 edition of Rowe, on which see Kathleen M. Lynch, *Jacob Tonson, Kit-Kat Publisher* (Knoxville, 1971), p. 131.

[9]  The act was passed in 1709, but its provisions took effect from 1 April 1710. See Plant, op. cit., p. 118.

[10]  It is possible that Humphrey Moseley acquired the copyright to Benson's text, or at least the unsold copies of it, in around 1655, since 'Poems Written by Mr William Shakespeare Gent.' figures in a catalogue of books for sale bound with the second part of James Howell's *Dodona's Grove*, which Moseley printed in 1650. See Harry Farr, 'Notes on Shakespeare's Printers and Publishers, with Special Reference to the Poems and *Hamlet*', *The Library*, 4th Series 3 (1923), 252. For a defence of Benson's methods, see Margreta de Grazia, 'The Scandal of Shakespeare's Sonnets', *Shakespeare Survey*, 46 (1993), 35–49, and Josephine Waters Bennett, 'Benson's Alleged Piracy of Shake-speares Sonnets and some of Jonson's Works', *Studies in Bibliography*, 21 (1968), 235–48.

Rowe's Shakespeare in 1714, one of which is said to be in eight volumes and is printed for that great collector of Shakespearean copyrights Jacob Tonson; the other includes the poems, and is said to be in nine volumes. The ninth volume is 'Printed by J. Darby . . . for E. Curll, K. Sanger and J. Pemberton. Sold by J. Tonson in the Strand'. The most probable explanation for the existence of these different versions is that by 1714 Tonson accepted *de facto* Curll and Sanger's ownership of the copyright of the poems and Sonnets, and came to some reciprocal arrangement with them as to the printing and selling of copies.

Subsequent high-profile editions of Shakespeare continued this tradition of shuffling the poems into supplements. When Pope's edition of the dramatic works appeared in 1725 it too was rapidly augmented by a supplementary volume of the poems, edited this time by George Sewell;[11] the presence of Pemberton's name on the title page of this volume marks a connection with the earlier consortium of printers. Title pages are not easy to interpret, but this evidence may indicate that a collected edition of Shakespeare's plays and poems could not be produced in the early eighteenth century without the collaboration of Curll, Sanger, or Pemberton. For copyright reasons as much as any other the non-dramatic verse had to shiver in a supplementary volume (and certainly by 1775 printers were recognising public demand for the poetical verse).[12] Tonson, otherwise an energetic pursuer of Shakespearean copyrights, simply failed to obtain the copyright of these works.

This may appear to be no more than bibliographical archaeology, but archaeology can sometimes reveal the foundations of our present attitudes. The majority of modern editions unthinkingly follow the precedent thus accidentally established. This is even true of Edmund Malone's revolutionary edition of the poems and Sonnets in 1780.[13] Malone returned the Sonnets to the order in which they appeared in 1609, and was the first to suggest that the

---

[11] The 1725 edition refers on its title page to 'Mr Shakespeare's miscellany poems'. Both Gildon and Sewell had been involved in producing miscellany poems: Gildon's 'Miscellany Poems upon various occasions' appeared in 1692; Sewell wrote the preface for Addison's 'Miscellanies in Verse and Prose' in 1725. They evidently thought that Shakespeare's poems could be presented to readers as contributions to this vogue. A reprint of 1728 of Sewell's edition is said to be printed for Tonson, who again appears to be manoeuvring for a stake in the poems.

[12] The 'Advertisement' to Thomas Evans's edition of *Poems Written by Mr William Shakespeare* (London, n.d. [1775]) states that 'several editions of the Poems of Shakespeare have been printed, but the eager desire to be possessed of the complete works of the noblest of poets, have rendered them scarce'.

[13] For a more sceptical account of Malone, see Margreta de Grazia, *Shakespeare Verbatim: The Reproduction of Authenticity and the 1790 Apparatus* (Oxford, 1991). De Grazia tells a convincing tale of how Malone transforms Shakespeare's works into historical documents, and how he denigrates the work of printers and players in order to elevate both Shakespeare's originary genius and his own editorial brilliance, but is less generous in her treatment of Malone than anyone who has attempted to edit the Sonnets must be.

first 126 of the Sonnets were addressed to a young man and that the remainder were directed to a mistress.[14] Malone's edition, despite its originality of editorial content, shows remarkable continuity with its predecessors: it is another supplementary volume, called a *Supplement to the Edition of Shakespeare's Plays Published in 1778 by Samuel Johnson and George Steevens*, in which the inferior labour of editing the non-dramatic verse was shuffled off onto a younger and less well-known man. The poems appeared annexed in this way partly because Steevens hated them: he famously stated that 'the strongest act of Parliament that could be framed, would fail to compel readers into their service'.[15] It is also more than likely that the analogy with Gildon and Sewell's volumes helped to determine the volume's marginal relation to the dramatic works: by 1780 a supplement was just where one put the non-dramatic verse. And editors, who are very good at being unthinking, have unthinkingly followed this august precedent, more or less to this day.[16]

What Malone also established was the idea that the narrative poems and the Sonnets had little in common and ought to be thought about in quite different ways. The Sonnets had a basis in autobiography; the narrative poems were mere genre pieces of antiquarian interest, which came well out of a comparison with Drayton and Daniel at their second best, but which seemed wearisome to an enlightened modern reader.[17] This aspect of Malone's work has scarcely been undone to this day. Editors and critics have often pointed out that Venus, when she persuades Adonis to breed, anticipates the 'procreation' Sonnets, and have diligently followed Malone in finding echoes of the dedication to *Lucrece* in Sonnet 26, but have done surprisingly little more to develop connections between the poems and Sonnets.[18] Some critics have sensed a recurrent interest in the perversities of sexual passion in all these poems, or

[14] *Supplement to the Edition of Shakespeare's Plays* (London, 1780), p. 579. On the aftershocks of this biographical reading, see Peter Stallybrass, 'Editing as Cultural Formation: The Sexing of Shakespeare's Sonnets', *Modern Language Quarterly*, 54 (1993), 91–103.

[15] Quoted in Hyder Edward Rollins (ed.), *The Sonnets*, A New Variorum Edition, 2 vols. (Philadelphia and London, 1944), ii, 337–8, from 'The Advertisement to the Plays of William Shakespeare' (1793).

[16] The Oxford Shakespeare embeds the poems in chronological position among the dramatic works. The effect of this is to invite readers to think of the Sonnets in conjunction with *Troilus and Cressida* and *Measure for Measure*, and the narrative poems in the context of *Richard III* and *the Comedy of Errors*. This is misleading given the high likelihood that at least Sonnets 127–54 were written in the mid-1590s (on which see Hieatt, Hieatt, and Prescott, see above, n. 6), and that one of the most satisfying contexts in which to read them is provided by *Love's Labour's Lost*.

[17] Malone concludes that although the narrative poems 'appear to me superior to any pieces of the same kind produced by Daniel or Drayton', nonetheless Shakespeare's 'disposition was more inclined to the drama than to the other kinds of poetry; that his genius for the one appears to have been almost a gift from heaven, his abilities for the other, only the same as those of other mortals.' The poems, he claims, are marred by 'the wearisome circumlocution with which the tale in each of them is told', *Supplement* (London, 1780), p. 575.

[18] Ibid., p. 602.

have drawn attention to the ways in which both in the Sonnets and in the narrative poems lovers are forced into passivity as a price of their desire.[19] But through the majority of their critical life these two groups of poems have sat apart from one another in the critical mind: Jonathan Bate's *The Genius of Shakespeare* follows this fashion and plunders the Sonnets for biographical clues while all but ignoring the narrative poems.[20] The poems and Sonnets suffer a longstanding critical need to be viewed together and pulled nearer to the front of our view of Shakespeare.

\* \* \*

But why not just take them, as Malone more or less did, and as tenaciously old-fashioned critics continue to do, as windows onto the life and mind of Shakespeare? The current critical climate is not hospitable to readings of this sort, and for good reasons. Many critics writing today would hold a version of a materialist and historicist thesis about human identity. This has three main prongs. The first is that personhood is not the same thing now as it was *c.*1600. The second is that personhood is both a material and a relational phenomenon: that is, you are what you are by virtue of how you stand in relation to other people, by virtue of what you possess and of what and how you earn. These material circumstances change through time so much that it makes no sense to speak of one's having the same experiences as Shakespeare. The third prong is that texts and minds do not mix: writers leave material textual traces behind, which echo other texts and other voices, which refract their social circumstances, and which are recorded by the quirky means of the early modern printing house. And the printing house was a place of messy labour:

> Two men are requisite about the presse, one to take, to gather, and order the sheetes, or leaves; thother to beate on the fourme which is on the presse, and to distribute or bray the ynke on the stone or block: which could not serve the turne by reason of the great travaile required therein, if they did not drawe the presse one after the other, and by turnes . . . The ynke is made of the smoke or sweat of oyle, which must be beaten, and distributed, because of the thicknes . . .[21]

---

[19] See Heather Dubrow, *Captive Victors: Shakespeare's Narrative Poems and Sonnets* (Ithaca and London, 1987); Jonathan Bate, 'Sexual Perversity in *Venus and Adonis*', *The Yearbook of English Studies*, 23 (1993), 80–92. For some suggestive links between attitudes to descriptive language in *Venus and Adonis* and the Sonnets, see Pauline Kiernan, 'Death by Rhetorical Trope: Poetry Metamorphosed in *Venus and Adonis* and the Sonnets', *Review of English Studies*, 184 (1995), 475–501.

[20] Jonathan Bate, *The Genius of Shakespeare* (London, 1997), pp. 34–64.

[21] Louis Le Roy, trans. R[obert] A[shley], *Of the Interchangeable Course, or Variety of Things in the Whole World* (London, 1594), fol. 22$^r$. (Usage of 'i' and 'j' and 'u' and 'v' have been modernised). The manufacture of printing ink from boiling linseed oil is described by Steve Wood, *The History of Printing Ink*, British Printing Society Jubilee Series of Monographs, 1 (London, 1994), pp. 2–3 and John Moxon, *Mechanick Exercises on the Whole Art of Printing*, ed. Herbert Davis and Harry Carter, 2nd edn. (London, 1962), pp. 82–6.

Here's work indeed: even the ink is made of sweat. And this is how Shakespeare's poems as artefacts were made. Critics in the materialist school would argue that texts are so thoroughly a material and social a production that they cannot be thought of as the work of one great genius, let alone as a key to unlock the heart of a single man.[22] To read Shakespeare now one should think about work—how Shakespeare was paid, about the labour of a compositor—and the material relics which result. One should look at typographical oddities in the early quartos, and how they complicate the concept of a single authorising genius. Rather than seeing the poems as transcriptions of life one should dwell on gems, jewels, and splodges of ink: acknowledge that you live in a material world.

This position has generated a large body of subtle work, and has shifted our focus on the literature of early modern England from the self and its demands, towards the many ways in which objects and material relations shape human needs and designs. A recent collection of essays called *Subject and Object in Renaissance Culture* is founded on the belief that personal identity in the Renaissance was rooted in a dialectical relation between agents and material objects: its varied essays suggest that in this period people established their identity through money, clothes, paper, ink, and the physical form of the book.[23] This movement has made us sceptical, if the New Criticism had not already achieved this, about any claims that poems relate simply to lives and minds. The materialist outlook also speaks directly to Shakespeare's period, in which material metaphors and aids were often invoked in discussions of how minds worked. Thomas Wright's discussion of memory in *The Passions of the Mind* is representative: 'for although true friends have always a secret cabinet in their memories to talk in their minds with them whom they love although absent, yet except the memory be revived by some external object oblivion entereth'.[24] Pictures and love tokens—material objects—help the memory, which is itself figured as a material space, a 'secret cabinet'.

[22] The mastermind of this movement is of course Jerome McGann, whose *A Critique of Modern Textual Criticism* (Chicago and London, 1983) has generated considerable interest in the sociology of text production. Analogous work on the Sonnets includes Randall McLeod (as Random Clod), 'Information Upon Information', *Text: Transactions of the Society for Textual Scholarship*, 5 (1991), 241–78, and Randall McLeod, 'Unemending Shakespeare's Sonnet 111', *Studies in English Literature*, 21 (1981), 75–96. See also Margreta de Grazia and Peter Stallybrass, 'The Materiality of the Shakespearean Text', *Shakespeare Quarterly*, 44 (1993), 255–83. The interest in the material realities of the Elizabethan print shop also, of course, owes much to D. F. McKenzie's detailed analysis of the erratic work-patterns of early modern compositors in 'Printers of the Mind: Some Notes on Bibliographical Theories and Printing House Practices', *Studies in Bibliography*, 22 (1969), 1–75.

[23] Margreta de Grazia, Maureen Quilligan, and Peter Stallybrass (eds.), *Subject and Object in Renaissance Culture* (Cambridge, 1996).

[24] William Webster Newbold (ed.), *The Passions of the Mind in General* (New York and London, 1986), p. 200.

But the materialist thesis also has its limitations. In its harder forms it finds it difficult to explain the reception history of the poems, particularly of the Sonnets, in the late eighteenth century and after, except by appealing to a rather wearied view of a romantic *Weltanschauung* which turns poems into autobiographical documents whether they will or nill. Is Borges interested in Shakespeare's memory simply because he was aware of generations of post-romantic biographic criticism? Did Edward Dowden talk insistently about Shakespeare's life ('I wish . . . to attain to some central principles of life in him which animate and control the rest') or his mind ('There is something higher and more wonderful than St Peter's, or the last judgement—namely the mind which flung these creations into the world') simply because he was smoking the fag end of Romanticism?[25] This seems unlikely. Earlier readers may be responding to some feature of the texts beyond those put there by their projective imaginations. There is, after all, in Shakespeare's poems a marked tendency to renounce material aids to mental functions, and a marked tendency to talk about the mind, that inner cabinet to which Wright alludes, as something which is interestingly unrevealed. The Sonnets which describe absences often stress the power of Shakespeare's memory rather than objects to recall the beloved:

> Since I left you, mine eye is in my mind,
> And that which governs me to go about
> Doth part his function, and is partly blind,
> Seems seeing, but effectually is out:
> For it no form delivers to the heart                              5
> Of bird, of flower, or shape which it doth latch;
> Of his quick objects hath the mind no part,
> Nor his own vision holds what it doth catch:
> For if it see the rud'st or gentlest sight,
> The most sweet-favour or deformèd'st creature,                    10
> The mountain, or the sea, the day, or night,
> The crow, or dove, it shapes them to your feature.
>     Incapable of more, replete with you,
>     My most true mind thus makes mine eye untrue.    (113)

To state the painfully obvious, Shakespeare does not here say that it is only by weeping into the handkerchief which his friend has given him that he is able to recall what his friend looks like. The memory is so strong that it turns every-thing into a cue, and in the process turns the world and its visual objects into representations of the friend. Shakespeare's memory, that record which is presented as being so incomparably vivid that it breaks the connection between

---

[25] Edward Dowden, *Shakespeare: A Critical Study of his Mind and Art* (London, 1875), pp. 2 and 5.

mind and the material world, matters more here than material things. The
poem presents us with what might be called a subjectivity effect, and it does so
by showing that its author knows what he sees, and knows what the world sees,
and knows that there is a disparity between what the world sees and what he
sees. This disparity establishes the power of love as a transformative force
which distinguishes the lover's experience from that of his readers: we see
crows or doves; he sees his beloved.

Sonnet 113, with its mind sinking into the eye, is also one of several
Sonnets which attach a peculiar—by which I mean idiosyncratically
Shakespearean—emphasis to the word 'mind'. 'Mind' is an extraordinarily
powerful word in the Sonnets: it can evoke the sinking of consciousness into
itself in the absence of the beloved ('Since I left you, mine eye is in my mind'),
or the alienness of strangers ('That I have frequent been with unknown minds'
(117. 5)). It is often used in contexts where its precise sense is extremely hard
to pin down: Sonnet 59 asks

> O that record could with a backward look,
> Even of five hundred courses of the sun,
> Show me your image in some antique book,
> Since mind at first in character was done,
> That I might see what the old world could say
> To this composèd wonder of your frame.   (59. 5–10)

The wishful transformation of the young man into an antiquity is odd enough,
but even odder is the suggestion that images or printed characters can bear the
stamp of mind. 'Mind' can mean 'disposition' or 'memory' in this period, but
still the suggestion that somewhere back then people were making material
images of 'mind' has the elusiveness which invites speculation about what
mind is and about how it relates to printed matter. What gives the poem its
teasing flavour is Shakespeare's responsiveness to the pliability of the word
'character' in the late sixteenth- and early seventeenth-centuries: its primary
sense is 'writing' or 'print', but the noun can also mean 'idiosyncratically
individual handwriting' (*OED* 4c, which aptly cites the Duke in *Measure* 4. 2.
192–3: 'Look you, sir, here is the hand and seal of the Duke. You know the
character, I doubt not').[26] The growing interest in Theophrastus' *Characters* in
the 1590s and early years of the seventeenth century may have helped to push
the word towards its later senses of 'personal qualities or distinguishing
attributes'.[27] The word occurs four times in different forms in the Sonnets,
and on each occasion it is used in a way that is slightly different from the

[26] All quotations from the dramatic works are from Stanley Wells and Gary Taylor (eds.),
*The Oxford Shakespeare* (Oxford, 1986).
[27] See J. W. Smeed, *The Theophrastan 'Character': A History of a Literary Genre* (Oxford,
1985), pp. 1–35.

usages in the dramatic verse.[28] When Shakespeare uses the verbal form of 'character' in the dramatic works to describe the operations of memory it tends to have a close connection with the processes of making a material record: Julia in *Two Gentlemen of Verona* addresses Lucetta as 'the table wherein all my thoughts I Are visibly charactered and engraved' (2. 7. 3–4), and Polonius, ever the technically correct schoolmarm, urges Laertes 'these few precepts in thy memory I See thou character' (*Hamlet* 1. 3. 58–9). The Sonnets tend to blur over the precise nature of the physical medium on which memories are charactered, leaving the word adrifting towards pure mental space: 'What's in the brain that ink may character I Which hath not figured to thee my true spirit?' begins Sonnet 108. The verb 'character' there does not bed thought down into print: it is raised towards an immaterial sense of 'body forth distinctively' by its proximity to 'spirit'. When the Sonnets describe records or emotions they often gently press the balance away from the materiality of table books and written texts towards the enigmatically mental: 'What's in the brain' becomes in itself a question and an object of enquiry for readers. This in turn can prompt the thought that there is something irretrievably private about mental realities, that memories and emotions can only be offered in the charactered form of print, and yet that the medium is their product rather than their master.

Here a pair of poems is particularly relevant. The first of them, Sonnet 77, has traditionally been thought (since Steevens in 1780) to have originally accompanied the gift of a blank commonplace book:

> Look what thy memory cannot contain,
> Commit to these waste blanks, and thou shalt find
> Those children nursed, delivered from thy brain,
> To take a new acquaintance of thy mind.
> These offices, so oft as thou wilt look,
> Shall profit thee, and much enrich thy book.   (77. 9–14)

On the face of it this poem offers much to materialistic critics: memory must be written down, and needs a material record. As critics are coming to recognise, the ways in which writers from this period recorded their thoughts in the physical form of a commonplace book have a profound effect on how they shaped their learning as they wrote, and on the ways in which they

---

[28] The other occurrences are 85. 3, 108. 1, 122. 2. 85. 3 is particularly obscure: 'My tongue-tied Muse in manners holds her still, I While comments of your praise, richly compiled, I Reserve their character with golden quill' is often emended to 'thy character', suggesting that the writings store away the distinguishing attributes of the young man. (On the 'their/thy' error in Q see n. 50 below). This emendation should be regarded with some suspicion, however, since it tallies so neatly with the view that the Sonnets are concerned with inner mental attributes. The unemended form suggests that the distinctive elegance of the writings is hoarded away like a hidden treasure.

conceptualised the workings of their minds.[29] But we should also notice here
that when memory *is* written down in a material form it becomes something
more than mere matter; it becomes alive, something, or even someone, that one
has to meet anew, like a new friend.[30] In the imagery of the Sonnets memory
more often accompanies the language of life than that of dead material; and as
a result the poems imply that there is something more vital to memory than
script, print, or matter.

The Sonnet which is often thought to be a companion poem to 77 is 122. It
considers what happens when one loses the externalised memory provided by a
commonplace book (which is presumably what 'thy tables' refers to in line 1):

> Thy gift, thy tables, are within my brain
> Full charactered with lasting memory,
> Which shall above that idle rank remain
> Beyond all date even to eternity;
> Or at the least so long as brain and heart                          5
> Have faculty by nature to subsist,
> 'Till each to razed oblivion yield his part
> Of thee, thy record never can be missed.
> That poor retention could not so much hold,
> Nor need I tallies thy dear love to score,                          10
> Therefore to give them from me was I bold
> To trust those tables that receive thee more.
>     To keep an adjunct to remember thee
>     Were to import forgetfulness in me.

John Benson in his edition of this poem sought to embed it in the life: he called
it 'Vpon the receit of a Table Booke from his Mistris',[31] assuming as he so
often does that the addressee of the poems is female. But what matters here is
less the material form of the lost book, than Shakespeare's memory, which
gives immortality to the young man as a fragile record could not. That memory
is again elusive, and it is again figured as at once a book ('those tables', 1. 12)
and as something organic, persisting 'so long as brain and heart | Have faculty
by nature to subsist'. And again that transitional word 'charactered' is used to
keep the poem teetering on the boundary between the impersonality of the
scripted and the singularity of a mental disposition. The memory has not just
the impersonality of an inky record, but a flavour too of the distinctively
individual: it is 'charactered' in the sense that it is written in the table of
the brain; but the biological metaphors also allow that there is something (as

---

[29] See e.g. Anne Moss, *Printed Commonplace Books and the Structuring of Renaissance
Thought* (Oxford, 1996).

[30] On the frequent association between childbirth and poetic creation in this period, see
Katherine Eisaman Maus, 'A Womb of his Own: Male Renaissance Poets in the Female
Body', in James Grantham Turner (ed.), *Sexuality and Gender in Early Modern Europe:
Institutions, Texts, Images* (Cambridge, 1993), pp. 266–88.

[31] *Poems Written by Wil. Shake-speare Gent.* (London, 1640), sig. E6[r].

we would put it) 'characterising' about the unique privacy of the memory. What it means to call Shakespeare *early* modern is to recognise the weight given to the former of these definitions; but what it means to call Shakespeare early *modern* is to insist that he is easing the verb 'charactered' towards its later senses. The later part of the poem suggests that the poem envisages its own future life: ''Till each to razed oblivion yield his part I Of thee, thy record never can be missed' might hint that the friend and his (or conceivably her) poems will only live for as long as the poet is alive to remember them. That same phrase also though admits the far grander possibility that the poet's memory of the works lost with the commonplace book will live as long as this poem has readers: ''Till each' could mean 'until all people'. Either way memory is linked to life; and either way a scripted 'character' blends into a personal record. But also either way we never discover what was actually written on the mysterious missing table book.

These examples suggest why generations of readers have speculated about what was in Shakespeare's mind, and what lay hidden in his memory. The poems raise urgent questions about the ways in which scripted and printed characters can hold on to life. But the poems I have just been discussing also show why no-one has definitively answered these questions, why Borges's narrator finds Shakespeare's memory so lacking in biographical content, and why so many commentators have thought that they alone held the key to Shakespeare's Sonnets. These poems raise questions about mind and its relations to matter. They suggest that there is a mental realm of memory beyond and above material records, that things can 'live in your memory' (as Hamlet puts it) even when their material record is lost. But, crucially, they do not tell their readers what is in the private realm of memory, or what the lost commonplace book actually had in it. If we think of Shakespeare's presentation of mind as a materialist one we should see his materialism as heuristic: that is, material objects are invoked to hint at the existence of mental realities which resist material embodiment.

Another example will clarify this rather difficult point. *A Lover's Complaint*, a poem which until quite recently was regarded as peripheral to the canon,[32] begins with the destruction of material objects, and those objects are again enigmatic and personal to an equal degree. A young woman is

[32] For arguments for the poem's authenticity, see Kenneth Muir, ' "A Lover's Complaint": A Reconsideration', in Edward A. Bloom (ed.), *Shakespeare 1564–1964* (Providence, Rhode Island, 1964), pp. 154–66; reprinted in *Shakespeare the Professional and Related Studies* (London, 1973), 204–19; MacD. P. Jackson, *Shakespeare's ' A Lover's Complaint': Its Date and Authenticity*, University of Auckland Bulletin, 72, English Series, 13 (Auckland, 1965). John Kerrigan's edition of *The Sonnets and A Lover's Complaint* (Harmondsworth, 1986) returned the poem to where it belongs, after the Sonnet sequence. His *Motives of Woe: Shakespeare and 'Female Complaint'* (Oxford, 1991) presents the most critically convincing account of the poem's relation to its tradition.

'Tearing of papers, breaking rings a-twain' (6), and 'Cracked many a ring of poesied gold and bone' (45). The poem, though, refuses to reveal what was actually in the papers or what was posied on the rings. (Thomas Whythorne, the Elizabethan music-master whose insatiable and disastrous courtships of widows are recorded in his autobiography, relates how he gave a ring engraved with the words 'The eye doth find, the heart doth choose, and love doth bind till death doth loose' to one of his would-be inamoratas:[33] Shakespeare is deliberately less revealing). And this air of material enigmas is further developed later in the poem, when we seem, by virtue of eavesdropping on a conversation between two lovers, to have discovered something about the prior history of these objects. The female narrator tells how the young man who courted and ruined her received gems and 'deep-brained Sonnets' from the many women who wooed him, which he then passed on to her:

> '"And lo, behold these talents of their hair,
> With twisted metal amorously impleached,
> I have received from many a several fair,
> Their kind acceptance weepingly beseeched
> With the annexions of fair gems enriched,
> And deep-brained sonnets that did amplify
> Each stone's dear nature, worth and quality.

> '"The Diamond? Why, 'twas beautiful and hard,
> Whereto his invised properties did tend.   (204–12)

It has been suggested that these tokens are what we see the young woman destroying at the start of the poem.[34] But they are a little less transparent than that. Certainly the language of this part of the poem is obscure even by the standards of *A Lover's Complaint*. 'Annexions' is a coinage, and the significance of the diamond is so arcane that it prompts a phrase which still nobody is quite sure they understand: 'invised properties' probably means 'hidden qualities', but it even hides its hiddenness in impenetrable obscurity. Seeing these objects does not give access to the emotions behind a love affair in material form. It gives readers all the intimacy of eavesdroppers, and all the eavesdropper's sense of puzzlement: we see apparently significant objects and apparently significant exchanges, and yet the specific significance of these things in the lives of those we observe is withheld from us. This might lead us to say that in Shakespeare's poems objects do not reveal emotions; they encrypt them intriguingly, and start his readers on a quest for mind. An object is held up as something which offers a point of access to an experience, but the experience which it signifies, and whatever those mysterious 'deep-brained sonnets' actually relate, is withheld from us.

---

[33] Thomas Whythorne, *The Autobiography*, ed. James M. Osborn (London, 1962), p. 159.
[34] So John Kerrigan (see above, n. 32), p. 18.

I have so far suggested that an interest in the limitations of material vehicles for conveying mental realities is a strong unifying thread in Shakespeare's poetic *oeuvre*. This creates enigmas, which have encouraged critics in the past to speculate about Shakespeare's life and mind. The next section of this lecture attempts to trace the roots of this interest in the enigmas of personal experience back to *Venus and Adonis* and *Lucrece*. I will also attempt to offer an explanation for Shakespeare's curious desire simultaneously to proffer and withhold the workings of the mind. The explanation I will present is in its way a materialist one. I shall suggest that this feature of his works can be related to the very odd demands of the early modern book-buying public. Briefly put, many of those who bought poems in this period wanted to obtain private and occasional material—exchanges between lovers, communications between poets and their patrons—but they also wished to obtain this material in cheap printed form. They wanted the accessibility and the economy of print, whilst also wishing to obtain works with the cachet of private manuscripts. What I think Shakespeare does is to insist more strongly and more delicately than any other poet in the period that those private exchanges, private documents like commonplace books, and the even more private mental realities to which they bear witness, remain private even when they are published in material forms. I will also suggest that in the narrative poems Shakespeare is worrying about the risks of publishing and selling a poem, and about the kinds of work which poems can perform.

* * *

*Venus and Adonis*, as I have said, was the first printed work to which Shakespeare's name was attached, and *Lucrece* was the second. These simple facts can give cues as to how these poems should be read: they are the first efforts of a young poet to make a name in print. And, as such attempts often are, they are anxious even despite their florid accomplishment. *Lucrece*, as has recently been recognised, is rich in metaphors both of trading and of publication. These metaphors often overlap with the horror at sexual impurity which hangs over the whole poem: Lucrece's beauty is 'published' by Colatine at the start of the poem ('why is Colatine the publisher I Of that rich jewel he should keep unknown?' (33–4)) and his rash willingness to vulgarise the beauty of his wife is what initially provokes Tarquin to assault her. The link between publication and prostitution is quite common in Shakespeare's plays, and a page smirched by an alien hand is often associated with sexual impurity (think of Othello's 'Was this fair paper, this most goodly book I Made to write "whore" upon?').[35]

---

[35] *Othello* 4. 2. 73–4. On the association in Shakespeare, see Ann Thompson and John O. Thompson, *Shakespeare: Meaning and Metaphor* (Brighton, 1987), pp. 163–70 and 177–83.

15

Wendy Wall has related this link between publishing and be-whoring to fears among writers in the 1590s that publication effeminised: to print a poem for money, rather than to allow it to circulate in manuscript among a small coterie, was akin to selling it on the streets in a sort of printed version of pimping.[36] As Wall suggests, being read, being published, becoming a material object for sale, and being sexually violated are all elements in Shakespeare's *Lucrece*. But the poem does not simply yield its secret character to a print audience: it publicly proclaims itself to be called *Lucrece* on its title page; the more risqué title *The Rape of Lucrece* is privily concealed within the volume's running-titles (until the edition of 1616). Characters in the poem also resist being read, and retain for themselves something of the reserve of a poem written for private circulation; or to put that more strongly, they resist translation of mental impulse into material form. Lucrece herself fears that her rape will be published in her face:

> Yea, the illiterate, that know not how
> To cipher what is writ in learnèd books,
> Will quote my loathsome trespass in my looks.   (810–12)

The verb 'to cipher', meaning 'to interpret a coded writing' is peculiar to *Lucrece*. It occurs three times in the poem in this sense but nowhere else in Shakespeare's works, and its frequency in the poem suggests that minds are harder to read than Lucrece allows. Indeed her responses to her rape are so opaquely ciphered that no-one whom she encounters can read them. Lucrece's maid sees 'sorrow's livery' (1222) on her face, but is unable to interpret the reasons for her grief, and it proves impossible throughout the poem to read the mind's construction in the face. When the groom to whom Lucrece consigns her letter to her husband blushes, Lucrece assumes he does so because he sees her shame ciphered in her face. Actually, Shakespeare tells us, he blushes because he is a bashful fellow ('it was defect | Of spirit, life, and bold audacity' (1345–6)). Lucrece misreads others, and she does so because she mistakenly believes that her shame is published in her appearance. Physiognomy is not as reliable a guide to character in life as it is in the depiction of the sack of Troy, where Ajax and Ulysses' faces 'ciphered either's heart; | Their face their manners most expressly told' (1396–7). Tarquin has forced upon Lucrece a state of near-derangement in which she thinks all her thoughts and actions are made immediately legible to others. In fact her mind is hidden, and material

---

[36] Wendy Wall, *The Imprint of Gender: Authorship and Publication in the English Renaissance* (Ithaca and London, 1993), p. 69: 'So feminized, the book became an appropriate object of male desire: desirable in its own right in the marketplace of sonnet sellers and buyers.' Wall's account of *Lucrece* develops some elements explored in Nancy Vickers's influential ' "The Blazon of Sweet Beauty's Beast": Shakespeare's *Lucrece*' in Patricia Parker, Geoffrey Hartman, and David Quint (eds.), *Shakespeare and the Question of Theory* (New York and London, 1985), pp. 95–115.

objects—from physiognomic signals, to letters to her husband, to the tapestry representation of the sack of Troy onto which she projects her grief—cannot contain or reveal it. This she discovers as she moves from the company of the maid and the groom (who are the two characters in the poem whose real life equivalents were most likely to have been illiterate in early modern England) to adopt a writerly relation to an audience. As she tries to compose a letter to her husband she discovers the difficulty of publishing even so public a shame as a rape, or even of saying simply 'come home':

> Her maid is gone, and she prepares to write,
> First hovering o'er the paper with her quill.
> Conceit and grief an eager combat fight:
> What wit sets down is blotted straight with will.
> This is too curious good; this blunt and ill.
> Much like a press of people at a door
> Throng her inventions which shall go before.   (1296–1302)

She revises and re-revises her letter, and eventually opts for a cryptic expression which holds 'her grief, but not her grief's true quality'. The cabinet of her mind remains closed to those who observe her, and at the end of the poem it closes its doors altogether to prying eyes:

> Immaculate and spotless is my mind;
> That was not forced, that never was inclined
> To accesary yieldings, but still pure,
> Doth in her poisoned closet yet endure.   (1656–9)

Hidden away, her mind resists the kind of public and published stigma which she fears by hiding in its closet. This was the most symbolically private of solitary places for Elizabethans of more than middling rank, and the place in which private papers and hidden tokens of love resided, and from which printed poems were often said to have been liberated.[37]

---

[37] On the ways in which closets could be used to present a zone of private experience to a select audience, see Patricia Fumerton, *Cultural Aesthetics: Renaissance Literature and the Practice of Social Adornment* (Chicago and London, 1991). On p. 69 she writes 'The history of the Elizabethan self, in short was a history of fragmentation in which the subject lived in public view but always withheld for itself a "secret" room, cabinet, case, or other recess locked away (in full view) in one corner of the house.' Fumerton also makes suggestive relations between the private treasuring of miniatures and the coy semi-self-revelations of the Elizabethan sonnet, although she does not extend her observations to include Shakespeare. More recent work on the closet, such as Alan Stewart, 'The Early Modern Closet Discovered', *Representations*, 50 (1995), 76–100, has emphasised its role as a space for collaborative male labour. Closets and chambers in Shakespeare's poems, however, do tend to be places in which, as Angel Day puts it in *The English Secretorie* (London, 1592), p. 109, 'we do solitarie and alone shutte up our selves'. Nashe's preface to the unauthorised first Quarto of *Astrophil and Stella* (London, 1591) describes how poetry 'although it be oftentimes imprisoned in Ladyes casks, & the president bookes of such as cannot see without another mans spectacles, yet at length it breakes foorth in spight of his keepers, and useth some private penne (instead of a picklock) to procure his violent enlargement'.

The most trenchant recent critique of *Lucrece* the poem is that by Ian Donaldson. He argues that the work is radically confused: sometimes its heroine appears to belong to a shame culture, in which her pollution by Tarquin matters because it will cause horror in those who see her and acquire a social stigma; at other times Shakespeare seems to represent pre-Republican Rome as a proto-Christian guilt culture, in which Lucrece's own perception of her moral weakness is the primary grounds of her misery.[38] The features of the poem which I have just been considering go some way towards countering this criticism. The poem delicately and quite deliberately suggests that Lucrece inhabits both these kinds of world. She thinks she lives in a shame culture in which all can see her violation published in her countenance; but guilt, her consciousness of what has been done to her and of what she feels about it, remains hidden within her. The poem refuses to publish her shame; indeed it keeps it in the closet, albeit a poisoned one. As Shakespeare never lets us forget, *Lucrece* is a chamber work: its main action, the rape, occurs within a private chamber, and readers are insistently reminded of the geography of the violation: the Argument plants the word: 'The same night he treacherously stealeth into her chamber'; it is then harped on throughout Tarquin's hesitant advance: 'The locks between her chamber and his will I Each one by him enforced retires his ward' (302–3); 'Now is he come unto the chamber door I That shuts him from the heaven of his thought' (338–8); until he arrives at Lucrece's inner sanctum: 'Into the chamber wickedly he stalks, I And gazeth on her yet unstainèd bed' (365–6). The first touch of Tarquin's hands on Lucrece create an inner privacy within her private chamber, as her veins shrink back into the private spaces of her body:

> They, must'ring to the quiet cabinet
> Where their dear governess and lady lies,
> Do tell her she is dreadfully beset,
> And fright her with confusion of their cries.   (442–5)

The dominant metaphor here, as so often in the poem, is of a city under siege; but the passage also places great emphasis on the domestic inner spaces of the citadel of that city. A cabinet, a closet, these hidden places of personal retreat, are where Lucrece habitually resides. The effect of the rape and its violation of her private spaces is to force her to generate more privacy and more privacy, until, at the end of her story, the mind hides from all eyes in its 'poisoned closet'.

The preoccupation of *Lucrece* with hidden spaces and private zones enables us to put the case against Wendy Wall's view of *Lucrece* a little more strongly: Wall occasionally overstates the commodity value of texts in

[38] Ian Donaldson, *The Rapes of Lucretia: A Myth and its Transformations* (Oxford, 1982), pp. 40–56.

the period and so can correspondingly underestimate what makes them critically intriguing to readers. The majority of those who bought verse in this period are unlikely to have done so in order to feel as they picked up a new collection of poems that they were enjoying complete material possession of a person or a poem or an experience or mental state. They did not, as Wall can suggest in her more enthusiastic moments, feel as though they were buying not just *Lucrece* the book, but also Lucrece the woman. It is likely that many of them bought poems in the hope of intimacy with elevated doings, but also in the knowledge that what they bought would present them with only a glittering carapace of greatness, which would leave them feeling more on the outside of a charmed circle than ever. Many of those who bought the strange volume of poems attributed to Shakespeare called *The Passionate Pilgrim* in 1599 are likely to have done so in the hope that it would contain what Francis Meres in the previous year had described as Shakespeare's 'sugred Sonnets among his private friends'.[39] Purchasers of poems might wish to feel as though they were just on the edges of an intimate circle of friends, not quite sure what private allusions meant, not perhaps even quite sure who the poems were originally for, but relishing them anyway. In the process of publishing Lucrece's story Shakespeare plays to these expectations among his readership: he intimates that material forms, faces, poems, tapestries, letters, will never completely deliver the imprint of mind. Minds and material entities do not marry in Shakespeare's verse or in life without impediments.

I have begun my account of Shakespeare's career as a poet with his second published poem *Lucrece* because it sets the outlines of my case so clearly: that Shakespeare's poems, to abuse a legal phrase, are poems of material non-disclosures. Shakespeare's first poem, *Venus and Adonis*, however, has a similar, though less explicit, plot of material vulgarisation and mental reservation. The verbal mannerisms, distinctive vocabulary and sheer sexiness of *Venus and Adonis* were immediately imitated by other poets. The poem determined the public view of Shakespeare for the next decade: one of the ways in which *The Passionate Pilgrim* volume of 1599 was designed to look as though it was by Shakespeare was by its inclusion of sonnets about Venus and Adonis of a richly erotic kind.[40] The frenzy of erotic writing to which *Venus and Adonis* gave rise, though, has all but obscured its more anxious side. This is a poem,

---

[39] Francis Meres, *Palladis Tamia* (London, 1598), sigs. 2O1$^v$–2O2$^r$.

[40] For an account of the reception of *Venus and Adonis*, see Katherine Duncan-Jones, 'Much Ado with Red and White: the Earliest Readers of Shakespeare's *Venus and Adonis* (1593)', *Review of English Studies*, 176 (1993), 479–501. On *The Passionate Pilgrim*, see Arthur F. Marotti, 'Shakespeare's Sonnets as Literary Property', in Elizabeth D. Harvey and Katharine Eisaman Maus (eds.), *Soliciting Interpretation: Literary Theory and Seventeenth-Century English Poetry* (Chicago and London, 1990), pp. 150–4, and C. H. Hobday, 'Shakespeare's Venus and Adonis Sonnets', *Shakespeare Survey*, 26 (1973), 103–9.

like *Lucrece*, which worries about publication, and which, like many poems
from the 1590s, is preoccupied with awkward questions about what kinds of
work words can achieve. So far I have concentrated more on life and minds
than on work; but *Venus and Adonis* is centrally preoccupied with what it is to
labour in words. The dedication to the Earl of Southampton promises that
Shakespeare will devote all 'idle hours' to the production of 'some graver
labour', which presumably is a reference to *Lucrece*, which was printed in the
next year. Shakespeare's way of describing his ambition has a hint of anxiety
to it, as it just glancingly suggests that hours might still be 'idle' even when
they are filled with the scribbling work of writing poetry.[41] The senses of 'idle'
in this period extend from 'Not engaged in work, doing nothing, unemployed'
(*OED* 4a), which might mark Shakespeare's use of it as glancingly a proud
claim to the leisured ease of a gentleman; but the darker range of the word,
'vain, frivolous, trifling' (*OED* 2a), points a recognition that writing may
achieve little. That association of words with vanity and material ineffectiveness shoots through the poem. Throughout *Venus and Adonis* words are trying
in vain to work. Venus begs and beseeches and bullies Adonis to sleep with
her—in vain. The poem confronts the active but ineffective eloquence of
Venus with Adonis's zealous interest in what many Elizabethans would
have thought of as 'real' work. Indeed Adonis has what could almost be called
a bourgeois preoccupation with honest labour. For him the sun does not simply
sink, but 'His day's hot task has ended in the west' (530). When his horse bolts
in pursuit of a mare he solemnly declares that 'all my mind, my thought, my
busy care, I Is how to get my palfrey from the mare' (383–4): for him mind and
urgent labour are inseparable. Adonis, the hoarder, declares 'The night is
spent' (717); Venus the eloquent spendthrift retorts 'Be prodigal' (755). The
poem dramatises a clash not just between Venus's life of leisure and Adonis's
life of active pursuit, but between someone who wants to work through words,
and someone who thinks the only way to live is by material labour. The
encounter between these two attitudes to labour can become wonderfully
corporeal, as when the ever-active Adonis thinks that Venus has passed out,
and assumes that the more frantically he works at it the better his chances of
reviving the languishing goddess ('He wrings her nose, he strikes her on the
cheeks, I He bends her fingers, holds her pulses hard. I He chafes her lips . . .'
(474–6)). But it can also become a tangled debate about how words can bear on
material realities. The one point at which the idle Venus thinks she is about to
get through to the stubbornly laborious Adonis is when she taps in to his
burgher mentality: she promises him 'increase' through reproduction, and
presents herself as an object for sale:

[41] The classic studies of this area of anxiety are Richard Helgerson, *The Elizabethan
Prodigals* (Berkeley and London, 1976) and the same author's account of the ways in which
poets attempted to fashion poetical careers for themselves, *Self-Crowned Laureates:
Spenser, Jonson, Milton and the Literary System* (Berkeley and London, 1983).

> To sell myself I can be well contented,
> So thou will buy, and pay, and use good dealing.
> Which purchase if thou make, for fear of slips,
> Set thy seal manual on my wax-red lips.   (513–6)

Nice goddesses, of course, do not sell themselves. Venus has trapped herself by accommodating her speech to the financial concerns of her audience. And once Adonis has kissed her she ups the price, like a genteel courtesan who pretends not to know the meaning of money: her 'vulture thought doth pitch the price so high I That she will draw his lips' rich treasure dry' (551–2). As she goes on to persuade Adonis to use his capital of beauty in procreation she meets her first real resistance. Adonis (finally) says 'You do it for increase — O strange excuse, I When reason is the bawd to lust's abuse' (791–2). 'Increase', as Adonis well knows, means both 'profit' (*OED* 4) and 'biological multi-plication, offspring' (*OED* 6: 'From fairest creatures we desire increase' as Sonnet 1 begins, at once urging marriage on the young man and stretching out a needy paw for reward). The pun here accuses Venus of taking payments for sex, and the way Venus is described after Adonis's rebuke hints at her metamorphosis into a fallen woman. When Adonis leaves her for the active business of the hunt her company becomes a throng of echoes, whom Shakespeare figures as servile barmen:

> For who hath she to spend the night withal
> But idle sounds resembling parasites,
> Like shrill-tongued tapsters answering every call?   (847–9)

These tapsters, like poor Francis in *1 Henry IV* who cries 'Anon, anon Sir' to every call, are the lowest sort of company. This is not a respectable joint. Venus, the goddess who does not even need to tread on the ground, has engaged her eloquence to achieve the simple goal of seduction, and then sinks to the status of Doll Tearsheet, selling herself in taverns. In a printed poem addressed to a noble patron, and a patron who was being persuaded to marry during the period of the poem's composition by the material means of financial penalties, this is a touching tale: it fuels Southampton's resistance to seduction, and invites a reward for doing so. But it also entertains the awkward sugges-tion that to put words too openly to work is to prostitute the muse.[42] This poem frisks lightly, but it also worries about the material efficacy of words, and the potential costs to an author of selling his works in public.

The poem, though, like *Lucrece*, is not simply a study in the materialities of work and print. It is also, like *Lucrece*, fascinated by the privacies of the mind. Adonis, as well as jealously hoarding his financial and sexual reserves,

[42] G. P. V. Akrigg, *Shakespeare and the Earl of Southampton* (London, 1968), pp. 31–3 and 195–6.

keenly preserves a little sanctum of mental space into which Venus's seductive eloquence can win no access:

> For know, my heart stands armèd in mine ear,
> And will not let a false sound enter there,
>
> Lest the deceiving harmony should run
> Into the quiet closure of my breast;
> And then my little heart were quite undone,
> In his bed-chamber to be barred of rest.   (779–84)

Adonis equates virginity with retaining a private retreat in 'the quiet closure of my breast', and when he finally escapes homeward from Venus's grasp it is presumably to his solitary bed-chamber. His retreat is reminiscent of Sonnet 48, in which the poet's love is hidden away as a secret treasure 'Within the gentle closure of my breast'. And this hidden intimacy is a state to which even Venus aspires: she too ends the poem retreating into a solitary chamber. Her eyes flee back from the sight of the dead Adonis, and the description of their flight is among the greatest passages in Shakespeare's non-dramatic verse:

> So at his bloody view her eyes are fled
> Into the deep-dark cabins of her head,
>
> Where they resign their office, and their light,
> To the disposing of her troubled brain,
> Who bids them still consort with ugly night,
> And never wound the heart with looks again,
> Who, like a king perplexèd in his throne,
> By their suggestion gives a deadly groan,
>
> Whereat each tributary subject quakes,
> As when the wind imprisoned in the ground,
> Struggling for passage, earth's foundation shakes,
> Which with cold terror doth men's minds confound.
> This mutiny each part doth so surprise
> That from their dark beds once more leap her eyes,
>
> And, being opened, threw unwilling light
> Upon the wide wound that the boar had trenched
> In his soft flank . . .   (1037–53)

What makes the passage so agile, so needful of its remarkable cross-stanzaic enjambement,[43] is its materialism, its rootedness in the material fact of battery and retreat, of guards excited by assault into entering the most secret inner reaches of the citadel. It takes us back to the landscape of *Lucrece*, in which

---

[43] The punctuation of Field's compositors generally follows stanzaic patterns. A full stop is routinely placed at the end of a stanza. Of the six exceptions to this rule, four are the result of the need to compress the line to fit the forme (lines 372, 432, 678, 1068), and two (lines 834 and 876) have no relation to the syntax. The comma which ends line 834 ('cry so,') is probably the result of eyeskip from the line above ('wo, wo,').

women flee into the depths of a secret chamber in order to escape an invading catastrophe. 'Cabin' is probably used in *OED* sense 3b: 'A small room, a bedroom, a boudoir', or it may have the same sense as 'cabinet': 'A small chamber or room; a private apartment, a boudoir' (*OED* 3). For Shakespeare those inner reaches were equated with areas of mental reservation. But the passage works by generating subjectivity from those material realities: it presents a woman whose perceptual apparatus is wrenched out of kilter with what is actually before her by the intensity of emotion. This is a privacy of the mind, and it is a form of subjectivity which owes its origins to the experience of being made to see the world in a uniquely separate way by suffering a distinctive pain. Venus, like Lucrece and like Adonis, is finally stung into solitude; at the end of the poem she hurries away 'In her light chariot' to Paphos 'where the queen | Means to immure herself and not be seen' (1192–4), and her eyes withdraw from the sight of the dead Adonis 'as the snail, whose tender horns being hit, | Shrinks backward in his shelly cave with pain' (1033–4). The snail, carrying a private bedroom on its back, is the perfect emblem of the wincing inwardness finally celebrated in this most adolescent of poems. *Venus and Adonis* offers its readers a deliciously public display of sexual desire, which, as the title-page boasts, one could buy as a material object 'at the signe of the white Greyhound in Paules Church-yard'; but at its end it shrinks back into the concealed cabinet of the mind.

\* \* \*

The narrative poems, then, lightly touch on questions of what it is to publish, and on what sorts of emotional reality remain private even in printed works. I have also suggested that this interest is distinctively tuned to the market for poetry in the 1590s. I would like now to return to Shakespeare's Sonnets, and explore in a little more detail the ways in which the extraordinarily enigmatic volume in which they first appeared can be related to some of the qualities I have found in the narrative poems.

There has been a huge amount of debate about the Sonnets, about whether they were illicitly printed, or whether Shakespeare authorised their publication. There has been even more debate about who, in real life, the 'Mr W. H.' might be who is referred to in the printer's dedication to the volume (and Jonathan Bate and Katherine Duncan-Jones have shown this year that there is still life in the old battles betwen advocates of Henry Wriothesley, Earl of Southampton and William Herbert, Earl of Pembroke).[44] I am by conviction a sceptic: my only firm belief about the Sonnets is that there must be something pretty remarkable about the volume which contains them to have stimulated

[44] See Katherine Duncan-Jones (ed.), *Shakespeare's Sonnets* (London, 1997), pp. 53–64 and Jonathan Bate, *The Genius of Shakespeare* (London, 1997), pp. 45–54.

this amount of debate. I would therefore not want to say, as most editors do, that the balance of probabilities must lie with one side or the other in these debates. I would rather want to understand why both sides might have a case. And this leads me to my root conviction about the volume called *Shake-speares Sonnets*. It is a volume which gives off such radically conflicting signals about its relations to the life of its author that it could have been designed to do so. Moreover it could have been designed to operate more or less exactly on the borderline between the published and the privately concealed on which I have attempted to locate *Venus and Adonis* and *Lucrece*. These features of the volume become apparent if it is inspected as a material object, through the eyes of a notional seventeenth century book-buyer. Once this inspection is over it might be possible to draw some conclusions about how best to read the poems.

A potential buyer who picked up a copy of *Shake-speares Sonnets* from the stall of William Apsley or John Wright in 1609 would immediately have recognised that they were holding a different kind of work from either *Lucrece* or *Venus and Adonis*. The volume at first sight would look like a real work: it seems monumental, with its author's name not tucked away at the end of the dedication, but blazoned on the title page and used as a running title for each opening. The first page of the volume contains the printer's dedication, studded with lapidary full stops designed to give it the appearance of a carving on stone.[45] Scattered through the volume are poems which proclaim their status as perdurable works: (55) 'Not marble, nor the gilded monuments | Of princes shall outlive this pow'rful rhyme . . .'. Individual poems too, draw voraciously on the vocabulary of labour: the language of the law, 'charters', 'sessions', 'leases', 'pleas', weaves into the metaphorical texture of the poems, as does the exchange of capital and interest. The arts of the parfumier, the painter, the dyer are all welded together in a collection which both looks like a work and is uniquely accommodating of labour and its language.

A reader who looked more closely at the volume, however, might begin to notice features which qualified this initial impression of the monumental. The dedication, with its teasing use of those initials W. H., might remind its would-be purchaser of a tradition of erotic fictions which use their preliminary matter to hint that the characters in the fiction might have some bearing on real life. George Gascoigne's *Adventures of Master F. J.* is found in a volume prefixed by an epistle, supposedly from someone called H. W., but almost certainly by Gascoigne himself, which relates how its manuscript passed to him from someone called G. T. to his printer A. B.[46] The proliferation of initials in

---

[45] This account of the volume owes much to the intriguing thoughts of Katherine Duncan-Jones, 'What Are Shakespeare's Sonnets Called?', *Essays in Criticism*, 47 (1997), 1–12, although I believe that the volume also gives off quite contrary signals.

[46] *A Hundreth Sundrie Flowres bound up in one Small Poesie* (London, 1573), fo. 201.

*F. J.* invites its readers to apply them to real people, although it is fairly clear that they are inventions of the author.[47] Some sonnet sequences, notably Giles Fletcher's *Licia*, invite readers to apply the generic name of the woman to whom they are addressed to real people, whilst also deliberately not making such identifications explicit:

> It may bee I am so devoted to some one, into whose hands these may light by chance, that she may say, which thou now saiest (that surelie he is in love) which if she does, then have I the full recompense of my labour . . . If thou muse what my LICIA is, take her to be some *Diana*, at the least chaste, or some *Minerva*, no *Venus*, fairer farre; it may be shee is Learnings image, or under some heavenlie woonder, which the precisest may not mislike; perhaps under that name I have shadowed *Discipline*. It may be, I meane that kinde courtesie which I found at the Patronesse of these Poems.[48]

In Fletcher's preface the invitation to muse on the identity, allegorical or otherwise, of his mistress is left teasingly open. This is how erotic fictions make themselves spicily real in the period: they simultaneously invite and shrink from what early modern writers would have termed 'application' of works to life. 'W. H.' is as likely to be a late contributor to this tradition as he is to be a real life nobleman.[49] His presence at the threshold of the volume

---

[47] See Adrian Weiss, 'Shared Printing, Printer's Copy, and the Text(s) of Gascoigne's *A Hundreth Sundrie Flowres*', *Studies in Bibliography*, 45 (1992), 71–104. On Gascoigne's prefatory manoeuvres, see John Kerrigan, 'The Editor as Reader: Constructing Renaissance Texts', in James Raven, Helen Small, and Naomi Tadmor (eds.), *The Practice and Representation of Reading in England* (Cambridge, 1996), pp. 102–24. Another notable example of the deliberately suggestive use of initials is Alexander B. Grosart (ed.), *Willobie his Avisa; or the True Picture of a Modest Maid, and of a Chaste and Constant Wife (1594)* (Manchester, 1880), p. 8, in which 'Hadrian Dorrell', almost certainly a fictional character, claims of the name 'AVISA' that 'I think it to be fained name, like unto *Ovids Corrinna*' and that it may be an acronym for 'Amans Uxor Inviolata Semper Amanda'. He goes on, in a gesture typical of the efforts of early modern erotic writers at once to detach their work from reality and at the same time to embed themselves in the stuff of life: 'Yet I would not have *Auisa* to be thought a politike fiction, nor a truethlesse invention, for it may be, that I have at least heard of one in the west of England, in whom the substance of all this has been verefied . . . This forceth me to conjecture, that though the matter be handled poetically, yet there is something under these fained names and showes that hath been done truly.' The poem famously contains a character called W. S., a player who is also an unsuccessful lover. This led the indefatigable Arthur Acheson, in *Mistress Davenant and the Dark Lady of Shakespeare's Sonnets* (London, 1913), to argue that the 'Dark Lady' was the wife of an Oxford landlord. For a characteristically judicious discussion of *Willobie* and the Sonnets, see Hyder Edward Rollins, ed., *The Sonnets*, A New Variorum Edition, 2 vols. (Philadelphia and London, 1944), ii, 295–313. The analogy between the two volumes lies in their shared willingness both to invite and eschew application, rather than in any common shared allusion to facts in Shakespeare's life.

[48] Giles Fletcher, *The English Works*, ed. Lloyd E. Berry (Madison, Wisconsin, 1964), pp. 78–80.

[49] For the engaging suggestion that he owes his life to a misprint of 'W. SH.', see Donald Foster, 'Mr W. H., RIP', *PMLA*, 102 (1987), 42–54.

invites readers to scrutinise it for signs of life, whilst also providing an
assurance that whatever biographical traces the volume offers will be well
concealed. If we look at the monumental volume of *Shake-speares Sonnets* as a
physical object we can see that it provokes—deliberately or not—niggling
questions about the life to which it relates.

The volume might also reasonably prompt speculation about where the text
of the poems came from. It contains the odd line that does not rhyme (25.9), a
couplet that is repeated in two poems (36 and 96), a fifteen line Sonnet (99), a
Sonnet with a second line which repeats, unmetrically, a phrase from its first
line (146), a repeated error in which 'their' is printed for 'thy', an error which
mysteriously stops at Sonnet 128, at a point in the sequence when some
unusual spellings also begin to appear.[50] These features would be less pro-
nounced to an early modern reading public, used to haphazard orthography and
accustomed to correcting and sometimes even rewriting printed texts as they
copied them into their own commonplace books;[51] but they might also qualify
the initial impression of the monumental. Whatever the origins of this volume

[50] Q confuses 'their' and 'thy' at 26. 12, 27. 10, 35. 8, 37. 7, 43. 11, 45. 12, 46. 3, 46. 8, 46.
13, 46. 14, 69. 5, 70. 6, 128. 11, 128. 14, and possibly also at 85. 3. As MacD. P. Jackson's
analysis of compositorial preferences in the Sonnets, 'Punctuation and the Compositors of
Shakespeare's *Sonnets*, 1609', *The Library*, 5th Series 30 (1975), 1–23, shows, the error is
usually made by compositor B, although 35. 8 and 37. 7 were set by compositor A. The most
probable explanation (offered by Malone) is that the copy contained two letter abbreviations
for the personal pronoun in which 'they' and 'thy' looked alike, but the absence of errors
after 128 is striking. The mistress is consistently addressed as 'thou', which may conceivably
have helped the compositor to unscramble difficult copy; but this would of course also make
instances of the possessive pronoun very high (around 2.1 instances per poem as against 1.5
instances per poem for the earlier part of the sequence, or 1.6 if one includes the occurrences
erroneously set as 'their') and so multiply the opportunity for error. This suggests that the
copy for the poems after 128 may have significantly differed in orthography from the early
part of the sequence. This is also suggested by some unique or unusual spellings: 'Broake' is
found only in 143. 2 and 152. 3; 'bouldness' is unique; 'ynough', 133. 3 occurs also in Q1 of
*Troilus* (also printed in 1609 by Eld, so this could be a compositorial quirk); 142. 14 'mai'st'
appears to be unique; 'wofull' occurs thirty-two times elsewhere in the canon and is usually
pre-1600. This hypothesis sits suggestively beside the recent claim on stylometric grounds
that Sonnets 126–54 are among the earliest poems in the sequence. See A. Kent Hieatt,
Charles W. Hieatt, and Anne Lake Prescott, 'When did Shakespeare Write *Sonnets* 1609?',
*Studies in Philology*, 88 (1991), 69–109. For the view that 'The 1609 edition represents not
that dream of a traditional textual editor, the author's final intention, but rather a set of poems
in various stages of composition', see Heather Dubrow ' "Incertainties now Crown Themselves Assur'd": The Politics of Plotting in Shakespeare's Sonnets', *Shakespeare Quarterly*,
47 (1996), 299. Marotti, 'Shakespeare's Sonnets as Literary Property' voices a similar
opinion about the miscellaneity of the Sonnet sequence.
[51] For scribal adaptations of some Sonnets, see John P. Cutts, 'Two Seventeenth Century
Versions of Shakespeare's Sonnet 116', *Shakespeare Studies*, 10 (1977), 9–16; Mary Hobbs,
'Shakespeare's Sonnet II—"A Sugred Sonnet"?', *Notes and Queries*, 224 (1979), 112–3;
R. H. A. Robbins, 'A Seventeenth Century Manuscript of Shakespeare's Sonnet 128', *Notes
and Queries*, 212 (1967), 137–8. For manuscript versions of individual Sonnets which may
reflect authorial variants, see Gary Taylor, 'Some Manuscripts of Shakespeare's Sonnets',
*Bulletin of the John Rylands Library*, 68 (1985), 210–46.

it does not have the appearance of a printed work which derives from a finely revised authorial fair copy (and here it will be clear that I am not as confident as Katherine Duncan-Jones that the volume is likely to have been authorised by Shakespeare: its physical appearance is more ambiguous than she allows).[52] It looks much more like the printed offshoot of a partially revised manuscript, which its author may have wished to keep private. A keen early modern collector of sonnet sequences might dig deep in his (or again, conceivably, her) memory when he brought the volume home: what other work, this person might ask, blazons its author's name on the running titles of each page? Most sonnet sequences have no running titles, or at most use the title of the fictional addressee at the top of each page. Most sonnet sequences have an authorial dedication, rather than one signed by the printer, and most sonnet sequences carefully dispose one or two complete poems onto each page, and add an ornamental border at the top and maybe at the bottom of each page.[53] *Shakespeares Sonnets* has none of these features, and to contemporary readers versed in the genre it would have looked unusual: Sonnets topped by the name of Shakespeare stagger across pages, their form broken by the printed page. Our Jacobean sonnet-buyer might recall that only one other printed sonnet sequence shares all these features, and that was the 1591 edition of *Sir P. S. His Astrophel and Stella*, an edition which was called in, and which is manifestly the printed offshoot of a manuscript which walked away from its rightful owner.[54] This unauthorised volume also blazons the unmistakable initials of Sir Philip Sidney over every page. As a physical object, the Quarto of *Shake-speares Sonnets* manages to look like a monumental achievement at

---

[52] See Appendix.

[53] Exceptions are rare: Barnabe Barnes' *Parthenophil and Pathenophe* (1593), sig. A2$^v$ contains an epistle from the Printer: 'The Author though at the first unknowne, yet enforced to accorde to certaine of his friendes importunity herein, to publish them by their meanes, and for their sakes . . .'. The poems that follow are disposed chaotically across openings. The general pattern, especially marked in sequences such as Bartholomew Griffin's *Fidessa* (1596) and Richard Barnfield's *Cynthia* which were printed for Humphrey and Matthew Lownes, is to present one sonnet per page with ornamental borders at the top and bottom of each page.

[54] The case for attending to physical similarities between these two volumes has been persuasively made by Marotti, 'Shakespeare's Sonnets as Literary Property', pp. 154–5. For the converse and equally defensible view, that the resemblances to the 1591 edition of *Astrophil and Stella* should be interpreted as signs that Shakespeare's sequence is the summation of its genre, at once recalling and overgoing its origin, see Katherine Duncan-Jones, 'What Are Shakespeare's Sonnets Called?', *Essays in Criticism*, 47 (1997), 1–12. For discussion of the first quarto of *Astrophel and Stella*, see H. R. Woudhuysen, *Sir Philip Sidney and the Circulation of Manuscripts 1558–1640* (Oxford, 1996), pp. 365–84, J. A. Lavin, 'The First Two Printers of Sidney's *Astrophil and Stella*', *The Library*, 5th Series 26 (1971), 249–55, and McDonald P. Jackson, 'The Printer of the First Quarto of *Astrophil and Stella* (1591)', *Studies in Bibliography*, 31 (1978), 201–3. For various accounts of why the volume was called in, see William A. Ringler (ed.), *The Poems of Sir Philip Sidney* (Oxford, 1962), pp. 542–3, and Germaine Warkentin, 'Patrons and Profiteers: Thomas Newman and the "Violent Enlargement" of *Astrophil and Stella*', *Book Collector*, 34 (1985), 461–87.

the same time as appearing to be a product of miscellaneous processes: it looks at once like a monument and like a heavily revised manuscript copy hyped into print by an eager printer, who may or may not have liberated it from the author's private closet.

If our Jacobean reader stopped his physical appraisal of the volume and began to read it, he would find this elusive blend of the monumental and the messily quotidian replicated in the poetic structure of the volume. The poems which seem to claim the most for the immortalising power of monumental verse often also suggest that organic frailties play across their surface, turning a marble monument into a work which lives by virtue of being continually re-read, and recreated in the hearts of new lovers. Sonnet 18 ('Shall I compare thee to a summer's day') ends not just with promise of a poetic monument, but with a claim that its subject's future life is dependent on the continuation of biological life:

> Nor shall Death brag thou wand'rest in his shade,
> When in eternal lines to time thou grow'st.
> So long as men can breathe or eyes can see,
> So long lives this, and this gives life to thee.   (18. 11–14)

Sonnet 55 begins proudly declaiming that 'Not marble, nor the gilded monuments | Of princes shall outlive this pow'rful rhyme'. But the couplet confesses that what guarantees the survival of 'The living record of your memory' is the poem's continuing appeal to readers. This is what makes it live: 'So, till the judgement that yourself arise, | You live in this, and dwell in lovers' eyes'. Possessive apostrophes are not used in the Quarto: its 'louers' could correspond to either the modern singular possessive form or to the possessive plural. The young man's vitality comes either from the singular gaze of his lover, whose claim to immortalise his subject thus dwindles to a hyperbole exchanged between friends, or from the repeated rehearsal of his beauty by subsequent readers, in which case the hyperbole is warranted. These senses hint that the life of this monumental poem depends upon its being re-read, re-lived, inscribed in new lives. They also generate uncertainty as to whether the poem was designed to hide in a private communication between friends, charactered in the idiosyncratic hand of Shakespeare, or to be blazoned in print for eternity.

What makes the volume *Shake-speares Sonnets* unique is the extent to which its every element can be seen under the marmoreal aspect of a work or in the shifting light of life: its appearance, its dedication, its willingness to link monuments with the quotidian, all these features invite from its readers a deliberate interplay between reading the collection for the life as a private manuscript record of a secret love, and reading it as a monumental printed work. Recent scholarship enables us to add to these features a multiplicity of other structures within which to read the poems. There are moments when the sequences seem to take a chronological pattern, relating a narrative which it is tempting to associate with autobiography. When the poet writes

> Three winters cold
> Have from the forests shook three summers' pride,
> Three beauteous springs to yellow autumn turned
> In process of the seasons have I seen,
> Three April perfumes in three hot Junes burned,
> Since first I saw you fresh, which yet are green.   (104. 3–8)

it is right to bear in mind the convention that sonneteers live life in multiples of three.[55] But recent stylometric tests have shown that Sonnet 104 begins a mini-sequence of poems which show a higher incidence of 'late rare words' and a lower incidence of 'early rare words' than the group which precedes it.[56] Stylistic analysis prompts the teasing suggestion that three years actually might have passed in Shakespeare's life since he wrote Sonnet 103. An autobiographical frame is one of the narrative structures which a reader of the Sonnets needs to keep in play, but this sort of living sequencing has to be allowed to coexist with an awareness of scrupulously artful shapeliness. So Sonnet 49 appears to be out of place to many readers, since it occurs among a group of poems about travel and absence. It begins anticipating a future cata-strophe with 'Against that time (if ever that time come) | When I shall see thee frown on my defects'; in doing so it anticipates 63, with its fearful opening 'Against my love shall be as I am now, | With Time's injurious hand crushed and o'er-worn'. And it does so in a manner which is artful despite the Sonnet's apparent oddity of placement: the human body was believed to suffer a 'grand climacteric' at 63 (and this fact has often been invoked in relation to Sonnet 63),[57] but (and this point has not to my knowledge been made about the poem before) it also was believed to suffer a minor climacteric at 49. The two poems are consciously linked as crisis poems. The effect of jutting this numerological artistry, reminding us of the frailty of life, in among the horsey business and packing away of jewels with which Sonnets 48–51 are concerned, is to juxtapose a craftsman's control over the pattern of his poem with the daily shocks of living bustle. The combination of miscellaneity and apparent artfulness which

---

[55] Horace's declaration in *Epodes*, XI. 5–6 ('This third December since I ceased to desire Inachia is shaking the leaves from the trees') was imitated by Desportes and Ronsard, on which see Rollins, *The Sonnets*, A New Variorum Edition. There are signs this was not simply a convention, however: Daniel refers in the 1592 text of *Delia* (31. 6) to three years of courtship, but extends it to five in 1594.

[56] See Hieatt, Hieatt, and Prescott, 'When did Shakespeare write *Sonnets* 1609?' 91. 'Zone 3', of which 104 marks the start, is however a section of the sequence with a relatively low instance of rare words, and so firm conclusions about the dates of poems in this part of the sequence are difficult to draw.

[57] See René Graziani, 'The Numbering of Shakespeare's Sonnets: 12, 60, and 126', *Shakespeare Quarterly*, 35 (1984), 79–82, which notes that the 126 poems to the young man equal twice the number of the grand climacteric.

governs the structure of the Sonnets volume, and what appears to have been the extraordinarily extended period of its composition, go to make the poems uniquely demanding: they tempt their readers to identify characters, to turn them into a unified narrative, to read for the life, to fancy they see an artful pattern behind the whole; but the poems always retreat at the last moment from a full revelation either of life or of a full shaping design.[58]

Since the 1960s the editorial tradition of the Sonnets has been unhealthily divided. Editors influenced by the New Criticism have concentrated, often to brilliantly illuminating effect, on the verbal complexity of the poems, but have sometimes shrunk from the intricacies of bibliographical analysis and have tended to dismiss biographical interpretations as 'gossip' or 'chit-chat'.[59] Editors in the biographical school have put much energy into determining the occasions and addressees of the poems, and have laboured with the empiricist's belief that truths are always single and always determinable—*either* Southampton, *or* Pembroke. The time has come for this division to end. It will only end when critics and editors appreciate two things: firstly, that there are no empirically ascertainable certainties about the addressees or the origins of the Sonnets; secondly that that indeterminacy is a very important part of the reading experience of the poems. The Sonnets draw a large measure of their power from their willingness to suggest that they offer clues to lives and mental experiences which remain nonetheless irretrievable. And given that they are by the author of *Venus and Adonis* and *Lucrece*, those poems preoccupied by not quite publishing mental secrecies, this is what one would expect. When Sonnet 53 begins

> What is your substance, whereof are you made,
> That millions of strange shadows on you tend?
> Since every one hath, every one, one shade,
> And you, but one, can every shadow lend.

---

[58] On the miscellaneity of sonnet sequences, see Germaine Warkentin, ' "Love's Sweetest Part, Variety": Petrarch and the Curious Frame of the Renaissance Sonnet Sequence', *Renaissance and Reformation*, 11 (1975), 14–23. Carol Thomas Neely, 'The Structure of English Renaissance Sonnet Sequences', *ELH*, 45 (1978), 359 notes that 'The Italian model—fragmentary composition followed by careful selection and arrangement into a sequence—both justifies the expectation of structure in the sequence and predicts its loose elastic nature'. On the origins of the term 'sonnet sequence', see William T. Going, 'Gascoigne and the Term "Sonnet Sequence"', *Notes and Queries*, 199 (1954), 189–91 and 'The Term "Sonnet Sequence"', *Modern Language Notes*, 62 (1947), 400–2. For arguments that individual Sonnets suit their positions in the sequence see Graziani, 'The Numbering of Shakespeare's Sonnets'. This approach yields more convincing fruit than the root-and-branch numerology of Alastair Fowler, *Triumphal Forms: Structural Patterns in Elizabethan Poetry* (Cambridge, 1970), pp. 174–97.

[59] John Kerrigan, *The Sonnets and A Lover's Complaint*, p. 11 says that biographical criticism 'soon finds itself spinning off the text into vacuous literary chit-chat'. L. C. Knights begins his essay on the Sonnets of 1934 with the sally 'That there is so little genuine criticism in the terrifying number of books and essays on Shakespeare's Sonnets can only be partly accounted for by the superior attractiveness of gossip', repr. in Peter Jones (ed.), *Shakespeare: The Sonnets. A Casebook* (London, 1977), p. 74.

the words 'substance' and 'shadow' seem at first to belong to the register of metaphysics, as they do generally in the Sonnets. 'Substance' carries the primary senses 'essential nature' or 'That of which a physical thing consists; the material of which a body is formed and in virtue of which it possesses certain properties' (*OED* 6a), which is opposed to the shadow, or insubstantial image, of a thing. The proximity of the poem to 54, which is about artistic representation, suggests that 'shadow' could mean 'artistic representation' (*OED* 6b) as well as having the daemonic overtones which commentators have sometimes found in the poem: so 'what are you made of that you generate so many representations?'. But then why 'tend', a word which can be used of the activities of servants or underlings (and which is so used in 57: 'Being your slave, what should I do but tend | Upon the hours and times of your desire?')? Does this word suggest that a more material scene is obliquely imaged in the lines, in which a person of miraculous 'substance' in *OED* sense 16a ('Possessions, goods, estate; means, wealth') is tended on by 'shadows', in the sense of 'parasites or toadies' (*OED* 8a)? This material scene of a rich patron thronged by scroungers is fleetingly registered in the poem. But, as so often happens in the Sonnets, the suggested presence of a material scenario forces a flurry of metaphorical activity from the poet. The material import of 'substance' prompts the poet to erect a barrage of defensive metaphors so thick that they momentarily suggest supernatural influence, or that a horde of Platonic shadows clusters around the true form of the addressee's beauty.[60] A game has nearly been given away, and the best way to hide it is with ghostly suggestion.

This example suggests that one should read the Sonnets experimentally, inventing for them possible circumstances, embedding the poems in those circumstances, and listening to how they sound. They will evade succumbing to those circumstances because their power lies in their ability to suggest that they could live in almost infinitely multiple circumstances. This form of experimental embedding, though, enables the range and depth of the poems' language to emerge at its richest. And this is how their earliest readers might well have responded to Sonnet sequences, as they copied individual sonnets into their commonplace books, or slipped copies of poems under the doors of their mistresses' chambers.[61] The poems in the sequence in which they appear

---

[60] For a reading of another Sonnet which is alive to its material circumstances, see John Barrell, 'Editing Out: The Discourse of Patronage in Shakespeare's Twenty-Ninth Sonnet', in *Poetry, Language and Politics* (Manchester, 1988), pp. 18–43.

[61] Thomas Whythorne, *Autobiography*, p. 21 describes how he left a poem for a lady 'between the strings of a gittern'. Whythorne's autobiography is frequently invoked as evidence for the social deployment of verse in the period. It was probably composed in 1575, shortly after the publication of George Gascoigne's *Adventures of Master F. J.*, to which it has more than passing resemblances. Both narratives may have roots in reality, or the 'factual' account of Whythorne's life may have roots in fiction. Shakespeare's fellow Warwickshireman Michael Drayton gives no less equivocal evidence of the practical utility

in Q and preceded by their dedication to Mr W. H. have a quality which one might call situational ambiguity. That is, they suggest a multiplicity of additional possible senses if their readers are prepared to try them out, to see how they fit, in different narrative settings. Let us finally consider one very famous example, Sonnet 116:

> Let me not to the marriage of true minds
> Admit impediments; love is not love
> Which alters when it alteration finds,
> Or bends with the remover to remove.
> O no, it is an ever-fixèd mark,                                            5
> That looks on tempests and is never shaken;
> It is the star to every wandering barque,
> Whose worth's unknown, although his height be taken.
> Love's not Time's fool, though rosy lips and cheeks
> Within his bending sickle's compass come.                                  10
> Love alters not with his brief hours and weeks,
> But bears it out even to the edge of doom.
>    If this be error and upon me proved,
>    I never writ, nor no man ever loved.

The greatness of the poem lies in its willingness to allow temporal effects to play across the surface of its vision of love as an immutable force. It does not simply assert the immutability of love; it suggests that there are specific temporal circumstances which make it necessary to state that immutability. Several critics have been prompted to embed this poem in the life: Seymour-Smith in his note imagined that 'The situation seemed to be that the Friend, no doubt flattered at first by Shakespeare's "return" to him, was soon puzzled by his obviously changed attitude. No doubt he upbraided Shakespeare for this . . . in some such petulant terms as: "You no longer love me as you used to, because I am older", and so on.'[62] Helen Vendler, in a rigorously aesthetic reading of this Sonnet, also feels that its form of love derives from a dramatic setting: she sees it as an answer to a declaration by the friend that loves do just end.[63] These critics are doing what readers of the Sonnets are invited to do. I

---

of sonnet-writing when he ruefully acknowledged that a sonnet he wrote for a 'witlesse Gallant' succeeded in winning the mistress over, but the poems he writes to his Idea miserably fail to gain her affection, *Idea. In Sixty Three Sonnets* (1619), Sonnet 21. Drayton's suggestion that poets wrote poems for friends and patrons to use, though, may be one further expression of the sonneteer's traditional sense of the ineffectiveness of his own verse in winning a mistress over.

[62] Martin Seymour-Smith (ed.), *Shakespeare's Sonnets* (London, 1963), p. 169.

[63] Helen Vendler, *Ways into Shakespeare's Sonnets* The Hilda Hulme Memorial Lecture, 3 December 1990 (London, 1990), pp. 20–4. She too is prompted to imagine an actual conversation: 'The young man has, after all, said, "I did love you once, but now impediments have arisen through alteration and removes." '

do not think either of them are right, because I believe that the success of the poem, and indeed the success of all the Sonnets, depends on its refusal to offer sufficient grounds for applying it to any one circumstance. Its opening lines raise practical problems of stress, emphasis, and sense which invite exploration of embedding the poem in a variety of possible dramatic scenarios. Its opening line probably means chiefly 'I will not acknowledge that there are any barriers to love'. But how strong is the stress on 'me'? Strong enough to carry a hint of rebuke? And the echo of the Solemnization of Matrimony makes this a particularly strong claim, turning it into a churchly vow, taken at that critical moment when the couple are asked if there is any impediment to their marriage. Why at such a sacred moment use the word 'admit', and why that emphasis on 'alteration'? Could one imagine that the poem was written by someone who is nobly forgoing a lover rather than simply reaffirming his vows, that the marriage of true minds alluded to in the first line is not between the poet and his addressee, but between the addressee and another person? 'Admit' on this reading would not mean 'confess' but 'allow to enter' (*OED* 1). The first lines would mean 'Do not allow *me* [and that is where a reader might well let the iambic stress fall] to come between you and the person with whom you have such a perfect mental affinity: I love you so truly that I can keep on loving you forever even when I forgo you.' When set in this sort of imaginary life the poem takes on new resonances, some noble, some bitter—or it wins its nobility through and despite of bitterness: to say that love alters not where it alteration finds becomes a rebuke (you have altered; I have not); the heroic 'bears it out even to the edge of doom' becomes deliberately strained, an instance of the scarcely suppressed irony masquerading as masochism in which the Sonnets abound. A love emerges which is above circumstance; but that expression of love is strategically directed to someone who has betrayed that ideal, and so is embedded in circumstance. I would not wish to present this as a new or even as a true hypothesis about the poem; rather I use it as an example to suggest that the life, the literary vitality, of the poem depends on one's willingness to experiment with its relations to the surrounding sequence, to its author's life, to other possible lives.

The Sonnets have fascinated so many for so long because of their unique ability, inscribed in their physical form, their order, their vocabulary, to be both monumental works and suggestive fragments of life at once. The life from which they spring can never, of course, be recaptured, but that does not mean that we should give up the chase. We should perhaps, though, devote less energy to fruitless attempts to associate Shakespeare, sexually or otherwise, with members of the English nobility, and put more energy into imagining the kinds of dramatic microclimate—the occasions, the emotional and social structures—which gave these poems their first life. Even if we know that the content of Shakespeare's memory will always elude us, even if we know that his life will never be known by us as it was by him, to keep looking for

33

these unfindable entities is a central criterion of a serious engagement with his poems. And, moreover, it is what his poems invite his readers to do.


## Appendix: Were Shakespeare's Sonnets Really Authorised?

Katherine Duncan-Jones has argued in 'Was the 1609 *SHAKE-SPEARES SON-NETS* Really Unauthorized?', *Review of English Studies*, NS, 34 (1983), 151–71, and in her edition of *Shakespeare's Sonnets* (London, 1997), pp. 32–41, against the received opinion that Shakespeare's Sonnets were printed without their author's consent. Her case rests in part on a revisionary account of the career of Thomas Thorpe. She notes Thorpe's close relations with theatrical circles, his work for the super-scrupulous Ben Jonson over *Volpone* and *Sejanus*, and his role in producing high quality printed editions of theatrical texts throughout the early years of the seventeenth century. The range and distinction of Thorpe's productions leads Duncan-Jones to conclude that it is likely that the printer came by his copy through personal contact with Shakespeare, possibly with Jonson as an intermediary.

If this case is accepted in its totality it has significant critical and editorial consequences: the order, the spelling, even the odd loose end of the text in Q might be seen as deriving from a copy which had authorial sanction. Duncan-Jones couches her argument strongly in order to counter the many attacks which have been launched against Thorpe, and this means that evidence which could be regarded as running against her case is given relatively light treatment. She does not discuss the fact that Thorpe's first effort with William Apsley to register a piece of copy, 'a panegyric or congratulation for the concord of the kingdomes of great Britaine in the unitie of religion under king JAMES' on 23 June 1603, was cancelled because the work was already registered to 'Master Seaton', Edward Arber, ed., *A Transcript of the Stationers' Register*, 5 vols. (London and Birmingham, 1875–94), iii, 37. This could, of course, have been a simple mistake by a young printer, but it may be an indicator that Thorpe was not at the start of his career completely scrupulous in his quest for copy to print (obtaining copy without an author's consent in this period was not a crime; to print copy registered in the name of another printer, however, violated one of the key principles of the stationers' company). Nor does Duncan-Jones give a very full account of Thorpe's apparent piracy of the copy of Marlowe's *Lucan's First Book Translated* from Blount, as discussed by W. W. Greg, 'The Copyright of *Hero and Leander*', *The Library*, 4th Ser., 24 (1944), 165–74. This case too is difficult: Thorpe's subsequent close relation with Blount may imply that the printers collaborated over the volume and tried to generate excitement by making the copy appear to have been stolen (Blount assigned his rights to print *Sejanus* to Thorpe on 6 August 1605, Arber, iii, 297). Taken in conjunction with Thorpe's unlicensed printing of *The Odcombian Banquet*, however, which Duncan-Jones dismisses as a harmless caper, the episode of Marlowe's Lucan might indicate that Thorpe was capable of seeking copy from other printers as well as directly from authors' hands (*contra* Duncan-Jones's claim that the evidence 'points to Thorpe as a publisher who bought his copy directly from authors', pp. 160–1), and/or that he was willing to use preliminary matter to feed an audience's taste for the illicitly obtained. That Q has been seen as having been printed without its author's consent, and that its publisher's prefatory matter has fuelled speculation about the origins of the volume is not entirely surprising in view of Thorpe's earlier career.

Duncan-Jones provides strong evidence that Thorpe was careful about the typographical accuracy of the texts which he published, and this finding is partly what prompts her decision to follow the Quarto at several points in her edition when the majority of editors choose to emend. The examples of *Volpone* and *Sejanus* are striking; but there are counter-examples. The translation of Lucan by Sir Arthur Gorges is referred to by Duncan-Jones as a 'finely-printed text of a most distinguished translation' (p. 163). Here one must qualify her opinion: the volume is sumptuous in its appearance, but the quality of typesetting is relatively poor, with many pages showing clear compositorial errors. Here too questions about the origins of the copy are deliberately raised in the preliminary matter: the preface, purportedly by Gorges's son Carew who was then only ten, states that he stumbled on the poem 'in my fathers study, amongst many other of his Manuscripts' (sig. A3$^v$) and arranged with his schoolmaster to have it printed. This too is difficult evidence to assess, and might reasonably be seen as an effort on the part of the author to avoid the stigma of print. But this example does also show that relatively inaccurately printed works which are presented as having arrived in the printer's hands through intermediaries were part of Thorpe's stock-in-trade, as well as carefully prepared play-texts.

Thorpe otherwise only signed prefatory matter for volumes whose authors were dead (as in the case of Marlowe's Lucan, and the 1616 edition of John Healey's translation of *Epictetus Manuall*) or out of the country (as appears to have been the case with the 1610 edition of Healey's *Epictetus* and the same author's translation of *The Citie of God*). There are three works for which Thorpe may have composed anonymous preliminary matter, two of which are consistent with this pattern: Arthur Dent died in 1607, and Thorpe printed his *The Hand-Maid of Repentance* with an anonymous preface 'To the Christian Reader' in 1614. This was despite the fact that the copy was entered to John Wright, who published a substantial number of Dent's posthumous works, on 23 July 1614 (Arber iii, 551). The claim in the preface that the copy 'hath by Gods goodnes come unto my handes' (sig. A4$^b$) is either a piece of Pecksniffery or a suggestion that Wright informally allowed Thorpe to publish the copy. Jan van Oldenbarnveld was a Dutchman who had no discernible connection with the printing of *Barnevels Apology* for Thorpe in 1618, and the unsigned epistle to the reader suggests there was no relation of any kind between author and printer, since it presents 'Barneveltius' as a dotard. Theophilus Field's *A Christians Preparation* (1622) is the only work for which Thorpe may have composed an epistle for a living author whom he knew. Its 'Epistle to the Reader', signed 'Anonymous' (in Greek), is, however, the least likely of the three unattributed epistles to be Thorpe's, since its author claims friendship with Field, who was then the Bishop of Llandaff. Even this epistle, though, claims that the copy for the work which follows was originally only intended for the eyes of certain 'High and Honourable personages', and was only printed by the 'incessant importunity' of the anonymous author of the preface.

Given the extent of the plague in 1609 it is quite likely that Shakespeare was not in London at the time the Quarto was going through the press, and so one should hesitate before inferring from the presence of a signed dedication by Thorpe that the printer obtained the manuscript without its author's consent. Yet the analogy with other sonnet sequences, which usually only have dedications by their printers in cases where piracy is clear or suspected, and with the other works for which Thorpe produced signed preliminary matter, does admit the possibility that the Quarto may have been printed with less involvement from its author than Duncan-Jones implies.

These facts taken together do not comprise proof that Shakespeare's Sonnets were unauthorised (and even if it could be proven that Shakespeare authorised the publication this would not necessarily imply that the copy from which Eld's compositors worked was finally revised, or that Thorpe's Quarto presents a miraculous incarnation of authorial final intentions). But the evidence presented in this appendix does constitute grounds for regarding the case as 'not proven', as the Scots would say. Thorpe was quite capable of producing a volume printed with its author's consent which accurately reflected its copy. He was also quite capable of producing volumes which offered the excitement of unauthorised publication. The appearance of the Quarto of *Shake-speares Sonnets* leaves it open to readers to opt for either of these alternatives, or to teeter uncertainly between the two.

# OVID AND THE SONNETS; OR, DID SHAKESPEARE FEEL THE ANXIETY OF INFLUENCE?

## JONATHAN BATE

Early in *The Anxiety of Influence*, Harold Bloom announces that 'the greatest poet in our language is excluded from the argument of this book'. He gives three reasons for this exclusion, one historical, one generic, and one individual. Historically, Bloom states, 'Shakespeare belongs to the giant age before the flood, before the anxiety of influence became central to poetic consciousness'; only with eighteenth-century and Romantic notions of genius and originality does 'the burden of the past' become the poet's overriding problem. Generically, Bloom thinks, drama is less susceptible to anxiety than is lyric: 'As poetry has become more subjective, the shadow cast by the precursors has become more dominant.' But for Bloom – and this accords with the essentially Freudian mode of his criticism – the most important cause is the individual one: 'Shakespeare's prime precursor was Marlowe, a poet very much smaller than his inheritor . . . Shakespeare is the largest instance in the language of a phenomenon that stands outside the concern of this book: the absolute absorption of the precursor. Battle between strong equals, father and son as mighty opposites, Laius and Oedipus at the crossroads; only this is my subject here.'[1]

I think that all three of these arguments are wrong. I believe that we *can* talk about Shakespeare and the anxiety of influence, though the dynamics of anxiety and confidence in his relationship with his precursors differ in certain respects from the Bloomian pattern.

To be fair to Bloom, it should be acknowledged that he has changed his mind about the historical argument concerning the giant race before the flood: he now thinks that the anxiety of influence 'is crucial in Euripides confronting Aeschylus or in Petrarch dreaming about Dante'.[2] As usual, Bloom boldly asserts rather than scrupulously demonstrates; I would like to historicize the matter and consider certain symptoms of anxiety in Renaissance imitation theory. As for the generic argument, Bloom has forgotten about the Sonnets, which have precisely the self-consciousness about themselves as poems in relation to other poems and poetic conventions that makes them readable in terms of what he calls the aboriginal poetic self. I do not wish to argue the case about Marlowe here, though it does seem to me that his influence needs to be thought about afresh in the light of Bloom. *Did* Shakespeare absolutely absorb Marlowe? How complete is the revision of *Hero and Leander* in *Venus and Adonis*, *Edward II* in *Richard II*, *The Jew of Malta* in *The Merchant of Venice*, and *Dido Queen of Carthage* in *Hamlet*? Might not Pistol's parodies be a symptom of anxiety? Did Shakespeare think of Laius at the crossroads when he heard that Marlowe had been stabbed to death in Deptford? After all, when Francis Meres sought a classical prece-

---

[1] Harold Bloom, *The Anxiety of Influence* (New York, 1973; reprinted 1975), p. 11.
[2] *The Breaking of the Vessels* (Chicago, 1982), p. 15.

dent for Marlowe's death, he remembered the poet Lycophron shot to death by a rival.[3] Bloom now thinks that Marlowe was Shakespeare's 'prime' precursor, but not the only one; I understand that in a Norton lecture at Harvard this year he added two others, Chaucer and the English Bible. Perhaps because he is a Hebraist and not a Latinist, he still has not seen that in fact Shakespeare's prime precursor was Ovid.

The Bloomian rhetorical ploy is to announce that x is the precursor of y and that poem B is a creative revision of poem A. By virtue of such bold juxtapositions, Francis Meres may be reclaimed as a kind of Elizabethan Yale critic. Thus he reads the civil war poems of Daniel and Drayton as revisions of Lucan's *Pharsalia*, proclaims Ausonius to be the precursor of William Warner, and so on.[4] Such associations as these are Bloomian in that they profess some affinity other than overt imitation. As in Bloom 'the profundities of poetic influence cannot be reduced to source-study' (*Anxiety*, p. 7), so in Meres the *Fasti* of Ausonius are not a source but a precedent for Warner's *Albion's Englande*. The trope used by Meres is that which Puttenham in his *Arte of English Poesie* denominated 'Paradigma, or a resemblance by example':

if in matter of counsell or perswasion we will seeme to liken one case to another . . . and doe compare the past with the present, gathering probabilitie of like successe to come in the things wee have presently in hand: or if ye will draw the judgements precedent and authorized by antiquitie as veritable, and peradventure fayned and imagined for some purpose, into similitude or dissimilitude with our present actions and affaires, it is called resemblance by example: as if one should say thus, *Alexander* the great in his expedition to Asia did thus, so did *Hanniball* coming into Spaine, so did *Caesar* in Egypt, therfore all great Captaines & Generals ought to doe it.[5]

Antiquity, then, offers a paradigm or an example which, by serving as a precedent, authorizes 'the things wee have presently in

hand'. The purpose of Meres's 'Comparative Discourse of our English Poets with the Greeke, Latine, and Italian Poets' is to dignify the poetry that is presently in hand in Elizabethan England by bringing paradigms to bear upon it. The structure with which he works is Puttenham's 'as . . . so . . .' formulation: 'As Virgil doth imitate Catullus in the like matter of *Ariadne* for his story of Queene *Dido*: so Michael Drayton doth imitate Ovid in his *England's Heroical Epistles*'; 'As the soule of Euphorbus was thought to live in Pythagoras: so the sweete wittie soule of Ovid lives in mellifluous and hony-tongued Shakespeare, witnes his *Venus and Adonis*, his *Lucrece*, his sugred *Sonnets* among his private friends, &c.' (Meres, pp. 316–17). Here, *paradigma* is both a figure of speech and a design for the construction of literary history.

Meres articulates two different kinds of relationship between English poets and their forebears, the specifically imitative and the grandly paradigmatic. *Imitatio* is a symptom of *paradigma*, but *paradigma* is not dependent on recognizable *imitatio* (Caesar's Egyptian expedition cannot really be described as an *imitation* of Alexander's Asian one). Thus *Englands Heroical Epistles* is an imitation of Ovid's *Heroides*, as *The Shepheardes Calender* is of Theocritus' *Idylls* and Virgil's *Eclogues*, whereas the affiliation of Shakespeare to Ovid

---

[3] Meres derived his information about Lycophron, as he did most of his classical allusions, from a popular handbook, the *Officina* of J. Ravisius Textor: see Don Cameron Allen, *Francis Meres's Treatise 'Poetrie': A Critical Edition* (Urbana, Illinois, 1933). Allen castigates Meres for lack of originality, failing to see that his value lies precisely in his status as a purveyor of Elizabethan *commonplaces*.

[4] Meres, 'A Comparative Discourse of our English Poets with the Greeke, Latine, and Italian Poets', in his *Palladis Tamia, Wits Treasury* (1598), reprinted in *Elizabethan Critical Essays*, ed. G. Gregory Smith, 2 vols. (Oxford and London, 1904), vol. 2, pp. 316–17.

[5] George Puttenham, *The Arte of English Poesie* (1589), ed. G. D. Willcock and Alice Walker (Cambridge, 1936), p. 245.

is more broadly paradigmatic. Meres cites not only *Venus and Adonis* and *Lucrece*, which may be seen as imitations of parts of the *Metamorphoses* and the *Fasti*, but also the Sonnets, which, being in a genre unknown to Ovid, cannot be so directly imitative. The metaphor used for this relationship is suggestively self-performing: the metamorphosis of Ovid into Shakespeare is imaged in an allusion to the fifteenth book of the *Metamorphoses*, where Pythagoras supports his theory of metempsychosis by claiming that he is a reincarnation of the soul of Euphorbus (*Metamorphoses*, 15.161). Meres, writing in 1598, lists *The Merchant of Venice* as Shakespeare's most recent comedy, and he may well be remembering Graziano's allusion in that play to the metempsychotic opinions of Pythagoras (4.1.130); whether or not this is the case, the comparison is an inspired one, for the fifteenth book of the *Metamorphoses* is the prime *paradigma* for the Sonnets. The principle of metempsychosis which book fifteen articulates is enacted in the metempsychosis of book fifteen into the Sonnets.[6]

Puttenham's figure of paradigm provides an Elizabethan equivalent for Bloom's concept of a precursor; Meres provides an instance of an Elizabethan reader of the Sonnets who believed that their paradigm was the *Metamorphoses*. This model offers an Elizabethan version of 'influence', but what about 'anxiety'? Here, I would suggest, Bloom's sixteenth-century precursor is Erasmus.[7] Indeed, Erasmus is far more of a Bloom than is Meres, since he writes a form of criticism that is itself creative: Bloom conjures up 'a theory of poetry that presents itself as a severe poem' (*Anxiety*, p. 13), and he would not admit that criticism is a secondary activity – 'all criticism is prose poetry' (p. 95). So too with Erasmus: his dialogues are severe poems, not mere critical diagnoses. The point about both Erasmus and Bloom is that they should never be taken entirely seriously; the strength of their criticism lies in its scandalous excess.

Here is the opening of the *Dialogus Ciceronianus*, first published in 1528:

BULEPHORUS

Who's that I see strolling about down there at the end of the arcade? Unless my eyes have lost their sharpness, it's our old friend and fellow student, Nosoponus.

HYPOLOGUS

Nosoponus? the fellow who once used to be the life and soul of our set, rosy-cheeked, a bit on the plump side, diffusing charm and amiability in every direction?

BULEPHORUS

The very same.

HYPOLOGUS

But whatever has made him look so different? He's more like a ghost than a human being. Is he suffering from some disease?

BULEPHORUS

Yes, a very serious one.

HYPOLOGUS

Whatever is it? Surely not dropsy?

BULEPHORUS

No, it's a malady that goes deeper than the skin.

HYPOLOGUS

You don't mean that new sort of ulcerating disease, the scab, as people euphemistically call it nowadays?

BULEPHORUS

No, this is eating him away deeper than that.

---

[6] The aim of this essay is to reread the relationship between Ovid and the Sonnets in the light of sixteenth-century imitation theory and late twentieth-century influence theory. It is not to enumerate Shakespeare's 'debt' in detail: there are accounts of Ovid as a 'source' for the Sonnets in Sidney Lee, 'Ovid and Shakespeare's Sonnets', *The Quarterly Review*, 210 (1910), 455–76, T. W. Baldwin, *On the Literary Genetics of Shakspere's Poems and Sonnets* (Urbana, Illinois, 1950), J. W. Lever, *The Elizabethan Love Sonnet* (London, 1956), pp. 248–72, and the commentary and appendix 2 of Stephen Booth's edition of *Shakespeare's Sonnets* (New Haven and London, 1977).

[7] The best account of Erasmus, and the *Ciceronianus* in particular, in relation to sixteenth-century imitation theory, is that of Terence Cave in chapter 2 of his *The Cornucopian Text: Problems of Writing in the French Renaissance* (Oxford, 1979). For the broader Renaissance context, Thomas M. Greene's *The Light in Troy: Imitation and Discovery in Renaissance Poetry* (New Haven and London, 1982) is indispensable.

HYPOLOGUS
He's not spitting blood?
BULEPHORUS
This illness has got a hold somewhere further in
than the lungs.
HYPOLOGUS
Not tuberculosis or jaundice?
BULEPHORUS
It's something more deep-seated than the liver.
HYPOLOGUS
Perhaps he's got a fever affecting his veins and
heart?
BULEPHORUS
Yes, it is a fever, but then it isn't: it's something
that burns deeper down than any fever raging in
the veins and heart – something with its source
in the brain, in the depths of the mind. But stop
making wrong guesses, it's a new sort of illness.
HYPOLOGUS
Hasn't it got a name yet then?
BULEPHORUS
Not a Latin one; the Greeks call it *zelodulea*,
'style-addiction'.
HYPOLOGUS
Did he catch it recently, or has he had it a long
time?
BULEPHORUS
It's had the poor fellow in its grip for more than
seven years. I say, we've been spotted. It looks
as if he's coming this way. You'll get a better
idea what's wrong from the man himself.[8]

Bulephorus cannot find a Latin name for this
peculiarly nasty illness which the Greeks call
*zelodulea*. But we now have an English one:
Nosoponus is suffering from the anxiety of
influence. However, as is the way with literary
diseases, its symptoms in the sixteenth and
seventeenth centuries are precisely the opposite of what they become in the nineteenth and
twentieth centuries. Romantic influenza
springs from the poet's realization that he has
failed to create himself, whereas *zelodulea* is the
melancholy that grows from the realization
that one cannot succeed in being created by
one's precursor. Romantic influenza is a form
of manic-depression, *zelodulea* of obsessional-
neurosis. Keats veers between triumph and
despair as he wrestles with Milton; Nosoponus

is ground down by a compulsion to imitate
Cicero.

*Zelodulea* is an obsessive desire not to be
original, or rather to find one's every origin in
a paradigm.[9] The paradigm for prose is
Cicero. Thus Nosoponus desires that every
word, phrase, clause, period, verbal inflection,
rhythmical pattern, and rhetorical structure he
uses should have a precedent somewhere in the
works of Cicero. If *amo, amas,* and *amat* are in
Cicero, but *amamus* is not, then *amamus* cannot
be used. Nosoponus is ill because he sits up all
night every night reading, analysing, index-
ing, and cataloguing his Cicero. Erasmus'
witty dialogue is an intervention in the celebrated debate about whether one should
imitate a single authority or range more
widely, taking choice morsels from a variety
of models; Nosoponus is a parody of the
extreme Ciceronianism of such humanists as
Christophe de Longueil and Pietro Bembo.
Bulephorus, the Erasmian voice, goes on to
make a number of distinctions that are traditional in classical and Renaissance imitation
theory: the ape is contrasted to the true son; the
bee gathering honey from many flowers is set
up as an ideal. But what is distinctive about the
*Ciceronianus* is its metaphor of illness, its sense
that influence is something profoundly
problematic. 'Ben Jonson has no anxiety as to
imitation', says Bloom, adopting the traditional view that influence was not problema-
tized prior to 'the post-Enlightenment passion
for Genius and the Sublime' (*Anxiety*, p. 27).
Yet in the *Ciceronianus* anxiety is a key term:

---

[8] *The Ciceronian: A Dialogue on the Ideal Latin Style*,
translated by Betty I. Knott, in *Collected Works of
Erasmus*, vol. 28; *Literary and Educational Writings 6*, ed.
A. H. T. Levi (Toronto, Buffalo, and London, 1986),
p. 342.
[9] For the shift from Renaissance quests for origins in an
authoritative, ultimately a divine, 'source' to the
Enlightenment desire for originality, and Milton's
pivotal position in this development, see David Quint,
*Origin and Originality in Renaissance Literature: Versions of
the Source* (New Haven and London, 1983).

'that carping anxious concern [*anxiam sollicitu-dinem*] for imitating Cicero'; 'this very anxiety [*haec anxietas*] makes one less likely to reach the goal one is aiming for' (*Ciceronianus*, p. 444).

In Erasmus, Nosoponus cannot write any-thing because he worries so much about finding a style that is answerable to Cicero: in Bloom, the post-Miltonic poet is inhibited because he worries so much about finding a style that is not answerable to Milton. In both Erasmus and Bloom, *revision* offers the only release from this stranglehold. Thus Bloom: 'Oedipus, blind, was on the path to oracular godhood, and the strong poets have followed him by transforming their blindness towards their precursors into the revisionary insights of their own work' (*Anxiety*, p. 10). And Erasmus: 'It may well be that the most Cicer-onian person is the one least like Cicero' (*Cicer-onianus*, p. 399). Both Bloom's 'blindness'/'insights' turn (itself a shameless revision of Paul de Man) and Erasmus' 'most'/'least like' paradox are riddling solutions to the problem of influence. Oedipus' cleverness, as well as his paternity, hovers over both texts: as Hypolo-gus puts it in the *Ciceronianus*, 'Now you're producing a riddle fit for the Sphinx, if a person is to be unlike someone else at the very point where he is like him' (p. 399). The proposition which I want to test is that among Elizabethan sonneteers weak poets are obsess-ive imitators like Nosoponus, while strong poets are those who are unlike their paradigm at the very point where they are like him.

At this juncture one needs a bridge between the theory and the poetry. It must be demon-strated that Elizabethan sonnets did invite their readers to think about imitation and paradigm. One does not have to look very far to find such a bridge, for Thomas Watson actually built one into the first Elizabethan sonnet-cycle, the *Hekatompathia* of 1582. Probably working under the influence of E.K.'s marginal glosses to *The Sheapheardes Calender*, he prefaced each poem with a brief critical account of its own imitative practices. In the headnote to 'Harke

you that list to heare what sainte I serve', the blazon of which 'My mistress' eyes are nothing like the sun' is a direct or indirect parody, he proclaims that he is proud to be a parasite:

This passion of love is lively expressed by the Authour, in that he lavishlie praiseth the person and beautifull ornamentes of his love, one after an other as they lie in order. He partly imitateth here in *Aeneas Silvius*, who setteth downe the like in des-cribing *Lucretia* the love of *Euryalus*; & partly followeth *Ariosto cant. 7.* where he describeth *Alcina*: & partly borroweth from some others where they describe the famous *Helen* of *Greece*: you may therefore, if you please aptlie call this sonnet as a Scholler of good judgement hath already Christened it *ainē parasitikē*.[10]

Further assistance is provided for the reader in the form of learned marginal references along the lines of 'Vide Chiliad. I. cent. 5 adag. 74. vbi. Erasm. ex Philostrati ad uxorem epistola mutuatur'. Watson is an eclectic rather than a Ciceronian in his imitative predilections, but these signpostings mark him out as a Noso-ponus.

In Erasmus' dialogue, Bulephorus attacks those who 'over-anxiously' try to emulate their idols; 'The industrious but incautious imitator risks finishing up with a style that is flashy and overdone instead ... I have known men who attempted to reproduce that won-derful fluency of Ovid's and merely spouted verses devoid of any substance and force' (*Ciceronianus*, p. 378). The criticism applies perfectly to the sonnet in *Hekatompathia* that immediately follows 'Harke you that list to heare what sainte I serve.' Watson's headnote includes a quotation from Ovid's *Tristia* (2.103–6) and an explication: 'The Author alluding in al this Passion unto the fault of *Actaeon*, and to the hurte, which hee susteined, setteth downe his owne amorous infelicitie; as *Ovid* did after his banishmente, when in an

---

[10] Thomas Watson, *The Hekatompathia or Passionate Cen-turie of Love* (London, 1582), sonnet 7, p. 21. Greek transliterated in both title and quotation.

other sense hee applied this fiction unto him-selfe, being exiled (as it should seeme) for having at unawares taken *Caesar* in some great fault'. The ensuing verses set down the poet's own amorous infelicity through the same allusion:

> Actaeon lost in middle of his sport
> Both shape and life, for looking but a wry,
> Diana was afraid he would report
> What secretes he had seene in passing by:
>   To tell but trueth, the selfe same hurt have I
>   By viewing her, for whome I dayly die.
>
> (*Hekatompathia*, sonnet 8, p. 22)

But the allusion is vapid, since there is no element of prohibition in the viewing of his mistress. Whether the 'error' (*Tristia*, 2.207) for which Ovid was exiled was something he saw in the imperial household or an actual involvement with the emperor's grand-daughter, the figure of Actaeon is a perfect image in which to convey it. Watson, however, alludes to Actaeon solely out of a desire to imitate Ovid's wit, and his lines are accordingly empty of substance and force.

Shakespeare did not parade the imitativeness of his sonnets in the Watsonian manner, but on one occasion he did write a piece of literary criticism of his own work. It suggests, as Meres does, that Ovid is the sonneteer's para-digm. The sonnet 'If love make me forsworn, how shall I swear to love?', later published by William Jaggard in *The Passionate Pilgrim*, is subjected to the astringent scrutiny of Holo-fernes: 'Here are only numbers ratified, but for the elegancy, facility, and golden cadence of poesy – *caret*. Ovidius Naso was the man. And why indeed "Naso" but for smelling out the odoriferous flowers of fancy, the jerks of invention? *Imitari* is nothing. So doth the hound his master, the ape his keeper, the tired horse his rider' (*Love's Labour's Lost*, 4.2.121–7). Holofernes may be a pedant, but he is not a fool: he sees that Berowne's sonnet is a catalogue of commonplaces and that these verses are, to follow Bulephorus again, spouted without any substance or force. Holo-

fernes also knows his imitation theory. He has been reading in the tenth book of Quintilian: 'imitatio per se ipsa non sufficit'; 'invenire primum fuit estque praecipuum' [imitation by itself is not sufficient; invention came first and is all-important].[11] Contained within Holo-fernes' analysis is Quintilian's distinction between imitation and emulation, which had also been picked up by Erasmus in the *Cicer-onianus*. The business of poesy is not ape-like imitation à-la-Watson but the emulation of Ovid's elegance and facility. Like Puttenham's figure of *paradigma*, emulation leaves room for dissimilitude as well as similitude.

The distinction may be made by contrasting the handling of Ovidian mythology in a repre-sentative piece by a weak Elizabethan and in a Shakespearian sonnet. Sonnet 63 of Barnabe Barnes's *Parthenophil and Parthenophe* begins as follows:

> JOVE for EUROPA's love, took shape of Bull;
> And for CALISTO, played DIANA's part:
> And in a golden shower, he filled full
> The lap of DANAE, with celestial art.
> Would I were changed but to my Mistress'
>   gloves,
> That those white lovely fingers I might hide!
> That I might kiss those hands, which mine
>   heart loves![12]

Thereafter the poet expresses the desire to be metamorphosed into his mistress's necklace or belt, or the wine that she is drinking. In an Ovidian conceit – indeed, an Ovidian indecency – he imagines being the wine that kisses her lips, trickles down her throat, runs through her veins, and finally 'pass[es] by Pleasure's part'. Ovidian metamorphic mythology has furnished Barnes with images through which to convey his desire for a metamorphosis in his own standing with

---

11 Quintilian, *Institutiones Oratoriae*, 10.2.4; 10.2.1 (all classical quotations are from Loeb editions).
12 Barnes, *Parthenophil and Parthenophe* (London, 1593), quoted from Sidney Lee's anthology of *Elizabethan Sonnets*, 2 vols. (London, 1904), vol. 1, p. 207.

regard to his lover.[13] Ovidian wit has furnished the sonnet with its tail. But the opening quatrain is formulaically dependent on Ovid and the final couplet crude in comparison with him. 'Weaker talents idealize; figures of capable imagination appropriate for themselves,' says Bloom (*Anxiety*, p. 5): the weak Barnes in no way advances on Ovid, in no way strives to outdo him.

But consider Shakespeare's Sonnet 53:

What is your substance, whereof are you made,
That millions of strange shadows on you tend?
Since every one hath, every one, one shade,
And you, but one, can every shadow lend.
Describe Adonis, and the counterfeit
Is poorly imitated after you.
On Helen's cheek all art of beauty set,
And you in Grecian tires are painted new.
Speak of the spring and foison of the year:
The one doth shadow of your beauty show,
The other as your bounty doth appear;
And you in every blessèd shape we know.

In Barnes the Ovidian mythological figures are fixed points, ideal substances which are shadowed in his own love. In Shakespeare the opposite is the case: the lovely boy is the substance, the mythological figure the shadow. 'Describe Adonis, and the counterfeit / Is poorly imitated after you': where Barnes offers counterfeits, poor imitations of Ovidian originals, Shakespeare makes the lovely boy into the ideal figure of beauty and Adonis into the counterfeit. The third quatrain performs a similar trumping, in this instance of those figures of natural plenty who are so central to Ovid's world: 'Speak of the spring and foison of the year', and one would usually speak of Proserpina and Ceres; but here nature is a shadow of the youth's beauty. The sonnet's strength derives from its appropriation of the term 'imitate'. Where a poet like Giles Fletcher announces on the title-page of his sonnet-sequence *Licia* (1593) that he is writing in 'imitation of the best Latin Poets, and others', Shakespeare claims within his poem that classical figures are imitations of his own

beloved. 'Figure' is an analogous term: *paradigma* is a figure of speech whereby classical figures serve as authorities, but Sonnet 106 goes so far as to make the claim that all praises of past beauties 'are but prophecies / Of this our time, all you prefiguring' (lines 9–10). The ideal figures are but prefigurings of the poet's present love.

When Shakespeare deploys this effect of inverted *paradigma*, he exercises a turn on the concept of metamorphosis. The paradigmatic function of myth is to provide poet and reader with a stock of archetypes. But where it is customary to suggest the force of a present change by comparing it to a traditional mythological metamorphosis that is known to be forceful, Shakespeare makes the myths into the shadow, the present change into the archetype or true substance. In Ovid, extreme emotion precipitates the metamorphosis of a person into an object of nature, whereas in Sonnet 113, extreme emotion precipitates the metamorphosis of the objects of nature into a person:

[Mine eye] no form delivers to the heart
Of bird, of flower, or shape which it doth
      latch.
Of his quick objects hath the mind no part,
Nor his own vision holds what it doth catch;
For if it see the rud'st or gentlest sight,
The most sweet favour or deformèd'st
      creature,
The mountain or the sea, the day or night,
The crow or dove, it shapes them to your
      feature.                              (lines 5–12)

---

[13] This is a much-used topos which may be traced back to Ronsard's 'Je vouldroy bien richement jaunissant' (*Amours*, 20), a lyric translated closely as sonnet 34 of Thomas Lodge's *Phillis* (1593) and more freely as 'Would I were chaung'd into that golden showre', a poem in *The Phoenix Nest* (1593) attributable to Ralegh. Sidney, who so often detaches himself from the literariness of other sonneteers, mocks the topos in *Astrophil*, 6: 'Some one his song in Jove, and Jove's strange tales, attires, / Broidered with bulls and swans, powdered with golden rain.'

This is Bloomian revision in that Ovid is being read antithetically. The Elizabethan would have used the term 'inversion' rather than 'revision', to judge from the headnote to the ninety-sixth poem of *Hekatompathia*, one of Thomas Watson's few revisionary strokes: 'In this Passion, the Authour in skoffing bitterly at *Venus*, and her sonne *Cupid*, alludeth unto certaine verses in *Ovid*, but inverteth them to an other sense, then Ovid used.' Bloom would call this *Tessera*, the second of his 'Six Revisionary Ratios': '*Tessera*, which is completion and antithesis . . . A poet antithetically "completes" his precursor, by so reading the parent-poem as to retain its terms but to mean them in another sense, as though the precursor had failed to go far enough' (*Anxiety*, p. 14).

Although on a few occasions such as this Watson swerves away from his models, he never approaches the climactic sixth revisionary ratio, '*Apophrades*, or the return of the dead', in which 'the new poem's achievement makes it seem to us, not as though the precursor were writing it, but as though the later poet himself had written the precursor's characteristic work' (*Anxiety*, p. 16). *Apophrades* is at work in the group of sonnets around Sonnets 59 to 64, for there it is as if Shakespeare has written Ovid.

Sonnet 59 opens with Shakespeare's darkest expression of poetic belatedness:

> If there be nothing new, but that which is
> Hath been before, how are our brains beguiled,
> Which, labouring for invention, bear amiss
> The second burden of a former child!

(lines 1–4)

The darkness of this is manifest if we recollect Holofernes' distinction between *imitari*, which is nothing, and 'the jerks of invention' to which the poet should aspire (*Love's Labour's Lost*, 4.2.125–6). Whereas Shakespeare proved his inventiveness in Sonnet 53 by appropriating the idea of imitation, now he laments that the labour for originality is fruitless since nothing is new, what one writes will be

already written, and what one imagines to be the child of one's invention will turn out to be the child of one's poetic father. 'Burden' is a key word: together with 'labouring' it establishes an image of writing as giving birth, but at the same time it suggests the burden of the past, the oppressive weight of the wits who have gone before. The notion of eternal repetition on which the sonnet rests carries the melancholy implication that all writing is mere imitation of previous writing. Line eight, 'Since mind at first in character was done', evokes an originary act of writing that can never be recovered. The sense of loss derives from the contrast between that '*at first*' and the poet's own '*second* burden'.

Sonnet 59 exemplifies its own contention that there is nothing new by means of its own nature as something that is not new. For what is its argument about repetition other than a repetition of Pythagoras' argument in book eleven of *Metamorphoses*? The image of birth as rebirth of something that has been before is itself the second birth of Ovid's 'nascique vocatur / incipere esse aliud, quam quod fuit ante' or, as Arthur Golding has it, 'For that which wee / Doo terme by name of being borne, is for too gin too bee / Another thing than that it was'.[14] Ovid's technique in the *Metamorphoses* is to slide from one story to the next in a process of repetition and variation that embodies the neo-Pythagorean theory of constancy and change. The structure of the Sonnets is the same: 60 picks up from 59.[15] In particular, it picks up on the language of Pythagoras' discourse. As every

---

[14] *Metamorphoses*, 15.255–6. Golding's 1567 translation is quoted from *Shakespeare's Ovid, being Arthur Golding's Translation of the Metamorphoses*, ed. W. H. D. Rouse (London, 1904; reprinted 1961), 4.279–81.

[15] I follow Katherine Duncan-Jones, 'Was the 1609 Shakespeares Sonnets Really Unauthorized?', *Review of English Studies*, NS 34 (1983), 151–71, and John Kerrigan, ed., *The Sonnets and A Lover's Complaint* (Harmondsworth, 1986), in ascribing authority to the 1609 order.

educated Elizabethan reader would have recognized,

> Like as the waves make towards the pebbled
> shore,
> So do our minutes hasten to their end,
> Each changing place with that which goes
> before;
> In sequent toil all forwards do contend.
>
> (Sonnet 60, 1–4)

is a version of

> But looke
> As every wave dryves other foorth, and that
> that commes behynd
> Bothe thrusteth and is thrust itself: Even so the
> tymes by kynd
> Doo fly and follow bothe at once, and
> evermore renew.   (Golding, 15.200–3)

Here Shakespeare is imitating closely: his 'sequent' derives from Ovid's 'sequuntur' (15.183) and 'in the main of light' in the following line translates 'editus in lucem' (15.221). He pursues a similar *imitatio* with the image of sea encroaching on land and land on sea in Sonnet 64. But he is also revising, for he undertakes an elision that is thoroughly Ovidian but which is never actually explicitly articulated by Ovid. It is in this sense that Shakespeare is, in Erasmus' terms, being most like his paradigm when he is unlike him, or, in Bloom's terms, making it seem as though he has written his precursor's own most characteristic work.

The elision consists of a movement from past to future. Where Sonnet 59 looks back, and ends with the rather half-hearted couplet 'O, sure I am the wits of former days / To subjects worse have given admiring praise', Sonnet 60 frees itself from eternal repetition by claiming that the verse itself will endure. A few sonnets earlier, in 55, Shakespeare had reiterated the great envoi of the *Metamorphoses*: 'Iamque opus exegi, quod nec Iovis ira nec ignis / nec poterit ferrum nec edax abolere vetustas' (15.871–2); 'Nor Mars his sword nor war's quick fire shall burn / The living record

of your memory' (lines 7–8).[16] Now in the couplet of Sonnet 60 this idea of triumphing through writing recurs and offers itself as the overcoming of time's inexorability: 'And yet to times in hope my verse shall stand, / Praising thy worth despite his cruel hand.' In book fifteen of *Metamorphoses*, the envoi stands alone, not as a reply to Pythagoras. It is Shakespeare who makes the connection and thus uses one part of Ovid to unwrite or rewrite another. Shakespeare thus both clears a space for himself, enables himself to say something new, and at the same time remains responsive to his paradigm. In the very act of asserting his own immortality, he asserts Ovid's. There is a kind of mutuality whereby imagining the past and imagining the future are one and the same; Ovid's paradigmatic status proves his immortality and implicitly opens the way for Shakespeare to achieve similar immortality through becoming paradigmatic to eyes not yet created and when rehearsed on tongues to be. As Puttenham put it in his account of *paradigma*, the example of the past gathers probability of like success for the present.

The idea that Ovid has been reborn in sonnets such as 60 effects a curious effacement of the poetic 'I'. The conceit of Shakespeare writing Ovid will not do here. Meres's image of 'the sweete wittie soule of Ovid liv[ing] in mellifluous and hony-tongued Shakespeare' carries the converse implication that it is Ovid who is writing Shakespeare. If it is Ovid who 'lives', Shakespeare has disappeared in the very moment of asserting his own enduring life. Consider the 'I' of Sonnet 64:

> When I have seen the hungry ocean gain
> Advantage on the kingdom of the shore,
> And the firm soil win of the wat'ry main,
> Increasing store with loss and loss with store;
> When I have seen such interchange of state . . .
>
> (lines 5–9)

---

16 Being an eclectic rather than a Ciceronian, Shakespeare has in this sonnet combined Ovid's envoi with Horace's 'Exegi monumentum aere perennius' (*Odes*, 3.30.1).

and so on. Who is this 'I'? Is it the speaker of the Sonnets, or is it Ovid's speaker, Pythagoras – or the speaker of the Englished Ovid, Arthur Golding?

> Even so have places oftentymes exchaunged
>    theyr estate.
> For I have seene it sea which was substanciall
>    ground alate,
> Ageine where sea was, I have seene the same
>    become dry lond,    (Golding, 15.287–9)

The 'I' has been transformed into a polyphony of voices. According to one view, this dissolution is a source of anxiety. One might apply to Sonnet 64 the conclusion of Terence Cave's chapter on Renaissance imitation theory in *The Cornucopian Text*: 'it recognizes the extent to which the production of any discourse is conditioned by pre-existing instances of discourse; the writer is always a rewriter, the problem then being to differentiate and authenticate the rewriting ... Rewriting betrays its own anxiety by personifying itself as the product of an author; it imprints on itself – one might even say *forges* – an identity' (Cave, pp. 76–7). But the polyphonic 'I' can equally well be seen as an expansion rather than a dissolution, a product of generosity rather than anxiety. There is, I think, a modesty about Shakespeare's self-effacement which is the counterpart to the arrogance of his inverted *paradigma*. Again, there is a process of repetition and variation in the movement from sonnet to sonnet: 60 overcomes the anxiety of 59, then 64 assuages the potential egotism of 60.

John Kerrigan sees modesty at work in Sonnet 55, and differentiates Shakespeare's claims for immortality from Ovid's. The final word of the *Metamorphoses* is in the egotistic first-person future: 'vivam', 'I shall live.' Golding renders the poem's last line 'My lyfe shall everlastingly bee lengthened still by fame' (Golding, 15.995). 'Strikingly, though,' says Kerrigan, 'Shakespeare promises to preserve the young man in verse, not himself.' Kerrigan notes that this difference has led to the citation of a third possible 'source' for Sonnet 55, an

elegy of Propertius (III.ii) where immortality is bestowed on the person praised, not the poet himself; he is rightly dismissive of this possibility, since Propertius was barely read in the 1590s. 'It seems more likely', Kerrigan concludes, 'that Shakespeare adapted Ovid and Horace in Sonnet 55, and virtually certain that early readers would have understood the lines that way.'[17] I am not so sure that early readers would have understood the lines this way. I think that, like nearly all modern commentators who have thought about Shakespeare and Ovid, Kerrigan has overlooked the fact that any Elizabethan who had been to a grammar school would have been well versed not only in the *Metamorphoses*, but also in Ovid's other works. I would suggest that in Sonnet 55 Shakespeare is again revising Ovid by making Ovid revise himself through the conflation of two different works. Images of the text outliving sword and fire derive from the end of the *Metamorphoses*, but the modesty of '*You* live in this' derives from the end of the *Tristia*:

> Quanta tibi dederim nostris monumenta
>    libellis,
>   o mihi me coniunx carior, ipsa vides.
> detrahat auctori multum fortuna licebit,
>   tu tamen ingenio clara ferere meo;
> dumque legar, mecum pariter tua fama legetur.
>           (V.xiv.1–5)

[What a monument I have raised to thee in my books, O my wife, dearer to me than myself, thou seest. Though fate may take much from their author, thou at least shall be made illustrious by my powers. As long as I am read, thy fame shall be read along with me.]    (Loeb trans., adapted)

It is from the tender 'tibi' and 'tu' of this passage, I would suggest, that Shakespeare works his immortalization of the beloved, just as it is from the structure of repetition in the

---

[17] *The Sonnets and A Lover's Complaint*, p. 241; see also p. 21. For the citation of Propertius, see J. B. Leishman, *Themes and Variations in Shakespeare's Sonnets* (London, 1961), p. 42.

last line of this – 'As long as I am read, thy fame shall be read along with me' – that he creates the couplet of Sonnet 18, 'So long as men can breathe or eyes can see, / So long lives this, and this gives life to thee.'[18] The transformation of Ovid's wife into Shakespeare's fair youth is another suggestive revision: between the antique and the modern pen there is a constancy in love but a change in the object of love.

In such patterns of reiteration and variation, there is a rapid interchange between *verba* and *res*. The language of such sonnets as 18 and 19, 60 and 64, is for ever shifting as it interlocks with and then extricates itself from the words, *verba*, of Ovid. And such shiftings furnish the alert reader with a reminder of the metamorphic substance, *res*, which Ovid and Shakespeare share. And in responding to the *res*, Shakespeare is going beyond the imitative poet like Watson who is stuck with the *verba* of his models. The Pythagoras of book fifteen has a figure which comes to the quintessence of the *res*, the matter, of both the *Metamorphoses* and the Sonnets:

> And even as supple wax with ease receyveth
> fygures straunge,
> And keepes not ay one shape, ne bydes assured
> ay from chaunge,
> And yit continueth alwayes wax in substaunce:
> So I say
> The soule is ay the selfsame thing it was, and
> yit astray
> It fleeteth intoo sundry shapes.
>
> (Golding, 15.188–92)

That the soul, the self, is like wax is an idea which possessed Shakespeare deeply. One thinks of Theseus addressing Hermia,

> you are but as a form in wax,
> By him imprinted, and within his power
> To leave the figure or disfigure it.
>
> (*A Midsummer Night's Dream*, 1.1.49–51)

And one thinks of related images of 'impression' and 'imprint' in the Sonnets (e.g. 112.1; 77.3). It is an idea that brings us to another kind of influence and another kind of anxiety.

I have been arguing that in his frequent references to antique books, and especially in Sonnet 59, Shakespeare reveals his susceptibility to the anxiety of literary influence, but that in most of the Ovidian sonnets, and especially Sonnet 60, he overcomes that anxiety by means of a process of reiteration and variation that corresponds to both Pythagorean metempsychosis and Bloomian 'revision'. But what the Sonnets cannot escape is the anxiety of personal influence. The real melancholy of the sequence comes from the way in which the poet is *impressed*, not by Ovid, not by the 'rival poet', but by the fair youth himself. The sense in which Ovid, and indeed the whole panegyric tradition, begets the Sonnets is far less troubling than that in which the youth himself begets them, in which he is the book that is the poet's burden. Nobody can take the poet's Ovid away from him; even if his library is burnt like Ben Jonson's, he can always buy a replacement copy. But the youth is a costly unique incunabulum:

> Farewell – thou art too dear for my possessing,
> And like enough thou know'st thy estimate.
> The charter of thy worth gives thee releasing;
> My bonds in thee are all determinate.
> For how do I hold thee but by thy granting,
> And for that riches where is my deserving?
> The cause of this fair gift in me is wanting,
> And so my patent back again is swerving.
> Thyself thou gav'st, thy own worth then not
> knowing,
> Or me to whom thou gav'st it else mistaking;
> So thy great gift, upon misprision growing,

---

[18] It is strange that scholars (e.g. Baldwin, *Literary Genetics*, p. 215; Lever, *Elizabethan Love Sonnet*, p. 201) have derived the first line of Sonnet 19, 'Devouring Time, blunt thou the lion's paws', from *Tristia*, 4.6.5, but not the couplet of Sonnet 18 from *Tristia*, 5.14.5. An earlier poem in the *Tristia* also gives immortality to the poet's wife: 'quantumcumque tamen praeconia nostra valebunt, / carminibus vives tempus in omne meis' [Yet so far as my praise has power, thou shalt live for all time in my song] (1.6.35–6, Loeb trans.).

Comes home again, on better judgement
  making.
Thus have I had thee as a dream doth
  flatter:
In sleep a king, but waking no such
  matter.

(Sonnet 87)

This sonnet is anxious not about books but
about the whims of the beloved. Like Hermia's
father, the youth has power to mould another
person's self; he is able to shape the poet, 'To
leave the figure or disfigure it'. Anxiety is
wrought by the fear of losing the beloved; the
really terrifying thought is that he has only
been possessed in a dream. This sonnet contains two words that are crucial to Bloom's
theory of poetry: 'swerving' and 'misprision'.
For Bloom, all poems are misprisions, mis-
interpretations, of other poems, and all poets
make room for themselves by swerving –
executing a *clinamen*, he calls it – away from
their precursors. One might say that the effect
of misprision is to guarantee the later poet's
copyright. But in Sonnet 87 there is a patent
rather than a copyright, and the swerve is in a
relationship on which writing only has some
bearing. In the last resort, the idea that our
loves are built on misprision is a much more
disturbing one than that our poems are built
on it.

# THOMAS M. GREENE

# Pitiful thrivers: failed husbandry in the Sonnets

Sonnet 125 of Shakespeare's collection ("Wer't ought to me I bore the canopy") is the penultimate poem in the series addressed to the male friend. It is the last complete sonnet in this series, and in comparison with its somewhat slighter successor, 126, it appears to offer a more substantial, dense, and conclusive instrument of retrospection. It opens by distinguishing the poet from those who court his friend's love by means of external gestures, "dwellers on forme and favor," but who see their calculations fail and are condemned to admire the young man from a distance: "Pittifull thrivors in their gazing spent." The poet's own devotion, he claims, consists purely of uncalculated internal gestures and it leads to a genuine, unmediated exchange.

> Noe, let me be obsequious in thy heart,
> And take thou my oblacion, poore but free,
> Which is not mixt with seconds, knows no art,
> But mutuall render onely me for thee.[1]

The couplet dismisses a "subbornd *Informer*," a slanderer who might accuse the poet himself of dwelling on form. But despite this calumny, the affirmation of the "mutuall render" between the two men acquires in the context of the whole collection a peculiar resonance. It can be regarded as a culminating moment in the twisting history of their relationship, and our understanding of the outcome of the "plot" in Sonnets 1–126 depends in part on our interpretation of this phrase. Contrariwise, fully to grasp the implications of the phrase and the sonnet requires consideration of all that precedes, and even to some degree what follows. An informed reading will necessitate a long swing backward before returning to 125.

Within its immediate context, this is the third of three successive sonnets affirming that the poet's love for his friend is untouched by external accidents. This succession (123–5) needs to be read in the light of an earlier group (109–12) alluding to the poet's shameful and scandalous conduct and another group (117–21) alluding to the poet's apparent neglect and betrayal of the friend. Thus, if one attributes validity to the Quarto sequence, the three protests of uncalculating devotion follow almost directly an experience of partial rupture, and they attempt to cement a reconciliation which has been to some degree in doubt.

But from a wider perspective, Sonnet 125 is responding to problems raised from the very opening of the collection. Its resolution of pure exchange could be said to respond to the anxiety of cosmic and existential economics which haunts the Sonnets and which marks their opening line: "From fairest creatures we desire increase." The paronomasia which links the two nouns translates phonetically the poet's obsessive concern with metaphorical wealth, profit, worth, value, expense, "store," "content." The "pittifull thrivors" of 125 take their place in a line of disappointed or misguided would-be thrivers distributed throughout the work. The "mutuall render," if in fact it is successful, would thus bring to a happy conclusion a quest for an adequate economic system which would avoid the "wast or ruining" and the excessive "rent" which burden those in 125 who vainly spend themselves. Up to the climactic reciprocity at the close of that sonnet, the sequence to the young man has provided very little by way of stable exchange systems.

The first of the pitiful thrivers is the onanistic friend as he appears in the opening 17 "procreation" sonnets. By refusing to marry and to beget children, he "makst wast in niggarding" (1); he becomes a "profitles userer" "having traffike with [him] selfe alone" (4). The procreation sonnets display with particular brilliance Shakespeare's ability to manipulate words which in his language belonged both to the economic and the sexual/biological semantic fields: among others, "increase," "use," "spend," "free," "live," "dear," "house," "usury," "endowed," along with their cognates. The umbrella-pun which covers them all, and which establishes a semantic node for the whole collection, lies in still another word: "husbandry":

> For where is she so faire whose un-eard wombe
> Disdaines the tillage of thy husbandry? (3)

The *ad hoc* meaning "marriage" joins the traditional meanings of "thrift," "estate management," "agriculture," and, by means of a conventional metaphor, coition as ploughing. When the pun returns ten sonnets later, the dominant meaning will emerge as management:

> Who lets so faire a house fall to decay,
> Which husbandry in honour might uphold,
> Against the stormy gusts of winters day
> And barren rage of deaths eternall cold? (13)

"House" means both the friend's body (the *banhus*, "bonehouse," of the Anglo-Saxon kenning) and the family line. The bourgeois poet accuses the aristocratic friend of a dereliction of those responsibilities incumbent on the land-owning class. The apparent implication is that through marriage the friend could "live" (4), could make a profit by perpetuating his family.

But if, in the procreation sonnets, thriving seems ostensibly within the young man's grasp, one must recognize nonetheless the disproportionate force of the thwarting power, the "barren rage of deaths eternall cold." Procreation progressively comes to appear as a desperate defense, a final maneuver against a principle which is ultimately irresistible.

> And nothing gainst Times sieth [scythe] can make defence
> Save breed to brave him, when he takes thee hence. (12)

The recurrent terror of "winters wragged hand" (6), particularly notable in this opening group, comes to cast doubt on the viability of marriage. Or rather, in view of the threatening "barenes everywhere" (5), husbandry emerges as a universal, existential concern that transcends the addressee's marital status. It even becomes a concern of the poetry we are reading, which alternately promises to "ingraft" the friend anew in the war with Time (15) only to describe itself as "barren" in the sequel (16). The friend, "making a famine where aboundance lies" (1), may after all be closer to the governing principle of the world, in which case the poet and his poetry are left in a confusing limbo.

Thus a terrible fear of cosmic destitution overshadows the husbandry of the procreation sonnets, a fear in excess of the announced argument, not easily circumscribed, rendering the bourgeois desire for "store" more urgent, eccentric, and obsessive. In the main body of the sonnets to the young man (18–126), this fear continues to find frequent expression but it is also localized much more explicitly in the poet's feelings about himself. The poetry reflects a sense of inner depletion, emptiness, poverty, which the friend is asked or stated to fill up; elsewhere it reflects a nakedness which the friend is asked to clothe. Sometimes the language evoking the friend's role might suggest literal patronage; elsewhere it might suggest a literal filling up through sex; but each of these literalizations taken alone would reduce the quality of the expressed need. The sense of depletion is more radical and more diffuse, and it is inseparable from feelings of worthlessness and deprivation. Sonnet 29 ("When in disgrace with Fortune . . .") represents the speaker

> Wishing me like to one more rich in hope,
> Featur'd like him, like him with friends possest,
> Desiring this mans art, and that mans skope,
> With what I most inioy contented least. . . .

The language faintly underscores the economic character of this despondency. Friends, if they existed, would be possessed. "Rich in hope" means both "endowed with hope" and "rich in prospect." "Inioy" here means "possess" as well as "take pleasure in" (Booth), thus justifying a secondary reading of "contented least": "poorest in whatever I own of worth." This privation is only relieved by thoughts of the friend: "thy sweet love remembred . . . welth brings," and this transfer is dramatized by the imagistic wealth of the lark simile interrupting the rhetorical bareness of the octave. In the following sonnet, 30 ("When to the Sessions . . ."), the poet laments the deaths of precious friends, moans the expense of many a vanished sight, pays anew "the sad account of fore-bemoned mone," until with remembrance of his friend "all losses are restord, and sorrowes end." In 26 ("Lord of my love . . ."), the poet sends his naked poetry as an offering to his liege lord, hoping that the friend will dress the drab language in "some good conceipt of thine," will "[put] apparell on my tottered loving." Dressing the tottered (tattered) loving might mean making the poet more eloquent or more rich or more accomplished as a lover, but the nakedness seems finally to transcend rhetoric or money or seductiveness. In 38 ("How can my Muse . . ."), the friend is once again filling a void:

> How can my Muse want subiect to invent
> While thou dost breath that poor'st into my verse
> Thine own sweet argument?

The friend plays the masculine role, pouring his worth into the otherwise barren verse, leaving the poet with the travail of giving birth but rightly taking credit for any success: "The paine be mine, but thine shal be the praise." In this economic system, all value seems to reside in the friend, or in *thoughts* of the friend, and the poet seems to be a leaky vessel constantly in need of replenishing, his personal and linguistic poverty never definitively abolished.

This system, however, rests on a shaky basis. The worth of the friend may reside after all in the poet's own fancy, as at least one passage may be understood to suggest:

> So then I am not lame, poore, nor dispis'd,
> Whilst that this shadow doth such substance give,
> That I in thy abundance am suffic'd. (37)

The substance of abundance may actually derive from the shadow of projection. This doubt becomes more plausible as fears of betrayal mount

> Thou best of deerest, and mine onely care,
> Art left the prey of every vulgar theefe. (48)

and as the fears are realized in the young man's affair with the poet's mistress (40–2): "Both finde each other, and I loose both twaine" (42). In other sonnets apparently free of jealousy, a threat to the friend's worth looms from the cosmic mutability already evoked in the procreation sonnets, and now an alternative economic system situates the source of value in the poetry of the Sonnets. The poetry, elsewhere naked, becomes in these poems an artifact that successfully resists time and death, assures eternal life to the one it celebrates, distills his truth for the ages, acts as a perpetuating force against "mortall rage" (64). In the sonnets which affirm this source of value, the young man is represented as a potential victim, helpless against the cosmic principle of destruction, passive, disarmed, doomed without the saving power of "my verse." Verse preserves, engrafts, refurbishes; it seems informed with a masculine force the friend lacks. He remains in this system the beneficiary of a gift his worth draws to itself, but this worth is not otherwise active. "Where alack, shall times best Iewell from times chest lie hid?" (65). The young man's excellence is a plunderable commodity, as it is elsewhere perishable; inert as a precious stone, it belongs to the world of basic elements in flux, "increasing store with losse, and losse with store" (64). The alleged source of genuine "store" in this class of sonnets is the poetry.

Yet it is noteworthy that the affirmations of this linguistic power tend to appear in the couplets of these sonnets (15, 18, 19, 54, 60, 63, 65; exceptions are 55 and 81). The couplets, moreover, tend to lack the energy of the negative vision in the 12 lines that precede them. The final affirmation in its flaccidity tends to refute itself; the *turn* fails to reverse the rhetorical momentum adequately, as the language loses its wealth and its potency while asserting them.

> His beautie shall in these blacke lines be seene,
> And they shall live, and he in them still greene. (63)

> O none, unlesse this miracle have might,
> That in black inck my love may still shine bright. (65)

The turn toward restoration can be read as a desperate bourgeois maneuver, struggling to shore up the cosmic economy against the mutability which instigates true verbal power. The poetry arguably fails to celebrate, refurbish the worth of the young man. The worth remains abstract, faceless, blurred, even when it is not tainted.

Thus we are left with two distinct sources of alleged value, the friend and the poetry, each the basis for a rudimentary economic system, each vulnerable to skepticism. The presence of each system tends to destabilize the other by casting doubt on the kind of value it attempts to establish. To cite the poetic convention behind each system does not adequately deal with its constituent presence in this work. At stake in this conflict of systems is the status and force of the poetic word, which alternately shares its maker's hollowness and serves his (narcissistic?) fantasies of power. The one system, the one relationship which is *not* to be found before the last sonnets to the friend is equal, direct, unmediated reciprocity. Reciprocity is unattainable partly because of the poet's social inferiority and, so to speak, his felt "human" inferiority, because the friend frequently appears in thought, fantasy, or memory rather than in the flesh, because the adulatory style intermittently gives way to suspicion, resentment, fear, anger (33–5, 40–2, 57–8, 67, 69, etc.) which militate negatively against equality, because the friend as an individual remains a "shadow," undescribed, voiceless, hazy, dehumanized by the very superlatives he attracts, and because the poetry, however unclear its status, is repeatedly presented as the binding agent of mediation, an essential go-between. It is not clear whether *any* of the sonnets is to be read as a spoken address, a dramatic monologue, rather than as a written communication. Many of them refer to themselves as written, refer to paper, ink, pens, and to poetic style. They may occasionally affirm a closeness between poet and friend, but their very existence suggests a distance which has to be crossed. We are never allowed to envision unambiguously the poet in the presence of his friend, as we are in love poems by Wyatt, Sidney, Spenser, and Donne.

The conflicting representations of the poetry's power (potent or weak?), its gender (male or female?), its durability (perennial or transient?) together with its mediating function between the two men raise questions about what might be called its rhetorical economics. The poetry is distinguished by its super-charged figurative density, its inexhaustible ramifications of suggestion, its insidious metaphoric multiplications, a superfetation which might have been accumulated to avoid at all cost the alleged danger of nakedness. The poetry could be working to refute its own self-accusations of dearth and repetition.

> Why is my verse so barren of new pride?
> So far from variation or quicke change? . . .
> So all my best is dressing old words new,
> Spending againe what is already spent. (76)

As though to adorn the monotony, every rift is loaded with ore, to the degree that the rhetorical density can be read as an extraordinary effort to exorcize that stylistic poverty the poetry imputes to itself. The poet may feel himself to be depleted, but he evidently owns enough wit to spend it extravagantly. Yet this very supercharging of language tends to heighten a certain impression of linguistic slippage. Metaphors are mixed, replaced by others, recalled, jostled, interfused, inverted, disguised, dangled, eroded, in ways which blur meanings as they are enriched.

> Nativity once in the maine of light,
> Crawles to maturity, wherewith being crown'd,
> Crooked eclipses gainst his glory fight,
> And time that gave, doth now his gift confound. (60)

The enriching of metaphor, a putative demonstration of the poet's real potency, is indistinguishable from a mutability of metaphor, a fragmentation which might be said to demonstrate instability. By this reading the process of verbal enrichment would coincide with a process of deterioration; indeed the enrichment might be perceived as leading to the slippage, "increasing store with losse, and losse with store." The poetry would then come to resemble a pail of the Danaids, and the questions regarding the poet's potency would remain open.

That poetic potency is related here to sexual potency is made clear beyond cavil by the rival poet group (78–80, 82–6). The other poet is a rival both for patronage and for sexual favors, and his rhetorical brilliance (or bombast) is associated with his glittering seductiveness. Thus the poetic speaker is doubly threatened by "the proud full saile of his great verse, bound for the prize of (al to precious) you" (86). The revealing word here is *proud*, which meant "lecherous" as well as "stately" and "ostentatious." Cognate forms have already appeared in 80, which constitutes a tissue of sexual double meanings and interweaves poetic competition inextricably with erotic:

> O how I faint when I of you do write,
> Knowing a better spirit doth use your name,
> And in the praise thereof spends all his might,
> To make me toung-tide speaking of your fame.
> But since your worth (wide as the Ocean is)
> The humble as the proudest saile doth beare,
> My sawsie barke (inferior farre to his)
> On your broad maine doth wilfully appeare.
> Your shallowest helpe will hold me up a floate,
> Whilst he upon your soundlesse deepe doth ride,
> Or (being wrackt) I am a worthlesse bote,
> He of tall building, and of goodly pride.
>> Then if he thrive and I be cast away,
>> The worst was this, my love was my decay.

So many words have sexual meanings ("use," "spends," "proudest," "saucy," "wilfully," "ride," "pride" – by attraction, "tall building") that the reader is tempted to interpret the sonnet primarily in erotic terms. But it opens with a contrast of the rivals as writers before shifting in ll. 11–12 to a presumptive contrast of physical endowments. It is true that the analogy of the possibly promiscuous love object with the ocean will return more crudely and unambiguously in the dark lady group (134). But if language is presented in 80 as a means to seduction, seduction on the other hand may consist simply of verbal overpowering. "Love" and poetic language are linked so closely that the primary meaning of the final clause would seem to be "my inadequate verse has led to my rejection." The contrast of the rivals underscores what the speaker will shortly call his *penury*, a word which brings together his financial, poetic, and sexual shortcomings but which leaves uncertain what is figure and what ground. At any rate the rival, however we regard his challenge, introduces a complicating factor in the economics of the Sonnets, by appearing to "thrive" (80, l. 13) while the speaker is ruined. In spending more, verbally, sartorially, and sexually, he may get more. Yet in the end he and his new patron will be revealed as devalued, the one by the vulgarity of his praise and the other by the vulgarity of the pleasure he takes in it. They are pitiful thrivers both. So at least the poet suggests, and he follows the rival poet group with a temporary kiss-off, not without sarcasm:

> Farewell thou art too deare for my possessing,
> And like enough thou knowst thy estimate. (87)

Farewell also to the theme of poetry's immortalizing power: with two brief exceptions (100, 107), it will disappear from the collection.

The rival poet group is of interest because it confirms the implicit linkage between monetary, verbal, and sexual "pride," and because it complicates the linkage between these forms of power and deeper, vaguer intrinsic "worth." The group is equally of interest because it throws up, almost incidentally, a revealing formulation of the Sonnets' essential vulnerability, a formulation which will prove useful when we return to our starting point in Sonnet 125:

> Who is it that sayes most, which can say more,
> Then this rich praise, that you alone, are you,
> In whose confine immured is the store,
> Which should example where your equall grew,
> Leane penurie within that Pen doth dwell,
> That to his subiect lends not some small glory,
> But he that writes of you, if he can tell,
> That you are you, so dignifies his story.
> Let him but coppy what in you is writ. (84)

The pen is penurious which cannot add to its subject, but a praiser of the friend is subject to this penury, since in him "are locked up all the qualities needed to provide an equal example."[2] The friend's alleged excellence is such that no metaphors are available, no imagistic equivalent is possible, and the authentic praiser will limit himself to pure representation ("Let him but coppy"). Only by representing accurately, achieving a perfect counterpart of the young man, will the poet overcome penury, "making his stile admired every where." But this last solution, in its context, proves to be unsatisfactory on several grounds. First it fails to escape epideictic drabness, by the poet's own showing. It leaves the poetry "barren of new pride," spending again the respent, "keep[ing] invention in a noted weed" (76). Second, he who is to be copied proves to be less of a Platonic idea than a changeable and fallible human; for that revelation we need go no further than the couplet of this sonnet (84), with its malicious glance at the rival's demeaning flattery.

> You to your beautious blessings adde a curse,
> Being fond on praise, which makes your praises worse.

A certain pathology of praise can infect both parties. But the third and most momentous reason why the copy solution fails is that pure representation in language is not of this world. Poetry depends on figuration, but precise figural adequation is unattainable. What is said with ostensible hyperbole in the opening quatrain – that no "example" can serve as "equall" to the young man – is universally true. To attempt not to add to one's subject may court penury, as Sonnet 84 argues, but the real failure lies in the necessity of accepting addition, of employing "compounds strange" (76), as the Sonnets most decidedly do and as all poetry does. Poetry as representation will always be vulnerable, because in its shifting mass of meanings it can never copy with absolute precision and because that which is copied changes, gains, and loses value. The economics of copying reserves its own pitfalls for aspirant thrivers; the pen is bound to be penurious.

Sonnet 105 betrays a similar vulnerability:

> Let not my love be cal'd Idolatrie,
> Nor my beloved as an Idoll show,
> Since all alike my songs and praises be
> To one, of one, still such, and ever so.
> Kinde is my love to day, to morrow kinde,
> Still constant in a wondrous excellence,
> Therefore my verse to constancie confin'de,
> One thing expressing, leaves out difference.
> Faire, kinde, and true, is all my argument,
> Faire, kinde and true, varrying to other words,
> And in this change is my invention spent,
> Three theams in one, which wondrous scope affords.
>     Faire, kinde, and true, have often liv'd alone.
>     Which three till now, never kept seate in one.

This appears to be another apology for an allegedly plain style. (I follow Ingram and Redpath in interpreting "since" in l. 3 as introducing the reason for the accusation, not its defense; the latter begins in l. 5.) Although the poet claims to hew singlemindedly to a unique theme with the same constant language, he cannot, he says, be accused of idolatry because the friend, in his inalterable generosity, deserves no less. The poetry "leaves out difference," spending its invention by varying three words in others. One might argue that *some* difference is already present in this variation. But there are differences in the word "difference" itself, as one learns from a glance at Booth's paragraph on the word; among its relevant meanings are "variety," "anything else," "disagreement," "hostility." *Constant* means both "invariable" and "faithful"; *kinde* means both "generous" and "true to his own nature"; *spent*, that ubiquitous word, means both "used" and "exhausted." The Sonnets escape the charge of idolatry, not because the man they celebrate remains correspondingly unchanging (he is nothing if not inconstant, in both senses), but because they fail to express one thing and systematically admit difference. They alternately valorize and deplore a plain stylistic constancy which they cannot achieve.

The problem of "difference," like the related problem of accurate representation, is pertinent to the affirmation of mutuality which concludes the long section of sonnets to the young man. Before we reach that affirmation, we hear of derelictions on both sides, derelictions grave enough to undermine the fragile economic systems in force earlier. The falsity of the friend, a mansion of vices (95), produces a policy of husbandry the precise reverse of that recommended in the procreation sonnets; now it is those who remain aloof from others like a stone who "husband natures ritches from expence" (94). The poet for his part has made himself a motley to the view, "sold cheap what is most deare" (110), blemished himself and his love. We have already noted the waning of poetry's asserted power as an immortalizing agent. As the Sonnets spiral downward in a vortex of betrayal, counter-betrayal, and justifications not untouched with sophistry, we look for an economic alternative to mere self-deception, that "alcumie . . . creating every bad a perfect best" (114). Something like this alternative can be glimpsed briefly in 120, where the mutuality of suffering and dishonor might produce mutual guilt in compassion and lead to an exchange of quasi-Christian redemption:

> But that your trespasse now becomes a fee,
> Mine ransoms yours, and yours must ransome mee.

This glimpse of reciprocity in shared weakness fades, however, and leads to the group of three (123–5) with which we began, a group essentially protesting the poet's freedom from self-interest and the enduring purity of his feelings, which will never flag and can dispense with ostentatious demonstrations. The last of this group culminates in the proffered "mutuall render" between poet and friend, before the very last poem to the friend, 126, returns to the theme of time and anticipates nature's final, mortal settling of accounts: "her *Quietus* is to render thee."

A skeptical reading of these concluding gambits would represent them as repressing artificially the pain and guilt which have already surfaced, and which will surface even more harshly in the dark lady group to follow. In their context these protests of fidelity, which "nor growes with heat, nor drownes with showres" (124), could be regarded as attempts to mask the real bankruptcy of the relationship. The negative stress of 123–5, lingering over that change (123), "policy" (124), form (125) the poet abjures, might well be read as symptomatic of a bad conscience whose spokesman would be the (internal) accusatory informer of 125. This repressive character of the final sonnets could plausibly be linked to their return to a relatively aureate style after the burst of directness earlier (as in 120 – "y'have past a hell of Time"). This *suspicion* of the excessive protest does hang over the concluding group, deepened by their conspicuous discontinuity with their context. Yet a purely cynical reading would strain out that element of real wishing which is also present. The reader can recognize the implausibility of the asserted constancy while regarding the struggle to hope, the conative pathos, with respect.

The crucial sonnet in this group is 125, since it seems to offer at last the possibility of a stable existential economics, a definitive end to penury, a compensation for the expense of living and feeling, even though it does this like its predecessors in large part by exclusion:

> Wer't ought to me I bore the canopy,
> With my extern the outward honoring,
> Or layd great bases for eternity,
> Which proves more short then wast or ruining?
> Have I not seene dwellers on forme and favor
> Lose all, and more by paying too much rent
> For compound sweet; Forgoing simple savor,
> Pittifull thrivors in their gazing spent.
> Noe, let me be obsequious in thy heart,
> And take thou my oblacion, poore but free,
> Which is not mixt with seconds, knows no art,
> But mutuall render onely me for thee.
>     Hence, thou subbornd *Informer*, a trew soule
>     When most impeacht, stands least in thy controule.

Lines 1–12 are ostensibly responding to the calumny of the unidentified informer of l. 13, a calumny whose content we can determine only through its refutation. This consists in a repudiation of what might be called affective formalism, external gestures of dutifulness like the carrying of a canopy of state over a monarch's head. Suitors who employ such external gestures may believe that they prepare in this way for an everlasting intimacy with him whose favor they court, but the intimacy "paradoxically turns out to be briefer than the time required to run through an estate by extravagance" (Ingram and Redpath). We have still another example of failed husbandry, combining formalism with the kind of decadent sophistication which would prefer cloying elaborate sauces ("compound sweet") to the familiar taste of homely fare. *Forme* (l. 5) brings together the young man's physical figure, the ceremonial of line 1, exaggerated courtesy, hollow gestures of servility, and the craft which produces "compound sweet," artificial confections of any sort, but which is allegedly absent from the poet's oblation. "Compound sweet" recalls the poetic "compounds strange" of 76, which the poet there reproached himself for omitting from his own verse. This suggests that dwellers on form are also ambitious poets whose style is overwrought. The image of the projected manor house (l. 3) is faintly sustained by "ruining" (l. 4), "dwellers" (l. 5), "rent" (l. 6), and the possible allusion to compound and simple interest (l. 7). This version of negative formalism ends with the loaded word "spent" (l. 8), in which so much meaning has sedimented throughout the work; here it means "bankrupted," "exhausted," "failed," ironically "summed up" in reliance on visual externals, and doubtless also "drained of semen," as the suitors' sexual designs are reduced to voyeurism. Unsuccessful entrepreneurs, with only the groundworks built of their mansion of love, the failure of their misguided, formalist generosity is symbolized by the suitors' symbolic distance from their prize, observable but not touchable.

Lines 9–12 supply the poet's redemptive version of erotic ceremonial, which substitutes the eucharistic oblation for the canopied court procession. In this secularized sacrament, the dutiful ("obsequious") poet freely makes an offering intended to manifest the inwardness and simplicity of his own devotion, knowing, or thinking that he knows, that his oblation will win him the unmediated, inner reciprocity which is his goal. The oblation which "knows no art," free from the charge of formalism, is that poetry which, as in 105, is confined to constancy, "to one, of one, still such, and ever so." Just as in 105 it "leaves out difference," in 125 it "is not mixt with seconds." Yet ironically and pathetically, the word "oblacion" is mixed with a transcendent "second," the deity of the communion service, so that the metaphor can only be regarded as a very strange, and somewhat ambiguous, compound. The use of the sacramental term leaves the reader uncertain just how much weight to accord it, and, by introducing the unbridgeable hierarchy of human and divine, would seem to annul in advance the pure reciprocity of the "mutuall render." To deny the operation of art requires art, and this art will prohibit the reciprocal affective mutuality toward which the whole work has seemed to want to move. To compose poetry is expensive, just as loving is expensive, and the unformulated implication of the work as a whole seems to be that expense is never truly recuperated. The increase we desire from fairest creatures never materializes. Spending leaves one spent, and it fails to buy immediacy; it places a residue of compound feeling and compound language between lover and beloved. Here in 125 the very word "seconds" is a compound. It means primarily "merchandise of inferior quality," but it associates itself with the "compound sweet" and thus with that formalist craft from which the oblation is supposedly pure. But banning "seconds"

61

from his poetry, the poet introduces a "second," which is to say a metaphor, and one which is complicated with still more implications. Language is condemned to be compound; poetry *is* art; it shapes and forms and distorts; it introduces inequalities, like the inequality between an offering and an exchange, or the inequality between a secular offering and the sacramental body of Christ.

Thus neither a "pure" offering (Booth discerns this "second" meaning in the word "poore") nor a pure mutuality is possible in a relationship which depends on the word; still less is it possible when the word, as here, is always presented as written. In a curious sonnet which immediately precedes the group 123–5, the poet reports that he has given away a gift he had received from the friend. This gift had been a notebook, "tables." It is unclear whether the notebook contained writing by the friend or memorials of the relationship by the poet, or had been so intended by the giver but been allowed to remain blank. The stress in any case falls on the superior retentiveness of the poet's mind and heart, in contrast to the limits of the "tables":

> That poore retention could not so much hold,
> Nor need I tallies thy deare love to skore. (122)

To dispose of the notebook which contained or might have contained a written record suggests a deep dissatisfaction with language as a mediating instrument. The verb "to skore," to keep a tally, is used contemptuously, as though to insinuate that writing involves a petty arithmetic of feeling. What is striking is that the writing before us has done precisely that, has supplied us with the tallies of an intimate cost accounting. The phrase in 122 may be scornful, and yet both inside and outside the poetic fiction the language of the poetry is all we have, keeping the score and keeping an ambiguous distance open between the tarnished lovers. As that space widens, the poet begins to look like the dwellers on form and favor, spent in his gazing across a distance. He and perhaps the friend as well become pitiful thrivers, barred from the absolute immediacy at least one of them yearns for, because poetry can never be idolatrously one and can never find the metaphor, the "example," which knows no difference. The poet's real enemy is not the "informer" as slanderer, but the voice within himself through whose forming action feeling comes into being.

In the sonnets to the dark lady that follow, poetic language is thematized less prominently; the poet's sense of inner poverty modulates to self-contempt; the physiological meanings of such words as "expense" and "will" are foregrounded. The mistress, who has "robd others beds revenues of their rents" (142), is perhaps the one thriver in the work who is not pitiful. Her role is antithetical to the young man's of the procreation sonnets; she is a "usurer that put'st forth all to use" (134) and her wealth is like the ocean's:

> The sea all water, yet receives raine still,
> And in aboundance addeth to his store,
> So thou beeing rich in *Will* adde to thy *Will*,
> One will of mine to make thy large *Will* more. (135)

But this inflationary economy leads to a depreciation of all values, and the only feasible policy apparently lies in a Christian husbandry:

> Why so large cost having so short a lease,
> Dost thou upon thy fading mansion spend? . . . .
> Buy tearmes divine in selling houres of drosse:
> Within be fed, without be rich no more. (146)

By the close of the sequence, however, the poet does not seem to have adopted this policy. In his disgust with sexuality and his own revolting entrapment in it, the poet tries systematically to subvert his own authority as poet and his perception of metaphoric congruence:

> O Me! what eyes hath love put in my head,
> Which have no correspondence with true sight. (148)

Language is systematically vulgarized, "abhored," and in the last regular sonnet to the mistress (152) the coherence of the poetic consciousness and the integrity of the poetic statement are simultaneously denied, as though the poetry had no legitimate source:

> For I have sworne thee faire; more perjurde eye,
> To swere against the truth so foule a lie.

The "eye" is perjured, but also the "I" and the "aye," the capacity to affirm. "Loves eye is not so true as all mens: no" (148). It is as though the pitiless obscenity, love-denying and love-blaspheming, had to expose the *pudenda* of language to register the meanness of the seamy loyalties and tawdry bargains.

The Sonnets can be read to the end as attempts to cope with progressively powerful and painful forms of cost and expense. The bourgeois desire to balance cosmic and human budgets seems to be thwarted by a radical flaw in the universe, in emotion, in value, and in language. This flaw is already acted out at the beginning by the onanistic friend who "feed'st thy lights flame with selfe substantiall fewell" (1). In Sonnet 73, the metaphoric fire lies in its ashes as on a deathbed, "consum'd with that which it was nurrisht by." This becomes, in the terrible Sonnet 129, "a blisse in proofe and proud and very wo," a line always, unnecessarily, emended. The vulnerability of the Sonnets lies in their ceaselessly resistant reflection of this flaw, their stubborn reliance on economies incapable of correcting it, their use of language so wealthy, so charged with "difference," as to be erosive. The vulnerability of the Sonnets might be said to resemble that nameless flaw that afflicts their speaker, but in their case the flaw is not ultimately disastrous. They are not consumed by the extravagant husbandry that produced them. Their effort to resist, to compensate, to register in spite of slippage, balances their loss with store. They leave us with the awesome cost, and reward, of their conative contention. The vulnerability is inseparable from the striving that leads us to them: the "poet's" expense and Shakespeare's expense.

# Notes

1. All quotations from the Sonnets are taken from the reproduction of the Quarto text in *Shakespeare's Sonnets*, ed. Stephen Booth (New Haven and London, 1980). I have normalized the usage of u/v. The glosses by Booth occasionally cited are taken from the compendious notes to this edition. I have also had occasion to cite glosses from the edition by W. G. Ingram and Theodore Redpath, *Shakespeare's Sonnets* (New York, 1965).
2. William Shakespeare, *Sonnets*, ed. Douglas Bush and Alfred Harbage (Baltimore, Md, 1967).

# The Scandal of Shakespeare's Sonnets

*Margreta de Grazia*

Of all the many defences against the scandal of Shakespeare's Sonnets—Platonism, for example, or the Renaissance ideal of friendship—John Benson's is undoubtedly the most radical. In order to cover up the fact that the first 126 of the Sonnets were written to a male, Benson in his 1640 *Poems: Written by Wil Shake-speare. Gent.* changed masculine pronouns to feminine and introduced titles which directed sonnets to the young man to a mistress. By these simple editorial interventions, he succeeded in converting a shameful homosexual love to an acceptable heterosexual one, a conversion reproduced in the numerous reprintings of the 1640 *Poems* up through the eighteenth century. The source for this account is Hyder E. Rollins's authoritative 1944 Variorum Sonnets, the first edition to detail Benson's pronominal changes and titular insertions.[1] Subsequent editions have reproduced his conclusions, for example John Kerrigan's 1986 edition which faults Benson for inflicting on the Sonnets 'a series of unforgivable injuries,' above all 'a single recurring revision: he emended the masculine pronouns used of the friend in 1 to 126 to "her," "hers," and "she."'[2] With varying degrees of indignation and amusement, critical works on the Sonnets have repeated the charge.

The charge, however, is wrong. Benson did not attempt to convert a male beloved to a female. To begin with, the number of his alterations

---

Reprinted by permission of Cambridge University Press and Margreta de Grazia from *Shakespeare Survey* 46 (1994), pp. 35-49.

has been greatly exaggerated. Of the seventy-five titles Benson assigned to Shakespeare's Sonnets, only three of them direct sonnets from the first group of the 1609 Quarto (sonnets 1-126) to a woman.[3] Furthermore, because none of the sonnets in question specifies the gender of the beloved, Benson had no reason to believe a male addressee was intended. As for the pronominal changes, Rollins himself within nine pages of his own commentary multiplies the number of sonnets 'with verbal changes designed to make the verses apply to a woman instead of a man' from 'some' to '*many*.'[4] Rollins gives three examples as if there were countless others, but three is all there are and those three appear to have been made to avoid solecism rather than homoeroticism. In only one sonnet are pronouns altered, though even there not uniformly. In Benson's printing of sonnet 101, masculine pronouns are altered to feminine in lines 11 and 14, but the masculine (or neutral) pronouns are retained in lines 6 and 9.[5] The alteration may have been made to distinguish the personification 'Truth' from the person of the beloved. In sonnet 104, 'friend' is emended to the more conventional 'fair love,' apparently for consistency: the 'fair love' of sonnet 104 corresponds to the twice repeated 'my love' of 105, the sonnet with which it is grouped (along with sonnet 106) to form a single poem entitled 'Constant Affection.' The only other alteration may also have been for the sake of consistency: the emendation of sonnet 108's nonce 'boy' to 'love' avoids the anomaly of a single sonnet addressed to a boy.[6]

Indeed the 1640 collection hardly seems concerned with covering up amatory poems to males. The very first fourteen lines printed in the 1640 *Poems* contain eleven male pronouns, more than any other sonnet, in celebrating an emphatically male beauty. If Benson had wished to censure homoerotic love, why did he not omit the notoriously titillating master-mistress sonnet (20)? Or emend the glamorizing sonnet 106 that praises the beloved—in blazon style, part by part—as the 'master' of beauty? Or the sexually loaded sonnet 110 that apologizes to a specifically male 'god in love' for promiscuity of a decidedly 'preposterous' cast?[7] The same question applies to the numerous sonnets in which references to a male beloved as 'my love,' 'sweet love,' 'lover,' and 'rose' are retained.

It is not Shakespeare's text, then, that has been falsified by Benson but rather Benson's edition that has been falsified by the modern tradition.[8] The question is, why has so patent an error not been challenged before? Certainly it is not for scarcity of copies: while only twelve copies exist of the original 1609 Sonnets, there are that many of the 1640 *Poems* in the Folger Library alone.

I wish to propose that modern treatments of the Sonnets have displaced onto Benson a singularly modern dilemma: what to do with the inadmissible secret of Shakespeare's deviant sexuality?[9] Benson is described as having put an end to that dark secret in the most radical way imaginable, by altering the sex of the beloved and thereby converting an ignominious homosexual passion into a respectable (albeit still adulterous) heterosexual one. In attributing such an act and motive to Benson, modern criticism curiously assumes—indeed posits—the secret it then reviles Benson for concealing. Quite simply, Benson's alleged act of editorial suppression presupposes something in need of suppression: there *must* be something horrible at the heart of the sonnets—the first 126 of them—to compel such a dire editorial manoeuvre.

I have dwelled on Benson only parenthetically to set the factual record straight. My real interest is not in factual error but in the kinds of cultural imperatives that motivate such errors. I see Benson's error as a glaring instance of the need to bury a shameful secret deep within the Sonnets. The need was not Shakespeare's. It has been rather that of Shakespeare criticism which for the past two centuries has been repeating variants of the repression it obsessively ascribes to Benson. This repression has, as I will proceed to argue, produced the very scandal it would deny. At the same time, it has overlooked the scandal that *is* there, not deep within the text but right on its surface.

## I

This has been the case from the time the Sonnets were first edited: by Edmond Malone in his 1780 edition.[10] Or, to be more precise, from the time the Sonnets were first not edited: by George Steevens who reprinted the 1609 Sonnets in a collection of early quartos in 1766 but refused to edit them for his 1793 edition of Shakespeare's complete works. While he could justify their publication as documents, he refused to honour them with an editorial apparatus, the trappings of a classic.[11] Though he maintained that it was their literary defects that disqualified them, his response to sonnet 20 points to something more visceral: 'It is impossible to read [it] without an equal mixture of disgust and indignation.'[12] Surely it is this kind of aversion that prompted his condemnation of Malone's decision to edit them:

Malone's 'implements of criticism, like the ivory rake and golden spade in Prudentius, are on this occasion disgraced by the objects of their culture.' For Steevens, Malone's attempt to cultivate such soiled objects as the Sonnets defiled the tools of editing. It was Steevens then and not Benson who first attempted to conceal the scandal of Shakespeare's dirty sexuality, not by changing pronouns but by reproducing the Sonnets in the form of a dusty document rather than of a lofty classic.

Malone, by providing the Sonnets with a textual apparatus in 1780 and then by including them in the canon proper in his 1790 edition of Shakespeare's plays and poems achieved precisely what Steevens had dreaded: he elevated the Sonnets to the status of literature. But the filth that embarrassed Steevens remained—remained to be covered up. In fact, as we shall see, Malone's major editorial ambition in regard to the Sonnets—to establish the connection between the first person and Shakespeare[13]—made the cover-up all the more urgent: if the Sonnets were in Shakespeare's own voice, what was to be done with the fact that the majority of them expressed desire for a young male?

Malone's driving project of identifying the experience of the Sonnets with Shakespeare's own is evident in all his major editorial interventions. Unlike Benson who expanded their contents to accommodate the experience of all lovers by giving them generic titles, Malone limited them so that they applied exclusively to Shakespeare.[14] His first step was to restrict the Sonnets to two addressees by introducing a division after sonnet 126. With only two beloveds, the task of identifying particulars could begin. First the young man was identified on the assumption that he was the same as the dedication's Mr W. H. Other identifications followed suit: of persons, time, things, circumstances. The dedicator's T. T. was Thomas Thorpe, Spenser was the rival poet, the 'now' of the sonnets was early in Shakespeare's career, the gift referred to in 122 was a table-book given to Shakespeare by his friend, sonnet 111's 'publick means, which publick manners breeds,' referred to Shakespeare's own lamentable ties to the theatre, the unfaithful lover of sonnet 93 was Shakespeare's own wife. All of these efforts to give particularity to the Sonnets contributed to Malone's project of personalizing them. His attempts to identify their abundant deictics, what Benveniste has called 'egocentric markers'— their hes and shes, thous and yous, this's and thats, heres and theres— fastened the Sonnets around Shakespeare's 'I.'[15] Thus the experience they recorded could be recognized as that which Shakespeare lived.

The identification proved, as might be anticipated, highly problematic, for there was one connection that could not be allowed: as Malone's own division emphasized, most of the Sonnets were addressed to a male. At each of the three points where Malone insisted upon the division at 126, circumlocutions betrayed his unease: although he referred to the addressee of the second group as a 'lady' and 'female,' the addressee of the first group was no man or male, but rather 'this person,' the majority of the Sonnets are '*not* addressed to a female.'[16] The unspeakable, that 126 sonnets were addressed to a male, remained literally unspoken; at the same time, the basic division according to the beloved's gender proclaimed it.

Within the text too, Malone had to dodge the implications of his own specification, indeed whenever any of the first 126 sonnets were explicitly erotic or amatory. Footnotes then must strain to distance Shakespeare from their content, as did the note to the notorious sonnet 20: 'such addresses to men, however indelicate, were customary in our author's time, and neither imported criminality, nor were esteemed indecorous' (p. 207). Even more belaboured was Malone's rationalization of Shakespeare's references to himself as the 'lover' of the male youth. Here, too, it is not Shakespeare who offends, but rather the custom of his age: and the customary offence was even then not at the level of conduct but at the level of speech. It was 'Such *addresses* to men,' '*expressions* of this kind,' as well as 'the general *tenour* of the greater part of them' that were 'common in Shakespeare's time, and . . . not thought indecorous' [my emphasis] (pp. 219-20). For Malone, nothing separated his present from Shakespeare's past more than the 'strange' custom among men of *speaking* of other men as their 'lovers.'[17] The offence was linguistic and literary and not behavioural; to censure the Sonnets would, therefore, be as 'unreasonable' as faulting the plays for violating Aristotle's *Poetics*—an anachronistic literary judgement (p. 207). Thus for Malone the greatest difference between his late eighteenth century and Shakespeare's late sixteenth century was that in Shakespeare's time, male/male desire was a manner of speaking and not doing, whereas in Malone's more enlightened time it was neither: not done, not even spoken of (hence his repeated euphemisms and circumlocutions).

There is another remarkable instance of how Malone embroils himself in his own editorial commitments. While wanting to read the Sonnets as personal poems, he must impersonalize what his edition foregrounds as their most salient feature: that most of them are addressed to a young male. His longest footnote stretching across six pages pertains to sonnet 93, 'So shall I live supposing thou art true,' a sonnet on sexual jealousy. He fastened on this sonnet in full conviction that Shakespeare, in the Sonnets as well as in the plays, wrote with particular intensity on the subject of jealousy because he himself had experienced it; it was his 'intimate knowledge' of jealousy that enabled him to write on the subject 'more immediately *from the heart*' (p. 266). Malone avoids the scandal that Shakespeare experienced sexual jealousy for a boy by replacing Shakespeare's *boy* to Shakespeare's *wife*, thereby violating his own ascription of the first 126 sonnets to a male, or rather 'not a female.' This weird displacement freed Malone to talk comfortably about Shakespeare's sexual experience—in heterosexual (Shakespeare as cuckold) rather than homosexual terms (Shakespeare as pederast). A digression on his wife's infidelity provided the additional benefit of justifying the adulterous liaison that the second group of sonnets recorded—Shakespeare was unfaithful to his wife because she had first been unfaithful to him. Realizing the danger of such inferences, Steevens (in the notes he contributed to Malone's edition) attempted to block it by insisting that the poem reflected not Shakespeare's *experience* but his *observation*, an impersonal rather than a personal relation (pp. 266-8). Malone stuck fast to his position, finding grounds for Shakespeare's experience of jealousy in documents, anecdotes, and the plays themselves.

James Boswell the younger, when he completed Malone's edition of *The Plays and Poems* in 1821, sided with Steevens, ruling Malone's conviction as 'uncomfortable conjecture.'[18] The judgement was unusual for Boswell, for throughout the twenty-one volume edition he rarely contradicted his friend and mentor. Yet his comments on the Sonnets opposed Malone with astonishing frequency. Indeed it would be fair to say that Boswell dismantled all of the connections Malone had worked so hard to forge between the Sonnets and Shakespeare's experience. The reason is clear: Boswell wanted to counteract the impression that Malone's 1780 edition, reissued in 1790, had produced: it is 'generally admitted that the poet speaks in his own person' (p. 219). Boswell, in the preliminary and concluding remarks with which he bracketed Malone's edition, as well as in scattered internal notes, attempted to stifle all autobiographical possibilities, beginning with Malone's opening identification of 'the individual to whom they were principally addressed, and the circumstances under which they were written.' The Sonnets could not have been addressed to any real nobleman for none, according to Boswell, would have tolerated such effeminizing verse. Any 'distinguished nobleman' would have taken offence at the 'encomiums on his beauty, and the fondling expressions' appropriate only to a 'cocker'd silken wanton' (p. 219). Thus such amorous language could not have been 'customary' between men in Shakespeare's time, as Malone had insisted, for it would have implied that men were effeminate. For Boswell, male desire for males could not have been an acceptable way of even speaking, even back then. For him, male/male desire existed nowhere (in England anyway), not in Shakespeare's past, not in his own present; not in language, not in deed. It was sheer make-believe: what Boswell terms, not unsalaciously, 'effusions of fancy . . . for the amusement of a private circle' (p. 220).

To establish their status as 'fancy,' Boswell must sever all the connections Malone had forged between the Sonnets and Shakespeare's life. And so he does, one by one: Shakespeare was as young as thirty-four or at most forty-five when writing the Sonnets so how could it be he who is represented as old and decrepit in several sonnets? Of course, it is not the association with old age (or with the theatre) that disturbed Boswell, but the logical extension of *any* connection: 'If Shakespeare was speaking of himself in this passage, it would follow that he is equally pointed at upon other occasions' (p. 220). More specifically, if it was Shakespeare who was old then it was also he who was 'grossly and notoriously profligate,' the perpetrator of '"harmful deeds,"' whose '"name had received a brand,"' and whose reputation suffered from the '"impression which vulgar scandal stamped upon his brow."' Such identifications were, Boswell insisted, absurd, for among the extant biographical materials 'not the slightest imputation [was] cast upon his character.' This is not surprising, for Malone and Boswell in their *New Life of Shakspeare* had rejected as factually inaccurate the numerous scandalous anecdotes that had cast him in the shady roles of poacher, adulterer, and carouser.[19]

If Boswell found any fault at all in Shakespeare, it was for his 'selection of topics,' his representation in any form of male/male desire. But Boswell legitimized this choice by attributing it to Shakespeare's altogether admirable 'fondness for classical imitation' (p. 221). Boswell now is at last able to name the unspeakable topic, though only in simultaneously disavowing it: and not in his own words, but in words properly removed from his own by quotation marks and from standard English by sixteenth-century old spelling. The quotation is from Webbe's *Discourse of English Poetrie* that defends Virgil's

second eclogue by insisting that the poet 'doth not meane . . . any
disordered loue, or the filthy lust of deuillish Pederastice' (p. 221).[20]
Boswell keeps a clean distance from the 'filthy' object as if afraid of
dirtying his ivory rake and golden spade. Having dismantled all of
Malone's connections, Boswell can conclude with a discussion of the
Sonnets' literary merits, the only relevant consideration after they have
been wrenched from toxic reality and consigned to innocuous fancy.

I have discussed the Malone (1780, 1790) and the Malone/Boswell
(1821) editions because it is with them that the modern history of the
Sonnets begins, and since no full edition of the 1609 Quarto was
printed prior to Malone's, that belated history can be considered their
only history.[21] They have the further importance of having established
the two critical approaches that have repeated themselves for two
centuries now—sometimes ingeniously, sometimes hysterically: (1)
Malone's—the Sonnets are about Shakespeare but not as a lover of
young men or, (2) Boswell's—the Sonnets are not about Shakespeare
or anything else, especially not about Shakespeare as a lover of young
men. Though these approaches are antithetical and mutually exclusive,
it must be stressed that both are motivated by the same urgency to deny
Shakespeare's desire for a male.

In this regard the history of the Sonnets' reception provides a
stunning example of the phenomenon Jonathan Dollimore has recently
identified: the centrality of homosexuality in a culture that denounces
it.[22] The denial of homosexuality in the Sonnets has produced the two
polarized approaches by which they have been traditionally read for
two centuries. Furthermore, what has been denied (by evasions,
displacements, circumlocutions, suppressions, abstractions, etc.) has
slipped into the text itself producing (as if from the Sonnets
themselves) an hermeneutical interior capable of concealing a sin, a
crime, a pathology. The unspeakable of Sonnets criticism has thus
become the unspoken of the Sonnets—to the exclusion of, as has yet to
be seen, what they quite forthrightly say.

## II

I now wish to turn to one of Malone's major editorial acts, his division
of the sonnets into two gendered groups, 126 to a young man, the
remaining twenty-eight to a woman. The division has been generally
accepted. It seems, after all, quite obvious: none of the first 126 sonnets
are addressed explicitly to a woman and none of the remaining twenty-

eight are addressed explicitly to a male. *Explicitly* is the key word, for what Malone's clear-cut division has obscured is the astonishing number of sonnets that do not make the gender of the addressee explicit.[23] Shakespeare is exceptional among the English sonneteers (Sidney, Spenser, and Daniel, for example) in leaving the beloved's gender unspecified in so many of the sonnets: about five-sixths of them in the first 126 and just less than that in the collection entire. The uncertainty of the beloved's gender is sustained by other types of ambiguity, most notoriously in the 'master-mistress' sonnet 20, but also in sonnet 53 in which the youth is described as a paragon of both masculine and feminine beauty, of both Adonis and Helen; similarly, a variety of epithets recur that apply to either sex: rose, friend, love, lover, sweet, fair.

The little evidence we have of how the Sonnets were read before Malone strongly suggests that the first 126 sonnets were not read as being exclusively to a male. Benson assumed that the Sonnets were to a female unless otherwise specified, as the titles he assigned to his groupings indicate.[24] So too did the numerous eighteenth-century editors who reprinted Benson: Gildon (1723) referred to them as 'being most to his Mistress' and Sewell (1725) believed them to have been inspired by 'a real, or an imaginary Lady.'[25] Independent of Benson, there is further and earlier evidence. Gary Taylor has discussed five manuscript versions of sonnet 2 from the early decades of the seventeenth century with the title 'To one that would die a maid';[26] there is also a 1711 reprint of the 1609 quarto that describes the collection as '154 Sonnets all of them in Praise of his Mistress.'[27] The eighteenth-century antiquarian William Oldys who possessed a copy of the quarto assumed that some of the first 126 sonnets were addressed to a female, and George Steevens defended his logic: 'From the complaints of *inconstancy*, and the praises of *beauty*, contained in them, [the Sonnets] should seem at first sight to be addressed by an inamorato to a mistress' (Malone and Boswell, p. 306). Malone's preliminary note announcing the division at 126 literally prevented such a 'first sight,' precluding the possibility open to earlier readers of assuming the ungendered sonnets to a female.

This is not, however, to say that Malone got it wrong: clearly no sonnets are addressed to a female in the first 126 and none to a male (except Cupid) in the subsequent twenty-eight. Just as clearly, the poet abandons the young man in 126 and declares his allegiance to a mistress in 127 and the formal irregularities (twelve pentameter lines in

couplets) may punctuate that shift.[28] Nor is there any reason not to take
144's announcement—'Two loves I have': 'a man right fair' and 'a
woman, colour'd ill'—at face value. Some kind of binary division
appears to be at work.[29] The question is whether that division is best
described in terms—or *only* in terms—of gender difference: in terms,
that is, of the object choices that have lent themselves so readily to the
modern distinction between homosexuality and heterosexuality.[30]

For that construction of desire—as Foucault's expansive history of
sexuality as well as Alan Bray's concentration on the Renaissance have
demonstrated[31]—depended on a construal of the body and of the
psyche that postdated Shakespeare, like Malone's edition itself, by
about two centuries. It may then be that Malone's overly emphatic
division of the Sonnets into male/female appears more in keeping with
the cultural preoccupations at the turn of the eighteenth century than of
the sixteenth. It may be symptomatic of a much later emphasis on
sexual differentiation, one that has been fully charted out recently in
Thomas Laqueur's *Making Sex: Body and Gender from the Greeks to
Freud.*[32]

According to Laqueur, 'Sometime in the eighteenth century, sex as
we know it was invented.'[33] What he means by this bold
pronouncement is that until then there was essentially one sex rather
than two. According to the classical or Galenic model, the female
possessed an inverted, interior, and inferior version of male genitalia;
as countless anatomical drawings attest, the uterus was imagined as an
inverted scrotum, the vagina an inverted penis, the vulva an inverted
foreskin. Reproductive processes as well as parts were also on par, so
that conception required orgasm from both male and female. Not until
the eighteenth century were male and female typically divided into two
discrete sexes with distinct reproductive parts and processes: hence the
invention of 'sex as we know it.' The shift is reflected in an array of
verbal and graphic representations: the construction of a different
skeleton for women than for men; anatomical drawings representing
incommensurate reproductive structures rather than homologous ones;
the division of formerly shared nomenclature into male and female so
that once ungendered sperm, testicles, and stones are gendered male
and differentiated from female eggs and ovaries. In short, a
reproductive biology was constructed based on *absolute* rather than
*relative* difference. It is only then, Laqueur notes, that the expression
'opposites attract' is coined, suggesting that 'natural' sexual attraction
is between unlikes rather than likes.[34]

As Laqueur points out, this reconstrual removed sexuality from a vast system of metaphysical correspondences based, like society itself, on hierarchical order and situated it firmly in the body or 'nature.' That a woman was previously imagined to possess less perfected versions of male genitalia legitimized her subordination to man. Biology thus upheld social hierarchy. Once difference was grounded in the body rather than in metaphysics, once male and female anatomy was perceived as incommensurate rather than homologous, then sexuality lost its 'social' bearings and became instead a matter of 'nature.' As Laqueur insists repeatedly, and as his characterization of the shift as an *invention* rather than as a *discovery* suggests, the change represents no empirical or scientific advance—'No discovery or group of discoveries dictated the rise of the two-sex model'[35]—but rather a cultural and political reorientation. Malone's division of the Sonnets may best be understood in the context of this reorientation.

There is another shift that strangely corresponds to both Malone's twofold division and biology's two-sex model, and it occurs at roughly the same point in time. In eighteenth-century grammars and discussions of grammar, a new attention to linguistic gender binaries appears. The hierarchy preserved in the one-sex model had also applied in questions of grammatical agreement: male gender prevailed over female because it was the 'more worthy' gender. In his popular rhetoric (1553), Thomas Wilson considered natural order violated when women preceded men in a syntactic construction, since man was clearly the dominant gender. In his official Latin grammar (1567), William Lyly assumed the same principle in explaining that an adjective describing both a male and female noun must agree with the male ('Rex et Regina Beati') because 'The masculine gender is more worthy than the feminine.'[36] In the eighteenth century, however, this ontological and grammatical hierarchy has ceased to be self-evident. And the reason appears to be that grammar now looks to biology rather than to metaphysics for its lead. New discoveries in biology are brought to bear on grammar, so that it is maintained that the discovery that plants have sexes introduced inconsistency into classical grammar's classification of plants as neuter.[37] In highly gendered languages like German, a general rethinking of conventional grammatical gender occurs. In English that possesses no conventional grammatical gendering, the problem took a more focused form. Towards the end of the eighteenth century, the first call for an epicene or gender-neutral pronoun is heard, in response to what is only then perceived as a problem: what to do with constructions like '*everyone* should go to *his* place' where a female and male antecedent is represented by the male 'his.'[38] As in biology, grammar can no longer assume an hierarchical relation between male and female to justify the predominance of male gender.

It is not only in relation to the third person that hierarchy disappears; in English, it had also by the start of the eighteenth century disappeared from the second person. In standard English, *thee/thou* had been dropped in favour of *you*, collapsing the complexly nuanced range of distinctions based on class relations. It is curious that Malone, who took great pride in noting philological difference in Shakespeare's age, ignored the second person pronoun while focusing on the third. Several recent critics, however, have discussed it, noting that the first 126 sonnets vacillate between *you* and *thou*, while the second twenty-eight consistently stick to *thou*.[39] Their explanations have been varied, contradictory and incomplete; the highly complex code remains unbroken. What can be ventured, however, is that the unwritten rules governing second person usage in the Renaissance were social and hierarchic.[40] They originated in social rank, though clearly were complicated by a calculus of differentials that included age, gender, education, experience, race, ethical worth, emotional stake, etc.[41]

This is not to propose a new division, the first 126 to 'you/thou,' the next twenty-eight to 'thou'[42]—but rather to suggest that gender difference is not the *only* way to differentiate the Sonnets' 'Two loves.' There are other forms of otherness that the Malonean or modern tradition has ignored. Sexual difference is only one differential category in these poems; class is another, so is age, reputation, marital status, moral probity, even physical availability. In each of these categories, the poet is more like the mistress than like the youth; love of like would, therefore, incline him more to the mistress than the boy. It is because Joel Fineman's awesome *Shakespeare's Perjured Eye: The Invention of Poetic Subjectivity in the Sonnets* limits difference to sexual difference that its argument is so troubling. For more relentlessly and consequentially than anyone since Malone, Fineman has emphasized the distinction between male and female; indeed, it is fundamental to his Lacanian account of the constitution of subjectivity. The rupturing transition required by this account occurs, for Fineman, in the move from homosexual love of the same to heterosexual love of the other, from the ideal specularity of the youth to the false linguistics of the mistress, a move that readily translates into the Lacanian break from the imaginary into the symbolic. In short, Fineman bases what may be the vastest claim ever made for the Sonnets—that they invent poetic subjectivity for the western tradition—on sexual difference, on that rupturing but constitutive transition from a like and admired object to an unlike and loathed one.[43] Yet in light of the biological and grammatical phenomena we have been attending, Fineman's construal of sexual difference is premature. The 'Invention of Poetic Subjectivity' he attributes to Shakespeare must await 'the invention of sex' Laqueur sees as an eighteenth-century phenomenon. Until male and female can be seen as two discrete sexes rather than variants on one sex, how can subjectivity be constituted in the break between the two?

It is because Fineman overstresses the gender division at sonnet 126 that his study might be seen as the culmination of the Malonean tradition. Focus on male/female difference lends itself too readily to a psychosexuality that excludes the psychosocial. If social distinctions like class or even age were introduced, for example, the entire Lacanian progression would be turned on its head, for the poet would experience the youth's aristocratic otherness *before* the mistress's bourgeois sameness, his extreme junior *before* his approximate peer. How, then, would it be possible to make the transition Lacanian subjectivity requires from imaginary identification to symbolic dislocation? I've put the burden of two centuries of criticism on Fineman's massively difficult book in order to make a very simple point: tradition has postulated (and concealed) in the Sonnets a sexual scandal that is based in the personal abstracted from the social, on a biology of two-sexes rather than on an epistemology of one-sex, on a division according to a gendered third person rather than a ranked second person. As I will show in the remainder of this paper by turning—at long last—to the Sonnets themselves, this has been a mistake . . . so *big* a mistake that the real scandal has been passed over.

## III

The ideological force of the imperious first line of the Sonnets has gone virtually unnoticed: 'From fairest creatures we desire increase.'[44] In the first seventeen poems which have traditionally (and rather preciously) been titled the procreation sonnets, there can be no pretence of fair being either an abstract value like the Platonic Good or a disinterested one like the Kantian Beautiful. *Fair* is the distinguishing attribute of the dominant class, not unlike Bourdieu's *taste* that serves both to distinguish the dominant class and, by distinguishing it, to keep it dominant.[45] The first seventeen sonnets urging the fair youth to marry and beget a son have an open and explicit social function: to reproduce, like an Althusserian state apparatus, the *status quo* by reproducing a fair young man, ideally 'ten for one' (6). The preservation of the youth preserves his aristocratic family line, dynasty or 'house': 'Who lets so faire a house fall to decay?' (13). If such houses are allowed to deteriorate, the social formation would itself be at risk: hence the general (and conservative) desire to increase 'fairest creatures' and to convince those privileged creatures that the repair of their 'beautious roofe' should be their 'chiefe desire' (10). Were these houses and roofs *un*fair, there would be no cultural imperative to maintain them, just as there is none to reproduce *un*fair (homely) persons: 'Let those whom nature hath not made for store, / Harsh featurelesse, and rude, barrenly perish' (11); while the youth is 'much too faire, / To be deaths conquest and make wormes thine heire' (6), the 'Harsh, featureless, and rude' can return to dust unlamented. 'Increase' is to be desired only from those whom Nature has 'best indow'd' with 'bountious guift' (11); and those gifts are not simply physical or spiritual riches but the social and material ones that structure society from the top. For this reason, it is only the fair lineaments of fair lineages that should be reproduced for posterity—'Thou shouldst print more, not let that coppy die.'

Underscoring the social concerns of this first group is their origin in pedagogical materials designed to cultivate fair young men. As has long been noted, these sonnets derive from Erasmus's 'Epistle to persuade a young gentleman to marriage,' Englished in Thomas Wilson's widely influential 1553 *The Arte of Rhetorique*.[46] The treatise was used in schools as a rhetorical exercise in persuasion. Languet repeated it in a letter to the young Sidney and Sidney in turn echoed it in his *Arcadia*, that consummate expression of aristocratic ethos. The treatise's tropes and arguments attained commonplace status, as is suggested by the seventeenth-century popularity of the sonnet that deploys the most of them, sonnet 2, copies of which survive in twelve early manuscripts.[47] It seems likely, then, that these opening sonnets would have evoked the pedagogical context which prepared fair young men to assume the social position to which high birth entitled them. The 'private friends' among whom according to Francis Meres these sonnets circulated as well as the patron to whom the collection is ostensibly dedicated can be assumed to have recognized this rhetoric as a blueprint for reproducing the fair values of the dominant class.[48] Shakespeare's 'Two loves' relate to this opening set piece quite explicitly: after sonnet 17, it is through his own poetic lines rather than the youth's generational loins that fair's lineaments are to be reproduced, fair's lineage extended.[49] The fair line ends, however, at 127 with the shocking declaration that 'now is blacke beauties successive heire.' As if a black child had been born of a fair parent, a miscegenating successor is announced, one who razes fair's lineage ('And Beautie slandered with a bastard shame') and seizes fair's language ('beauty hath no name')—genealogy and etymology. Desire inverts its object at this breaking point: from an embodiment of a social ideal to an embodiment of a social atrocity. In praising the youth's fair lineaments, social distinction had been maintained; in praising the mistress's dark colours, social distinction is confounded. This reverses the modern ranking of the 'Two loves' that has found one unspeakable and the other simply regrettable. For the love of the youth 'right fair' which tradition has deemed scandalous promotes a social programme while the love for the mistress 'collour'd ill' which tradition has allowed threatens to annihilate it.

This is a sign, I think, that there is something misleading about the male/female categories by which Malone divided the collection: they too easily slip into the post-Enlightenment categories of homosexual and heterosexual which provoke responses that are precisely the inverse of what the Sonnets themselves call for. I would like to propose instead that the two groups be reconsidered under rubrics available in the period, appearing in E. K.'s note to the *Shepherdes Calendar* defending Hobbinol's passion for young Colin Clout on the grounds that 'paederastice [is] much to be preferred before gynerastice, that is the love that inflameth men with lust toward womankind.'[50] Unlike homosexual and heterosexual, the terms better correspond with Shakespeare's 'better' and 'worser' loves, his pederastic love of a boy ('my lovely Boy,' 126) and gynerastic love of a womb (the irresistible 'waste of shame,' 129).[51] As E. K. specifies, pederastic love is 'much to be preferred' over gynerastic, and the Sonnets demonstrate why: because it does not imperil social distinction.

Indeed the poet's main task in the first group is to protect those distinctions, a task that takes the specific form of preserving the youth's lineaments from Time's disfigurations. Shakespeare's 'pupil pen' is in contest with 'Times pensel' (16). In his own verse lines, he would transcribe the youth's fair features before 'confounding Age' unfairs them by cross-hatching his physiognomic lineaments with 'lines and wrincles' (63), cancelling or deleting the youth's fair copy, rendering him thereby 'featurelesse' like those consigned to perish barrenly—as if to make him indistinguishable from the 'Harsh' and 'rude.' In the gynerastic group, however, it is not Time but Lust that threatens distinction. Lust mars not through the sharp incisions of Time's stylus—its pen-knife—but through the obscuring adulterations of 'a woman colour'd ill.' While Time's deadly scriptings disfigure what is seen, Lust's murky adulterations confound what is known. Once a black mistress preempts the fair youth, a whole range of epistemological distinctions collapse: between black and fair (131, 132) to be sure, but also between truth and lies (138); private and public (137); first person and second, first person and third (135-6); past, present, and future (129); is and is not (147), worst and best (150), angel and friend (144). In the first group, though aging himself ('Beated and chopt with tand antiquitie' (62), the poet sets himself up as Time's adversary, his own glamourizing lines counteracting Time's disfiguring marks; in the second group, however, Lust and Will are familiars rather than adversaries, so much so that Will is literally synonymous with Lust in 135 and 136, and Lust personified blurs into Will's person in 129. The pederastic 'pupil pen' reinscribes the pedagogical ideal with which the Sonnets begin; while the gynerastic 'waste of shame' adulterates even the most black and white distinctions.

This is not to say that love of the youth is altogether 'of comfort.' The majority of the sonnets to him register intense longing, humiliation, loss felt and anticipated, betrayal, and even worse, self-betrayal—all the result, perhaps, of a cultural overinvestment in 'fairest creatures.' Yet the cost is nothing in comparison with what gynerasty exacts.[52] As the promiscuous womb threatens social order, so too gynerasty threatens psychic stability. Will himself takes on the hysterical attributes of the womb that obsesses him, in the breathlessly frantic copulatives of 129, in the semantic confusions listed above which in sonnet 147 he calls 'mad mans' discourse. There could be no more shocking manifestation of his hysteria than sonnet 136 in which every word could be said to signal his desire, homonymically or synonymically.[53] This maniacal repetition is audible in '*Will*, will fulfill the treasure of thy loue, / I fill it full with wils, and my will one,' but it is present in all the sonnet's phonetic variables as well, reducing their signification to the tautological deadlock of 'Will wills will.' Nor is Will ever released from this uterine obsession; like all men in sonnet 129, he does not know how to avoid the sulphuric pit (144), how 'To shun the heauen that leads men to this hell' (129); hence the fatal return in the final two Anacreontics to his mistress's genital 'eye,' her inflammatory and unquenchable 'Well.'[54]

But the real horror of gynerasty is social and general rather than personal and particular. Edgar in *Lear* contemns Goneril's royal womb adulterated by the bastard Edmund as 'indinguish'd [*sic*] space of Womans will.'[55] It is precisely this failure of discrimination that characterizes the dark lady's sexual capacity, as is evidenced by her indiscrete admission of Wills. In these sonnets it is not only common names that lose distinction, but also proper. Men named Will are indistinguishable: Will Shakespeare would be among them, and perhaps Will of the dedication's Mr W. H., and perhaps the mistress's husband is also Will, but what difference does it make when Will like *Homo* (like 'sausie Iackes' too) is a common name to all?[56] Repeatedly in these sonnets the indiscriminate womb is contrasted with that exclusive treasured 'place' or 'viall' (6) in which the youth's purely aristocratic seed would be antiseptically distilled or 'pent in walls of glasse' (5). The 'large and spacious' place that is the focus of desire in the second group is no such discerning 'seuerall plot': it is 'the wide worlds common place' (137) and primarily an incontinently liquid one—'the baye where all men ride' (137) and 'sea all water, [that] yet receiues raine still' (135)—in which all distinctions of blood bleed into one another.

As the law itself under Elizabeth confirmed by more severely prosecuting fornication between men and women than between men, nothing threatens a patriarchal and hierarchic social formation more than a promiscuous womb. By commingling blood-lines, it has the potential to destroy the social fabric itself. The gynecrasty of the Sonnets, then, needs to be considered in terms of the range of sexual practices Alan Bray has foregrounded (among them, bestiality, adultery, rape, and prostitution) that were in the period termed 'sodomy' and associated with such crimes against the state as sorcery, heresy, and treason.[57] There is good reason, therefore, to credit Jonathan Goldberg's recent suggestion that in Renaissance terms, it is Shakespeare's sonnets to the dark lady rather than those to the young man that are sodomitic.[58]

The dark lady's indiscriminate womb images social anarchy no less than Lear's invocation of cosmic cataclysm: 'all germains spill at once.'[59] The germains spill serially in the mistress rather than all 'at once,' but with the same helter-skelter randomness, *including those of the fair youth*, so that his noble seed is intermixed with that of common 'sausie Iackes' (128) and of unnumbered intercoursing 'Wills.'[60] The patriarchal dream of producing fair young men turns into the patriarchal nightmare of a social melting pot, made all the more horrific by the fact that the mistress's *black* is the antithesis not just of fair but of *white*. Tradition has been ever slower to entertain the possibility that these poems express desire for a black woman rather than desire for a boy. But the important work that is being done on England's contact with Africa and on its cultural representations of that contact is making it increasingly difficult to dissociate in this period blackness from racial blackness—black from blackamoor—promiscuity from miscegenation, especially in a work that begins by arguing for the perpetuation of pure fair blood.[61]

This paper began with one traditional error and ends with another. The first was minor, an erroneous representation of Benson's publishing efforts. The last, however, is quite major. The scandal in the Sonnets had been misidentified. It is not Shakespeare's desire for a boy; for in upholding social distinctions, that desire proves quite conservative and safe. It is Shakespeare's gynerastic longings for a black mistress that are perverse and menacing, precisely because they threaten to raze the very distinctions his poems to the fair boy strain to preserve. As with the Benson falsification, it is the motive behind the error that is worth thinking about. And I will end by doing so.

   Since the eighteenth century, sexuality has been seen in biological and psychological terms rather than social.[62] Perversion, therefore, is seen as pathological rather than subversive. But in a period in which the distribution of power and property depended on orderly sexuality, it remained imperative that sexuality be understood and judged in social terms. The social consequences of sexual arrangements (whether male-female marriages or male-male alliances) and derangements (male-female adultery or male-male sodomy) were too basic to allow them to become merely personal matters—to become, that is, what they have become in modern sexual discourse: the precondition of personal identity. Modern readings of the Sonnets (the only kind we have) have skewed the relation of Shakespeare's 'Two loves' to conform with this classification. The result is quite topsy-turvy: readings of the young man sonnets have concealed a personal scandal that was never there; and readings of dark mistress sonnets have been blank to the shocking social peril they promulgate. A category mistake lies at the bottom of this odd hermeneutic: the Sonnets' 'Two loves' have been misclassified, the 'love of comfort' avoided as abnormal and unnatural and the 'love of despaire' countenanced as normal and natural. This essay has argued that a reclassification is in order according to a different system altogether, one that would replace the personal categories of normalcy and abnormalcy with the social ones of hierarchy and anarchy—of desired generation and abhorred miscegenation.

## NOTES

1. *A New Variorum Edition of Shakespeare: The Sonnets*, 2 vols. (Philadelphia, Pa. and London, 1944), vol. 2, p. 20, n. 1. Sidney Lee in his introduction to a 1905 facsimile of the Sonnets noted Benson's changes but without itemizing them or speculating on Benson's motives: *Shakespeare's Sonnets: Being a Reproduction in Facsimile of the First Edition* (Oxford, 1905), pp. 57-8.

2. *The Sonnets and A Lover's Complaint* (Middlesex and New York, 1986), p. 46.

3. Benson gives the title 'Selfe flattery of her beautie' to sonnets 113-15, 'Upon receit of a Table Booke from his Mistris' to sonnet 122, 'An intreatie for her acceptance' to sonnet 125. See Rollins, vol. 2, pp. 20-1 for a list of Benson's titles.

4. Cf. Rollins, pp. 20 and 29.

5. Benson alters the pronoun from male to female only in the last four lines of the sonnet: 'To make *her* much out-live a gilded tombe'; 'To make *her* seeme, long hence, as *she* showes now' (emphasis added). The masculine pronoun is retained in lines 6 and 9: 'Truth needs no colour with *his* colour fix'd'; 'Because *he* needs no praise wilt thou be dumbe?' (emphasis added). Benson, *Poems: Written by Wil. Shake-speare. Gent.* (London, 1640), E$^v$.

6. The only other sonnet referring to the beloved as 'boy' (sonnet 126, 'O thou my lovely boy') was with seven others dropped from the 1640 collection, perhaps by accident.

7. See Stephen Booth's gloss to sonnet 110, lines 9-12, pp. 356-7 as well as to sonnet 109, lines 9, 10, 13, 14, pp. 352-3 in *Shakespeare's Sonnets* (New Haven, Conn. and London, 1977).

8. For accounts of how Benson's printing-house and editorial practices have also been maligned, see Josephine Waters Bennett, 'Benson's Alleged Piracy of *Shakespeares Sonnets* and of Some of Jonson's Works,' *Studies in Bibliography*, 21 (1968), pp. 235-48. See also Margreta de Grazia, *Shakespeare*

*Verbatim: The Reproduction of Authenticity and the 1790 Apparatus* (Oxford, 1991), p. 49, n. 1, pp. 163-73.

9. On the hysterical response to this problem in modern readings of the Sonnets, see Peter Stallybrass, 'Editing as Cultural Formation: The Sexing of Shakespeare's Sonnets,' *Modern Language Quarterly*, 54 (March, 1993), 91-103, reprinted in this volume.

10. *Supplement to the Edition of Shakespeare's Plays Published in 1778 by Samuel Johnson and George Steevens*, 2 vols. (1780), vol. 2.

11. *Twenty of the Plays of Shakespeare*, 4 vols., ed. George Steevens (1766).

12. Quoted by Rollins, vol. 1, p. 55.

13. See de Grazia, p. 154.

14. See de Grazia, pp. 155-6.

15. For the profusion of deictics in the Sonnets, see Joel Fineman, *Shakespeare's Perjured Eye: The Invention of Poetic Subjectivity in the Sonnets* (Berkeley, Los Angeles, London, 1986), pp. 8-9, p. 311, n. 6.

16. *The Plays and Poems of William Shakspeare*, 10 vols. (1790; facs. rpt., New York, 1968), vol. 10, pp. 191, 265, 294. Subsequent references to this volume will appear in text.

17. On 'lover,' see Booth, p. 432.

18. *The Plays and Poems of William Shakspeare* (1821; facs. rpt., New York, 1966), vol. 20, p. 309. Page references to this volume will henceforth appear parenthetically in text.

19. For Malone's invalidation of the inculpatory anecdotes, see de Grazia, pp. 104-7, pp. 135-41.

20. Boswell corrects Webbe for referring to the eclogue as the sixth ('by a slip of memory, or the printer's mistake') when it should be the fourth (p. 221). Bruce R. Smith situates this eclogue in Renaissance pastoral in 'The Passionate Shepherd,' *Homosexual Desire in Shakespeare's England: A Cultural Poetics* (Chicago and London, 1991), pp. 79-115.

21. The 1609 Sonnets were reprinted but without an apparatus by Bernard Lintott in 1711 and by George Steevens in 1766.

22. *Sexual Dissidence: Augustine to Wilde, Freud to Foucault* (Oxford, 1991).

23. See Booth's scrupulous account of the division, p. 430.

24. Rollins aligns the 1640 titles with the 1609 sonnet numbers, vol. 2, pp. 21-2.

25. See de Grazia, p. 155, n. 57.

26. 'Some Manuscripts of Shakespeare's Sonnets,' *Bulletin of The John Rylands University Library*, 68, I (1985), 217.

27. Bernard Lintott, *A Collection of poems in Two Volumes . . . Being all the Miscellanies of Mr William Shakespeare, which were Publish'd by himself in the Year 1609 . . .*, 2 vols.

28. In the 1609 quarto, the irregularity is rendered typographically conspicuous by two sets of empty brackets in place of the final couplet.

29. On the possibility that the Sonnets were organized according to a tripartite structure (152 Sonnets, 2 Anacreontics, a Complaint) based on generic rather than gender difference following the model of Daniel, Spenser, Lodge, and others, see Kerrigan's Introduction to *Sonnets*, pp. 13-14 and the bibliographic references on p. 66.

30. On the taxonomy of 'homo' and 'hetero,' see Eve Kosofsky Sedgwick, *The Epistemology of the Closet* (Berkeley and Los Angeles, 1990).

31. Michel Foucault, *The History of Sexuality*, vol. I: *An Introduction*, trans., Robert Hurley (New York, 1978) and Alan Bray, *Homosexuality in Renaissance England* (London, 1982).

32. (Cambridge, Mass. and London, 1990).

33. P. 149. Laqueur notes the agreement of Michel Foucault, Lawrence Stone, and Ivan Illich in identifying the late eighteenth century as the point at which human sexuality was reconceptualized, p. 5 and n. 14.

34. Ibid. p. 152

35. Ibid. p. 153.

36. *A Short Introduction of Grammar* (London, 1530), p. 47.

37. See Dennis Barron, *Grammar and Gender* (New Haven, Conn., 1986), p. 35.

38. Ibid. pp. 190-1.

39. See G. P. Jones, 'You, Thou, He or She? The Master Mistress in Shakespearian and Elizabethan Sonnet Sequences,' *Cahiers Élisabéthains*, 19 (1981), 73-84 and Andrew Gurr, 'You and Thou in Shakespeare's Sonnets,' *Essays in Criticism*, 32 (1982), 9-25. Arthur F. Marotti is sensitive to the tonal effects of such positionalities in his discussion of how Shakespeare's artistry can compensate for his inferior social rank, in 'Love Is not Love: Elizabethan Sonnet Sequences and The Social Order,' *Journal of English Literary History*, 49 (1982), 413-16.

40. On the origins of the distinction between *tu/vos* in Latin and *thou/you* in English, see R. Brown and A. Gilman, 'The Pronouns of Power and Solidarity,' in T. A. Sebeok, ed., *Style in Language* (Amherst, Mass., 1960), pp. 253-76.

41. The same perplexing instability of address characterizes another male/male couple divided by rank, not to mention age, experience, and size: Falstaff and Hal, who shift constantly from one form to the other as they

uneasily jockey for position in a relationship characterized by jockeying, a relationship in which male/male erotic desire is, as Jonathan Goldberg has recently argued, not entirely absent; 'Hal's Desire, Shakespeare's Idaho,' in *Henry IV, Parts One and Two*, ed. Nigel Wood (Philadelphia, Pa., 1995), 145-75. I wish to thank him for letting me read the typescript.

42. Sonnet 145 is the sole exception; it substitutes 'you' for 'thou' in the interest of preserving rhyme: 'I hate, from hate away she threw, / And sau'd my life saying not you.'

43. The book's overinvestment in gender binaries raises troubling political and hermeneutic questions. Its argument that subjectivity is attained through the renunciation of the imaginary realm of homosexual sameness bears a disturbing resemblance to a pseudo-Freudianism that perceives homosexuality as stunted or incomplete development. It also requires that sonnets 1-126 be read as univocal and 127-52 as equivocal, though Fineman later revises this programme by maintaining that equivocation is present in both groups, though only latently in the first.

44. The Sonnets will henceforth be quoted from the facsimile of the 1609 *Shake-speares Sonnets* printed in Stephen Booth's edition. Lars Engle has recently discussed this first line as inaugurating the Sonnets' concern with 'human value in time,' but without noting the specific class inflection of this value, 'Afloat in Thick Deeps: Shakespeare's Sonnets on Certainty,' *Publications of the Modern Language Association*, 104 (1989), 832-43.

45. Pierre Bourdieu, *Distinction: A Social Critique of the Judgement of Taste*, trans. Richard Nice (Cambridge, Mass., 1984).

46. For the influence of this epistle on Shakespeare and others, see Rollins, *Variorum* I, p. 7 and II, p. 192, T. W. Baldwin, *The Literary Genetics of Shakespeare's Poems and Sonnets* (Urbana, Ill., 1950), pp. 183-5, and Katharine M. Wilson, *Shakespeare's Sugared Sonnets* (London and New York, 1974), pp. 146-67.

47. See Taylor, pp. 210-46.

48. This is not to say that the Sonnets unequivocally reproduce aristocratic value. As Thomas M. Greene points out, the thrift and husbandry urged upon the young man in the first seventeen sonnets is decidedly bourgeois ('Pitiful Thrivers: Failed Husbandry in the Sonnets,' *Shakespeare and the Question of Theory*, ed. Patricia Parker and Geoffrey Hartman [New York and London, 1985], pp. 230-44). Furthermore, the socially inferior poet (sonnets 25 and 110) by taking on the youth's responsibility for reproducing fair in effect assumes aristocracy's genetic privilege: his inky poetic lines preempt the youth's fair genealogical ones: 'His beautie shall in these blacke lines be seene' (63).

49. For the semantic and homonymic connections between lines and lineaments, see William Empson, *Seven Types of Ambiguity* (New York, 1947), pp. 54-5, cited by Booth, p. xiii. For the line/loin resonances, see Additional Notes to Booth's 1978 edition, p. 579.

50. Kerrigan brings E. K.'s gloss to bear on the Sonnets to conclude that the Sonnets register a 'profound homosexual attachment of a scarcely sensual, almost unrealized kind,' p. 51; Stephen Orgel comments briefly on the psychological and legal advantages of 'paederastice' over 'gynerastice' in 'Call Me Ganymede,' *Impersonations: The Performance of Gender in Shakespeare's England* (Cambridge, 1996), p. 71. See also Smith's discussion of the quote in relation to Virgil and Spenser, pp. 95-8.

51. On the identification of woman with womb, see Richard Verstegan: 'And as Homo in Latin doth signifie both man and woman, so in our toung the feminyne creature also hath as we see the same of man, but more aptly in that it is for due distinction composed with womb, *she being that kynde of mann that is wombed*, or hath the womb of conception, which the man of the male kynd hath not,' *The Restitution of Decayed Intelligence* (Antwerp, 1605), p. 194.

52. Stephen Orgel, in commenting on the 'all but axiomatic' love of men for boys in the period, refers to the Sonnets as evidence that 'the problem of sex between men involves a good deal less anxiety' than between men and women, 'Call Me Ganymede,' p. 71.

53. No special case has to be made for 'loue' or 'loue-sute' as synonyms for will, and Booth's commentary supports the equivalence of the sonnet's other nouns ('soule,' 'things of great receit,' 'stores account,' 'treasure,' 'number,' 'one,' 'nothing,' and 'none'), pp. 469-73. Verbs also relate to lust: 'come' to climax; 'check' to its deferral; 'knows,' 'proved,' 'reckon'd' to forms of carnal knowing; 'fulfill' and 'fill' to orgasm; 'is admitted' and 'hold' to sexual entry. Adjectives express sexual desirables—'sweet,' 'great,' 'blind'—and adverbs modify the sexual act, 'so neere,' 'thus farre,' 'with ease.'

54. On eye as vulva, see Booth, p. 521.

55. *The Tragedie of King Lear*, The Norton Facsimile *The First Folio of Shakespeare*, prepared by Charlton Hinman (New York, 1968), TLN 2724.

56. Paul Ramsey notes that 22 1/2 per cent of all Englishmen were named Will at the end of the sixteenth century, *The Fickle Glass: A Study of Shakespeare's Sonnets* (New York, 1979), p. 23.

57. See Smith, esp. pp. 41-53 and Jonathan Goldberg, *Sodometries: Renaissance Texts, Modern Sexualities* (Berkeley, 1992), pp. 18-23.

58. 'Hal's Desire,' p. 41.

59. *The Tragedie of King Lear*, TLN 1663.

60. The promiscuous dark lady is not unlike Spenser's miscegenating Acrasia ('bad mixture') who razes the estates of her noble lovers in *FQ*, Bk. II, 12.

61. On the racial inflections of fair/dark and black/white in the early modern period, see Ania Loomba, *Gender, Race, Renaissance Drama* (Manchester and New York, 1989), pp. 42-5 and Kim Hall, *Things of Darkness: Economies of Race and Gender in Early Modern England* (Ithaca and London, 1995), pp. 6-15.

62. This paragraph owes much to Dollimore, pp. 23-40 et passim.

SEL 21 (1981)
ISSN 0039-3657

# Unemending Shakespeare's Sonnet 111

## RANDALL McLEOD

Until some curious inquirer makes a thorough investigation into all the technical details of Elizabethan printing, and from this and a comparision of
handwritings arrives at some definite statement of the relative probability of
various misreadings and misprintings, emendation must remain in much the
same state as medicine was before dissection was practised.

R.B. McKerrow

For 250 years editors of *Shakespeare's Sonnets* invariably concurred
with Charles Gildon's edition of 1709 in the crux of Sonnet 111.1, reading "with" where the first quarto gives "wish:"[1]

O For my fake doe you wifh fortune chide,

If editors comment on the first-quarto reading, they usually dismiss its
"obvious misprint," "obvious corruption," or "obvious typographical
error;" frequently it is silently altered.[2] I will show that there is no good
reason to suppose that the author did not write "wish," that the manuscript copy for Q1 did not read so, or that the compositor did not set the
word he read. Nor is the emendation, "with," obviously right even if
"wish" were an obvious corruption. Not only is the Q1 crux intelligible
(which fact must recommend it over any emendation, however

---

Professor McLeod teaches at Erindale College of the University of Toronto. He has
published articles on Renaissance typography in *SB* and in *Ren&R*.

[1] An early draft of this paper was presented at the 1978 annual meeting of The Shakespeare Association of America (Textual Seminar), Toronto, Canada. Extracts from the
paper and its argument were subsequently given in Stephen Booth's *Shakespeare's Sonnets, With Analytic Commentary*, second printing, with "Additional Notes (1978)"
(New Haven: Yale Univ. Press, 1978), pp. 580–82. The revised essay is dedicated to him
in thanks for his generous interest.

The epigraph is quoted from F. P. Wilson, *Shakespeare and the New Bibliography*,
rev. Helen Gardner (Oxford: The Clarendon Press, 1970), p. 5.

[2] See for example, editions by Hadow (1907), Alden (1913), Tucker Brooke (1936),
Rollins (1951), Harbage and Bush (1961), and Barnet and Burto (1964).

The 250 years of editorial fidelity to the emendation ended in M. Seymour-Smith's
valuable edition (London: 1963). His "old-spelling" text retained the Q1 reading and
justified the retention with this note, here given in full (p. 165): "*wish*. All editors except
Lintott (ed. 1711) have followed Gildon's emendation (ed. 1710) to 'with'; but Q means
simply: 'It is for my sake that you wish fortune to scold . . .'; or more colloquially and
perhaps more precisely: 'You are correct when you say that I, or what I have represented,
deserve this criticism.'" This note seems to have been ignored by subsequent editors.

time-honored), but also the rhetorical structure of the sonnet is revealed only when this line is stripped of the early eighteenth-century corruption. Finally I shall argue that with this new clarity of structure we must countenance a multiplication of syntactical ambiguities in the poem. The text becomes more sure, but the range of its meanings multiplies.

To begin, let us set aside the meaning of the crux to analyze the problem bibliographically. Through examination of the textual traditions we can determine authorities for the readings. This done, we will be able to turn, confident in the Q1 text, to a literary analysis of it. I am not unaware that the threat of a textual argument conducted outside the footnotes will discourage many readers. I have chosen, however, to put the bibliographic work horse before the more elegant cart of literary criticism partly because its strength can pull the quarto from the slough of emendation, and partly so that its lucidity and conclusiveness might draw non-specialists to this critical approach. Without some such hitching of critical methods, scholars will continue to reject a surprisingly large number of readings in Renaissance texts merely on the inappropriate grounds of taste. (Those who are prepared to take the quarto reading on faith, however, shall be spared this time, and may turn ahead to its literary interpretation on p. 87.)

Since there is no known manuscript tradition for Sonnet 111, authority clearly resides in a printed edition.[3] In the first half of the eighteenth century, when the emendation took hold, the stemma for *Shakespeare's Sonnets* was not clear. There were two drastically different active branches, one of which derived from Q1, the quarto printed by Elde in 1609, and the other from O1, the octavo printed by Benson in 1640; and for all anyone knew, these were collateral editions, each with its own authority. It was not until this century that Alden demonstrated conclusively that, as had long been suspected, O1 derived mostly from Q1, and thus generally lacked independent authority.[4] This fact does not preclude the theoretical chance that a small number of its readings can preserve authoritative press variants of Q1, readings that are no longer evidenced in the surviving copies of that edition. Of course, such authoritative readings preserved in O1 would be hard to tell apart from

---

[3]Unless otherwise stated the bibliographic information has been culled from Hyder Rollins, ed., *The Sonnets, A New Variorum Edition of Shakespeare*, (Philadelphia and London: 1944), vols. 24, 25. Information on press variants is found in vol. 25, p. 8. I have found several more (Randall McLeod, "A Technique of Headline Analysis, with Application to *Shakespeares Sonnets, 1609*," *SB* 29 (1978):197-210, but an exhaustive post-Hinman analysis has yet to be undertaken.

[4]R. M. Alden, "The 1640 Text of *Shakespeare's Sonnets*," *MP* 14, no. 1 (May 1916):17-30.

errors originating there, but the question of their detection is quite separate from the theoretical issue of their existence. In the discussion to
follow it will be useful, therefore, to inquire into the O1 line even if it is
derivative; but we may begin here with the crux in Q1.

Of the thirteen copies of Q1 that survive, none is reported to show
variation in the text of this poem, or indeed of its forme, G(i). Here,
then, is a typical image of Sonnet 111 (approximate size):

> **111**
>
> O For my fake doe you wifh fortune chide,
>  The guiltie goddeffe of my harmfull deeds,
> That did not better for my life prouide,
> Then publick meanes which publick manners breeds.
> Thence comes it that my name receiues a brand,
> And almoft thence my nature is fubdu'd
> To what it workes in,like the Dyers hand,
> Pitty me then,and wifh I were renu'de,
> Whilft like a willing pacient I will drinke,
> Potions of Eyfell gainft my ftrong infection,
> No bitterneffe that I will bitter thinke,
> Nor double pennance to correct correction.
>  Pittie me then deare friend,and I affure yee,
>  Euen that your pittie is enough to cure mee.

The following diagram will aid discussion of the derivation of this
text; it traces in outline the stemma of the earliest editions, and indicates
their readings of the crux. In analyzing these derivative editions we will
be able to shed light on the question of whether the reading "with" arose
in them in response to a variant reading in Q1.

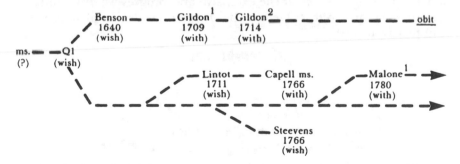

The upper line of descent is the less conservative. After Benson the
editors do not seem to have collated with Q1. The conservative line,
below, begins with what might now be called facsimile editions of Q1 by
Lintot and Steevens, for they retained old–fashioned spelling and resisted emendation. Subsequently Capell and Malone collated with Q1
(as their notes show), and their scholarship quickly undermined the

reputation of the upper line, hitherto the more popular, though it persisted well into the nineteenth century.

The reading "with" in the crux of Sonnet 111.1 first appears in the less conservative line, in Gildon 1, but curiously it is soon found in the more conservative line, first in Capell and then in Malone 1. Capell's textual notes give no specific evidence of collation with the texts of the upper line, but his introduction does criticize the spurious arrangement that originates with the Benson edition "in impressions of all sizes" which "now pass upon the world for the genuine poems of Shakespeare." At the time he wrote that remark, there were some five editions in the upper line after Benson's that Capell could have been referring to, any one of which reads "with." Fourteen years later Malone's collations refer pejoratively a half dozen times (though not in the present crux) to the readings of "all modern editions." This vague phrase could refer to three more editions in the upper line since Capell's time. Finally, Malone has been suspected of seeing Capell's manuscript and more probably of corresponding with him about *Sonnets.* Thus a strong circumstantial argument can be made that these two bibliographically-minded scholars derived the emendation in Sonnet 111.1 rather than reinvented it. And if this is so we see the limitations in stemmata like that adduced above, for they leave out the incest between the lines.

How many times the emendation "with" was actually arrived at independently may be of interest as evidence for the divergence of eighteenth-century English from what was, as I shall argue later, the Shakespearean idiomatic use of "wish." But the bibliographic argument need only concern itself with the textual authority of the readings in the crux. So let us turn now to trace the derivation in the upper line down to Gildon, glancing as we go at the extensive and progressive differentiation from the quarto text. Here is the image of a portion of Benson's 1640 text from E(i).

*A complaint.*

O For my fake doe you wifh fortune chide,
  The guiltie goddeffe of my harmeleffe deeds,
That did not better for my life pruvide,
Then publick meanes which publicke manners breeds.

As we already noted, the crux is invariant in Q1 and O1;[5] but the impor-

[5] Readers who refer to the type facsimile of Benson's edition (London: A.R. Smith, 1885) may doubt the validity of my assessment of Benson's reading in the crux. However the "with" that it reports in Sonnet 111.1 is not found in its copy-text, one of the British Library copies, neither of which deviates from Q1's "wifh." (My thanks to Wilson C. McLeod, Jr., for collation of the BL copies.) The emendation seems to have been re-invented by Smith's compositor.

tance for us of looking at the latter setting of the crux is to see the invariant text of the crux in its variant context. In Benson the sonnet number is replaced with a title. Astonishingly, instead of "harmful" in line two of Q1 we now read its direct opposite in O1: "harmlesse." Lastly, something not shown in the illustration, this sonnet runs into Sonnet 112 in O1 to make a single poem of twenty-eight lines. But the crux still reads "wish."

If we look for a moment beyond the immediate issue of Sonnet 111 on G4r of Q1 to consider its whole forme, G(i), and then collate this with its reflex in O1, we will find eight substantive differences.[6] This is higher than Benson's usual rate of variation. (Alden held that he corrected the text nineteen times, and corrupted it forty-eight times: one correction and three new errors per Q1 forme.)[7] Even if some of these eight differences between the first two editions originated in Q1 in lost press variants, and not in Benson, we have the security of knowing that the crux in Sonnet 111 is not in question and was therefore not likely variant even if there were variants in G(i) of Q1. If, for example, the differences between Q1 and O1 in the collation "harmful"/"harmlesse" stemmed from Q1 press variation, we would assume proofreading during the printing of Q's G(i). If we knew of such proofreading here (and surviving variants elsewhere in Q1 testify to proofreading in this edition) then we would know something even more important — that our crux survived it, and is therefore more likely to be true to the manuscript than we might otherwise have thought.

If this surmise is too speculative, we may suppose more surely the existence of a fourteenth exemplar of Q1 (now lost), which served Benson as copy text in 1640, and which confirms the quarto reading in the crux. The same logic argues for a fifteenth exemplar (now lost) that served Lintot as copy text in 1711, and which also read "wish" in the crux.[8] Bibliographic reconstruction of lost exemplars cannot produce

| [6]Sonnet | Q | Benson |
|---|---|---|
| 100.8 | giues | give |
| 101.3 | Both | But |
| .11 | him | her |
| .14 | him | her |
| .14 | he | she |
| 108.10 | iniury | injuries |
| 111.2 | harmfull | harmlesse |

[7]Of course, the changes in gender of the pronouns in Sonnet 101 (see note four) are editorial alterations rather than errors or corrections.

[8]Only one of the surviving exemplars seems to have served as printer's copy. I conclude that the cryptic marginal marks in the Huntington's Wright imprint are in fact marks of casting or marking off for George Steevens's edition, *Twenty of the Plays of Shakespeare*, etc., 4 vols. (London: J. and R. Tonson, 1766).

I assume that if any other copy texts survived they would show printer's marks like that of the Huntington Wright copy. I have not found such in microfilms of eleven other hard evidence, but at least it allows us to project some possibilities and probabilities of the first printing and the subsequent transmission of the text of the crux and of its forme. It does not prove that the quarto reading is correct, for that cannot be proven by any means; but it argues that it is more likely correct than the surviving evidence can lead us to believe. A greater test of the quarto reading lies in our consideration of the next edition.

Gildon's first edition came exactly a century after the publication of the original quarto. It was derived from Benson's O1, as its omissions, re-ordering, titling, for example, clearly indicated. Gildon introduces the now standard "with" in the crux.

## A Complaint.

OH! For my Sake do you with Fortune chide,
    The guilty Goddefs of my harmlefs Deeds,
That did not better for my Life provide,
Than publick Means which publick Manners breeds.

But there is always the remote chance that Gildon coud have collated his Benson copy-text against yet another lost copy of Q1, one that did read "with" as a press variant in the crux. If he did, then his "with" would be a candidate for a status more exalted than that of emendation. I will devote the rest of the paragraph to denying this chance. We may begin with a passage in Gildon's "Remarks on the Poems of Shakespeare" (p. 449). Here he attacks a publication of Lintot's—not the second volume (of 1711), which contains our text, "One Hundred and Fifty Four Sonnets, all of them in Praise of his Mistress"—but the first volume (of 1709) (not shown in the stemma) containing among other texts *The Passionate Pilgrim*. Gildon's attack begins:

> This leads me to a Book lately publish'd containing only some few of his Poems confusedly put together; for what is there call'd *The Passionate Pilgrim* is no more than a medly of *Shakespear's* thrown into a Heap without any Distinction, tho' they are on several and different Subjects as for Example. The first *Stanza*, in these Poems, is call'd *The false Relief.* The next Stanza is call'd *The Temptation* and on quite another Subject tho' incorporated into one under that general Title of *The Passionate Pilgrim.*

---

copies. The last copy (which may not be photocopied), The British Library Aspley imprint, has been kindly investigated for me by Nicolas Barker, Head of Conservation, and has no such marks.

And so on he goes giving Benson's unauthentic titles, reproving Lintot for removing them and lumping all the poems out of order under the title, *The Passionate Pilgrim*. Gildon could not have read carefully Lintot's *"Advertisement"* (A2r), where he states that his copy text was "a little stich'd Book, printed at *London* for *W. Jaggard* in the Year 1599," during Shakespeare's lifetime, as Lintot notes. We may conclude that Gildon was willfully ignorant of the textual authority of *The Passionate Pilgrim*. Moreover, as Benson intermixes poems from *Sonnets* and *The Passionate Pilgrim*, Gildon's ignorance of the textual authority of one text implies his ignorance of the authority of the other. This implication is rendered all the more certain since the first two poems of *The Passionate Pilgrim* are substantive variants of Sonnets 138 and 144. Ultimately we must conclude that Gildon knew nothing of Q1, and that therefore his reading of "with" in the present crux cannot derive from a supposed variant sixteenth copy of Q1 (now lost), with which, we might have supposed, he collated his Benson copy-text. Had Gildon found the "with" reading in his copy-text, it would have to have been a variant in Benson's O1, not in Q1. Now, possibly there may be such a Benson variant, though certainly no such variation is reported.[9] But in any case, for it to have authority, it would have to reflect the same variant in Q1 — an absurd idea, and one inconsistent with the reconstruction conjectured above.

Luckily there are two Gildon editions, and if we scrutinize the second we have another basis for triangulation on the crux and on Gildon's editorial practice. Gildon's second edition (of 1714) attests to his lack of restraint in improving Shakespeare; note in line four that "Manners," the reading of his first edition, gives way to "Custom" in the second — a reading (like "with" in the crux in line one) that we know — all the more strongly — can have no textual authority.

## *A Complaint.*

O H! for my fake do you with Fortune chide
The guilty Goddefs of my harmlefs Deeds,
That did not better for my Life provide,
'Than publick Means which publick Cuftom breeds.

Let us step back from these details to see them in historical perspective. Benson substantively corrupts about six percent of the 135 lines in G(i) of Q1 — in which occurs Sonnet 111; and Gildon's editions combined cor-

---

[9]Textual variants are reported in Benson only in sigs. A, D, and H (Rollins, 25:19) and none of these suggests unknown Q variants.

rupt about fifteen percent of the 202 lines in Benson's E(i), which also
contains the crux. To calculate the ultimate deviation from Q we must
remember that the errors are compounded. Thus, by the time Gildon's
work came to serve as copy-text for subsequent editions in his line, above
one line in five from Q1 had been corrupted. And this calculation does
not include the corruption of the sequence and integrity of each poem,
or the eight sonnets omitted from Benson's edition, or the two taken
from *The Passionate Pilgrim* rather than from *Sonnets*. Corruption in
three lines of the first quatrain alone of Sonnet 111—"with" in line 1,
"harmless" in line two, and "Custom" in line four—marks Gildon's editions as signally inauspicious places to divine Shakespearean text.

   Analysis of the family tree of Gildon's texts thus decisively determines
his authority for "with." He had none. It is purely editorial taste—or the
lack of it.


   Let us now pass from the subsequent to the prior history of the crux,
and entertain the thought that the manuscript may have read "with."
Could Elde's compositor have confused this supposed "with" with "wish"
by virtue of a so-called "muscular" error, that is, by reaching into the
wrong compartment of the case when setting or distributing? This question might seem to offer scope for flights of academic fancy, but in fact it
pulls us sharply to the ground with an unequivocal answer: No. We have
been wrong to talk of the reading of Q1 as "wish," for it is
                                    wiſh
—to give it back its ligatured face and to countenance it for the first
time. It is a three-sort word, with two of its letters, ſ and h, tied, and
printed by a single type,    ſh . The "with," however, is a four-sort word
with no ligatures. The letters t + h never form a ligature in this fount (or
any that I have seen), whereas the letters    ſ + h are never set without
ligation in this text, though they can be occasionally found untied in
contemporary English texts.[10] It is strange but true that this simplest of
physical facts, ligation, completely undercuts the only rationale editors
have ever used to justify their emendations in Sonnet 111, that "wish"—

---

[10]Look, for example, in the dedication to Shakespeare's *Venus and Adonis* Q1 (1593),
where long *s* + *h* are never tied, and where we also find combinations of round *s* + *h*,
also untied. This latter setting serves to avoid fouling of the kern (or protuberant typeface) that comes with the long *s* sort. I suppose that the printer, Field, inherited the italic
fount from his French master, Vautrollier, and that the fount is of French origin. French
composition does not usually require this combination of letters. (French expresses [ ſ ]
by ch not sh (trèshaulte *vs* la chemise), except in loan words (le T-shirt, le shift).

   The ligature is not frequently seen in short supply in English books, but Daniel's *Delia*
(Q1) offers an interesting contemporary example. See Randall McLeod, "Spellbound:
Typography and the Concept of Old-Spelling Editions," *Ren&R* n.s. 3, no. 1(1979):
50-65 (throughout for kerning and ligatures, p. 61 for *Delia*).

as they print it — is an obvious typo. The editors have committed a blunder equivalent to saying "4 = 3."

Ligatures should not come as a surprise if only we would look at the text and not read merely the rumors of it offered in modern editions and their collations, the founts of which frequently obscure the decisive evidence, and which do not stimulate visual thinking about text. The need for visual thinking is not a rare thing. Why, only two pages away in Q1 in Sonnet 106.11 we find ſtill usually emended to "skill," and again no one seems to notice that the emendation runs against typographical logic; for there was a ligature for ſt, but not one for sk, which was usually set with a round s before k. Of course, it may be pedantic to require everyone to read old editions, but if the editors and scholars themselves are so ill-adept at understanding the power of physical evidence and the distinction between spelling and typesetting, there can be little hope of accuracy and validity in the texts that now dominate education and literary criticism.

A glance at Q1 will show that on the average any given line of it contains one of a dozen ligatures. There are, for example, twelve occurrences of four ligatured sorts in Sonnet 111 alone— ſh ſt ct ſſ — and over 2,000 ligature uses in the whole quarto. Of these the mis-setting ſtall evidently for ſhall in 90.11 (photoquoted on p. 89, below) seems the only typographical error involving a ligature, and this is, crucially, an error of ligature for ligature, and of one for one.[11] There are several ways such a typo could have come about, but the most likely is that the ſt was misdistributed into the ſh compartment of the case, and subsequently taken in error for it. Such an error is facilitated by their being both ligatures and of similar set, for they thus can be misread for each other (in mirror image) during distribution. Although many ligatures, including ſh, lay adjacent in the upper right-hand corner of the old lower case (see illustration below), and were frequently taken one for another by virtue of tiny muscular errors in setting, ſt could not have been taken up for ſh for this reason; for ſt actually lay in the upper case, and well to the left. Thus, misdistribution of ſt into the compartment for ſh provides the most likely explanation of the crux in Sonnet 90.11 (if the error is indeed a typo rather than a misreading, mis-remembering or uncorrected setting of a manuscript error).

Types can be confused in other ways too. It is reported that in the 1703 quarto of *Hamlet* the hero enjoins Ophelia to be "as Chaste as Ice, as puer as Snosh," the latter phrase being a mis-setting of "pure as Snow."[12] Here the reported sh in "Snosh" must be the ligature, and thus

[11]The same typo is found in *Romeo*, Q2, 1.2.17.
[12]H. Farr, "Notes on Shakespeare's Printers and Publishers, with Special Reference to the Poems and *Hamlet*," *The Library*, 4th ser., 3, no. 4 (March 1923): 225-60 (see p. 260).

the confusion is between a ligature and a non-ligatured type.[13] A glance at the early lay of the case shows how the ſh ligature and the w could have been confused; the compartment of the former lay directly above that of the latter, and types could easily have spilled over into it. The two types had, moreover, almost identical set; and thus the compositor's fingers would not have detected a mis-setting, as they would have if he had taken a type with a kern (protuberant typeface), when he had thought to take one without. Thus, in the error of "Snoſh" for "Snow" the set, the lay, and gravity conspire to offer ready explanations of how the mis-setting occurred; and these same facts point to what seems to be true from casual observation of Renaissance books, that ſh is mis-set for w more often than *vice versa*. To conclude, "wiſh" can be an easy typo for the nonsense word "wiw," but not for the legitimate word "with."[14] Practical examples like these show that the editor's obligation in cruxes like this of Sonnet 111 is to forestall the abstract notions which too readily proffer emendations like "with," and to think in terms of practical things—*to thingk*. Texts do not fall from the sky; and if editors conceive of their function as installing them there, they would do well to remember Raphael's account to Adam of "sublimation gradual," whereby "body up to spirit works."

Here, for interest, is the first English illustration of the lay of the case,

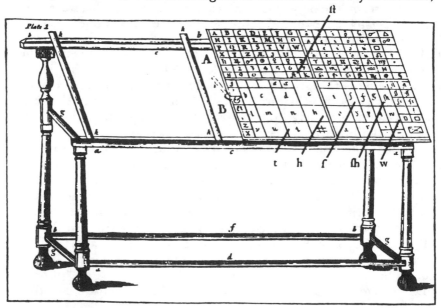

[13]We may consider that w is a ligature in name only, though when types ran short it was set as vv. In Q1 the essential equation still operates: one type in the original setting for one type in the emendation.
[14]The typographical argument does not mean that ligatured ſh and non-ligatured th

Joseph Moxon's of 1683, with locations for some types referred to in discussion. Until fairly recently (in historical terms) printing has been a conservative profession; the fact that the lay changed little in the century after Moxon argues that its prior history was also conservative, and that Elde's lay resembled the one shown here. Renaissance typos (like the frequent confusion of ſh and w) argue the same conclusion.

As the evidence of ligatures rules out decisively the "obvious typographical error" alleged by the editors, we may ask whether the hypothetical "with" in the manuscript could have been misread as "wish." As the error seems unlikely in italic hand, suppose we conjecture that the lost manuscript was in secretarial hand, like all of Shakespeare's surviving signatures. As it is supposed that the secretarial Hand D in *The Booke of Sir Thomas Moore* is Shakespeare's, we can examine this manuscript to see how the relevant clusters are formed.[15] Consider the left margin of folio 9r, lines 107–10.[16]

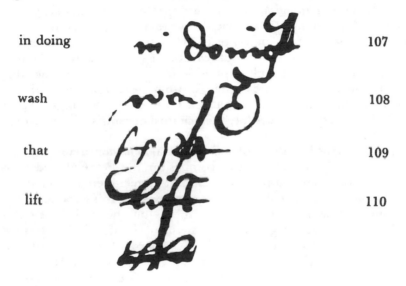

| in doing |  | 107 |
| wash |  | 108 |
| that |  | 109 |
| lift |  | 110 |

---

can never be confused, only that they will not be confused by muscular error. We must seek another explanation. After looking casually for such confusion for four years, I have found only one example. In Dekker's *Patient Grissil* (Q1) Bowers reports a press-variant in I1ʳ. Three texts read "ſhall" and one reads "thall." The explanation for the setting seems obvious as soon as we see the corrected line: "But that faire issue that shall now be borne" (4.3.263). The original setting, "thall," seems to have been influenced by the "th" of the preceding word, "that." It is not, then, a muscular error. See Fredson Bowers, ed., *The Dramatic Works of Thomas Dekker*, 4 vols. (Cambridge: 1953–1961) 1:276 (for text) and 295 (for collation).

[15]Recent assessment of the Shakespearean claim (still a claim by default) is found in Thomas Clayton, *The "Shakespearean" Addition in "The Booke of Sir Thomas Moore": Some Aids to Scholarly and Critical Shakespearean Studies (ShakS, Monograph Series:*

(The first and last words are not directly relevant to the crux, but they cannot be eliminated without cropping the relevant shapes. In any case, the post linking of the f in "lift," the last word, is analogous to what I will say about the corresponding link of the ſ in "wash.")

Students of the subtlety of handwriting will notice that I have chosen one example with a terminal and one with a medial h, and that this has an effect on the final arc of the letter in question; the convenient grouping of evidence in the manuscript is adequate to the point I wish to make, however. The example clearly shows the difference not only of the high-riding t in "that" and the deeply descending ſ in "wash," but also this crucial differentiation: the t joins the subsequent letter, h, directly and close to the base line, whereas the ſ joins the subsequent h with an arc, not a straight line, which ventures from the top of its shape, not the middle. This argues that "wish" and "with" are not readily confusable in what we imagine to be Shakespeare's hand.

Finally, the *Sir Thomas Moore* manuscript throws additional light on this obscure question in that "with" always appears in abbreviation there, either as "w$^t$" (five times) or as "w$^{th}$" (twice). It is pointless, of course, to argue too precisely about features of a lost manuscript; but at least reasonable bibliographic suppositions show that there is nothing obviously confusable in these clusters in what we surmise to be Shakespearean handwriting and abbreviation. If there were, we might expect to find what no editor argues for, such confusion rampant elsewhere in the first quarto.

If, and this is the last aspect of compositorial behavior to consider, the manuscript read "with," but the compositor mis-remembered it as "wish," we still might suspect that the mis-remembered form made sense of some sort, and we should strive to know what this sense could be. Sometimes, of course, one mis-remembers on the basis of similar sounds; and thus one might argue that the [ʃ] of "wish" is formed under the influence of the [tʃ] in the next word, "fortune," and thus that the manuscript may have read "with." Such an argument is surely plausible, and is attractive to my skeptical disposition; but I know of no method of assigning it a statistical probability either in detecting corruption or reconstructing the supposed copy reading. How does one prove, for example, that the manuscript read "with" and not "will" — a

---

*Studies in the Bibliography of Renaissance Dramatic Texts*, 1, Dubuque, Iowa, 1969). The pioneer work in the field is A.W. Pollard, W.W. Greg, E.M. Thompson, J.D. Wilson, R.W. Chambers, *Shakespeare's Hand in the Play of Sir Thomas More* (Cambridge: Cambridge Univ. Press, 1923).

[16]The manuscript is Harleian MS. 7368, a portion of which is reproduced here with the kind permission of the British Library. Folio 9r is well reproduced in G. B. Evans's *The Riverside Shakespeare*.

synonym of "wish?" Like all arguments for emendation in this crux, this phonetic one arises only from the prejudicial assumption of inadequate text. The ultimate defence against such rationalization of emendation is simply to read the quarto sensitively as a text that exists, not as evidence of some other text that does not.

With this the bibliographic argument comes to a close. It cannot prove the quarto reading to be correct, but to adapt McKerrow's analogy to medicine, it can anatomize the crux, systematically calling in question the assumptions that must support the allegation of error, and driving us to look harder at the text.

We can now return to the question of meaning, deferred while bibliography cleared our vision of the text. The difficulty now, I assert, lies in syntax and grammar rather than in diction. A note on the history of the relevant grammatical constructions will prepare us for appreciating the Shakespearean idiom. Let us begin with "chide," the last word in the first line of Sonnet 111, and demonstrate the differences between its old and modern usage. In Old English the person chided was grammatically dative.[17] In the collapse of the inflectional system after the Conquest the verb became predominantly transitive — its only modern usage. Shakespeare used "chide" and its conjugates about 100 times, and eighty percent of his usage is transitive. The verb is often used absolutely, but in the few intransitive uses with indirect object it is completed by the prepositions "with" only twice, but "at" four or possibly five times. A scanty account in the *Oxford English Dictionary* suggests that "chide with" was a dialect or biblical usage. In one of Shakespeare's two uses of the construction, in *Cymbeline* 5.4.82, Jupiter is asked to chide with Mars and Juno; this divine "chiding with" may have been an evocation of its biblical usage, and, the emendors may argue, explains its use in Sonnet 111 in connection with the goddess Fortune. We must agree that Gildon's reading does indeed have this philological appeal. But this truth does not guarantee that the manuscript reading is thereby regained. The fact that "chide at" is more common in Shakespeare than "chide with," and that the verb is only rarely intransitive should warn us of the dangers of emending anachronistically. This counter-argument perhaps leads to a stand-off.

But luckily the case does not end here, for (are you ready?) the quarto construction is quite simply meaningful as it stands! It can be

---

[17]For the history of "chide" see *OED*. For "chide at" in Shakespeare see *LLL* 4.3.130, *AYL* 3.5.129, *WT* 4.4.6, *Rom.* 3.2.95, and (questionably) *Shr.* 1.2.225. "Chides with thinking" (*Oth.* 2.1.107) is not an example of this construction. References are to *The Riverside Shakespeare,* and were found with the help of the Spevack concordance to this edition.

paraphrased, for example, as "Wish *that* fortune chide." The inserted conjunction, "that," could be regarded, if we chose, as restoring the author's ellipsis; but the *Oxford English Dictionary* ("wish" vb. 1.b) assures us that in the Renaissance "wish" regularly did not need to be followed with "that." Regarding the grammar as normal, we may proceed to read "chide" either as a root infinitive or as a finite verb. There are other examples in Shakespeare of both of these usages:

1) To wish him wrastle with affection   *Ado* 3.1.42
2) Say that I wish he never find more cause   *Antony* 4.5.15
3) In that good path that I would wish it go   *Measure* 4.3.133
4) I wish my brother make good time with him   *Cymbeline* 4.2.108
5) I will not wish thy wishes thrive   *John* 3.1.334

The "him" of the first example indicates an accusative-and-infinitive construction. By contrast, the "he" of the second example indicates that "find" is a finite verb in the third person. As it lacks the "-s" ending of the indicative conjugation, it must be subjunctive . Of the remaining examples, the third and fourth do not distinguish between infinitive and subjunctive moods, nor does the fifth distinguish among infinitive, subjunctive, or indicative. In conclusion, we can read "fortune chide" in Sonnet 111 as either or both of two constructions:

a) (elliptical "that" + ) nominative "fortune" + subjunctive "chide"

b)                   accusative "fortune" + infinitive "chide"

Neither grammatical analysis makes much literary difference, of course; my point is merely that we recognize any legitimate Shakespearean construction in the crux and the tension between the reader's alternative understandings of its grammar. The modern reader's difficulties with the grammar of the crux is not, of course, a reason to entertain the emendation.

Now that the grammatical options are clear and vouched for by other examples in Shakespeare's text, where emendors have feared to tread, we must try to understand what it means to appeal to someone to "wish for one's sake that fortune chide." In the apparent absence of an object for the absolute intransitive verb "chide," I imagine that most readers understand the first line of Sonnet 111 (without grammatical warrant) as if it were transitive: "Wish that fortune chide *me* for my sake," reading in the first person pronoun "me" from the adjective phrase "for my sake." If so they are likely to reject this reading, and head directly for the emendation—as who should want to experience the anger of fortune? The problem cannot be solved, however, by Gildon's emendation, for the ambiguity of his "with" (meaning either "alongside" or "against" or both) surely raises the same problem. As for the question "Who would ever solicit fortune's chiding?" Sonnet 90 provides a perverse answer: this very persona. Note the references to antagonistic fortune in line twelve and especially in line three, where the friend is asked to "Ioyne with the spight of fortune"—a phrase that anticipates the crux in Sonnet 111, "wish fortune chide."

### 90

THen hate me when thou wilt, if euer, now,
  Now while the world is bent my deeds to croſſe,
Ioyne with the ſpight of fortune, make me bow,
And doe not drop in for an after loſſe:
Ah doe not, when my heart hath ſcapte this ſorrow,
Come in the rereward of a conquerd woe,
Giue not a windy night a rainie morrow,
To linger out a purpoſd ouer-throw.
If thou wilt leaue me, do not leaue me laſt,
When other pettie griefes haue done their ſpight,
But in the onſet come, ſo ſtall I taſte
At firſt the very worſt of fortunes might.
    And other ſtraines of woe, which now ſeeme woe,
    Compar'd with loſſe of thee, will not ſeeme ſo.

In this sonnet the persona asks the friend paradoxically to join with spiteful fortune by hating him. The irony is transparent, of course, as the sonnet concludes with a statement of the persona's love, which appeals for love not for hate.

The phrase "for my sake" in Sonnet 111.1 can also be ironic. Witness the hammering of it in Sonnet 42, lines seven, eight, and twelve.

### 42

THat thou haſt her it is not all my griefe,
  And yet it may be ſaid I lou'd her deerely,
That ſhe hath thee is of my wayling cheefe,
A loſſe in loue that touches me more neerely.
Louing offendors thus I will excuſe yee,
Thou dooſt loue her, becauſe thou knowſt I loue her,
And for my ſake euen ſo doth ſhe abuſe me,
Suffring my friend for my ſake to approoue her,
If I looſe thee, my loſſe is my loues gaine,
And looſing her, my friend hath found that loſſe,
Both finde each other, and I looſe both twaine,
And both for my ſake lay on me this croſſe,
    But here's the ioy, my friend and I are one,
    Sweete flattery, then ſhe loues but me alone.

This is the language of foolosophy, the kind of tone we associate with the Clown of *All's Well* (1.3) and his paradoxical praise of cuckoldry. Coming from the mouth of a sonneteer it sounds more savage and desperate. The examples of Sonnets 90 and 42 surely mean that the tone of Sonnet 111, which sonnet employs the same diction as those earlier sonnets, also admits of ironic interpretation.

I raise this point because it seems reasonable to assume (in the face of their silence) that the eighteenth–century emendors of Sonnet 111 may have been repelled by blatant "masochism" in the first quatrain of the quarto version.[18] But such moralistic interpretation as may be alleged is certainly shallow, for it fails to read the first quatrain of Sonnet 111 against not only the contexts I have just adduced, but also the development of this very sonnet, as I shall now show.

At this point in the essay it is imperative to begin a sketch of the overall meaning of the sonnet and of its tones, for these issues bear on how we expect "wish" or "with" to function in the sonnet. Contrast for a moment Sonnet 92.

### 92

> BVt doe thy worſt to ſteale thy ſelfe away,
> For tearme of life thou art aſſured mine,
> And life no longer then thy loue will ſtay,
> For it depends vpon that loue of thine.
> Then need I not to feare the worſt of wrongs,
> When in the leaſt of them my life hath end,
> I ſee, a better ſtate to me belongs
> Then that, which on thy humor doth depend.
> Thou canſt not vex me with inconſtant minde,
> Since that my life on thy reuolt doth lie,
> Oh what a happy title do I finde,
> Happy to haue thy loue, happy to die!
>     But whats ſo bleſſed faire that feares no blot,
>     Thou maiſt be falce, and yet I know it not,

This sonnet implies that the persona knows of the friend's humor (line 8), but that by striving to make his own consciousness and the term of his life dependent on the humor's absence, the persona exhibits a reluctance to deal with his actual knowledge and to shape his life independently. This position is morally dubious if we take it at face value.[19]

Sonnet 111 shows a sharp contrast to Sonnet 92. Here, in one of many vacillations, the friend's humor is now solicited rather than denied. On

---

[18]Of course the rejection of the quarto reading may have been prompted by a desire for metrical smoothness, for Gildon's reading finishes the line with regular iambic stresses.

[19]I stress "at face value" because the present analysis is of this sonnet in isolation, and it

the face of it, the masochism may seem as much a failure to deal with this aspect of the friend as is the mere denial of it in Sonnet 92. But the solicitation is part of a large, dialectical design in which the friend's humor is engaged seemingly in order to be transformed into pity (see lines 8, 13, 14), and to be endured by a persona who is now the patient of a cure rather than one who denies-the disease. The change from masochism to patience is signaled not only by the word "pacient" in line nine, but more crucially for the present argument by the pivotal wish for pity that just precedes it. The word "wish" in line eight—or wiſh rather—certainly catches the eye, as should the repetition of "pittie" in the couplet. Attending to these features of the Q1 version yields a clear perception of the poem's structure that has been eclipsed for the two-and-a-half-century reign of the emendation; for the whole poem contrasts two wishes, one for chiding (line 1) and one for pity (line 8). The friend's behavior enjoined in Q1 is thus the attitudinal and the volitional, and indeed the persona responds in kind. Our loving Will, as he is elsewhere called,[20] is a "willing pacient" (line 9), who "will" drink potions (lines 9-10), who will think no bitterness bitter (line 11), and who will think double penance not too correct correction (lines 11-12). The sequence of wishes asked of the friend expresses a contradiction through time: first he is to have one wish (line 1), "then" its opposite (line 8). The solicited behavior of the friend leads to a similarly contradictory activity (staged as a re-activity) in the persona; but here the contradiction is embodied simultaneously, as in the contradictory attitude that bitter is not bitter (line 11), and in such an oxymoron as the "willing pacient" (line 11), the paradox of which we perceive when we remember that the Latin etymon of "pacient" is *pati*, "to suffer." (The word is cognate with "passion," which is punned on complexly in Sonnet 20.2.) The transformational desire to suffer is the prerequisite of "pennance" (line 12) and of submitting to a "cure" (line 14). This contrasts with the usual fare of static and unredemptive paradoxes in love sonnets—of hot ice and cold fire. This dynamic paradox of patience must be seen to transvalue the initial and partial assumption of masochism.

Surely part of the difficulty in assessing the moral capability of the persona in this sonnet lies in the love-sonnet genre itself. The cruel lover and the suffering persona who anatomizes his pain are conventional. The vocabulary of sadism and masochism is simply a given, a corollary

---

may be only in the succession of sonnets that we have an adequate basis for moral evaluation. Also, the author's showing this poem to the friend (if ever he existed) would render it part of another symbolic structure (social behavior), in which its meaning would be vastly transformed.

[20]See for example Sonnets 57, 135, 136, etc., often with a pun on "will" meaning "desire" or "sexual organ," or on "Will," the personal name.

of the politics of exalting the lover and abasing the self. Reinforcing the politics of love in the narrative of *Shakespeare's Sonnets* is something that more closely resembles social politics. In various poems we gather that the lover (if there is only one) is perhaps the patron; he seems high-born, and therefore holds all the rights in the relationship. He is projected as chartered, as secure in his being, and condescending to the persona; he is associated with eternal life and identified as the tenth muse. To the solicitous persona, by contrast, falls the labor of love; he is of the class that supports all this gaudy luxury, and he is dirty-handed like the dyer. His intense efforts, psychological, moral, and aesthetic, regularly have, in his eyes if not in ours, but problematic success; he is divided against himself; his end is death and oblivion. With R. D. Laing we can see that to call the victim of love or of society a neurotic is to be blind to the "neuro-genic" system of relations which exalts by debasing—exalts some by debasing others. *Shakespeare's Sonnets,* dwelling in irony and innuendo and self-doubt, suggests but never unleashes the full criticism towards which it points, criticism of the conventions of society, of love, and of love poetry that render unequal those whom love could unite, and which explain why the persona takes on problems which do not seem to be (or seem to be only) his own, and why he does not press the friend's face in his own dirt. The reader cannot escape the sense that the persona often seems to pull his punches, and sometimes even make little effort to hide that fact, as in Sonnet 42. This all suggests that nothing in *Sonnets* is to be taken at face value; these poems are not necessarily to be judged by canons of sincerity. Against this complex background of paradox and contrived expression, dictated by, but also pitted against, both the genre and the social codes, the masochism of the first quatrain of Sonnet 111 may have to be interpreted as strategic gesture, and not (or not only) as raw psychological data.

I have ventured thus far into the domain of literary interpretation of Sonnet 111 to deal with questions of tone, of masochism, and incidentally, though crucially, of "wishing," in line eight, which in typesetting, diction, and meaning illuminates the crux in line one. But we cannot tarry here, for the text of the first line contains so many more problems that criticism is well warned to forego large-scale interpretation until the minute complexities of the text are sounded.

Let me return, then, to questions of syntax and grammar. Thus far the interpretation of Sonnet 111 has rested on the supposition that the first line of the poem is an imperative construction like the eighth line, that "wish fortune chide" is like "wish I were renu'de." Such it may be, surely, but it can also be a simple indicative, for inversion of subject and verb is not an infrequent feature of *Sonnets,* as for example, "Then of thy beauty do I question make" (Sonnet 12.9), a phrase which has never tempted any editor to point with a question mark. Thus, the indicative paraphrase: "You do wish fortune chide." In this interpretation of the verb "chide," a sadistic friend replaces the masochistic persona; but the poem still hinges on the changing of the first wish to one of pity (in line 8 and again in lines 13 and 14).[21]

Finally, we cannot dismiss the interrogative construction either—even though there is no question mark in Q1. Only about seventy percent of the Q1 interrogative constructions (so deemed by the consensus of modern editors) are pointed with a query in Q1. The only compositorial analysis of Q1 to date suggests that the compositor setting this sonnet was slightly more accurate—by *our* standards—(seventy-four percent) than his mate (sixty-six percent); but the record of both of them suggests that the manuscript lacked consistent pointing in interrogative constructions.[22] The portions of the *Sir Thomas Moore* manuscript in Hand D have, by the way, some twenty questions (half of which are rhetorical), and none of these is pointed with a query. If the *Sonnets* manuscript was so deficient, and if the bulk of question marks are compositorial, then the presence or absence of one in the first quatrain cannot be deemed to determine the construction. Given these internal characteristics of the punctuation and grammar of Q1, we are free to consider the interrogative interpretation of the crux as equally valid as the imperative or indicative. Perhaps the easiest way to read the quatrain as a queston is with the tone of incredulity: "Surely you don't wish fortune to chide for my sake; don't you know what she has done to me already?" But reflection will quickly suggest other valid readings of the interrogation.

It is interesting to note that the consistent pointing with question marks in *Sonnets* was begun and, with only a few exceptions, finished by the very Gildon whose corruption of Sonnet 111 we have just seen. As all subsequent eighteenth-century editions (as opposed to conservative reprints of Q1 like Lintot's or Steevens's) followed Gildon's reading in the crux, it is not unreasonable to assume that their editors were familiar with his text or its derivatives, and that they may have taken his attitude toward the construction, as evidenced by his punctuation of line four, along with his emendation in line one. I do not see that there is any criterion that serves to decide among these ambiguities of construction in Q1, and the best course seems to be to countenance them all.

[21]See note 2 for Seymour-Smith's indicative interpretation.

[22]Compositor analysis is found in MacD. P. Jackson, "Punctuation and the Compositors of Shakespeare's *Sonnets*, 1609," *The Library*, 5th ser., 30, no. 1 (March 1975): 1-24. Identification of some of the workers in this shop is to be found in Theodore Redpath, "The Punctuation of Shakespeare's *Sonnets*," 218-51 (notes 272-76) in Hilton Landry, ed., *New Essays in Shakespeare's Sonnets* (New York: AMS Press, 1976), see esp. note 13, pp. 273-74.

Before we leave this sonnet there is one further unturning of the screw. Thus far we have assumed, as apparently did Gildon and his followers, that "chide" is, strictly speaking, intransitive, and that "guiltie goddesse" is in apposition to "fortune." Need this be so? We could paraphrase lines one and two to read, "Wish for my sake that fortune chide the goddess guilty of my harmful deeds." Thus there would be two goddesses, fortune, and another unnamed, who was specifically responsible for the persona's ill fortune—something like his personal bad angel. It is also possible that we have here a roundabout way of asking fortune to chide herself, in which case we are dealing with a "friendly friend" and not the humorous one. There are two hurdles to clear before we can accept this: 1) can the comma which to our modern eyes differentiates intransitive from transitive constructions be so equivocal in the quarto system of punctuation, and 2) is the reading theologically appropriate?

The second question is answered positively by reference to the various deities of *Shakespeare's Sonnets*. There is "that God . . . that made me first your slaue" in Sonnet 58.1, who may or. may not be the "little Loue-God" of Sonnet 154.1, who may or may not be the "God in loue" of Sonnet 110.12. Perhaps in Sonnet 58 we are not to think of any specific deity invoked in his own right, but simply to realize that the persona is projecting his own state metaphysically. He does this elsewhere, in Sonnet 144, for example, with mention of his "better" and "worser" "spirits," and by projecting the love triangle as a struggle among "angell," "diuel," and "finde." The easy modulation in Sonnet 58 from the "God" that enslaves the persona (line 1) to the "charter" of the friend that justifies the slavery of the persona (line 9) suggests that, however these metaphors function locally, they serve globally in the sonnet merely to signify the power of the friend and the bondage of the persona. Closer to home, Sonnet 110.12 speaks of the friend, it seems, as a "God in loue" to whom the persona is "confin'd." Curiously the speaker says, this "God" is "next my heaven the best." The persona seems to draw a distinction between the gods of idolatrous love and of orthodox religion. If Sonnet 111 is taken as a continuation of Sonnet 110, "fortune" (111.2) may appear as an intermediary between on the one hand the "God in loue," who is to give the persona welcome (110.13) and pity (111.8, 13), and on the other hand the "guiltie goddesse" of his "harmful deeds" (111.2), who is to be chided by fortune at the instigation of the "God in loue." This is the structure (if not the content) of the triangle in Sonnet 144. It all suggests to me that there is a sufficiently confused pantheon in *Shakespeare's Sonnets* to accommodate both "fortune" and another "goddesse" in Sonnet 111.2.[23]

[23]Seymour-Smith suggests that the "goddesse" is the "Goddess of Success, . . . that which the Friend has pursued."

The first question, that of punctuation, is too complicated to treat in more than a sketch in the footnote,[24] but this will be enough to show that it too admits of positive answer. The problem must be assessed across the whole quarto and with a theory of the stints of the compositors; but consider here an example from this very sonnet. The comma at the end of line nine divides a subject from the verb and thus obscures the syntax: "I will drinke, / Potions." As we are dealing with enjambment here we ought not "stand upon points," and I doubt that any logical or poetic purpose can be detected in the comma. Its lack of function here hardly impedes interpretation, since the eye always stops at the end of a line, enjambment or no enjambment. But that the comma in line one does not require "chide" to read intransitively must come as a surprise to most readers, who read Shakespeare only in modern editions, which point with a comma. The only modern defence for the comma in 111.1 or for the period in 111.4 is editorial interpretation of the text. The argument that these marks of punctuation are merely derived by the modern editor from the Q1 copy-text is quite misleading, since a comma and period in Q1 are not the same as a comma and period in a modern edition. The function of individual marks of punctuation must be understood in relationship to the whole system of such marks in each edition. In Q1, for example, commas can point sentences; periods, questions; queries, exclamations. For the modern editor to transcribe the first-quarto punctuation in lines one and four into the system of punctuation of a modern edition is already to have interpreted the poem and reduced its ambiguity, even though it appears to be a conservative approach.

The two questions are now answered positively, and accordingly we must regard as possible the reading which does not equate "fortune" and "goddesse" in line two. More and more ambiguity.

[24]Here are selected examples of intrusive pointing by both compositors, "corrected" early in editing history. Sonnet 111 is set by Compositor B according to Jackson.

| Q1 compositor | Q1 page | sonnet and line | Q1 reading | modern reading | first modernizer | Q1 punct. divides |
|---|---|---|---|---|---|---|
| A | C3v | 32.3 | re-suruay: | re-survay | Gildon | vb-obj |
| B | D2r | 44.12 | attend, | attend | Lintot | vb-obj |
| A | D4r | 55.7 | burne: | burn | Gildon | vb-obj |
| A | D4v | 56.11 | see: | see | Capell and Malone | vb-obj |
| B | E4r | 74.5 | reuew, | review | Malone l* | sub-vb |
| B | F2r | 84.2 | alone, | alone | Malone l* | sub-vb |
| B | H3r | 126.7 | skill. | skill | Lintot | sub-vb |

(* = Information lacking in Rollins; Malone may not be the first)
With deficient pointing as in Sonnet 62.11 ("read" needs to be at least "read,") we cannot be sure that there is not simply an inking problem. But with the inked punctuation in this table we have positive evidence of intrusive pointing, which evidence justifies the supposition that the comma in Sonnet 111.1 need not force "chide" to be intransitive.

The crux in Sonnet 111.1 and its context can now be understood to equivocate at least among three different kinds of sentence—assertive, interrogative, and imperative, and between transitive and intransitive verbs—six constructions in all, to be precise about the equivocal. And this does not take into account the alleged interpretation of "chide" as a transitive verb with ellipsis of the object, "me." Whether we read "goddesse" in apposition to "fortune" multiplies the ambiguity further, as does the uncertainty of whether "chide" is an infinitive or subjunctive. No doubt some of these readings will seem more plausible to some, others to others. But the further ambiguity of words "thence" (lines 5 and 6) and "then" (lines 8 and 13), and in general the loose hold of logic on the poem seem to mean that none of these constructions and their combinations can be denied—except, of course, by modern editorial practice, which denies all manner of quarto subtleties—specifically by emending and generally by modernizing. I am sure we are all prepared on general principles to greet the restoration of a Shakespearean text, but there will be many who will wish it could be had with less ambiguity. It is not my purpose to argue here that the victory is not pyrrhic, though I do not believe it is. But I will assert that almost any sonnet of Shakespeare's is of equal ambiguity and complexity, if only one will approach it free of prior interpretation. In the present state of Shakespearean criticism this means that we must sidestep the editors.

# WAS THE 1609 *SHAKE-SPEARES SONNETS* REALLY UNAUTHORIZED?

## By Katherine Duncan-Jones

### I. THE TEXT OF THE *SONNETS*

MODERN editors of the *Sonnets* have often given the impression that what these poems need is not so much editing as fundamental rewriting; or, failing that, the provision of a voluminous accompanying text of commentary and explication. While it would be most unwise to claim, as Hazlitt did of *The Faerie Queene*, that 'it is all as plain as a pike-staff', the time may have come for a more direct and simple approach to the text. What I propose here is a fresh look at the 1609 Quarto edition, published by Thomas Thorpe and printed by George Eld. Although this is in practice the only text on which any edition of the *Sonnets* can be based, it has become traditional to suggest that it is an 'unauthorized' publication, which may have been 'suppressed'. Dover Wilson, for example, thought more highly of the 1609 Quarto than most modern editors have done, but still thought it unbelievable that Shakespeare could have authorized the publication, asserting that it must have been suppressed almost as soon as printed.[1] Yet it is striking not only that there is no evidence whatsoever of suppression, but also that so large a number as thirteen copies of the book survive. This is a substantial figure when we consider how many comparable texts in the period have either vanished entirely, or, like the first edition of *Venus and Adonis*, or Barnabe Barnes's sonnet sequence *Parthenophil and Parthenophe*, survive only in unique copies. Of the first authorized edition of *Astrophel and Stella*, published by William Ponsonby, only three copies survive. The conventional aspersions on the Thorpe text need to be investigated. They are often, it seems, based on preconceptions about Shakespeare, rather than on historical or bibliographical evidence.

Thomas Thorpe and his text have had a very rough ride over the last 350 years. The publisher John Benson in 1640 was the first of many editors who have seen fit to treat the individual sonnets like cards in a pack, reshuffling them to produce a layout—often, as in the Benson text, heterosexual—felt to be worthy of the Swan of Avon.

---

[1] *The Sonnets*, ed. J. Dover Wilson (1963), p. xlii.

RES New Series, Vol. XXXIV, No. 134 (1983)

One of the most systematic reorderings of recent years, that of Brents Stirling in 1968, is founded on the firm assumption that Thorpe's text is 'pirated or at least unauthorized'.[2] Sir Sidney Lee's biography of Thorpe in the *DNB* (1905) built up a picture of systematic roguery and sharp practice. Using such epithets as 'predatory' and 'irresponsible', Lee suggested that Thorpe specialized in handling 'neglected copy', being unscrupulous even by the standards of the day. While few editors have gone the whole way with Lee, his picture has never been seriously challenged. The only attempt to rehabilitate Thorpe, by Leona Rostenberg in 1960, after furnishing a useful account of his publishing career, founders in confusion in uncritical acceptance of the theories of Arthur Acheson (1920).[3] Miss Rostenberg concludes her article by suggesting that Thorpe published the *Sonnets* at the instigation of Florio, Chapman, and others out of malice to Shakespeare. She appears to assume, as many from Benson onwards have done, that the *Sonnets* as they stand in the 1609 Quarto are self-evidently damaging to Shakespeare's reputation. Among other wild hypotheses about Shakespeare's personal life, she touches on his supposed affair with Mrs Anne Davenant. It is a sadly instructive example of the power of the *Sonnets* to undermine reason that this article, which begins as an interesting and careful bibliographical study, collapses into such fantastic and improbable speculations. On the text of the *Sonnets*, Miss Rostenberg claims that it is

well established that Shakespeare played no part in the publication and never gave his approval . . . Had the poet endorsed the publication, the registration would have appeared with his full name.

Actually, these conclusions are by no means 'well established'. Such a majestic scholar as Chambers has considered that Shakespeare may have sold Thorpe the copy for the *Sonnets*, and Miss Rostenberg's interpretation of the Register entry is very dubious. Many entries in the Stationers' Register are extremely abbreviated, and since Shakespeare was well known by 1609, as well as being the only writer bearing his surname, there would be no need to identify him by Christian name. Many of the plays were entered without any author's name at all. *Troilus and Cressida*, for instance, both when entered on 7 February 1602/3 and on its second entry, 28 January 1608/9, was decribed merely as 'a booke called *the history of* TROYLUS *and* CRESSIDA'. Yet there is no doubt of Shakespeare's authorship, announced on the title-page of the 1609 Quarto, and Alexander and

---

[2] Brents Stirling, *The Shakespeare Sonnet Order : Poems and Groups* (Los Angeles, 1968), p. 1.
[3] Leona Rostenberg, 'Thomas Thorpe, Publisher of "Shake-speares Sonnets"', *Papers of the Bibliographical Society of America*, liv (1960), 16–37.

others have even thought that this may have been set up from Shakespeare's autograph. All that the Stationers' Register entry of 'a booke called SHAKESPEARES sonnettes' (20 May 1609) really tells us about the manuscript Thorpe was handling is that, unlike any other Elizabethan sonnet sequence, this collection had no identifying title or names of participants. The namelessness of the poet, the friend, and the mistress, as well as of the seducer and maiden in *A Lover's Complaint*, is one of the most distinctive features of Shakespeare's sequence. But it was presumably Shakespeare, not Thorpe, who refrained from naming them. Had there been any form of title, such as 'Will and Emilia', Thorpe would presumably have wished to identify the work more precisely by using it. If anything, the namelessness of the *Sonnets* testifies to Thorpe's careful attitude to his copy. We have no evidence, for instance, that Sidney intended his sonnet sequence to be entitled *Astrophel and Stella*, but its publishers in 1591 found it convenient so to entitle it.[4]

It is time Thorpe and his text received fundamental scrutiny, with the help of fuller bibliographical aids than were available to Lee and his immediate successors. A particularly useful reference work is Paul G. Morrison's *Index of Printers, Publishers and Booksellers* (Chicago, 1961), which supplements the great Pollard and Redgrave *Short-Title Catalogue*. With the help of Morrison's *Index*, we can quickly gain a broader picture of Thorpe's publishing career than was possible for Lee. In drawing conclusions from the evidence, we should if possible approach the *Sonnets* without any idealized preconception about what kind of thing our national poet might do. Charles Knight in 1841 led the way for many others who have felt it out of the question that the respectable dramatist, withdrawing to the bosom of his family in Stratford, could have wished to associate himself with these poems.[5] Such an assumption seems to lie behind many editors' assertions that the text was unauthorized. Lee spelt out the fears on which this conviction was based:

a purely literal interpretation of the impassioned protestations of affection for a 'lovely boy', which course through the sonnets, casts a slur on the dignity of the poet's name which scarcely bears discussion.[6]

---

[4] Cf. *The Poems of Sir Philip Sidney*, ed. W. A. Ringler (1962), p. 458.

[5] *The Sonnets*, ed. Charles Knight (1841), p. 126; quoted by H. E. Rollins, Variorum edition of *The Sonnets* (1944), ii. 6. Rollins summarizes the textual and critical history of the *Sonnets* so fully that I have not attempted to do so here. Some of the major editions since Rollins have been those of Seymour-Smith (1963), Ingram and Redpath (1964), and Stephen Booth (1977).

[6] *Sonnets of Shakespeare*, ed. Sidney Lee (1905), p. 11.

Yet the poet himself tells us, in Sonnet 110, that he is shameless, caring little for his reputation or the integrity of his own image:

> Alas 'tis true, I have gone here and there,
> And made my selfe a motley to the view,
> Gor'd mine own thoughts, sold cheap what is most deare,
> Made old offences of affections new.

We have no reason to suppose that Shakespeare was particularly concerned with the literary image he presented to the world. In this, as in so many respects, he offers a striking contrast to Jonson. Where Jonson, through such a figure as Horace in *The Poetaster*, makes a clear definition of his artistic personality and ideals, Shakespeare nowhere asserts his presence in the plays, either as a writer or a personality. We should therefore be wary of making assumptions about what he was like when approaching the *Sonnets*. Nor, perhaps, should we be too ready to assume that Shakespeare would have carelessly released marketable manuscripts without payment. A non-dramatic text such as the *Sonnets*, having no reason to pass through the hands of the dramatic companies, might, one would imagine, travel from author to printer with comparatively few intermediaries. In spite of Meres's remark about Shakespeare's 'sugar'd sonnets among his private friends', there are no surviving manuscript copies even of individual sonnets from a date earlier than 1620. This is especially striking in a period when so many 'loose' sonnets, and sequences variously ordered, did circulate in manuscript. Jaggard's scoop in getting texts of only two of the *Sonnets*, 138 and 144, for *The Passionate Pilgrim* (1599) may point to their being, as a whole, kept close. I am not much persuaded by Peter Beal's suggestion, in his invaluable *Index of Literary Manuscripts*, that

It is at least a possibility that certain of the texts found in the miscellanies of the 1620s and '30s ultimately derive from early MS copies of individual sonnets and have no connexion with the 1609 edition.[7]

The manuscript miscellanies catalogued by Beal contain among them texts of only eleven individual sonnets, and even from his own accounts all appear to be based either on the 1609 text, or, in a very large number of cases, on each other.

There are two main grounds on which I would argue for the substantial integrity of the 1609 Quarto. The first is Thorpe's practice and associations as a publisher. *Pace* Lee and many others, I suggest that Thorpe was a publisher of some deserved status and

---

[7] Peter Beal, *Index of Literary Manuscripts* (1980), ii. 450.

prestige, handling works by close associates of Shakespeare, and producing, in many cases, highly authoritative texts. In the course of twenty-five years he published an impressive list of dramatic, theological, and poetic texts and translations, striking for the augustness of the persons to whom they are dedicated and, in many cases, for the care with which they have been authorially proof-read. Like many able men closely concerned with the trade of letters, Thorpe seems to have been something of a prankster. The one clear example of his publishing an unauthorized text—Coryate's *Odcombian Banquet* (1611; like the *Sonnets*, this was printed by Eld) in which all the prefatory material was included, but none of the text— seems to have been a deliberate prank, rather than sharp practice. It seems possible that Jonson and Thorpe together devised this joke publication.[8] But among Thorpe's forty-three other books, this seems to be the only documented example of unauthorized publication.

The second ground of my argument is structural. Within the 1609 text many elements of thematic and structural coherence are to be found which commentators have failed to recognize. The *Sonnets* fall into recognizable numerological units, the last two 'Anacreontic' sonnets (153, 154) have some warrant in traditional sonnet-ordering, and so, even more, does the sub-Ovidian afterpiece *A Lover's Complaint*, often bypassed as an embarrassing irrelevance. The sequence may not, to a modern eye, read as a wholly satisfactory continuum. Even such a sensitive and conservative commentator as Stephen Booth has some sympathy with the impulse to rearrange.[9] But there are probably no sonnet sequences of the period which do satisfy a modern reader's desire for continuity. The structural principles on which the Elizabethans built their sequences were only partly thematic or narrative. In profound ways, Shakespeare's sequence is very unlike all the others: but in such a superficial matter as ordering, I suggest, it would have been recognized by contemporaries as adequately answering expectations of continuity and coherence. Careful and unbiased reading of the whole volume as it stood in 1609 should be the preliminary to any investigation of the more rarefied mysteries offered by the *Sonnets*.

[8] Michael Strachan, *The Life and Adventures of Thomas Coryate* (1962), pp. 134-7, accepts Lee's view of Thorpe as an unscrupulous entrepreneur, holding Thorpe and Edward Blount jointly responsible for *The Odcombian Banquet*, about which, he says, Coryate was 'furious'. I think Strachan takes Coryate's fury too seriously. Then as now, public literary squabbles must have made for good sales, and the jocular tone of the final section of *Coryats Cramb* suggests to me that this was some such deliberate literary combat, to which Coryate himself may have been a party.

[9] Stephen Booth, *Shakespeare's Sonnets Edited with Analytic Commentary* (New Haven and London, 1977), pp. 545-6.

## II. THE CAREER OF THOMAS THORPE

Between 1600 and 1625 Thomas Thorpe, who was born in about 1569, was the publisher of at least forty-five books. Like most young publishers, he began his professional life as the close associate of an older man. He worked with Edward Blount, who in turn had been apprenticed to the highly successful and reputable William Ponsonby, publisher of *The Faerie Queene* and the *Arcadia*.[10] As his third book, Edward Blount had published Marlowe's *Hero and Leander* (1598); the culmination of his career was his work, with Jaggard, on the printing of the First Folio of Shakespeare's plays in 1623. This was not the first time Blount had handled Shakespearian material, however, for in 1601 he had published Chester's *Loves Martyr*, whose ascription of *The Phoenix and the Turtle* to Shakespeare is not questioned. Like Blount, Thorpe began his career with Marlowe, moving on to Shakespeare at a later stage. In 1600 he was associated with Marlowe's wonderful blank-verse translation of *Lucans First Booke*, dedicating the work to Blount, and referring to Blount's 'old right' in the book. His florid and quipping epistle to Blount is the first of the eccentric, rather self-assertive epistles and dedications which characterize some of Thorpe's publications. We shall probably never know precisely by what means a manuscript of Marlowe's *Lucan*, a work which had originally been entered in the Stationers' Register by John Wolfe in September 1593, reached Edward Blount, and in turn Thomas Thorpe. But we do know that the text appears to be an excellent one, in which editors have felt the need to make very few conjectural emendations. High standards of textual accuracy seem to be usual in the works Thorpe published. Most strikingly, he was for four crucial years Ben Jonson's publisher. After four comparatively minor works, his career as a publisher began in earnest in 1605, with his publication of Chapman's *All fooles* and Jonson's *Sejanus his falle*, entered by Blount and Thorpe on 6 August. Both works were printed by George Eld, who was to print the *Sonnets* four years later, and both are unusually good texts. In the most recent edition of Chapman's comedies G. Blakemore Evans suggests that the copy-text for *All fooles* 'was Chapman's own fair copy, or at least a transcript of that manuscript': the play seems therefore to have been purchased from the author, not from the players, and the heavy proof-corrections are likely to be

[10] Cf. Philip Gaskell, *A New Introduction to Bibliography* (1972), p. 180. There is an article on Blount by Sidney Lee, 'An Elizabethan Bookseller', in *Bibliographica*, iv (1895). Like Thorpe, Blount deserves fundamental re-examination with fuller information than Lee provides.

authorial.[11] The evidence for authorized publication of *Sejanus* is even stronger. Herford and Simpson remark on the excellence of the text, and so do more recent editors, such as Jonas Barish:

*Sejanus* was . . . published by Thomas Thorp [*sic*] in 1605, in an extremely accurate text. The exactness of the marginal annotations, the closeness with which the typography conveyed Jonson's metrical intentions, and the corrections made in proof all suggest that Jonson oversaw the printing himself.[12]

Shakespeare was one of the principal actors in *Sejanus* when it was performed by the King's Men in 1603 (others included Burbage, Heming, and Condell). It seems probable that he would have known of Jonson's decision to sell the play to Thorpe two years later, and he might have learned at that time of Thorpe's possible usefulness as a publisher of texts by dramatists. One small typographical feature of the 1605 Quarto is perhaps worth noticing, bearing in mind the fact that the same publisher and printer produced the baffling capitalized dedication to the *Sonnets* four years later. In Act V the Senate's proclamation, though in English, is printed after the manner of a Roman inscription, capitalized, and with a stop after each word:

MEMMIVS REGVLVS. AND . FVLCINIVS. TRIO. CONSVL'S, THESE. PRESENT. KALENDES. OF. IVNE. WITH. THE. FIRST. LIGHT. SHALL. HOLD. A. SENATE. IN. THE. TEMPLE. OF. APOLLO.[13]

This feature disappeared in the 1616 Folio of Jonson's works, where capitals were used only for proper names, the rest being italicized. Given the closeness with which Jonson oversaw the text of *Sejanus*— Herford and Simpson detected at least twenty-five press-corrections —the use of capitals in 1605 probably answered to his intentions. Thorpe and Eld may have learned from the Westminster-educated Jonson how to set out a 'Latinate' inscription in English. Jonson's satisfaction with the 1605 *Sejanus* is suggested by the survival of two authorial presentation copies, one to Sir Robert Townshend, the other to Francis Crane, the Prince of Wales's secretary.[14] One further play was entered to Thorpe in 1605, on 4 September: the collaborative *Eastward Ho*, by Chapman, Jonson, and Marston. It was entered

[11] *The Plays of George Chapman: The Comedies*, ed. Alan Holaday (Urbana, 1970), pp. 227–9.
[12] *Sejanus*, ed. Jonas A. Barish (Yale, 1965), p. 205; cf. also *Ben Jonson*, ed. C. H. Herford and P. and E. Simpson (Oxford, 1925–52), iv. 331–5.
[13] Jonson, *Sejanus his falle* (1605), sig. M.
[14] Herford and Simpson, ed. cit., iv. 333–4.

jointly to William Aspley and Thomas Thorpe, but in the event published by Aspley alone. Thorpe seems to have ceded his rights to Aspley, possibly because he was fully occupied with *All fooles* and *Sejanus*. An amicable arrangement is suggested by the fact that he continued to work in association with Aspley, who was to be one of the two booksellers assigned to sell the *Sonnets*. It is perhaps worth noting that the latest editor of *Eastward Ho*, R. W. Van Fossen, concludes that the copy for the Quarto was 'the authors' foul papers or a scribal transcript thereof rather than prompt copy'.[15]

Thorpe's next two publications were again for Chapman and Jonson: Chapman's *The Gentleman Usher* (1606) and in the same year Jonson's *Hymenaei*. For some reason neither of these was entered in the Stationers' Register. The printer for both was Valentine Simmes. *Hymenaei* is another corrected text, which Herford and Simpson describe as 'authoritative', and *The Gentleman Usher* is described by its latest editor as a 'reasonably careful' piece of printing which has been heavily corrected in proof, and in one section, at least, authorially revised.[16] A further publication in 1606 sheds an interesting light on Lee's assertion that Thorpe 'specialized in procuring "neglected copy"'. The work is a sermon entitled *The Life and Death of Jesus Christ*, by a Cambridge man, Samuel Walsall, of Corpus, which had been preached before the King at Royston in October 1606. In a prefatory epistle to the King, Walsall says that His Majesty had asked for a personal copy of the sermon: in a second epistle *To the Reader* he justifies his decision to allow the sermon to be printed. It is abundantly clear that the decision to publish was his own, and that it was precisely to avoid 'surreptitious' publication that he did so:

> Fear suggested, that, copies of the Sermon being already extorted, it might chance without my knowledge be PRESSED (so I presently apprehended it) To DEATH: which (were I touched with ordinary regard of reputation) might have made deeper *impression* of griefe in mee, then of letters in the paper . . . To stoppe the detracting mouth, or if not, to set it wider open, see here I have exposed this . . . to viewe, to censure, and had sooner, had the PRINTER sooner dared to adventure his Mart.[17]

In spite of the final hint of irritation at the dilatoriness of the printer or bookseller, common in new authors, this epistle points to an amicable arrangement between Walsall and Thorpe, since it indicates that the publication is one firmly authorized by himself. This helps to strengthen the impression of trust between author and

---

[15] George Chapman and others, *Eastward Ho*, ed. R. W. Van Fossen (1979), p. 47.
[16] *The Plays of George Chapman: The Comedies*, ed. Alan Holaday (Urbana, 1970), p. 131.
[17] Samuel Walsall, *The Life and Death of Jesus Christ* (1606), sig. A4.

publisher given by the clearly authorized Jonson–Thorpe publications. Walsall's sermon was published simultaneously in Cambridge by J. Porter. It seems to have been fairly popular, endorsing Walsall's fears of surreptitious publication, since another edition of it was published by Thorpe in 1615. A third, in 1622, was by J. Wright.

In 1607 Marston, the third member of the *Eastward Ho* triumvirate, joined the company of dramatists published by Thorpe. His *What you will* was printed by Eld and entered to Thorpe in the Register on 6 August. A rather better-remembered play was also published by Thorpe in the same year (printer unknown): Jonson's *Volpone, or the Foxe*. Thorpe's university connections, already indicated by his publication of the Walsall sermon, are perhaps expanded here by Jonson's confident dedication of *Volpone* jointly to the universities of Oxford and Cambridge. This elaborate capitalized dedication, set out like a lapidary inscription, but in English, is perhaps worth quoting in full for its visual and syntactical resemblance to that of the *Sonnets*:

TO THE MOST NOBLE

AND MOST AEQVALL

SISTERS

THE TWO FAMOVS VNIVERSITIES,

FOR THEIR LOVE

AND

ACCEPTANCE

SHEWN TO HIS POEME

IN THE PRESENTATION :

BEN: IONSON

THE GRATEFVLL ACKNOWLEDGER

DEDICATES

BOTH IT, AND HIMSELFE.

As a whole, *Volpone* is an excellent text, in which Jonson made twenty-three corrections in the course of printing. Herford and Simpson observe that 'It is significant that, when Jonson returned to this play after such an interval [for the 1616 Folio] he found nothing to recast'.[18] The Quarto is set far above the common run of 'playbooks' both by the dedication, quoted above, and by Jonson's dedicatory epistle, which claims a high status for all good poets, and in particular for dramatic and satiric poets working on classical models and with serious didactic aims. Its appearance is further enhanced by the inclusion of ten laudatory poems by Jonson's friends, who include Donne, Chapman, Beaumont, and Fletcher.

[18] Herford and Simpson, ed. cit., v. 8.

The 1607 *Volpone* is scarcely the sort of back-door publication in which, according to Lee, Thorpe specialized, since it is so confidently heralded by the author and his friends, and accepted by Jonson later as the definitive text. The still unresolved question of whether Jonson at this period used 'legal' or 'calendar' dating makes it impossible to be certain how close in time *Volpone* is to Shakespeare's *Sonnets*.[19] Jonson's epistle is dated 11 February 1607, and the title-page date is 1607. Should Greg's conjecture that Jonson used new-style dating be wrong, however, this would denote 1607/8, bringing *Volpone* to within a year of the *Sonnets*.

The year 1608 undoubtedly did see two more major dramatic texts published by Thorpe: Jonson's *Masques of Blacknesse and of Beautie*, and Chapman's *The Conspiracie and Tragedie of Charles Duke of Byron*. The latter was printed by George Eld and contains a dedication to Sir Thomas Walsingham. Jonson's *Masques* were entered in the Register on 21 April 1608. No press-variants were discovered in the copies collated by Herford and Simpson, but they found the important manuscript version of the *Masque of Blacknesse* to offer only two small improvements on the printed text.[20] There has been no very recent edition of Chapman's two-part drama of *Byron*, but the collations of T. M. Parrott in 1910 indicated that the 1608 text was corrected authorially in press. He found it greatly superior to the 1625 edition (also a Thorpe publication) which Chapman, though still alive, seems not to have overseen.[21] The year 1608 saw one further publication by Thorpe, suggesting his continued university connections: *Wits ABC*, a collection of epigrams by one Richard West of Magdalen College, Oxford. This was entered on the same day as Jonson's *Masques*, 21 April 1608. This volume has the distinction of being the only collection of original non-dramatic verse published by Thorpe besides Shakespeare's *Sonnets*.

A gap of almost a year ensued between Chapman's *Conspiracie and Tragedie of Byron* (entered on 5 June 1608) and *Shake-speares Sonnets*, entered in the Register on 20 May 1609. One further work, Bishop Joseph Hall's allegorical *Discovery of a newe world*, had been entered to Thorpe on 18 January 1608/9, but was in the event brought out under the imprint of Edward Blount, indicating a continued association between Thorpe and Blount. Coming at last to the *Sonnets*, I think we can place their appearance in a fairly clear context in Thorpe's publishing career. The evidence so far points to Thorpe as

[19] W. W. Greg, 'The Riddle of Jonson's Chronology', *The Library*, 4th Ser. vi (1925), 340-7.
[20] Herford and Simpson, ed. cit., vii. 163-5.
[21] *Chapman's Tragedies*, ed. T. M. Parrott (1910), p. 623.

a publisher who bought his copy directly from authors, judging by the frequency of authorial press-correction, and whose two main areas of association were the theatres and the universities. The former, clearly, is the more relevant to Shakespeare, but the latter is worth noting, as indicating a level of respectability which we would not normally expect in a publisher of plays. Thorpe's publications for Jonson, Chapman, and Marston identify him as a man to whom the most intellectual of the leading dramatists were willing to sell their texts. Jonson, in particular, had notoriously exacting standards, and in the case of the five works he sold to Thorpe he clearly took great pains to ensure that the text was excellent in all respects. He would scarcely have been in a position to do this if the copy had been procured by Thorpe in an undercover way. Are we really to believe that the man to whom the martinet Jonson entrusted these works would in the following year snatch and maul a collection of poems by Shakespeare? The fact that there is no sign of authorial press-correction in the thirteen surviving copies of the *Sonnets* should not surprise us. Even Shakespeare's narrative poems, universally accepted as authorized texts, with their authorial dedications to Southampton, offer no evidence that the poet bothered to oversee the printing. Of the first edition of *Venus and Adonis* only one copy survives, so there is little to go on. But in the case of *The Rape of Lucrece* there is positive evidence that, whoever was responsible for the few corrections that were made, it was certainly not Shakespeare, but some rather unobservant pedant.[22] Physically, *Shake-speares Sonnets* strongly resembles other Thorpe–Eld publications, such as Marston's *What you will* (1607) or Chapman's *Conspiracie and Tragedie of Byron* (1608). The typeface of the text, though not of title-page or headlines, is identical in all three, and there is the same tendency to crowd a page regardless of units of sense. Scholars have complained of the insensitive way in which the 1609 *Sonnets* are set out, often with one or two lines of a sonnet separated from the rest. On sig. 1ᵛ, for instance, we have only the opening line of Sonnet 137, and have to turn the leaf to read the other thirteen lines. Similar fragmentations occur in the Marston and Chapman texts. For instance, in *The Conspiracie of Byron*, Act 2, scene i (sig. C3ᵛ) we have the first line of Savoy's speech which opens the scene, and have to turn the leaf for the rest. On sig. M4ᵛ a single line by Soisson is separated from Byron's speech to which it is a reply. In mitigation of Eld's printing-house methods, we could perhaps point to the arbitrary dissections of verse and sense in many of the modern Arden editions—the less excusable since

[22] *Shakespeare's Poems*, ed. J. C. Maxwell (1966), pp. 146-8.

Shakespeare's works are now so highly valued. The printing of the *Sonnets* has been the subject of a detailed investigation by Macd. P. Jackson. In particular, he analyses the work of the two compositors who set it up, and who may have been responsible for *Troilus and Cressida*, printed by Eld in the same year.[23] Exhaustive investigation of all the Thorpe–Eld texts might tell us much more about what kind of copy Thorpe most often handled, as well as about the ways of Eld's printing-house. But even a superficial survey suggests that physically *Shake-speares Sonnets* is not an uncharacteristic Thorpe–Eld publication. Its distinctiveness in the 'list' springs from its genre rather than from its physical make-up. It is one of only two volumes of original and non-dramatic poetry published by Thorpe. We should perhaps deduce from this that Thorpe may have obtained this non-dramatic piece through links he had already formed, since there is no evidence of previous or subsequent handling of this kind of poetry— which was in any case a little old-fashioned by 1609. The most likely link would be through the playwrights, in particular Jonson, Chapman, and Marston—not, as has often been suggested, through Mr W. H. himself, unless he was also an actor or playwright. The person who might most probably have brought Shakespeare or his manuscript to Thorpe's notice is Jonson. If Shakespeare in 1608-9 wanted to raise some money by selling an unpublished literary manuscript, Jonson, as an active overseer of his own works in print, and no doubt a man who drove a keen bargain, would have been an obvious friend to consult on the matter. If Jonson were asked for such advice at this date, we can be fairly sure that he would have recommended Thorpe. There is a practical reason why Shakespeare might particularly have wanted to raise some cash from a non-dramatic work in the early summer of 1609. An injunction which appears to belong to May 1609 prohibited the performing of plays and other public spectacles in London.[24] This was no doubt because of the severe outbreak of plague which had infested London throughout the winter of 1608-9, with redoubled severity in April 1609. Anticipating a loss of income from the theatre, Shakespeare might well have decided that the moment had come to dispose of a non-dramatic manuscript. All this is mere hypothesis. But all the circumstantial evidence points to some such above-board transaction as likely, rather than to deliberate piracy by Thorpe.

[23] Macd. P. Jackson, 'Punctuation and the Compositors of Shakespeare's *Sonnets, 1609*', *The Library*, 5th Ser. xxx (1975), 1-24.

[24] *Malone Society Collections*, II. iii (1931), 319; cf. also F. P. Wilson, *The Plague in Shakespeare's London* (1927), pp. 120-1. I am indebted to Miss Jean Robertson for drawing my attention to these references.

The rest of Thorpe's career can be briefly summarized. His theatrical connections seem to have declined after his publication of the anonymous *Histrio-mastix* in 1610, and he turned increasingly to theological and travel books, often of a very distinguished character. Cartwright's *The Preacher's Travels* (1611) combined the two, being an account of travels in the Middle East by a clergyman who was a graduate of Magdalen College, Oxford; there may be some continuous link with Magdalen, since Thorpe had published the epigrams of Richard West, of the same college, in 1608. Two publications in 1610 were of remarkable quality: the late John Healey's translations of *St. Augustine of the Citie of God* (entered in 1608) and of *Epictetus his manuell.* The florid and somewhat obscure dedications of these works by Thorpe to William Herbert, Earl of Pembroke, were held against him by Lee, who described them as 'extravagantly subservient in tone'. But if Thorpe is to be held blameworthy for his obsequiousness towards this eminent statesman and man of letters, so are Heming and Condell, who dedicated the First Folio to Pembroke and his brother in 1623. While I have no wish to become entangled in the search for 'Mr W. H.', I think it striking that the two works published by Thorpe immediately after the *Sonnets* both bear dedications to William Herbert, said by Heming and Condell to have favoured Shakespeare and his works.

The next Thorpe publication, Coryate's *Odcombian Banquet* (1611), seems to be a deliberate piece of mischief, perhaps perpetrated with the connivance of Jonson (see above, p. 155). Among the later publications Nashe's *Christ's teares over Jerusalem* (1613; previously published by Roberts in 1593 and Wise in 1594) stands out for its literary quality. More striking still is Thorpe's share in the publication of Sir Arthur Gorges's translation of Lucan's *Pharsalia* (1614). This is a finely-printed text of a most distinguished translation, now strangely forgotten. Lucan's epic was of particular importance to 'republican' political thinking in the Civil War period, and Gorges's version, in rhyming tetrameters, is clear, powerful, and readable. Metrical and verbal similarities suggest to me that this version, rather than the Thomas May translation of 1626, may lie behind the Cromwell–Caesar passage in Marvell's *Horatian Ode*, especially since May's version and the pretensions he based on it are mocked in *Tom May's Death*.[25] Be that as it may, the book is self-evidently a 'quality' publication. It was entered to Walter Burre on 27 May 1614, and published jointly under three separate imprints by Burre,

[25] The editors of the revised edition of Marvell's poems make no reference to the Gorges version: *Poems and Letters*, ed. Margoliouth and Legouis (1971), i. 301, 305, and *passim*.

Edward Blount, and Thorpe. It is quite clearly an authorized publication, though Gorges avoids the stigma of print by having a dedicatory epistle, describing the preparation of the text for publication, written by his ten-year-old son, Carew Gorges.[26] The dedicatee is Lucy Harington, Countess of Bedford. The first of the six poems *To the Translator* is by Ralegh, whose *History of the World* appeared in the same year as Gorges's Lucan, also published by Burre. It was probably Burre, rather than Thorpe, who made the initial contact with Gorges, but I imagine that Thorpe would have viewed his third share in this enterprise as a considerable source of pride. To Thorpe *Lucans Pharsalia* may well have seemed the high point of his publishing career, rather than *Shake-speares Sonnets*.

Between 1614 and 1625 Thorpe published eleven more books, the last being the second edition of Chapman's *Conspiracie and Tragedie of Byron*. He seems to have sustained his connections with the University of Oxford, for in 1635 he was assigned a lodging in the beautiful fifteenth-century almshouse at Ewelme, which was administered by dignitaries of the University. It may also be relevant that he had published a book on such an establishment of more recent foundation, *The Charterhouse* (1614; printed by Eld), published also under the title of *King James his hospitall* in the same year. Miss Rostenberg writes of Thorpe's retirement as if it were something of a disgrace: 'Thomas Thorpe died a pauper, a ward of his country's largesse.'[27] But it must surely have been a very fortunate old man at that period who, after an extremely hazardous professional career, could end his days in such a well-ordered and secure establishment. Ben Jonson, who died apparently in lonely misery in his chamber by Westminster Abbey, was scarcely so fortunate.[28] Jonson's former publisher may have succeeded in securing a more stable form of patronage for his declining years than did the more talented dramatist.

Thorpe's publishing career would be worth studying in considerably more detail: but I hope I have gone far enough to show that he was probably not the unscrupulous entrepreneur for which he has been taken. Shakespeare must surely have known of him, at the very least, because of his publication of a play (*Sejanus*) in which he had played a leading role; and he could well have viewed favourably a man who had published such writers as Marlowe, Chapman, Jonson, and Marston. I see no real reason why Shakespeare could not himself have

[26] The only full survey of Gorges's works seems to be that by H. E. Sandison, 'Arthur Gorges, Spenser's Alcyon and Ralegh's friend', *PMLA* xliii (1928), 645-74. *Lucans Pharsalia* is briefly noticed on p. 673.

[27] Leona Rostenberg, art. cit., p. 37.

[28] Herford and Simpson, ed. cit., i. 102-15.

sold the manuscript of the *Sonnets* and *A Lover's Complaint* to Thorpe, unless it is clear that the texts as they stand cannot be authorial. My reasons for feeling that they do in fact make very good sense as they stand in the 1609 Quarto are the subject of the next section.

### III. THE STRUCTURE OF *SHAKE-SPEARES SONNETS*, 1609

The 1609 *Shake-speares Sonnets* is, as a formal whole, comparable structurally with Sidney's *Astrophel and Stella*, Spenser's *Amoretti*, Daniel's *Delia*, and Lodge's *Phillis*. Many later collections offer structural and numerological parallels. For instance, John Davies of Hereford's highly derivative sequence *Wittes Pilgrimage* (entered in the Stationers' Register on 27 September 1605) totals 152 sonnets, the same number as Shakespeare's sequence if we except the two Diana/Cupid sonnets at the end. It is also interesting in having strong Pembroke–Herbert associations. But in examining the structure of the 1609 volume as a whole, it is the sequences of Sidney, Spenser, Daniel, and Lodge which seem most closely relevant. Whatever we may think of more refined structural features, Shakespeare's *Sonnets* fall very obviously into three sections. There is an opening section of 17 sonnets of persuasion to marriage, a central section of 108 sonnets of friendship, in which time, love, and beauty are profoundly explored, rounded off by a twelve-line envoi, and followed by the final section of 28 'Dark Lady' sonnets, which includes, as final sections often did, some rather miscellaneous material. The last two poems are 'Anacreontic'—the two sonnets, perhaps referring to Bath, on Diana's cooling fountain. The central sequence opens very clearly with the radiantly confident 'Shall I compare thee to a Summers day?', which, after the seventeen suasory sonnets, is pure unmitigated eulogy. The 'this' of its final line—'so long lives this'— may refer both to the sonnet whose first thirteen lines we have just read, and to the whole Friendship sequence which ensues. The twelve-line poem 126 (not a sonnet) 'O thou my lovely boy' has been generally felt to terminate the central phase of the sequence, being described by Dover Wilson and many others as an 'envoi':[29] a clear fresh start is marked by Sonnet 127, 'In the ould age blacke was not counted faire'. The number of sonnets in the first section, 17, is not of obvious significance unless we accept Dover Wilson's attractive but quite unsupported hypothesis that these sonnets were commissioned by the Countess of Pembroke to mark her son's seventeenth birthday,

---

[29] J. Dover Wilson, ed. cit., pp. 240-1.

which certainly fell in a period when pressure on the young man to marry was very intense.[30] Nor does 28, the number of sonnets in the third section, seem significant, though one could build a card-house on Dover Wilson's hypothesis by conjecturing that the Dark Lady's age might be imagined as 28—this is the age of Lady Capulet in *Romeo and Juliet*, and might conceivably be a formulaic age for the 'older woman'. It is also the age of Iago in *Othello* (I. iii. 311-12). But numerologically the opening and closing sections do not seem to fall into a clearly recognizable pattern. The middle section of 108 sonnets, however, conforms to the precedent set by Sidney in *Astrophel and Stella*, which in the authoritative 1598 text, overseen by his sister, has 108 sonnets. It is clear that this figure was felt to be of significance and authority in Sidney's immediate circle, since Fulke Greville took pains in the Warwick Castle MS to bring his *Caelica* also to the total of 108.[31] In the posthumous printed text the number is 110. (Shakespeare's middle sequence is 108 or 109, according to whether or not we include the 'envoi'.) Alexander Craig's *Amorose Songes, Sonets, and Elegies* (1606) also totals 108 poems, and there are 108 lines in Spenser's *Dolefull Lay of Clorinda*, in which the Countess of Pembroke is imagined as lamenting the death of her brother. Whether or not we accept Adrian Benjamin and Alastair Fowler's theories about the reason for this number,[32] it is too distinctive a total to have recurred by chance in Sidney, Greville, Spenser, Craig, and Shakespeare. Shakespeare could have aimed, as several sonneteers did, at a round hundred or 'century' of sonnets— compare Barnabe Barnes's *Divine Centurie of Spirituall Sonnets* (1595), for instance. It seems highly unlikely that he aimed roughly at a hundred, but instead overshot it and by chance reached a figure identical to that of *Astrophel and Stella*. In totalling 108/9 in his central section he must surely have intended to label his sequence as belonging in some sense to the august tradition established by Sidney and followed by Greville and others. Shakespeare may not have directly known *Caelica*, which was not printed until 1633, but he must surely have known at least *Astrophel and Stella* and *The Dolefull Lay of Clorinda*. The recurrence of the figure in Shakespeare makes it seem less likely that 108, here at least, has particular associations with Penelope Rich, as Benjamin's discoveries relating to the 'Penelope

[30] J. Dover Wilson, ed. cit., pp. 99-100.

[31] Cf. W. H. Kelliher, 'The Warwick Castle Manuscripts of Fulke Greville', *BMQ* xxxiv (1970), 107-221; and *Poems and Dramas of Fulke Greville*, ed. G. Bullough (1938), i. 331-4 and *passim*.

[32] Alastair Fowler, *Triumphal Forms: Structural Patterns in Elizabethan Poetry* (1970), pp. 174-80.

game' suggest, since it is most unlikely that Shakespeare's Friendship sonnets are closely linked with her: though I suppose it is possible that Shakespeare mimicked the figure without being aware of its more intimate associations in the Sidney–Greville circle. The ultimate rationale of the figure must be admitted to be still pretty mysterious. But its use by Shakespeare must mark his central sonnet sequence as a deliberately fashioned structure. Both externally and internally the central sequence is a coherent whole, with at least as much continuity from sonnet to sonnet as *Astrophel and Stella*, and more than is to be found in many other sequences. There are frequent 'runs' of two, three, or more sonnets which read either as continuous meditations on single themes, or seem to spring out of single events or situations. Some examples are 27, 28, on sleeplessness; 33–6, on the friend's treachery; 48, 50, 51, on the poet's journey; 63–7, on the operation of time; 71–4, in which the poet anticipates his death; 78–86, the 'Rival Poet' section; 100–3, on the poet's silence. There is if anything rather less continuity of thought than this in Sidney's *Astrophel and Stella*. While the debate between reason and passion is a continually recurring theme in the first thirty or so sonnets, for instance, there is very rarely any sense of one sonnet building on the previous one, such as we often have in Shakespeare's sequence. Particularly clear examples of continuous thought are the two pairs 44, 45 and 46, 47. In Sidney, while we do have a general sense of Astrophel's movement deeper and deeper into an acceptance of the intellectual and emotional bondage of his love for Stella, each sonnet seems like a fresh start: there is very rarely any immediate linking of sonnet to sonnet by words and images. Late in the sequence, from the point where the songs begin to appear, there are some local patches of continuity: *AS* 66 and 67 are linked reflections on Astrophel's self-blinded hope, for instance, and the next three sonnets are on his joy. But the only clearly continuous passage which seems to spring from an imagined event or situation, as many of Shakespeare's linked sonnets do, is the section of eleven sonnets, 73–83, between the second and third songs. All of these arise out of Astrophel's stolen kiss, evoked in the second song, though even in this section Sonnet 75, a paradoxical eulogy of Edward IV, is not specifically related to the theme of the kiss. Sonnets 87–9 are on Astrophel's absence; 96–9 on his sleeplessness; 101–2 on Stella's sickness. But the placing of 103, on Stella's Cleopatra-like journey on the Thames, with no reference to her having been ill, suggests (if the order is authorial) that variety of effect was one of Sidney's aims, quite as much as continuity or coherence. Variety was certainly one of

127

the qualities most prized in collections of sonnets, from Watson's pedantic *Hekatompathia* onwards. Drayton, for instance, boasted of his versatility and range of effect:

> My wanton verse nere keepes one certain stay,
> But now, at hand; then seekes invention far,
> And with each little motion runnes astray,
> Wilde, madding, jocond, & irreguler.[33]

Shakespeare could almost have been replying to such claims when he wrote in Sonnet 76:

> Why is my verse so barren of new pride?
> So far from variation or quicke change?
> Why with the time do I not glance aside
> To new found methods, and to compounds strange?

Shakespeare's central sequence, Sonnets 18 to 126, is if anything more tightly knit thematically than most of the sonnet sequences printed earlier. The many attempts, from Benson onwards, to fragment and rearrange the *Sonnets* seem to spring from a reluctance to recognize the habitual looseness of the accepted form of the Elizabethan sonnet sequence, as well as from a desire to see if rearranging will exonerate Shakespeare from affection for a 'lovely boy'.

Looking at the 1609 volume as a whole, it is possible to perceive other structuring devices which are not unlike those of the sequences printed in the 1590s. The two final sonnets, 153 and 154, on the sleeping Cupid's firebrand being plunged in cold water by one of Diana's nymphs, have often been felt to be irrelevant, substandard, and perhaps not authorial. But several other authors used similar 'Anacreontic' verses to divide off their collections of sonnets from the continuous lyric or complaint which followed. Daniel's *Delia* (1592) has an Anacreontic 'Ode', 'Nowe each creature joyes the other', which divides the sonnets from *The Complaint of Rosamond* (sig. H2–H2ᵛ). Lodge's *Phillis*, published in the following year, also has an 'Ode', in the trochaic metre which the Elizabethans associated with 'Anacreon', dividing the sonnets and lyrics of *Phillis* from the topographical narrative poem *The Complaint of Elstred* (sig. H3ᵛ). Spenser also used this device. In the *Amoretti* (1595) four little

---

[33] Sonnet appended to *Englands Heroicall Epistles* (1599); the better-known version of this boast was not published until Drayton's last revision of *Idea*, in 1619:

> My Muse is rightly of the English strain,
> That cannot long one fashion entertain.

Cf. Drayton, *Works*, ed. J. W. Hebel (1931), i. 485, ii. 310.

Anacreontic poems, the longest a version of the familiar 'Cupid and the bee' lyric, divide the sonnets of the *Amoretti* from the lyrical *Epithalamion* (F6ᵛ–G2). Although I cannot explain why these writers felt it appropriate to 'sign off' their sonnet sequences with lightweight Anacreontic poems, often fancies about Cupid which seem to bear no relation to the more naturalistic treatment of love which has gone before, there is clearly a tradition of so doing, and it is one which Shakespeare, in Sonnets 153 and 154, can be seen to have followed.

Most editors have reluctantly conceded that *A Lover's Complaint* is, as its separate title in the 1609 text asserts, by Shakespeare.[34] But Alastair Fowler is one of only a very small number of commentators who have suggested that it forms part of the same structural unit as the *Sonnets*.[35] In general, editors of the *Sonnets* have separated them from *A Lover's Complaint*, either omitting the *Complaint* altogether, or placing it with the poems published earlier. In 1794 Malone placed it after *The Passionate Pilgrim*; more recently, in the New Cambridge edition, it has been placed with *Venus and Adonis* and *The Rape of Lucrece*, so that readers of the companion edition of the *Sonnets* would not even see it. Yet, whatever we may think of its poetic quality, it is, I suggest, an intended component of the volume as first published. Daniel's *Delia* volume of 1592 proceeds, after the Anacreontic 'Ode', to *The Complaint of Rosamond* (in rhyme royal); Lodge's *Phillis*, also after such an ode, is followed by *The Complaint of Elstred* (in sixains). Both of these are, like *A Lover's Complaint*, narratives by seduced women who find some justification for their fault in the great rank and power of their lovers. A rather feebler example of this two-part structure is Richard Lynch's *Diella* (1596), where the final sonnet of the sequence invites the chaste Diella to contemplate the love story which follows: *The Love of Don Diego and Ginevra*, a narrative in sixains with a happy ending. Shakespeare's *A Lover's Complaint* (which, like *Rosamond*, is in rhyme royal) can be seen to fall into the general structural pattern established by Daniel, although its heroine is nameless and the setting indistinct in time and place. In both Daniel and Lodge there appears to be some deliberate counterpointing of a sonnet sequence in which a male lover reflects on his unrequited love, and a verse narrative in which a woman reflects on her betrayal by a man. Shakespeare's narrative poems offered an analogous contrast, unrequited female desire in *Venus and Adonis* being contrasted with male lust and female chastity in *The Rape of Lucrece*. Lucrece's complaint in lines 764–1036 forms an almost

[34] Maxwell, ed. cit., p. xxxv.
[35] Alastair Fowler, op. cit., pp. 183–97.

detachable 'complaint' comparable with *Rosamond*. The *Sonnets* and *A Lover's Complaint* seem to contain the seeds of such a contrast between the male lover and the female victim, though the great intricacy and thematic profundity of the *Sonnets* makes it much less apparent. There must, surely, be some intended connection or parallel between the young seducer whom the girl finds so enchanting that she fears she could well submit again to his wiles, and the unreliable young Friend of the central sequence of *Sonnets* who is universally admired and adored (16, 31), and to whom the poet is a willing vassal or slave (26, 57, 58). Both the poet of the *Sonnets* and the maiden of the *Complaint* declare themselves willing to submit repeatedly to the charms of a young man whom they know to be untrustworthy. The seducer has one rather distinctive characteristic which can be linked with the Friend: he has a capacity for sudden rage which is seen as positively attractive, almost like the 'rich anger' of the poet's mistress in Keats's *Ode to Melancholy*:

> Yet if men mov'd him, was he such a storme
> As oft twixt May and Aprill is to see,
> When windes breath sweet, unruly though they be.

This attractive irritability, evoked in terms of weather, seems strongly reminiscent of Sonnet 34 ('Why didst thou promise such a beautious day') which, with the sonnets immediately before and after it, describes and condones some 'fault' of the Friend in largely meteorological terms. I do not want to press the parallels between the *Complaint* and the *Sonnets* too far. For instance, I would not wish to press an analogy between the poet, 'Beated and chopped with tand antiquitie' (Sonnet 62) and the reverend old man leaning on his 'greined bat' in the *Complaint* who listens to the maiden's narrative. But there certainly are parallels and connections, as well as a general tradition of presenting a Complaint as an afterpiece to a sonnet sequence. The editorial practice of separating the works from each other seems very dubious.

To readers of Daniel's *Delia* and *Rosamond*, or of Lodge's *Phillis* and *Elstred* volume, the overall look of the 1609 *Sonnets* volume would have been by no means strange. Malone observed that 'Daniel's Sonnets . . . appear to me to have been the model that Shakespeare followed',[36] and this suggestion should perhaps have been more vigorously pursued. Had *Shake-speares Sonnets* appeared in the late 1590s, it would no doubt have taken its place clearly among the sonnet sequences of that period. Much of its strangeness

[36] *The plays and poems of William Shakespeare*, ed. Edmond Malone (1794), xvi. 5.

springs from its date and, as I have suggested, from the fact that none of the characters are given names. These are among the many mysteries in the *Sonnets* which will no doubt continue to excite curiosity and hypothesis 'So long as men can breath or eyes can see'. But whoever next undertakes to plumb their depths, I suggest that he should do so in the context of an exhaustive reading of the 1609 text as it stands in its entirety. It seems more than possible that Shakespeare himself sold the copy to Jonson's friend Thorpe entire, though without troubling himself to correct the normal crop of errors which appeared in Eld's text. Kenneth Muir has suggested cogently that many of what Lee described as 'misprints' can be more plausibly explained as faithful renderings of the accidentals of an authorial manuscript, though one 'presumably' published without the author's permission.[37] I hope I have shown that this presumption is one we need not make. Shakespeare may have done as he said in Sonnet 110, and 'sold cheap what is most deare'.

[37] Kenneth Muir, *Shakespeare the Professional and Related Studies* (1973), pp. 214 and 233.

# Editing as Cultural Formation:
# The Sexing of Shakespeare's Sonnets

Peter Stallybrass

For the past two years, I have been trying to understand the work of bibliographers and editors. I undertook this "retraining" for two contradictory but related reasons. The first is that as I became increasingly engaged in the teaching and organization of cultural studies courses, I began to wonder what the strengths of specific disciplinary trainings might be. That is, one of the obvious dangers of interdisciplinary work is that one ends up doing history, anthropology, economics—badly. It is hard to gather the technical skills of another discipline on the side: the historical skills, for instance, of finding sources, let alone knowing how to read them. I began to wonder what exactly the technical skills of someone teaching in a department of English might be. Whatever they were, I didn't seem to know about them or have them. (By contrast, I did have at least the rudiments of a historical training through having worked with various historians in England.) I found that the librarians at the University of Pennsylvania had an extraordinary range of skills that, as someone who worked on and with books, I felt I should know. The second reason for my turn to editing and bibliography is that I came to believe that the material culture of books was central to any cultural analysis of "literature" and therefore to one aspect of cultural studies.[1] Questions of, say, the for-

---

[1] Formative work in this field has been done by Roger Chartier, Jerome J. McGann, and Donald F. McKenzie. See, for instance, Chartier, *The Cultural Uses of Print in Early Modern France*, trans. Lydia G. Cochrane (Princeton, N.J.: Princeton University Press, 1987); Chartier, ed., *The Culture of Print: Power and the Uses of Print in Early Modern Europe*, trans. Lydia G. Cochrane (Princeton, N.J.: Princeton University Press, 1989); McGann, *A Critique of Modern Textual Criticism* (Chicago: University of

*Modern Language Quarterly* 54:1, March 1993. © 1993 University of Washington.

mation of nationalism (and national languages), the construction of the individual, and the making of genders and sexualities are materially embedded in the historical production and reproduction of texts.

A further reason to shift interests has been to interrogate a notion of historicity that emphasizes the *punctual* emergence of its objects of study. That is, a course on the seventeenth century would be about writers who wrote ("on time") in the period one was studying (Milton, Donne, Behn). In such a course, one might incorporate "precursors" or earlier writing as "background," but that only reproduces the notion of a series of punctual moments that can be related chronologically through their dates of origination. Margreta de Grazia powerfully challenges this view in *Shakespeare Verbatim*.[2] She contends that the Shakespeare we still study is the construction of the late eighteenth century and, above all, of the editorial labors of Malone. In other words, "our" Shakespeare is (or until recently was) the contemporary of the French Revolution rather than of the Armada. What I attempt to do here is to give a working example of the implications of such a proposition. I argue that in an important sense, if we take seriously the labor of production (editorial work, theatrical stagings, critical commentary, the global production and distribution of books, the incorporation of texts into the educational apparatus), Shakespeare is a central nineteenth-century author. But what is being authored remains a question. In the case of the *Sonnets*, which I shall examine, we can read the inscription of a new history of sexuality and "character." But that new history emerges unpunctually, dislocated by its need to write itself

---

Chicago Press, 1983); *The Textual Condition* (Princeton, N.J.: Princeton University Press, 1991); and McKenzie, *Bibliography and the Sociology of Texts* (London: British Library, 1986).

　　[2] De Grazia, *Shakespeare Verbatim: The Reproduction of Authenticity and the 1790 Apparatus* (Oxford: Clarendon, 1991).

**Peter Stallybrass is professor of English and chair of the Cultural Studies Committee at the University of Pennsylvania. He is coauthor with Allon White of *The Politics and Poetics of Transgression* (1986) and coeditor with David Scott Kastan of *Staging the Renaissance* (1991).**

over the culturally valued but culturally disturbing body of the *Sonnets*.[3]

Until Edmond Malone's 1780 edition, the history of the publication of the *Sonnets* was that of the reproduction of John Benson's edition of 1640, in which Benson had radically reordered the sonnets, given titles to individual sonnets, conflated sonnets to create longer poems, changed at least some pronouns so as to render the beloved female rather than male, and added many other poems that modern editors do not regard as Shakespearean(de Grazia, *Shakespeare Verbatim*, 132–76). In returning to the 1609 quarto of the *Sonnets*, Malone was intent upon rescripting Shakespeare's poems to show the contours of the man behind them. That is, he was inventing the character Shakespeare as he is still visible to us. Above all he turned, as de Grazia has argued, to the *Sonnets*, which he believed gave a crucial key to Shakespeare's inner life;[4] now, much to Malone's credit, the "boy," the "friend," "he" appear as central figures. But they do so as the site of moral panic. Once created, the "authentic" character of Shakespeare steps into the spotlight as a potential sodomite.

The 1821 edition of Malone prints the sonnets together with the remarks of John Boswell, Jr., who presents the characters of the new edition (Shakespeare, the young man, the rival poet, the dark lady) *and* the panic that attends their presentation. Boswell seems appalled at the prospect of what the reader will make of Malone's Shakespeare: the Bard has been given a rich interiority, but at the cost of impugned reputation. In the final page of his remarks Boswell dedicates himself to proving that Shakespeare was not a pederast. In the process, as hysterical symptom, he draws the lines of defense that have governed nearly all subsequent readings of the *Sonnets*: (1) In the Renaissance, male-male friendship was expressed through the rhetoric of amorous

---

[3] For other work on the *Sonnets* to which I am indebted, see Gregory W. Bredbeck, *Sodomy and Interpretation: Marlowe to Milton* (Ithaca, N.Y.: Cornell University Press, 1991), 167–80; Bruce R. Smith, *Homosexual Desire in Shakespeare's England: A Cultural Poetics* (Chicago: University of Chicago Press, 1991), 228–70; and de Grazia, "The Scandal of Shakespeare's Sonnets," *Shakespeare Survey*, forthcoming.

[4] Malone, *Supplement to the Edition of Shakespeare's Plays Published in 1778 by Samuel Johnson and George Steevens* (London: Bathurst, 1780); and John Benson, *Poems: Written by Wil Shake-speare. Gent.* (London, 1640).

love. (2) Shakespeare didn't love the young man anyway, because he was his patron, and the poems are therefore written in pursuit of patronage. (3) The poems are not really about love or friendship, because sonnets are conventional. They are, then, less about a young man or a dark lady than about Petrarch, Ronsard, Sidney, and the like (a boy's club, but not *that* kind of boy's club). (4) Malone was wrong, and the sonnets are, after all, a miscellany. They "had neither the poet himself nor any individual in view; but were merely the effusions of his fancy, written upon various topicks for the amusement of a private circle."[5]

Now there is nothing necessarily wrong with any of these readings. I'm not concerned here with their truth or their scholarly credentials but with their emergence as attempted solutions to a crisis. As these readings get established, the crisis that produced them gets progressively buried, only to reemerge at junctures like the trial of Oscar Wilde in the 1890s.

At the moment of the formation of "Shakespeare" through a reading of the *Sonnets* in the 1780s and 1790s, it is striking how nakedly the issues are presented. Malone prints his commentary at the bottom of the page, but his own remarks are frequently framed as a response to the criticisms of George Steevens, who thought that the *Sonnets* should not be published at all. Malone's footnote to sonnet 20, for instance, reads as follows:

> —the MASTER-MISTRESS of my passion;] It is impossible to read this fulsome panegyrick, addressed to a male object, without an equal mixture of disgust and indignation. We may remark also, that the same phrase employed by Shakespeare to denote the height of encomium, is used by Dryden to express the extreme of reproach:
>> "That woman, but more daub'd; or, if a man,
>> "Corrupted to a woman; thy *man-mistress*."
>>> *Don Sebastian.*
>
> Let me be just, however, to our author, who has made a proper use of the term *male varlet*, in Troilus and Cressida. See that play, Act V. Sc. I. STEEVENS.
>
> Some part of this indignation might perhaps have been abated, if it

5 Boswell, "Preliminary Remarks," in *The Plays and Poems of William Shakspeare*, ed. Edmond Malone (London, 1821), 20:220.

had been considered that such addresses to men, however indelicate, were customary in our author's time, and neither imported criminality, nor were esteemed indecorous. See a note on the words—"thy deceased *lover*," in the 32d Sonnet. To regulate our judgement of Shakespeare's poems by the modes of modern times, is surely as unreasonable as to try his plays by the rules of Aristotle.

 *Master-mistress* does not perhaps mean *man*-mistress, but *sovereign* mistress. See Mr. Tyrwhitt's note on the 165th verse of the Canterbury Tales, vol. iv. p. 197. MALONE. (20:241)

In the most literal sense, character assassination precedes the construction of character: Malone's justification of Shakespeare comes after (both temporally and upon the printed page) Steevens's assault.

 Nor did Malone's response satisfy Steevens, who, in his 1793 edition of Shakespeare, wrote: "We have not reprinted the Sonnets etc. of Shakespeare, because the strongest act of Parliament that could be framed, would fail to compel readers into their service; notwithstanding these miscellaneous Poems have derived every possible advantage from the literature and judgement of their only intelligent editor, Mr. Malone, whose implements of criticism, like the ivory rake and golden spade in Prudentius, are on this occasion disgraced by the objects of their culture."[6] The passage is a paradoxical mixture of the direct and indirect: the word *sodomy* nowhere appears, and yet everywhere it underpins the argument in a curiously inverted form. The acts of Parliament by which sodomites were persecuted and punished are here magically displaced by imaginary decrees that, however strong, will have no force to make the reader turn to Shakespeare's *Sonnets*. Readers cannot be "compel[led]" to the "service" of these poems; that is, they will refuse to be seduced, corrupted, sodomized. A familiar scenario, in which the state apparatus contrives to represent its victims as the agents of oppression, has been invoked.[7] But Steevens limits the danger of those demonic agents by transforming them into the objects of "culture," by which he surely means the excrement that contami-

---

 [6] Steevens, "Advertisement," in *Plays*, by William Shakespeare, ed. Samuel Johnson and George Steevens (London, 1793), 1:vii–viii.

 [7] See Jonathan Dollimore, "Transgression and Surveillance in *Measure for Measure*," in *Political Shakespeare: New Essays in Cultural Materialism*, ed. Jonathan Dollimore and Alan Sinfield (Manchester: Manchester University Press, 1985), 72–87.

nates even that distinguished "culture-critic," Edmond Malone, despite the long handles of his ivory rake and golden spade.

Culture as contamination. The gentle Shakespeare as contaminator and corrupter of youth. But if this character is reiterated throughout the nineteenth century, it is above all as a character denied. Critics, in other words, worked *from* what they imagined as character assassination (e.g., Shakespeare as pederast) *to* character. But how many character assassinators are there to be reproduced and ritually denounced? In the nineteenth century, as for Malone at the end of the eighteenth, Steevens is virtually alone as the assassinator who must be endlessly named, denounced, put straight. From this distance, the repeated act of putting straight appears as a form of cultural hysteria, but its excesses inscribe a crisis in the attempt to form a normative character and sexuality through Malone's Shakespeare.

One of the most drastic responses to Malone's edition of the *Sonnets* was William Henry Ireland's forgery of a letter purporting to be from Elizabeth I to Shakespeare, thanking him for his sonnets.[8] The *Sonnets*, in other words, were addressed neither to a male beloved nor to a common woman but to the monarch herself. The forgery was only one of several by Ireland, so what is perhaps more remarkable is that the supposition that Shakespeare's beloved was Elizabeth I was justified at great length (and with considerable learning) in two books by George Chalmers.[9] In the latter, *A Supplemental Apology,* Chalmers marvels at the assumption of Steevens and Malone that "Shakespeare, a husband, a father, a moral man, addressed a hundred and twenty six *Amorous* Sonnets to a *male* object!" (55). Chalmers, rightly noting that Malone was the first editor to posit a male beloved, sets out to erase that defamation: "Every fair construction ought to be made, rather than consider Shakespeare as a miscreant, who could address amatory Verses to a man, with a romantic *platonism of affection.* But I have freed him, I trust, from that stain, in opposition to his commentators, by shewing, distinctly, his real object. This object, being once known,

    [8] *Miscellaneous Papers and Legal Instruments under the hand and seal of William Shakespeare* (London: Egerton, 1796), 30.

    [9] Chalmers, *An Apology for the Believers in the Shakespeare Papers* (London: Egerton, 1797); and *A Supplemental Apology* (London: Egerton, 1799).

darkness brightens into light, order springs out of confusion, and contradiction settles into sense" (73–74).

If Chalmers's position gained little support, the structure of his
argument was endlessly repeatable. First, the claim that Shakespeare is
heterosexual is always supplementary. Indeed, heterosexuality is itself
constructed as a back-formation from the prior imagination of pederasty and sodomy. Secondly, it is simply assumed that the taint of
male-male love will destroy the character of the national bard. So just
as heterosexuality is the belated defense against sodomy, so "character"
is the belated defense against an imagined character assassination that
has preceded it. The *Sonnets* thus produce in the nineteenth century a
formidable apparatus to invent a new self: the interiorized heterosexual, projected back onto (or formed in opposition to) Shakespeare.

That apparatus can be seen at its most spectacularly troubled in
the writing of Coleridge. On "Wed. morning, half past three, Nov. 2,
1803," Coleridge picked up a volume of Wordsworth's set of Ander-
son's *British Poets,* which contained Shakespeare's *Sonnets.* In the margin he found a pencil note by Wordsworth, objecting to the later sonnets (that is, to the sonnets addressed, according to Malone, to the
dark lady and thus "heterosexual"). Coleridge wrote: "I can by no
means subscribe to the above pencil mark of W. Wordsworth; which,
however, it is my wish should never be erased. It is *his* and grievously
am I mistaken, and deplorably will Englishmen have degenerated if
the being *his* will not in time give it a value, as of a little reverential relic
—the rude mark of his hand left by the sweat of haste in a St. Veronica
handkerchief."[10] Wordsworth is wrong about Shakespeare; but his
error is encoded in the enduring, sexualized mark of his hand, which
Coleridge reveres as a "relic" of his friend (the paper on which he has
written becomes the handkerchief that, like St. Veronica's, immortal-
izes his physical being). Writing as masturbation with eternal effects. In
response to Wordsworth's comments on the later sonnets, then,
Coleridge fetishizes the material trace that homoerotically binds him
to his friend.

But at this point Coleridge seems to forget that Wordsworth is writ-

---

[10] *Coleridge's Miscellaneous Criticism,* ed. T. M. Raysor (Cambridge, Mass.: Harvard University Press, 1936), 454.

ing about the *later* poems, as if what names his relation to Wordsworth were the name that Steevens silently attributes to the *earlier* sonnets and to the relationship between Shakespeare and the young man. Abruptly, Coleridge veers from his meditations upon his friend to an apostrophe to his own infant son, Hartley, who is being christened that very day:

> These sonnets thou, I trust, if God preserve thy life, Hartley! thou wilt read with a deep interest. . . . To thee, I trust, they will help to explain the mind of Shakespeare, and if thou wouldst understand these sonnets, thou must read the chapter in Potter's *Antiquities* on the Greek lovers—of whom were that Theban band of brothers over whom Philip, their victor, stood weeping; and surveying their dead bodies, each with his shield over the body of his friend, all dead in the place where they fought, solemnly cursed those whose base, fleshly, and most calumnious fancies had suspected their love of desire against nature. This pure love Shakespeare appears to have felt—to have been in no way ashamed of it—or even to have suspected that others could have suspected it. Yet at the same time he knew that so strong a love would have been more completely a thing of permanence and reality, and have been more blessed by nature and taken under her more especial protection, if this object of his love had been at the same time a possible object of desire—for nature is not soul only. In this feeling he must have written the twentieth sonnet; but its possibility seems never to have entered even his imagination. . . . O my son! I pray that thou may'st know inwardly how impossible it was for a Shakespeare not to have been in his heart's heart chaste. (*Miscellaneous Criticism,* 455)

Wordsworth writes about the late sonnets; Coleridge responds by writing about the early sonnets as they had been read by Steevens and Malone. And Coleridge's reading is a tortuous and tortured reading of the possibility or impossibility of a sexual relation between men. But every move by which he attempts to erase the specter of sodomy conjures it up. To set one's mind at rest, one needs, of all things, to read a commentary on the Greeks (by no less a person than the archbishop of Canterbury, despite Coleridge's denunciation of christening in the same note as "unchristian . . . foolery"), as if the "purity" of the Greeks were sufficiently secure to secure the "purity" of Shakespeare. Even more strange is Coleridge's attempts to deny the function of the "imagination" to the poet to whom he attributed it in the highest degree. The possibility of sodomy "seems never to have entered even his imagination"; he could not "have suspected that others could have suspected" his love.

Which makes it the more remarkable that later, in a note of 14 May 1833, Coleridge decided not only that all the sonnets were written to a woman but also (more remarkably still) that Shakespeare inserted the twentieth sonnet to *obscure* his heterosexuality (and thus to raise, seemingly unnecessarily, the thought of pederasty, which before he could not "have suspected that others could have suspected"). Again, the movement of Coleridge's thinking is revealing. His note in 1833 begins with the reflection that "it is possible that a man may under certain states of the moral feeling, entertain something deserving the name of love towards a male object—an affection beyond friendship and wholly aloof from appetite."[11] When he turns to the friendship between Musidorus and Pyrocles in Sidney's *Arcadia*, it looks as if he is preparing his way for a restatement of Malone's position on the sonnets. "In Elizabeth's and James's time," Coleridge remarks, "it seems to have been almost fashionable to cherish such a feeling" (*Table Talk*, 178). But Malone's "defense" of Shakespeare is no longer adequate as a defense for Coleridge. Shakespeare must be purified even of the "rhetorical" male-male love that is said to characterize his age. To the extent that his sonnets are "sincere," they must be heterosexual: "It seems to me that the sonnets could only have come from a man deeply in love, and in love with a woman; and there is one sonnet which from its incongruity, I take to be a purposed blind" (*Table Talk*, 180–81). Shakespeare, in other words, disguises himself as a pederast to avoid detection as a man "deeply in love" with a woman.

If Coleridge's later interpretation of the *Sonnets* seems incredible, it testifies to the great *obstacle* that they formed in the smooth reproduction of the national bard. That there should be such a smooth reproduction was, of course, increasingly important as Shakespeare was inscribed within a national and colonial pedagogy. If strategies as desperate as Coleridge's could not command assent, what could one do with the sonnets? Steevens had a rare follower. Henry Hallam, in his *Introduction to the Literature of Europe*, describes Coleridge's "hetero-

---

[11] Coleridge, *Table Talk* (London: Murray, 1835), 2:178.

sexualizing" of the sonnets as "absolutely untenable."[12] But Hallam, like Steevens, consequently finds the "frequent beauties" of the sonnets "greatly diminished" by the supposed "circumstances" of their production. "It is impossible," Hallam concludes, "not to wish that Shakespeare had never written them" (264).

What Hallam and other nineteenth-century critics wanted to unwrite was the primal scene in the modern production of Shakespeare: the scene conjured up by Steevens's denunciation. Strangely, although Steevens had taken aim at the Quarto and at Malone's edition, his polemic came to color even Benson's, which continued to be reprinted in the early nineteenth century. In 1808 there appeared an edition of love poems by "William Shakspeare" (the spelling of the author's name itself testified to the influence of Malone).[13] The second volume included Benson's edition of the sonnets, but many of Steevens's and Malone's notes were incongruously affixed to these significantly different poems. Even stranger perhaps is the case of Dr. Sherwin of Bath, who sometime after 1818 wrote a series of marginal comments in his 1774 copy of the *Poems* (i.e., the sonnets in their pre-Malone, Benson form).[14] Sherwin, in other words, was reading an edition of the sonnets from which it would have been *impossible* to abstract the story of Shakespeare, the young man, the rival poet, and the dark lady, since the sonnets had been totally reordered, sometimes run together so that two or more sonnets were made into a single poem, and given titles that pointed in quite other directions, as well as occasionally having their pronouns changed. Moreover, the poems Sherwin read in his copy were entitled "Poems *on Several Occasions.*"

Yet what Sherwin responded to was not the text before him but the mode of interpretation that Steevens and Malone had instituted and "the unaccountable Prejudices of the late Mr. Steevens": "When Mr. Steevens compliments his Brother-Commentator [Malone] at the Expence of the Poet, when he tells us, that his Implements of Criticism are on *this Occasion disgraced by the objects of their Culture,* who can avoid a mingled Emotion

---

[12] Hallam, *Introduction to the Literature of Europe in the Fifteenth, Sixteenth, and Seventeenth Centuries,* 263n.

[13] Shakspere, *Love Poems* (London: Cundee, 1808).

[14] Shakespeare, *Poems* (London: Etherington, 1774). Sherwin's copy, with his marginalia, is in the Folger Shakespeare Library.

of Wonder and Disgust? Who can, in short forbear a Smile of Derision and Contempt at the folly of such a declaration?" (2: flyleaf). Steevens and Malone between them had constructed and passed down an impossible legacy: a legacy from Malone of the *Sonnets* as crucial documents of the interior life of the national bard; a legacy from Steevens of that interior life as one that would destroy the life of the nation.

The effects of this impossible legacy were complex. David Lester Richardson, for instance, blamed the "flippant insolence of Steevens" for the neglect of the *Sonnets* (which Richardson still referred to as "a volume of Miscellaneous Poems").[15] Yet even as he promoted them, he was embarrassed by them. A registering of their beauty is, he writes, "accompanied by [a] disagreeable feeling, bordering on disgust" at the "indelicate" expressions of love between man and man (p. 26). Sonnet 20 is "one of the most painful and perplexing I ever read. It is a truly disagreeable enigma. If I have caught any glimpse of the real meaning, I could heartily wish that Shakespeare had never written it" (38). A hundred years later the same sonnet, according to Walter Thomson, "threatened to mislead us and sent us searching for almost twelve months," until he could reassure himself that the word *passion* in the sonnet meant "emotional poem" rather than "amorous desire": "'Passion' is the crucial word, the foundation whereon the fantastic edifice is built in which it is alleged that Shakespeare was perverse in his morals. No more subversive mis-statement could be disseminated about any author or man, and not its least pernicious feature is that it places in the minds and mouths of the perverse a defence of their perversities. . . . We have it from a doctor of wide experience that it is no uncommon thing for perverse persons to cite Shakespeare as their exemplar."[16]

Thomson's last claim is not as wild as it may first appear. For as Alan Sinfield has argued, one of the effects of the Oscar Wilde trial was to help constitute a gay subculture with its own privileged texts and modes of reading.[17]

[15] Richardson, *Literary Leaves* (Calcutta: Thacker, 1840), 1, 3.

[16] Thomson, *The Sonnets of William Shakespeare and Henry Wriothesley* (Oxford: Blackwell, 1938), 2–3.

[17] Sinfield, lecture delivered at Georgetown University, 23 April 1992. For related considerations, see his *Faultlines: Cultural Materialism and the Politics of Dissident Reading* (Berkeley: University of California Press, 1992), 290–302.

What particularly frightens Thomson is the connection between that new subculture and the uses of Shakespeare as a colonial text. In Calcutta in 1840 Richardson could write of the *Sonnets* as an unread text (1), but the educational apparatus of imperialism transformed that. The *Sonnets* by the late nineteenth century were being reproduced in school editions that quoted Dowden as saying that "in the Renascence epoch, among natural products of a time when life ran swift and free, touching with its current high and difficult places, the ardent friendship of man with man was one."[18] Thomson found just such an interpretation unacceptable. "We have information," he complains, "which justifies the statement that about 40 per cent of the people who buy and read Shakespeare entertain the belief that he was a moral pervert" (9). "The supreme literary ornament of our race" (12) had become a contaminated source that subverted the colonial project: "What, for instance, of the many tens of thousands of students who, since Lord Macaulay's day, have come to our universities from India? They are frequently of literary bent and Shakespeare strongly attracts them. How many of them must return to India with these fallacies planted in their minds?" (7). But it is, of course, the "fallacy" of "perversity" that drives the writing of Thomson (as of Malone and Chalmers before him). The justification of Shakespeare is always subsequent to the charge of deviation—just as the concept of the "heterosexual" is a belated response to the *prior* concept of the "homosexual."

The *Sonnets*, I believe, played a central role in the constitution of a new "history of sexuality." Since Foucault, we have been accustomed to trace such a history through religious confessions, through medical discourse, through architecture. But one primary site in the formation of sexualities was the post-Enlightenment formation of "literature." If the *Sonnets* were crucial to it, then in their post–Steevens-Malone variant they lent themselves to intense critical and editorial labors that brought forth narratives of "normal" and "deviant" sexualities. The two great spurs to such narratives were the Steevens-Malone debate (and the Malone edition) at the end of the eighteenth century and Oscar Wilde's "Portrait of Mr. W. H." and trial at the end of the nineteenth century. Wilde published the piece in *Blackwood's* in 1889 after Frank

---

[18] W. J. Rolfe, ed., *Shakespeare's Sonnets* (New York: Harper, 1883), 15–16.

Harris's *Fortnightly Review* had rejected it. As Harris notes in his biography of Wilde: "'The Portrait of Mr. W. H.' did Oscar incalculable injury. It gave his enemies *for the first time* the very weapon they wanted, and they used it unscrupulously and untiringly with the fierce delight of hatred."[19] Balfour and Asquith, to whom Wilde sent the story, advised against publication on the grounds that it would corrupt English homes.[20] Wilde created a specter that produced, by reactionary back-formation, not only the "normal" Shakespeare but "normality" itself.

That "normality," I have been arguing, was a hysterical symptom that accompanied Malone's construction of a unified character attributable to Shakespeare (and to the "characters" in his writing). But the narrative of characterological unity that Malone assembled was ideologically fruitful. That is, it did not merely erase the prior text of the *Sonnets* but prepared the site of a new kind of struggle. For the drive toward unity of character (Shakespeare's character, the characters of the *Sonnets*) led to more and more dramatic consequences at the level of sexual identity. The *Sonnets*, previously a marginal aspect of Shakespeare's corpus, became the ground on which "sexual identity" was invented and contested. If we need now to reconstruct the cultural history of Shakespeare, it is to understand how the imaginary terrain of our own bodies came into being.

[19] Frank Harris, *Oscar Wilde* (East Lansing: Michigan State University Press, 1959), 69.

[20] Richard Ellman, *Oscar Wilde* (New York: Knopf, 1988), 298.

# Shakespeare's "Perjur'd Eye"

IN THE FIRST PORTION of his sonnet sequence—in the subsequence of sonnets addressed to a young man—Shakespeare writes a matching pair of sonnets that develop the way in which his eye and heart initially are enemies but then are subsequently friends. The first sonnet of the pair begins: "Mine eye and heart are at a mortal war, / How to divide the conquest of thy sight" (46).[1] In contrast, the second sonnet, relying on a "verdict" that "is determined" at the conclusion of sonnet 46, begins: "Betwixt mine eye and heart a league is took, / And each doth good turns now unto the other" (47).

Taken together and in sequence, the two sonnets compose an argument *in utramque partem,* with their poet placing himself on both sides of a rhetorical question that is a commonplace in the tradition of the Renaissance sonnet.[2] Despite the conventional opposition, however, the two sonnets confidently argue to what is the same, and equally conventional, conclusion: namely, that their poet's eye and heart do "good turns now unto the other" (47). Thus, in the first sonnet, after meditating on the war between his eye and heart, the poet syllogistically and Neo-Platonically derives the moral that: "As thus: mine eye's due is thy outward part, / And my heart's right thy inward love of heart." In turn, in the second sonnet, from thinking on the amity between his eye and heart, the poet reassuringly discovers that "thy picture in my sight / Awakes my heart to heart's and eye's delight." Taken together and in sequence, therefore, the two sonnets respond to the rhetorical question that they raise by juxtaposing a *concordia discors* and a *coincidentia oppositorum* each against the other. Both sonnets speak to the fact that their poet's eye and heart, however much they differ from or with each other, are equally "delighted." In both sonnets, eye and heart will peacefully "divide the conquest of thy sight," as though, from the ideal perspective shared by the two sonnets, eye and heart are complementary and coordinated aspects of each other.

In a straightforward way, the rhetorical wit of these two sonnets consists of thus hendiadystically arriving, from different starting points, at a common destination, for in this way the two sonnets manage to resolve, or to beg the question raised by, a traditional *débat.* Yet, however witty, the poems take seriously the equivalence of the conclusions that they share. In both cases the relationship of eye and heart, whether initially antipathetic or sympathetic, leads immediately, via complementary antithesis, to a recuperative and benign assessment of yet

REPRESENTATIONS 7 • Summer 1984 © THE REGENTS OF THE UNIVERSITY OF CALIFORNIA other differences adduced. In war or peace the sonnets' several binaries combine to generate a clarity of eye and purity of heart whose own discrete proprieties and properties in turn reciprocally establish, or are established by, the integrity and integration of the other categorical oppositions to which the poems refer. In the first sonnet, for example, sonnet 46, the difference between "outward" and "inward" is secured and reconciled because the vision of the eye and the "thinking" of the heart can be harmoniously apportioned between the clear-cut opposition of "The clear eye's moiety and the dear heart's part." In the second sonnet, 47, the absence of the beloved is converted or transmuted into presence because: "So either by thy picture or my love, / Thyself away are present still with me." This systematic complementarity—whereby opposites either are the same or, as opposites, still somehow go compatibly together—speaks to a general, indeed, a generic, homogeneity subtending both sonnets, something that informs them more deeply than the thematic heterogeneity that the two sonnets only provisionally or momentarily evoke. In the first sonnet it is the difference between eye and heart that establishes the concord between them, whereas in the second sonnet the concord derives from their similarity. But this difference, which is the difference between difference and similarity, turns out not to make much difference. In both sonnets the eye is "clear" and the heart is "dear" by virtue of a governing structure of likeness and contrast, of identity and difference, of similarity and contrariety, that both sonnets equally and isomorphically employ.

What these two young man sonnets, 46 and 47, share, therefore, as Lévi-Strauss might say, is the sameness of their differences: what joins them together is a structural identity, or a structure of identity that is yet more fundamental and more powerful than their apparent opposition. At the level of theme and of poetic psychology, this yields the Petrarchan commonplace in accord with which the poet's eye and heart come instantly to complement each other, moving from war to peace, from antipathy to sympathy, in a progress that constitutes a kind of shorthand summary of the amatory assumptions of ideal admiration, e.g., the way Cupid shoots his arrows through the lover's eye into the lover's heart.[3] This is a specifically *visual* desire, for in both sonnets it is as something of the eye that the young man's "fair appearance lies" within the poet's heart. In both sonnets "thy picture in my sight" indifferently "Awakes my heart to heart's and eye's delight."

Such homogenizing visual imagery, applied to the poet's love, to his beloved, and to his poetry, pervades the sequence of sonnets addressed to the young man, and this imagery is regularly employed, as in sonnets 46 and 47, to characterize a material likeness or sameness that conjoins or renders consubstantial two distinctive yet univocally collated terms: not only the poet's eye and heart, but, also, the poet and his young man (e.g., " 'Tis thee (myself) that for myself I praise, / Painting my age with beauty of thy days" [62]), the young man and, in the opening sonnets which urge the young man to procreate, *his* young man (e.g., "Look in thy glass and tell the face thou viewest, / Now is the time that face should form another" [3]), as well as the poet's poetry and that of which the poetry speaks (e.g., "So long as men can breathe or eyes can see, / So long lives this, and this gives life to thee" [18]). In general, the poet identifies his first-person "I" with the ideal eye of the young man—"Now see what good turns eyes for eyes have done" (24)—and then proceeds to identify these both with the "wondrous scope" (105) of his visionary verse: "So till the judgement that yourself arise, / You live in this, and dwell in lovers' eyes" (55).

In all these cases the visual imagery that Shakespeare employs is, of course, nothing but conventional. Indeed, the sonnets addressed to the young man regularly allude to the conventionality of their visual imagery, often characterizing such imagery, as well as that of which it is an image, as something old-fashioned, even antiquated, as in the literary retrospection of sonnet 59:

> O that record could with a backward look,
> Even of five hundreth courses of the sun.
> Show me your image in some antique book,
> Since mind at first in character was done!

There are a good many reasons why the young man's poet might "look" in this "backward" way to specifically visual imagery, to imagery of vision, in order, as sonnet 59 goes on to say, to "see what the old world could say / To this composed wonder of your frame." With regard to the poet's ideal desire, which aims to conjoin poetic subject with poetic object—"thou mine, I thine" (108)—the young man's poet can rely upon a familiar Petrarchist motif, derived from Stoic optics, of eroticized *eidōla* or likenesses, intromissive and extromissive, whose very physics establishes a *special* (from *specere*, "to look at") coincidence of lover and beloved, as, for example, when Astrophil, at the beginning of Sidney's sonnet sequence, looks into his heart to write, and finds there pre-engraved or "stell'd" upon it the stylized image or *imago* of the Stella whom he loves. In turn, this physics of the *eidōlon* presupposes an equally familiar and specifically idealist metaphysics of genus and species whereby individual particulars are but subspecies of a universal form or type, declensions of a paradigmatic archetype whose immanent universality is regularly and perennially conceived in terms of light, as in Platonic *eidos*, from *idein*, "to see," or as the end of the *Paradiso*, where Dante sees "La forma universal" in his vision of "luce etterna" and "semplice lume" (in this divine light, we can add, Dante also sees the painted "likeness," the "effige," of himself).[4] Moreover, again in ways that are nothing but conventional, the poetry of idealization, especially as it develops in the self-consciously literary tradition of the Renaissance sonnet, characteristically assimilates such visual imagery, which is its imagery *of* the ideal, to itself, so as thereby to idealize itself as effective *simulacrum,*

physical and metaphysical, of that which it admires. As an activity of "stelling,"—
e.g., "Mine eye hath play'd the painter and hath stell'd / Thy beauty's form in
table of my heart" (24)—such poetry is *Ideas Mirrour*, as Drayton called his sonnet
sequence, and it is so precisely because, being something visual and visionary, it
can claim to be not only the reflection of, but also the objectification of, its idea
of its ideal.[5]

Speaking very generally, it is fair to say that this is the regular force of visual
imagery in the tradition of the literature or poetry of praise—a tradition that
goes back to the praise of love in the *Symposium* or *Phaedrus*, but one that is
especially vital in the particular literary genre of the sonnet, where it goes without
saying that the poet is a lover who desires only that which he admires. With
regard to poetic procedure or, rather, with regard to what is the common and
long-standing understanding of poetic procedure, this is a tradition of specifically
visionary poetic likeness, either mimetic likeness, whereby poetry is the simulat-
ing representation of that which it presents—"ut pictura poesis," speaking picture—or figural likeness, as when Aristotle defines metaphor (whether based on
analogy or commutative proportion) as the capacity "to see the same" (*theōrein
homoion*), metaphor being for Aristotle, as for the tradition of rhetorical theory
that derives from him, an activity of speculative likening that, quite literally,
"theorizes sameness."[6] Correspondingly, with regard to poetic subjectivity, this is
a literary tradition in which the poet is a panegyric *vates* or seer who, at least
ideally, is the same as that which he sees (e.g. Dante's reflexively reflective "effige"),
just as, with regard to poetic semiosis, poetic language, as *eikōn, speculum, imago,
eidōlon*, etc., is Cratylitically the same as that of which it speaks, for example, the
way Dante identifies his own "beatitude" with "those words that praise my Lady,"
his "lodano" with "la donna," or the way Petrarch puns on "Laura," "laud," and
"laurel,"[7] These are general themes and motifs by reference to which the poetry
of praise characteristically become a praise of poetry itself.[8]

It is possible to get some sense of how very familiar, over-familiar, this received
literary tradition is to Shakespeare if we register the formulaic way the young
man's poet in sonnet 105 identifies, one with the others, his "love," his "beloved,"
and his "songs and praises":

> Let not my love be called idolatry,
> Nor my beloved as an idol show,
> Since all alike my songs and praises be.

What joins these three together is the ideality they share, an ideality that establishes a three-term correspondence between the speaking, the spoken, and the
speech of praise. " 'Fair,' 'kind,' and 'true' is all my argument," says the poet in
sonnet 105, and these "Three themes in one, which wondrous scope affords"
("Three themes" that sonnet 105 repeats three times) amount to a phenome-

nological summary, an eidetic reduction, of a Petrarchist metaphysical, erotic, and poetic Ideal: "Fair" identifies the visibility, the *Sichtigkeit,* of an ideal sight (*idein,* "to see"); "kind" identifies the homogeneous categoriality, the formal elementality, of an ideal essence (Platonic *eidos*); "true" identifies the coincidence of ideal knowledge and knowing (*oida,* which is also from *idein*). It is by reference to such precisely conceived and conceited ideality, an ideality that in effect recapitulates the history of ideas up through the Renaissance, that sonnet 105 manages to identify "my love," "my beloved," and "my songs and praises," each one of these being " 'Fair,' 'kind,' and 'true,' " and therefore, by commutation, each one of these being the same and truthful mirror-image of the other two. In the same idealizing way, this is how sonnets 46 and 47 manage to eliminate the difference between their eye and heart, and thereby manage, despite the difference with which they begin, to say the same thing. More generally, we can say that this is how Shakespeare's poetry of visionary praise, because it is a "wondrous scope" and because it is addressed to a "wondrous scope," is always, as sonnet 105 puts it, monotheistically, monogamously, monosyllabically, and monotonously "To one, of one, still such, and ever so." This is an ideological poetry, as sonnet 105 seems almost to complain, whose virtue consists in the way its copiousness always copies the same ideal sameness—"Since all alike my songs and praises be"—a universal and uni-versing poetic and erotic practice whose very ideality is what renders it incapable of manifesting difference, for, as the poet puts it in sonnet 105:

> Kind is my love to-day, to-morrow kind,
> Still constant in a wondrous excellence,
> Therefore my verse, to constancy confin'd,
> One thing expressing, leaves out difference.

However, as the palpable claustrophobia of sonnet 105 suggests, it would be possible to look more closely at the sonnets addressed to the young man so as to see the way they characteristically resist and conflictedly inflect their most ideal expressions of visionary unity, the way they chafe against the "constancy" to which they are "confin'd," the way that they implicitly "express" the "difference" that they explicitly "leave out." If, as Murray Krieger has suggested, we are supposed to hear the "one" in sonnet 105's *wondrous scope,*" then so too do we also hear the "two" in its "T(w)o one, of one, still such, and ever so."[9] So too, the entire sonnet is colored by the ambiguous logic of its opening "Since"—"Since all alike my songs and praises be"—since this concessive particle explains both why the young man is an idol as well as why he is not. Such complications, though they are implicit, have their effect. As complications, they add a reservation or a wrinkle to the poet's otherwise straightforward rhetoric of compliment. In such oblique, yet obvious, ways the young man sonnets will regularly situate themselves

Shakespeare's "Perjur'd Eye"

151

and their admiration at one affective and temporal remove from the ideality that they repeatedly and repetitiously invoke, with the peculiar result that in these sonnets an apparently traditionary poetics of ideal light comes regularly to seem what sonnet 123 calls "The dressings of a former sight."

This peculiar retrospection is a consistent aspect of the young man sonnets' imagery of the visual and the visible, imagery that is characteristically presented in the young man sonnets as though it were so tarnished with age that its very reiteration is what interferes with the poet's scopic or specular identification of his poetic "I" with the ideal "eye" of the young man: "For as you were when first your eye I ey'd" (104). In general, the young man's poet, *as* a visionary poet, seems capable of expressing only a love at second sight; his identification of his ego with his ego-ideal seems worn out by repetition, as though it were the very practice by the poet of an old-fashioned poetry of visionary praise that effectively differentiates the poet as a panegyricizing subject from what he takes to be his ideal and his praiseworthy object. We can take as an example the mixed-up deictic and epideictic compact of the couplet to sonnet 62 which has already been cited— " 'Tis thee (myself) that for myself I praise, / Painting my age with beauty of thy days"—where the confused identification of the poet's "I" and "thou" effectively identifies the first person of the poet with the youth and age of visionary praise. The same thing goes, however, to take another example, for the "stelling" of sonnet 24. At the beginning of the sonnet the poet remembers how, in the past, "Mine eye hath play'd the painter and hath stell'd / Thy beauty's form in table of my heart." At the end of the sonnet, however, speaking in and for the present, the poet observes: "Yet eyes this cunning want to grace their art. / They draw but what they see, know not the heart" (24).

In this context, we can recall the fact that Shakespeare writes his sonnet sequence, for the most part, after the Elizabethan sonnet sequence vogue has passed, in what we might call the literary aftermath of the poetry of praise, when such Petrarchist panegyric has come to seem, to some extent, *passé*. This is the historical literary context within which the sonnets addressed to the young man— which are conceived long after what even Sidney, at the inaugural moment of the Elizabethan sonnet sequence, called "Poor Petrarch's long-deceased woes"— make a personal issue out of their self-remarked literary belatedness, regularly associating what they themselves characterize as their old-fashioned literary matter and manner with their poet's sense of his senescence.[10] In sonnet 76, for example, the poet asks:

> Why is my verse so barren of new pride?
> So far from variation or quick change?
> Why with the time do I not glance aside
> To new-found methods and to compounds strange?

As the poet first poses them, these are rhetorical questions, questions about rhetoric, but these questions then will press themselves upon the poet's person; they define for him his sense of superannuated self:

> Why write I still all one, ever the same,
> And keep invention in a noted weed,
> That every word doth almost tell my name,
> Showing their birth and where they did proceed?

A good many young man sonnets are concerned with just this kind of literary question, and, as in sonnet 76, in these sonnets it appears as though it is the very asking of the question that turns out to empty out the poet's praising self. It is as though, because he is committed to an ancient poetry of praise, the poet feels himself obliged to pay the debts incurred by a bankrupt literary tradition—as though the poet, as a person, is himself entropically exhausted by the tired tropes with which, according to an old poetic custom, he ornaments himself:

> So all my best is dressing old words new,
> Spending again what is already spent:
> For as the sun is daily new and old,
> So is my love still telling what is told. (76)

This is significant because it introduces a new kind of self-consciousness into the already highly self-conscious tradition of the Renaissance sonnet. In familiar ways, the poet in sonnet 76 identifies himself with his own literariness. At the same time, however, it is in an unfamiliar way that the poet's subjectivity here seems worn out by the heavy burden of the literary history that his literariness both examples and extends. For what is novel in a sonnet such as 76 is not so much the way the poet takes the ever-renewed sameness of the sun, its perennially revivified vivacity, as a dead metaphor for the animating *energeia* and *enargia* of an ideal metaphoricity. Rather, what is striking, and what is genuinely novel, is the way the visionary poet takes this faded brightness personally, the way he identifies his own poetic person, his own poetic identity, with the after-light of this dead metaphoric sun. Identifying himself with an aged eternality—which is itself the image of an ideal and an unchanging identity—the young man's poet is like a bleached Dante: he is a visionary poet, but he is so, as it were, after the visionary fact, a seer who now sees in a too-frequently reiterated "luce etterna" a vivid image, an *effige* or an *eidōlon*, of the death of both his light and life, as in sonnet 73: "In me thou seest the twilight of such day / As after sunset fadeth in the west, / Which by and by black night doth take away, / Death's second self, that seals up all in rest." This is the peculiarly inflected imagery of light with which the young man's poet assimilates to his own poetic psychology the self-consuming logic of "Spending again what is already spent," for it is with this imagery of after-light that the poet makes his own poetic introspection into something retrospective:

> In me thou seest the glowing of such fire,
> That on the ashes of his youth doth lie
> As the death-bed whereon it must expire,
> Consum'd with that which it was nourish'd by. (73)

In terms of what we can think of as the conventional visual imagery of the poetry of praise, it is as though in Shakespeare's sonnets to the young man *Ideas Mirrour* had now become the "glass" of sonnet 62, a "glass," however, that rather horrifyingly "shows me myself indeed, / Beated and chopp'd with tann'd antiquity," with the subjective consequence of this for the poet being that, as sonnet 62 goes on to say, "Mine own self-love quite contrary I read."

There is much more that might be said about this imagery of tired light, or tired imagery of light, for it can be argued that such imagery not only determines the young man's poet's sense of space and time, but also his erotic sensibility as well (consider, for example, "A liquid prisoner pent in walls of glass" [5]). As it is, however, it seems clear that we cannot overlook—as sentimental readings often do—the novel coloring that Shakespeare's young man sonnets give to their visual imagery, to their imagery *of* the visual, for this is responsible, to a considerable degree, for the pathos of poetic persona that these sonnets regularly exhibit. By the same token, however, it would be a mistake to overemphasize this darkness that informs these sonnets' literary, visionary light. If the young man sonnets are suspicious of their visual imagery, this is not a suspicion that they put directly into words. Quite the contrary, whatever reservations attach to the young man sonnets' imagery of vision, these reservations, like those that shade the poet's various characterizations of the ideality of the young man, are implicit rather than explicit, something we read between what the young man sonnets call their "eternal lines to time" (18).

It is important to insist upon this indirection, upon the fact that the young man sonnets do not explicitly speak against their light, because this accounts for the residual idealism with which the young man sonnets always turn, heliotropically, to "that sun, thine eye" (49). At least ideally, the young man sonnets would like to be like the courtly "marigold" of sonnet 25, whose "fair leaves spread . . . at the sun's eye." Like such flowers of fancy, the young man sonnets would like to look exactly like the ideal that they look at, just as the poet would like his "I" to be "as you were when first your eye I ey'd" (104). Hence the nostalgia of the poet's introspection: the poet sees his difference from an eternal visionary sameness, his difference from a visionary poetics that would always be the same because, as Aristotle says of metaphor, it always "see(s) the same." But this insight serves only to make the poet's ideal bygone vision seem all the more ideal, an image of poetic presence that is always in the past, even when this ancient past is the present in the future tense, as in the prospective retrospection of sonnet 104, where the poet tells "thou age unbred: / Ere you were born was beauty's summer dead." This loyally retrospective visuality, a poetry of re-turn rather than of turn, accounts for the complex texture of the young man sonnets' imagery of vision, a complexity that derives from the fact that the young man sonnets never entirely reject the ideality from which they are estranged. If the young man sonnets characteristically distance themselves from their visual imagery even as they employ it, this distanciation possesses poetic force precisely to the extent that such imagery of light continues to retain, specifically in retrospect, at a distance, its originary and traditionary ideal connotations.

I stress the vestigial power of such visual ideality in the young man sonnets, its "present-absent" (45) presence, because this both measures and prepares for the difference between the sonnets addressed to the young man and those addressed to the dark lady. As is well known, in the subsequence of sonnets addressed to the dark lady such ideal imagery of light is explicitly—Shakespeare's word here is important—"forsworn" (152). What gives this "forswearing" its power, however, and what distinguishes it, tonally as well as thematically, from the implicit visual reservations informing the sonnets addressed to the young man, is the way the dark lady's poet puts these heretofore unspoken visionary suspicions directly into words. In the young man sonnets, the young man, whatever his faults, is an "image" whose idealization effectively can represent an ideal that is lost, as in sonnet 31: "Their images I lov'd I view in thee, / And thou (all they) hast all the all of me," or the young man is a "shadow" who to the poet's "imaginary sight . . . makes black night beauteous, and her old face new" (27). In contrast, in the dark lady sonnets, though as something that is more complicated and more unsettling than a simple opposition, the dark lady has the "power," as in sonnet 149, "To make me give the lie to my true sight, / And swear that brightness doth not grace the day."

We broach here what is often called the anti-Petrarchanism of the sonnets to the dark lady, and it is certainly the case that the dark lady sonnets regularly characterize their literary peculiarity and novelty in terms of the way they differ from the specular ideality of a previous Petrarchist poetics. When the poet looks at the young man, he sees "That sun, thine eye" (49). In contrast, when he looks at the dark lady, what he sees is the way she is unlike the ideal brightness of the young man: "My mistress' eyes are nothing like the sun" (130). On the face of it, this amounts to a straightforward difference, for, on the one hand, there is brightness, whereas, on the other, there is darkness. What makes this difference complicated, however, is that when the poet makes an issue of it, when he gives explicit expression to it, he presents the darkness of the lady as itself the image of this difference, as an image, precisely, of the difference between the black that it is and the light that it is not.

This is why the difference between the lady's stressedly unconventional darkness and the young man's emphatically conventional brightness produces something that is both more and less than a straightforward black and white antithesis of the kind suggested by the "anti-" of anti-Petrarchanism. On the one hand, there is brightness, but, on the other, is a darkness that, in a peculiar or what Troilus calls a "bi-fold" way, is both these hands together both at once.[11] Such is the strangeness of a lady whom the poet alternately praises and blames for being other than what at first sight she appears. As an image of that which she is not, the lady is presented as the likeness of a difference, at once a version of, but at the same time a perversion of, that to which she is, on the one hand, both positively and negatively compared, and that to which she is, on the other, both positively and negatively opposed. For this reason, as she is presented, the lady is, strictly speaking, beyond both comparison and opposition. The lady both is and is not what she is, and because she is in this way, *in* herself, something double, the lady cannot be comprehended by a poetics of "To one, of one, still such, and ever so." As the poet puts it in sonnet 130—this the consequence of the fact that his "mistress' eyes are nothing like the sun"—the lady is a "love," just as she inspires a "love," that is "as rare, / As any she belied with false compare." The irrational ratio of the formula defines the peculiarity of the lady. She is a "she" who is logically, as well as grammatically, both subject and object of "belied with false compare," comparable, therefore, only to the way comparison has failed.

From the beginning, this effective doubleness of the lady, defined in specifically literary terms, i.e., in terms of a new kind of poetics, is what the poet finds distinctive about her, as in the first sonnet he addresses to her:

> In the old age black was not counted fair,
> Or if it were it bore not beauty's name;
> But now is black beauty's successive heir,
> And beauty slander'd with a bastard shame. (127)

What we are supposed to recognize here as officially surprising is that the lady's traditional foul is now characterized as something that is fair, just as in later sonnets this novel fair will be yet more surprisingly foul: "For I have sworn thee fair, and thought thee bright, / Who art as black as hell, as dark as night" (147). In either case, however, whether fair or foul, it is always as images of that which they are not, as something double, fair *and* foul, as something duplicitous and heterogeneous, that the lady and her darkness acquire their erotic and their literary charge.

Thus "black" is "now" "beauty's successive heir," now that "beauty" is "slander'd with a bastard shame." In the context of the sequence as a whole, the force of this unconventional "succession" is that it repeats, but with a difference, the themes of reiterated and legitimately procreated likeness with reference to which the young man at the opening of his subsequence is supposed, as an *imago*, to "prove his beauty by succession thine" (2): "Die single, and thine image dies with thee" (3). Instead of the ideal multiplication of kind with kind, the ongoing reproduction of the visual same, by means of which the young man is supposed to "breed another thee" (6)—a breeding implicitly associated in the young man sonnets with a kind of homosexual usury: "that use is not forbidden usury" (6)—the novel beauty of the lady instead exemplifies a novelly miscegenating "successivity"—novel *because* successive to such Platonized "succession"—whereby black becomes the differential substitute, the unkind "heir," of what is "fair."[12] So too with the blackness of the lady's "raven" eyes, a darkness that replaces at the same time as it thus displaces the brightness it sequentially succeeds:

> Therefore my mistress' eyes are raven black,
> Her eyes so suited and they mourners seem
> At such who, not born fair, no beauty lack,
> Slandering creation with a false esteem. (127)

This, in little, defines the structural and temporal relationship of the dark lady sonnets to the young man sonnets. The second subsequence is a repetition of the first, but it is a discordant and a disturbing repetition because the latter subsequence, stressing itself as a repetition, represents the former (as also the former's themes of visionary presence—"So either by thy picture or my love / Thyself away are present still with me" [47]—in such a way that its memorial repetition explicitly calls up the poignant absence of that which it recalls. To the degree that this articulates the silent reservations that darken the idealism of the young man sonnets, to this extent we register the way in which the "black" of the second subsequence is continuous with the elegaically retrospective visuality of the first. Yet there is also an emphatic difference between the two, a difference that derives precisely from the fact that the dark lady's poet explicitly expresses what the young man's poet preferred to leave implicit. For what the dark lady's poet sees in the darkness of the lady's mourning eyes is the death of ideal visionary presence; her darkness is for him an image or *imago* of the loss of vision. But, according to the poet, it is this very vision of the loss of vision that now thrusts him into novel speech—the discourse of "black beauty"—making him now no longer a poet of the eye, but, instead, a poet of the tongue: "Yet so they mourn, becoming of their woe, / That every tongue says beauty should look so" (127).

As Ulysses says of wanton Cressida, therefore, "There's language in her eye."[13] But what is odd about this language is what is odd about the lady's eye, namely, that it is opposed to vision. The difference between this and the way that language is characterized in the young man sonnets is, of course, considerable, and we may say that this difference at once examples and defines the novelty of the way a poet speaks in a post-Petrarchist poetics. In the young man sonnets the poet ideally speaks a visionary speech, and therefore, when he speaks about this speech he speaks of it as something of the eye: "O, learn to read what silent love hath writ: / To hear with eyes belongs to love's fine wit" (23). In contrast, but again as something that is more complicated than a simple opposition, the poet in the dark lady subsequence will speak about his speech *as* speech, and as something that, for just this very reason, is different from a visual ideal. It is in this "forswearing" way that the dark lady, with the "pow'r" of her "insufficiency," will "make me give the lie to my true sight, / And swear that brightness doth not grace the day" (150). The double way the lady looks is like the double way that language speaks, which is why, for example, when the poet looks at the lady's far too common "common place" (137), a place that is at once erotic and poetic, he tells us how "mine eyes seeing this, say this is not" (137).

Thematized in this way, as something radically discrepant to the truth of ideal vision, as the *voice* of "eyes . . . which have no correspondence with true sight" (148), language is regularly presented in the dark lady sonnets as something whose truth consists not only in saying, but in *being*, something false: "My thoughts and my discourse as madman's are, / At random from the truth vainly express'd: / For I have sworn thee fair, and thought thee bright, / Who art as black as hell, as dark as night" (147). Correspondingly, because no longer something visual, because no longer the iconic likeness or the *eidōlon* of what it speaks about, verbal language now defines itself as its forswearing difference from what is " 'Fair,' 'kind,' and 'true' ": "For I have sworn deep oaths of thy deep kindness, / Oaths of thy love, thy truth, thy constancy, / And to enlighten thee gave eyes to blindness, / Or made them swear against the thing they see" (152). And, as a further and more personal result, the poet now identifies himself with the difference that his language thus bespeaks. He is no longer a visionary poet who identifies his "I" and "eye." Instead, *because* he speaks, the poet comes to inhabit the space of difference between poetic language and poetic vision, a difference generated *by* the speech he speaks. The poet's subjectivity, his "I," is precipitated in or as the slippage between his eye and tongue. The poet becomes, in the phrase I take as title for this paper, the subject of a "perjur'd eye": "For I have sworn thee fair: more perjur'd eye, / To swear against the truth so foul a lie!" (152).

It is fair to say, therefore, that in the dark lady sonnets we encounter a poetics in which true vision is captured by false language, and that the conflict thus engendered—between sight and word, between being and meaning, between poetic presentation and poetic representation—in turn determines specific variations on, or mutations of, traditionary sonneteering claims and motifs. A poetics of verbal re-presentation, stressing the repetition of the *re-*, spells the end of the poetics of visual presentation, thereby constituting the Idea of poetic presence as something that is lost. To the extent that this is the case, Shakespeare's sonnet sequence marks a decisive moment in the history of lyric, for when the dark lady sonnets forswear the ideally visionary poetics of the young man sonnets, when poetic language comes in this way to be characterized as something verbal, not visual, we see what happens to poetry when it gives over a perennial poetics of *ut pictura poesis* for (literally, *so as* to speak) a poetics of *ut poesis poesis*, a transition that writes itself out in Shakespeare's sonnets as an unhappy progress from a poetry based on visual likeness—whose adequation to that which it admires is figured by a "wondrous scope" by means of which "One thing expressing, leaves out difference" (105)—to a poetry based on verbal difference—whose inadequate relation to that which it bespeaks is figured by an "insufficiency" that "make(s) me give the lie to my true sight" (150). In the sequence as a whole, this progress from a homogeneous poetics of vision to a heterogeneous poetics of language is fleshed out as a progress from an ideally homosexual desire, however conflicted, for what is " 'Fair,' 'kind,' and 'true' " to a frankly misogynistic, heterosexual desire for what is fair *and* unfair, kind *and* unkind, true *and* false—a progress, in other words, from man to woman. Here again, however, it is explicitly and literally as a figure *of* speech that the lady becomes the novel "hetero-" opposed as such to an ideal and a familiar Neo-Platonic "homo-," as when: "When my love swears that she is made of truth, / I do believe her though I know she lies" (138). It is in this way, by making each the figure of the other, that the poet collates his corrupting Eros with his corrupting Logos. When the poet "credit[s] her false-speaking tongue," the result is that "On both sides thus is simple truth suppress'd" (138). But the consequence of this false correspondence, of this traducement of the Cratylism of the poetry of praise—e.g., of the "beatitudinizing" power of Dante's "Beatrice," or of the self-applauding circularities of Petrarch's puns on "Laura," "laud," and "laurel"—is that the poet comes to express, in terms of a specific desire of language, the novel duplicity of a specifically linguistic language of desire: "Therefore I lie with her, and she with me, / And in our faults by lies we flattered be" (138).

Again there is more that might be said about the way the dark lady sonnets thematize their lady's and their poet's speech as speech, and draw from this the moral that such speech is radically excessive to an orthodox poetics of admiration. As with the implicit reservations that inform the young man sonnets' visionary themes, it would be possible to show how Shakespeare's explicitly paradoxical version of a traditionary poetics of praise not only affects the poet's expressions of desire—leading him from a homosexual desire for that which is admired to a heterosexual desire for that which is not admired—but, again, his sense of space and time as well. If we could follow this out in sufficient detail we would develop a more textured phenomenology of the psychology of the Shakespearean subject. This would help not only to describe the ways in which poetic person or lyric subjectivity in Shakespeare's sonnet sequence is altogether foreign to the kind of poetic person we find in first-person poetry up through the Renaissance, but also to explain why this novel Shakespearean subjectivity—not only as it appears in Shakespeare's first-person sonnets but also as it manifests itself in Shakespeare's zero-person plays—subsequently becomes (since Shakespeare, which is to say since the decisive conclusion of an epideictic poetics, which is to say since the end of a poetic tradition in which all poetry is a poetry of praise) the dominant and canonical version in our literary tradition of literary subjectivity per se.

For obvious reasons an essay is not the place to develop the details of such an account, an account that necessarily calls for all the particularity and specificity of extended practical and historical literary criticism.[14] However, for the sake of an outline of such an account, one point seems especially important: namely, that this novel Shakespearean subjectivity, for all its difference from that which it succeeds, is nevertheless constrained by the traditionary lyric literariness to which it stands as epitaph. In this sense, we might say that "poor Petrarch's long deceased woes" exert a posthumous power, prescribing in advance the details of their own forswearing. This point, too, can only be developed here in a schematic and perfunctory fashion. But it is possible, by looking at the way the dark lady's poet revises the visionary logic and psychologic of the young man's poet's eye and heart, to get some sense of the way Shakespeare's paradoxical invention of a heterogeneous and heterosexual poetics of paradoxical praise amounts to an orthodox mutation of a conventionally homogeneous and homosexual poetics of orthodox idealization:

> Thine eyes I love, and they as pitying me,
> Knowing my heart torment me with disdain,
> Have put on black, and loving mourners be,
> Looking with pretty ruth upon my pain.
> And truly not the morning sun of heaven
> Better becomes the grey cheeks of th' east,
> Nor that full star that ushers in the even
> Doth half that glory to the sober west,
> As those two mourning eyes become thy face.
> O, let it then as well beseem thy heart
> To mourn for me, since mourning doth thee grace,
> And suit thy pity like in every part.
> > Then will I swear beauty herself is black,
> > And all they foul that thy complexion lack.

As in sonnets 46 and 47, the general conceit of sonnet 123, with its frustrated lover addressing his pitiless, disdaining beloved, is a Petrarchan commonplace, going back beyond Petrarch to the *rime petrose* of Arnault Daniel. Equally common is the intricate development of the imagery of sympathetically erotic vision. In this sense we deal here with the same poetics Shakespeare presupposes in the young man sonnets, where, for example, he can speak familiarly of "that sun, thine eye" (49) precisely because a long-standing tradition of metaphysical and sexual allegory authorizes an iconographic equating of the two. On the other hand, but in an equally insistent way, sonnet 132 further plays upon this convention and these traditional light-sight metaphors when, as a result of comparing the beloved's eyes to the sun, it turns out not that her eyes are lamps, but that the sun to which they are compared is therefore black. This too is, in part, conventional (e.g., Stella's eyes are black), but what concerns us is the stressed contrast to what has come before. In the young man sonnets the morning is "sacred," "new-appearing" (7), "golden" and "green" (33). Here, instead, "the morning sun of heaven" is obscuring complement to "the grey cheeks of the east," shining in the morning like the evening star at night, because it is a brightness in an encroaching darkness of which it is itself the cause and sign. Where in the sonnets addressed to the young man the sun is a "gracious light" (7) to the morning, here, instead, the morning is a "mourning" whose inversion is a darkening "grace"; "Since mourning doth thee grace." This pun on "mo[u]rning," which explains why in the dark lady sonnets "brightness doth not grace the day," is the kind of motivated homophone that Shakespeare is often either faulted or appreciated for, either the sort for which, in Johnson's phrase, he threw away the world, or the sort with which he generates the resonant ambiguities that critics like to list. The point that is emphasized by the sonnet, however, is that the pun, which must be noticed as such for it to work its poetic effect, does in little what the poem does rhetorically as a whole: repeating itself *in* itself so as to undo itself with its own echo, discovering and producing its own loss at the very moment of calling to our attention the way language, theme, and image displace themselves by folding over upon themselves in paradox. So too, this is precisely the mourning paradox of what is epideictically orthodox for which the poem will sadly say that it was written: "Then will I swear beauty herself is black, / And all they foul that thy complexion lack."

In obvious ways, therefore, all this—morning *and* melancholia—results in something that is much more complex than a simple negation of Petrarchan themes and images, and for this reason the poem possesses a tonality unlike even the most self-consciously witty Petrarchan lovers' complaint. The system of logical oppositions and conventional antitheses into which we might be tempted to organize the sonnet's courtly courtship argument falls to pieces as soon as the sonnet brings antithesis into play. Just as the lady's eyes by turning black express a pity occasioned by her heart's disdain, so too does the poet here thematize the fact that he here expresses his heart's desire with a language of disdain. In the same way that the stain of the lady's eyes is both image of and answer to the disdain of her heart, so too does the poet here amplify the lady's beauty by fouling the

Shakespeare's "Perjur'd Eye"

161

conventional images of fairness. The relationship between the lady's eye and the lady's heart, or of the poet to the lady, is a matter, therefore, neither of similarity and contrast nor of pity and disdain, and, for this reason, there is no way either poet or lady might "suit thy pity like in every part." Pity is a figure of disdain just as morning is a version of the night, each of them the homeopathic mirror of the heteropathy of the other. As a result, with likeness emerging as the instance, rather than the antithesis, of difference, with pity the *complement* to disdain, the sonnet forces its reader to deal with oddly asymmetrical oppositions whereby each polarized side or half of every opposition that the sonnet adduces already includes, and therefore changes by encapsulating, the larger dichotomy of which it is a part. With regard to the lady, this means that she cannot treat the poet either with pity or with disdain, or even with an oxymoronic combination of the two. For her "charm" consists precisely of the way these two apparently anti-thetical modalities, empathy and antipathy, each turn out to be, within their singular propriety, the contrary double not only of its other but also of itself, the two together thus composing a double doubling whose reduplicating logic fore-closes the possibility of ever isolating either modality in itself. With regard to the poet, this means that he cannot speak of his lady with a simple rhetoric of simi-larity and contrast, for his language undercuts the logic of likeness and difference even as it advances complementary contrarieties.[15]

The difference between this and what happens when sonnets 46 and 47 develop their eye-heart topos is pointed enough, a difference now that *makes* a difference. Where the two young man sonnets see both eye and heart as each the figure and occasion of the other, sonnet 132 instead both literally and fig-uratively describes a desire at odds with itself because at odds with what it sees. Where the two young man sonnets bring out the syncretic identity built into their differences, the dark lady sonnet instead brings out the diacritical difference built into its identities. Where the two young man sonnets develop an ideal logic of sympathetic opposition, the dark lady sonnet gives us instead what is the paradoxical opposite, if we can call it that, to such a logic of sympathetic oppo-sition. In terms of form, of theme, of tone, these are all significant differences. But it is important to realize that these differences derive not only their force but also their specific qualities, their content as well as their contours, from the structurally systematic way in which sonnet 132 understands its language para-doxically to redouble, with a difference, the orthodox dual unities with which it begins—i.e., from the way in which the double doubling of sonnet 132 tropes, re-turns, re-verses, the unifying tropes of an idealizing, homogeneous poetics, this way inverting the reciprocal way that eye and heart in sonnets 46 and 47 "each doth good turns now unto the other" (47). "Mourning" its "morning," the sonnet puts into words, literally puts *into* words, the duplicity of its speech, and this duplicity, thus bespoken, in turn divides the original bright desire and golden poetics presupposed by the young man sonnets. By means of this remarked duplication, the sonnet undoes both erotic and rhetorical identification, and thereby, *through* its language, justifies the chiasmic inversion of the poet's eye and heart. In sonnet 132 the content of "mourning" *is* the loss of "morning," and this hole built into a double language, this difference sounded in a sameness, is what functions both to blind the poet's eye and to break the poet's heart. Developed in this way, as the forswearing double of a visual ideal, as "morning" *manqué*, language acquires in the sonnet, and at the same time also proclaims, its novel motives and motifs, precisely those that the poet defines, logically and psychologically, as "Then will I swear beauty herself is black."

It is language, therefore, conceived and conceited as something linguistic, as something of the *tongue*, as both like and unlike the vision to which it is opposed and on which it is superimposed, that in the dark lady sonnets describes and names the redoubling of unity that leads to division, the mimic likeness of a likeness that leads to difference, the representation of presentation that spells the end of presence. Writing at or as the conclusion of a tradition of poetic idealism and idealization, when poetic imitation no longer functions as *Ideas Mirrour*, when poetic metaphor no longer "see(s) the same," Shakespeare in his sonnets draws the formal and thematic consequences that follow from the death of visual admiration. In the poetics of the sequence as a whole, at the level of its rhetorical figures, the dark lady sonnets explicitly break the amatory metaphorics of "Two distincts, division none" (*The Phoenix and the Turtle*) by substituting for such a unitary duality a tropic system of triangular, chiasmic duplicity: "A torment thrice threefold thus to be crossed" (133). In the narrative the sequence tells, this figural double duplication, which brings out the difference built into binary identities, is thematically embodied in the ambiguously duplicitous dark lady—darker and older, almost by structural necessity, than the fair young man—and then projected into the double cuckoldry story itself, where the poet is betrayed by both his objects of desire when they couple or cross-couple with each other, and when the sequence as a whole moves from the unity of *folie à deux* to the duality of *ménage à trois*. In terms of the sonnets' own literary self-consciousness, there is an analogous contrast, again thematic, between the traditional poetry of erotic idealization addressed to the young man and the parodic undoing of that tradition by means of the radically *para-*, not *anti-*, Petrarchanism addressed to the dark lady, which repeats, but with a difference, the "sameness" of traditional idealizing themes. Finally, because the self-conscious tradition of the poetry of praise assumes that the language of poetic desire is itself identical to the object of poetic desire—which is why an orthodox poetry of love characteristically writes itself out as a love of poetry—Shakespeare's paradoxical version of the poetry of

Shakespeare's "Perjur'd Eye"

163

praise brings out even the difference built into the identity of literary and sexual admiration, which is how the dark lady sonnets describe a poetic desire whose Eros and Logos are themselves thematically out of joint.

It would be possible, of course, to find literary precedents for what seems novel in Shakespeare's sonnets. The kind of chiasmic (not oxymoronic) figurality that governs so many of Shakespeare's sonnets, the darksome light of the young man sonnets and their conflicted response to idealism, the general sense of literary belatedness that runs through the sequence as a whole—such features are already present in Dante, and they are yet more insistently and urgently emphatic in Petrarch, where the intractably heterogeneous relation of poetic signifier to poetic signified defines, to some extent, the central worry of the "scattered" songs to Laura. (In *The Secretum*, Petrarch's private and unpublished imaginary dialogue with Saint Augustine, Augustine accuses Petrarch of having fallen in love with Laura *only* on account of her name). So too, we could readily trace the way the Renaissance sonnet grows increasingly arch in its presentation of the Cratylitic correspondence of signifier to signified. This archness develops in so smooth and continuous a way as to suggest an unbroken line linking Beatrice, through Laura, through Stella (and through others) to, finally, what Shakespeare in several voluptuary sonnets calls his "Will."[16] So too, we could correlate the development of such literary self-consciousness with the increasingly intentional artificiality of the later "golden" sonnet, the way such sonnets strive, quite frankly, to present the conventionally reflexive reflections of orthodox epideixis as something *merely* literary, for prime example, the over-written way that Astrophil looks deep into his heart and in this way underwrites his introspective astrophilia. Even more obviously, we could find in the Renaissance vogue for the mock encomium, in the widespread enthusiasm for comically paradoxical praises of that which is low, not only the hyper-rhetorical temperament that Shakespeare's sonnets presuppose, but, also, a regularly reiterated interest in the specific themes that Shakespeare develops in the sonnets to the dark lady—e.g., the paradoxical praise of blindness, darkness, nymphomania, cuckoldry, false language, and so forth.[17]

The existence of such precedents is evidence of the fact that what Shakespeare "invents" in his sonnets is what he "comes upon" in a literary tradition and a literary history of which he is well aware and to which his sonnets are, again in a conventional way, intended as response. Yet it is important to recognize the genuine novelty that Shakespeare introduces into this literary tradition when he puts into words, as I have put it, his suspicions—truly, *sub-spicere*—of the visual and visionary poetics of idealism. For when Shakespeare thus outspokenly articulates, thematically as well as formally, the "insufficiency" that "make[s] me give the lie to my true sight" (150), when he makes his language literally as well as figuratively "mourn" the "morning," he manages, on the one hand, to render explicit reservations that in the orthodox Renaissance sonnet are serious but always implicit, just as, on the other, he manages to take seriously what in the tradition of the paradoxical mock encomium is explicit but always merely comic. He can do so because the thematic innovation has more than thematic consequence. By "expressing" the "difference" that the idealizing and homogeneous Renaissance sonnet necessarily "leaves out," the peculiar matter of Shakespearean paradox finds itself instantiated, exampled, by the corresponding paradox of Shakespearean poetic manner. Language thus speaks *for* its own gainsaying. The result is a new kind of Cratylism, a second degree of Cratylism, that, like the Liar's Paradox Shakespeare often flirts with in his sonnets—"Those lines that I before have writ do lie" (115), "When my love swears that she is made of truth" (138)—is proof of its own paradoxicality. In this gainsaying way—a speech acquired on condition that it speak against itself—Shakespeare accomplishes a limit case of the correspondence of signifier to signified. As the self-belying likeness of a difference, language becomes in Shakespeare's sonnets the true icon of an idol. Shakespeare's poetics of the word in this way acquires the "power" of its "insufficiency" (150), for every word the poet speaks effectively presents, is demonstration of, the loss of his ideal.[18]

With regard to Shakespearean subjectivity, two points follow from this, one practical, the other theoretical. First of all, the poet who speaks such a "forswearing" speech is no longer the speaking "eye" of the traditional sonnet. As a result, the poetic persona of Shakespeare's sonnets can no longer elaborate his subjectivity in accord with the ideal model of a self composed of the specular identification of poetic ego and poetic ego-ideal, of "I" and "you," or of eye and eyed. Instead, identifying himself with the heterogeneous look of the lady, or with the duplicity of her speech, the poet identifies himself with difference, with that which resists or breaks identification. The result is that the poet's identity is defined, by chiasmic triangulation, as the disruption or fracture of identity: "Me from myself thy cruel eye hath taken, / And my next self thou harder hast engrossed" (133). In terms of poetic erotics, we can say that this is why the poet of Shakespeare's sonnet sequence possesses a doubly divided desire—"Two loves I have of comfort and despair" (144)—and why the one is purchased dialectically, measure for measure, at the expense of the other, as "Th' expense of spirit in a waste of shame" (129). Speaking more generally, we can say that such a poetic self identifies himself with an inescapable, because constitutive, "insufficiency." Built up on or out of the loss of itself, its identity defined as its difference from itself, a hole opens up within the whole of poetic first-person self-presence. This "hole" within the "whole" (and also without, see sonnet 134: "He pays the whole, and yet am I not free") inserts into the poet a space of personal interiority, a palpable syncope, that justifies and warrants poetic introspection. This accounts for the strong personal affect of Shakespeare's lyric persona, what is called its "depth." By joining the rhetorical form of triangular chiasmus to the thematic

165

heartbreak of a "perjur'd eye" (a phrase that, for this reason, we can think of as a "Shakespeareme," i.e., the smallest minimal unit of Shakespearean self), Shakespeare's sonnets give off the subjectivity effect called for by a post-idealist literariness. This is also how Shakespeare produces subjectivity in his plays, where, to take a simple example, the cross-coupling of pairs of lovers, their "star-cross'd" fate regularly explained in terms of a thematic disjunction between vision and language, characteristically generates what are taken to be Shakespeare's deeply realized, psychologistically authentic, dramatic personae. Moreover, to the extent that the characterologies of these characters continue to retain their specifically characterological or subjective appeal, to this extent we have evidence of the abiding, though posthumous, power of the idealism and the idealization to which the logic of their unhappy psychologies attest—an ideality all the more powerful for being constituted retrospectively, as a "remembrance of things past," as "th' expense of many a vanish'd sight," as a "fore-bemoaned moan," "Which I new pay as if not paid before" (30).

This leads, however, to a concluding theoretical observation. It has no doubt already been noticed that this reading of Shakespeare's sonnets, perfunctory as it is, has many affinities with various literary theories that have been labeled, somewhat simplistically, Structuralist and Post-Structuralist. My concern with the way the "languageness" of language is stressed by Shakespeare's sonnets is related to accounts of literariness that have been developed by such formalists as Roman Jakobson, Gérard Genette, Michael Riffaterre. My concern with cross-coupling chiasmus is related in very obvious ways to A. J. Greimas's "semantic square," to Paul De Man's discussions of figural chiasmus, and also to Jacques Lacan's "Schema L," which Lacan draws as a quaternary "Z." So too, my discussion of the way in which an idealist homogeneity is disrupted by a supplementary heterogeneity is in many ways like, and is certainly indebted to, Jacques Derrida's various essays in deconstructive phenomenology. Most obviously and most importantly, my account of a subjectivity precipitated by the paradoxical relationship of language to vision, my understanding of a language of desire and a desire of language, is very much influenced by Lacan's psychoanalytic account of what he calls the capture of the Imaginary by what he calls the Symbolic.

It is possible to recognize, therefore, a considerable overlap between certain contemporary literary, and not only literary, theorizations and both the formal and thematic peculiarities of Shakespeare's "perjur'd eye." This suggests either that Shakespeare was very theoretically acute or, instead, that contemporary theory is itself very Shakespearean. However, before choosing between either of these alternatives, we should recall the fact that contemporary literary theory, as it has thought itself out, has enacted a development very similar not only to the development we can discern in Shakespeare's sonnets as they move from the sonnets addressed to the young man to those addressed to the dark lady, but similar also to the larger literary development within which we can locate the historical significance of Shakespeare's sonnet sequence as a whole. Responding to Husserl's Dantesque phenomenology of *Ideas,* to Husserl's concern with eidetic reduction and a transcendental Ego, Sartre developed a psychology of imagination whose logic and metaphors very much resemble the paranoiac visionary thematics of a good many of Shakespeare's sonnets to the young man. The subjective optics of the Sartrian "gaze" and its melodrama of mutually persecutory master-slave relations subsequently receives in the thought of Merleau-Ponty, especially in late works such as *Le Visible et l'Invisible,* an ironically comic revision whose chiasmic marriage of subject and object is reminiscent of more than a few of Shakespeare's most genuinely poignant sonneteering conceits; it was Merleau-Ponty, after all, who introduced "chiasmus" into contemporary critical discourse, as a way to explain the way Cézanne paints the trees watching Cézanne.[19] Lacan, Merleau-Ponty's friend, broke with Merleau-Ponty on just this point, seeing in the fully lived "flesh" and "visibility" of Merleau-Ponty's chiasmus a psychological and a phenomenological sentimentality. Instead, Lacan developed an account of the way subjectivity is born in the place where chiasmus breaks. Lacan's anamorphic "gaze," very different from "*le regard*" of Sartre or of Merleau-Ponty, along with Lacan's account of the way language potentiates and inherits this rupture of the imaginary, rather perfectly repeats the formal as well as the thematic logic of Shakespeare's "perjur'd eye."[20] So too, Derrida's attempt to rupture this rupture, Derrida's putatively post-subjective account of a supplemental *différence,* seems, from the point of view of Shakespeare's sonnets, nothing but another "increase" that "From fairest creatures we desire" (1), assuming we recognize the wrinkle, literally the "crease," that Shakespeare introduces into the perennial poetics of copious "increase."

This is significant because it raises the possibility that current thought works to transfer into a theoretical register a constellated set of literary themes, metaphors, motifs, that Shakespeare introduces into literature, in response to specific literary exigencies, at and as the beginning of the end of the Humanist Renaissance. If so, it is possible that current theorizations are important not because they offer a method or even a point of view with which to look back at Shakespeare, but, instead, because they participate in the very same literary history within which Shakespeare writes his sonnets, emerging now as a symptomatic and epiphenomenal consequence of the way, at the beginning of the modernist epoch, Shakespeare rethinks the literature he succeeds. Putting the question more strongly, we can ask whether, repeating Shakespeare's repetition, it is possible for contemporary theory to do so with a difference.

These are not questions I mean fully either to answer or even to address in this essay. But I would like at least to raise them, for it seems important that such a sense of repetition is itself a distinctive mark of Renaissance sensibility, especially

Shakespeare's "Perjur'd Eye"

167

of a good many literary minds for whom the project of their present is to give rebirth to the past. The very great Humanist Leone Ebreo—precursor to Spinoza, and in this way an important influence on Freud—in his dialogue *D'amore e desiderio* distinguishes—the topic is an old one—between love and desire on the the grounds that love is an emotion one feels for that which one possesses, whereas desire is the emotion one feels for that which one does not possess.[21] Returning to the subject sometime later, in a dialogue called *De l'origine d'amore*, Ebreo emends his original distinction, reformulating it on the grounds that even that which one possesses, because it is possessed in transient time, carries with it, even at the moment of possession, a sense of loss.[22] This possession of loss, an emotion which is half love and half desire—what we might call a desire for love, but what we cannot call a love of desire—grows increasingly strong when the later and post-Humanist Renaissance returns to rethink a good many other topics relating to the origin of love. In time, in Shakespeare's sonnets, the rebirth of the Renaissance turns into the death of remorse, for in Shakespeare's sonnets "desire is death" (147) *because* "now is black beauty's successive heir" (127).[23]

It is because this is so central a theme in them, because they fully realize their *re-*, that Shakespeare's sonnets possess more than merely local interest. In Shakespeare's sonnets we hear how a literature of repetition, rather than a literature *de l'origine*, explains its desire to itself. With regard to the matter of poetic person, this is important because it allows us to understand how Shakespeare's response to secondariness leads him to introduce into literature a subjectivity altogether novel in the history of the lyric, or, as Shakespeare puts it, "Since mind at first in character was done" (59). For this very reason, however, the constitution of Shakespearean poetic self necessarily recalls the imperatives of a literariness larger even than the Shakespearean:

> If there be nothing new, but that which is
> Hath been before, how are our brains beguil'd
> Which laboring for invention bear amiss
> The second burthen of a former child! (59)

"The second burthen of a former child" very well characterizes the subjectivity fathered in the late Renaissance by the burden of a belated literariness. There is good reason to compare the rebirth of this aborted subject that "invention bear(s) amiss" with "Death's second self, that seals up all in rest" (73). However, to the extent that it is not only Shakespeare who looks, as sonnet 59 puts it, "with a backward look," to see "Your image in some antique book," the revolutionary question raised by such Shakespearean retrospection will continue to retain the ongoing urgency of a perennial and, it seems fair to say, since even Shakespeare now is "nothing new," an increasingly important literary commonplace:

REPRESENTATIONS

That I might see what the old world could say
To this composed wonder of your frame,
Whether we are mended, or whe'er better they,
Or whether revolution be the same.
    O, sure I am the wits of former days
    To subjects worse have given admiring praise. (59)

# Notes

1. All Shakespeare references are to *The Riverside Shakespeare*, ed. G.B. Evans, et al. (Boston, 1974). Sonnet numbers are indicated within parentheses.
2. See Lisle C. John, *The Elizabethan Sonnet Sequences: Studies in Conventional Conceits* (New York, 1938), pp. 93–95; J.H. Hanford, "The Debate of Eye and Heart," *Modern Language Notes*, 26:6 (1911), 161–65.
3. Petrarch, 174; compare to 86 and 87; references are to *Petrarch's Lyric Poems: The Rime Sparse and other Lyrics,* ed. and trans. R.M. Durling (Cambridge, Mass., 1976). *Le Roman de la Rose,* ed. F. Lecoy (Paris, 1914), pp. 1684–87; see notes for background of the motif.
4. Dante, *Paradiso,* Canto 33, lines 91–131; references are to *Dante's Paradiso,* ed. and trans. John D. Sinclair (New York, 1977).
5. "Idea" is a sonneteering commonplace: J.W. Hebel, in his edition of *The Works of Michael Drayton* (Oxford, 1961) cites parallels in de Pontoux's *L'Idée,* in du Bellay, Desportes, Daniel; see vol. 5, p. 13. The Quarto prints "steeld"; Stephen Booth summarizes the range of connotations in *Shakespeare's Sonnets* (New Haven, 1977), pp. 172–73. The conflicting ensemble of motifs attaching to "steeld"—visual, metallic, inscriptive, all those also referring to "stolen" and to "styled"—themselves stage the tensions that sonnet 24 develops out of its general visual conceit, especially the sonnet's play on "perspective."
6. Simonides' saying is already a cliché for Plutarch, *De aud. poet.* 3. In *Elizabethan Critical Essays* (London, 1937), vol. 1, pp. 386–87, G.G. Smith cites the many Renaissance parallels. Aristotle, *Poetics* 1459a 5–8; "But the greatest thing by far is to be a master of metaphor. It is the one thing that cannot be learnt from others; and it is also a sign of genius, since a good metaphor implies an intuitive perception of the similarity in dissimilars *(to gar eu metapherein to to homoion theōrein estin),*" *Aristotle on the Art of Poetry,* ed. and trans. I. Bywater (Oxford, 1909), p. 71.
7. " 'We beg you to tell us wherein this bliss of yours *(tua beatitudine)* now lies.' And I answered her by saying: 'In those words that praise my lady (In quelle parole che lodano la donna mia)'. . . . Therefore I resolved that from now on I would choose material for my poems that should be in praise of this most gracious one." *La Vita nuova,* (XVIII), F. Chapelli, ed., *Opere di Dante Alighiere* (Milan, 1967); M. Musa, trans., *La Vita Nuova of Dante Alighieri* (Bloomington, Ind., 1965). Acting on this resolve, Dante composes the first canzone of *La Vita Nuova,* "*Donne ch'avete inteletto d'amore,*" which later, in *Purg.* 24, 49–63, in conversation with Buonagiunta, will be remem-

bered as marking the beginning of *"le nove rime"* of the *"dolce stil nuovo."* For Petrarch's puns on "Laura," see, for example, *Rime Sparse,* 5, 6, 7, 194, 196, 246, 327, 356.

8. Because the sonnet begins as a poetry of erotic praise, and because praise is also a central thematic issue in the orthodox Renaissance sonnet, the genre is a particularly focused instance of the poetry of praise. This is a significant fact because from antiquity up through the Renaissance, praise or, more generally, the epideictic (praise or blame), is taken to be the master literary genre of literature as such, the single genre under which all other, more particular, literary genres are properly subsumed. This is the basis for the hierarchy of literary genres or "kinds" in Renaissance literary theory, a typology that goes back to Aristotle, who derived all poetry from primal, epideictic imitation: praise of the high and blame of the low. We can identify the idealist assumptions at stake here by recalling the fact that the only poetry Socrates allows into the republic is "praise of gods and virtuous men."

The epideictic bias of traditional poetics—e.g., reading the *Aeneid* as a praise of Aeneas—is usually understood to reflect a concern on the part of the theoreticians with the didactic function of the poetical and the rhetorical; this is to understand the poetical or rhetorical in terms of effective moral persuasion. There is a more formal reason, however, with which traditional poetic theory accounts for the generic importance of the epideictic. Epi-deictic or de-monstrative rhetoric is called such because it is a rhetoric of "show" and "showing forth." The Greek is *epideiknunai,* "to show," "display"; in the middle voice, "to show off," "to display for oneself." The Indo-European root is *\*deik,* with variant *\*deig,* "to show," which gives Greek *dikē,* "justice," and the verb *deiknunai,* "bring to light," "show forth," "represent," "portray," "point out," "show," leading to English "deictic," "paradigmatic," "apodeictic," etc. So too, *deiknunai* is also closely related to *deikeilon,* "representation," "exhibition," "reflection," "image," "phantom," "sculpted figure."

Aristotle brings out the significance of this semantic field, the Heideggerean resonance of which is obvious enough, when he distinguishes epideictic rhetoric from the two other kinds, forensic and deliberative, on the grounds that in the former the audience serves as "observer" (*theōron*), whereas in the latter two the audience serves as "judge" (*kritēn*), *Rhetoric,* 1358b2. Aristotle's point, brought out by his distinguishing between a rhetoric addressed to vision and a rhetoric addressed to judgment, is that epideictic or demonstrative oratory, as distinct from the transparent language of the law courts or the assembly, is a rhetoric both of display and self-display, a spectacular speech that we "observe" precisely because its manner calls attention to itself, a pointing "there" that points ego-centrically to "here," an objective "showing" that amounts to a subjective "showing-off." This explains why the epi-deictic is an extraordinary, not an ordinary, language. The point could be put in more contemporary terms by recalling the way Jakobson defines the specifically literary function as that message which stresses itself as merely message. The Renaissance sonnet characteristically amplifies this formal circularity of the language of praise, its recursive reflexivity, through various psychologistic conceits all designed to demonstrate the correlation of admiring subject with admired object. The point to realize is that when Shakespeare gives over the poetry of praise, when he distances himself from a visionary poetics, he not only gives over the themes and imagery of a perennial poetics, but also gives over the semiosis of this profoundly orthodox (and structuralist) literariness.

For the visual imagery employed by Renaissance poetic theory, especially theory of epideixis, see O.B. Hardison Jr., *The Enduring Monument: A Study of the Idea of Praise in Renaissance Literary Theory and Practice* (Westport, Conn., 1962), pp. 51–67. For general background see R. Tuve, *Elizabethan and Metaphysical Imagery* (Chicago, 1947), chaps. 2, 3; R.W. Lee, "*Ut Pictura Poesis*: The Humanistic Theory of Painting," *Art Bulletin* 22 (1940), 197–269; E.H. Gombrich, "*Icones Symbolicae*: The Visual Image in Neo-Platonic Thought," *Journal of the Warburg and Courtauld Institutes* 11 (1948); R.J. Clements, "*Picta Poesis: Literary and Humanistic Theory in Renaissance Emblem Books* (Rome, 1960).

9. Murray Krieger, "Poetic Presence and Illusion: Renaissance Theory and the Duplicity of Metaphor," *Critical Inquiry* 5:4 (1979), 619.

10. *Astrophil and Stella*, No. 15.

11. *Troilus and Cressida*, V.2.144.

12. Dante puts homosexuals and usurers in the same circle of hell, on the grounds that they couple, for sterile profit, kind with kind. For a very plausible explanation of why Brunetto Latini is also included here, see Eugene Vance, "Désir, rhétorique et texte," *Poétique* 42 (April, 1980), 137–55.

13. *Troilus and Cressida*, IV.5.55–57. With regard to the way Shakespeare represents Petrarchism in the plays, compare this with Longaville's sonnet in *Love's Labor's Lost*: "Did not the heavenly rhetoric of thine eye, / 'Gainst whom the world cannot hold argument, / Persuade my heart to this false perjury" (IV.3. 58–60), or with Romeo's "She speaks, yet she says nothing; what of that? / Her eye discourses, I will answer it," *Romeo and Juliet*, II.2.12–13.

14. I develop such an account in *Shakespeare's Perjured Eye: The Invention of Poetic Subjectivity in Shakespeare's Sonnets* (forthcoming, University of California Press); this contains a fuller account of visual metaphors in traditional poetics, especially the way such metaphors are employed in the literature of orthodox and paradoxical praise.

15. From Aristotle on, rhetoricians regularly identify comparison as the distinctive, characteristic trope of praise, this because comparison allows a speaker to amplify his referent. It is possible to double the two terms of a comparison so that the four terms thus produced stand to each other in a chiasmic relation. This is what happens to eye and heart in sonnet 132. This kind of chiasmic trope is especially characteristic of paradoxical, comic praises of that which is low, this because such paradoxical praises present themselves as mimic repetitions of orthodox praise. The technical term for this kind of reduplicating trope—tropes that break, by redoubling, the dual unities of metaphors that "see the same"—is *syneciosis*. Puttenham calls this the "cross-coupler," and associates it with the erotic, unkind mixture of kinds: "Ye have another figure which me thinkes may well be called (not much swerving from his originall in sence) the *Crosse-couple*, because it takes me two contrary words, and tieth them as it were in a paire of couples, and so makes them agree like good fellowes, as I saw once in Fraunce a wolfe coupled with a mastiffe, and a foxe with a hounde," in George Puttenham, *The Arte of Englishe Poesie* (1589), facsimile reproduction (Kent, Ohio, 1970), p. 216.

16. With their puns on "Will" the dark lady sonnets render explicit a good deal of what is left implicit in the young man sonnets. To begin with, the dark lady sonnets play on the fact that in Elizabethan slang "Will" refers to both the male and female genitals: "Wilt thou, whose will is large and spacious, / Not once vouchsafe to hide my will in

thine?" (135). This picks up and extends, by doubling, several *doubles entendres* that run through the sonnets addressed to the young man. In the young man sonnets, for example, Shakespeare develops, in various ways, not only sexual, the image of the "pricked prick"—"But since she prick'd these out for women's pleasure, / Mine be thy love, and thy love's use their treasure" (20)—and uses this to characterize a desire which stands somewhere between the homosexual and the heterosexual. It is the same image, really, as "stell'd" in sonnet 24, or the time-marking "dial hand" of sonnet 104, but Shakespeare clearly enjoys the erotic connotations of the "pricked prick"—consider, for example, the fate of Adonis: "And nousling in his flank, the loving swine / Sheath'd unaware the tusk in his soft groin" (*Venus and Adonis*, lines 1115–1116), or the bawdy puns of *Love's Labor's Lost*, e.g., "Let the mark have a prick in't" (IV.1.132), "The preyful Princess pierc'd and prick'd a pretty pleasing pricket" (IV.2.56), or, more elaborately, the way Othello takes as well as "took . . . by the throat the circumcised dog / And smote him—thus" (V.2.355–356). In the dark lady sonnets, however, by virtue of the pun on "Will," the poet becomes not only a "pricked prick," but also, again exploiting Elizabethan slang, the "cut cunt" (compare Malvolio in *Twelfth Night*: "These be her very c's, her u's, and her t's, and thus makes she her great P's" (II.5.86–88). This double doubling, whereby "Will" performs the copulation that the poet speaks about, enables Shakespeare explicitly to develop some of the thematic consequences, not only erotic, that the subject of a verbal name *must* suffer. As a "Will," the poet becomes the chiasmic copula between male and female, presence and absence, inside and outside, waxing and waning, showing and hiding, whole and hole, one and none:

> Among a number one is reckon'd none:
> Then in the number let me pass untold,
> Though in thy store's account I one must be,
> For nothing hold me, so it please thee hold
> That nothing me, a something sweet to thee.
>     Make but my name thy love, and love that still,
>     And then thou lovest me, for my name is Will (136).

Quite apart from the various themes and images that are thus put into crosscoupling play, the "Will" sonnets are significant precisely because they mark the first person of the poet with a name, not a deictic, for this identifies the person of the poet through a system of representational, not presentational, reference. This is quite different from the kind of immediate reference achieved by deictic, I-you, indication, for, as has often been pointed out (e.g., Bertrand Russell on egocentric particulars, Jakobson on shifters, and E. Benveniste on pronouns and relationships of person in the verb), such egocentric reference requires the presence of the speaker to his speech. In contrast, a name retains a stable referent regardless of who speaks it. In ways which I discuss in *Shakespeare's Perjured Eye*, it can be shown, first, that deixis is the mode of first-person speaking required by an epideictic poetics, second, that a post-epideictic poetry, such as Shakespeare experiments with in the dark lady sonnets, acquires its subjective effects from the contest it stages between self-displaying visual deictics and self-belying verbal names, as in sonnet 151, where "flesh . . . rising at thy name doth point out thee / As his triumphant prize," but is also obliged "thy poor drudge to be, / To stand in thy affairs, fall by thy side."

REPRESENTATIONS

There is more to say about these disappointing pointers, but I would like to note here that it was Oscar Wilde who first insisted in a strong way on the importance for Shakespeare's sonnets of this quarrel between verbal name and visual deictic. It was Wilde who, reading between the lines, and picking up an old conjecture (going back to Thomas Tyrwhitt in 1766), named the poet's catamite "Willie Hughes," doing this in order to draw out the important and pervasive Shakespearean pun on double "hue," "view," "use," and "you"—the same double-U whose present-absent presence distinguishes "whole" from "hole" in sonnet 134. These are the signifiers through which Shakespeare thinks the large narrative of the sonnets. By doubling the dual unity of first and second person, Shakespeare introduces, for the very first time, a third person into epideictic lyric. This formally *absent* third person—a "he" or "she" or "it"—who stands in between, as missing connection, the poet's first and second person, is what the poet becomes to himself when he becomes his name. Compare, for example, the progress of Othello from "all in all sufficient" (IV.1.265) to "That's he that was Othello; here I am" (V.2.283). Recognizing this, it becomes possible to understand why Wilde's *Portrait of W.H.* is the only genuinely literary criticism that Shakespeare's sonnets have ever yet received. Wilde's novella narrates the argument between the metaphorics of visual presentation, the "Portrait," and the signifiers of linguistic representation, "W.H." In the same way, Wilde's *The Importance of Being Earnest* acts out the question of what is *in* a Shakespearean name, thereby putting an end to a theatrical tradition that begins, at least in English drama, with *The Comedy of Errors*. I discuss the relation of Wilde to Shakespeare more fully in *Shakespeare's Perjured Eye*. I also discuss Wilde's concern with the issue of specifically literary naming in "The Significance of Literature: *The Importance of Being Ernest*," October 15 (1980), pp. 79–90.

17. For a discussion of the classical mock encomium, see T.C. Burgess, *Epideictic Literature* (Chicago, 1902), pp. 157–66. For discussions of Renaissance praise paradox, see A.E. Mallock, "The Techniques and Functions of the Renaissance Paradox," *Studies in Philology* 53 (1956), 191–203; E.N. Thompson, "The Seventeenth Century English Essay," *University of Iowa Humanistic Studies*, 3:3 (1926), 94–105; A.S. Pease, "Things Without Honor," *Classical Philology* 21 (1926), 27–42; H.K. Miler, "The Paradoxical Encomium with Special Reference to its Vogue in England: 1600–1800," *Modern Philology* 53:3 (1956), 145–78; A.H. Stockton, "The Paradoxical Encomium in Elizabethan Drama" *University of Texas Studies in English* 28 (1949), 83–104; R.E. Bennet, "Four Paradoxes by Sir William Cornwallis, the Younger," *Harvard Studies and Notes in Philology and Literature* 13 (1931) 219–40; W.G. Rice, "The *Paradossi* of Ortensio Landi," *University of Michigan Essays and Studies in English and Comparative Literature* 8 (1932), 59–74; "Erasmus and the Tradition of Paradox," *Studies in Philology* 53 (1964), 191–203; W. Kaiser, *Praisers of Folly* (Cambridge, Mass., 1963); B. Vickers, "*King Lear* and Renaissance Paradoxes," *Modern Language Notes* 63:2 (1968), 305–14; R. Colie, *Paradoxia Epidemica: The Renaissance Tradition of Praise Paradox* (Princeton, N.J., 1966).

18. At stake here is the difference between a rhetorical paradox and a merely logical paradox, for these are not the same, though in the Renaissance they are, of course, very much related. In contemporary philosophical terminology, this is something like the distinction between a real logical paradox (which would carry, if such a thing exists, some of the weight of the rhetorical paradox) and a merely semantic paradox (e.g., The Liar's Paradox).

19. See especially the discussion of *entrelacs* in *Le Visible et l'Invisible* (Paris, 1964), chap. 4.

Shakespeare's "Perjur'd Eye"

20. I refer here not only to Lacan's explicit formulations, but also to the development of Lacan's thought, from the early emphasis on visual themes, as in the essay on the "mirror-stage" and accompanying discussions of aggressivity, to the later emphasis on language, anamorphosis, and accompanying discussions of (male) desire, to, finally, as a third term added to the opposition of the Imaginary and the Symbolic, Lacan's emphasis on the "Real," the limits of representation, and accompanying discussions of (female) *jouissance*. Lacan's sense of the Renaissance is colored, however, by a very Catholic and Counter-reformational, a very French, conception of the Baroque: "Le baroque, c'est la régulation de l'âme par la scopie corporelle," *Encore* (Paris, 1975), p. 105, which is why Lacan's direct comments on Shakespeare are often disappointing.

21. Leone Ebreo, *Dialoghi d'amore*, ed. Santino Caramella (Bari, 1929), p. 5, cited by J.C. Nelson, *Renaissance Theory of Love* (New York, 1958), p. 86. Ebreo's distinction remains a strong challenge to subsequent writers on the subject. Consider, for example, "Love, universally taken, is defined to be a desire, as a word of more ample signification; and though Leon Hebraeus, the most copious writer of this subject, in his third dialogue makes no difference, yet in his first he distinguisheth them again, and defines love by desire." Robert Burton, *The Anatomy of Melancholy*, ed. A. Shilleto (London, 1903), Part III, sect. 1, mem. 1, subs. 2; vol. III, p. 10.

22. Ebreo, *Dialoghi*, p. 207, cited by Nelson, pp. 86–87.

23. That desire is death is of course a commonplace, e.g., Ronsard's "Car l'Amour et la Mort n'est qu'une mesme chose," *Sonnets Pour Hélène*, II:77, *Oeuvres complètes de Ronsard*, ed. G. Cohen (Paris, 1950). What is important is the specifically double way in which Shakespearean revision revives this dead metaphor.

# "Incertainties now crown themselves assur'd": The Politics of Plotting Shakespeare's Sonnets

### HEATHER DUBROW

### I

INDETERMINATE IN THEIR CHRONOLOGY, DESTABILIZED BY their textual cruxes, and opaque in much of their language, Shakespeare's sonnets have nonetheless attracted curiously positivistic claims. In particular, critics who differ on many interpretive problems are nevertheless likely to agree that the direction of address of these poems can be established with certainty: the first 126 sonnets refer to and are generally addressed to the Friend, while the succeeding ones concern the Dark Lady. The past thirty years have witnessed trenchant challenges to many assertions in John Dover Wilson's book on these lyrics, such as his identification of the Friend with William Herbert; but his observation that "most readers . . . will not be disposed to deny authority to . . . [the] division into two sections" remains accurate.[1]

The axiom that the first 126 poems involve the Friend and subsequent lyrics concern the Dark Lady generates assumptions about the presence of a linear plot: poet meets Friend, and they enjoy a period of happiness; their joy is, however, shadowed by a period of absence and by the fault alluded to in Sonnet 35 ("No more be griev'd at that which thou hast done") and elsewhere. The entrance of the Dark Lady, who is as untrustworthy as she is attractive, disrupts the idyll celebrated in the joyous sonnets. She, the poet, and the Friend become embroiled in a triangle of jealousy and deceit. To be sure, critics disagree on the details of this plot, such as the exact nature of the "sensual fault" (35.9).[2] And, indeed, many students of these poems admit that their narrative line is sometimes obscure or submerged. Moreover, practitioners of gay and lesbian studies and queer theory have recently reformulated the story in question in order to emphasize the moments acknowledging homoerotic attraction.[3] But, despite such inter-

---

This essay is based on a paper I delivered at the 1992 annual meeting of the Shakespeare Association of America in Kansas City, Kansas. I am grateful to the audience for useful comments, and I would also like to thank David Loewenstein for his incisive commentary on an earlier version.

[1] John Dover Wilson, *An Introduction to the Sonnets of Shakespeare for the Use of Historians and Others* (Cambridge: Cambridge UP, 1963), 14.

[2] All citations of the sonnets follow *The Riverside Shakespeare*, ed. G. Blakemore Evans (Boston: Houghton Mifflin, 1974). I identify each sonnet by number and initial line the first time I refer to it and thereafter by number only.

[3] Bruce R. Smith, for example, discerns a crucial break after Sonnet 20; see *Homosexual Desire in Shakespeare's England: A Cultural Poetics* (Chicago and London: U of Chicago P, 1991), esp. 256.

pretive debates and doubts, the basic assumptions about structure and plot that I have identified are still widely and firmly accepted.

On the surface at least, it is surprising that those assumptions have been interrogated so rarely. Their pedigree is far from reassuring: the division at Sonnet 126 ("O thou, my lovely boy, who in thy power") was established by Malone, whose work on Shakespeare's lyrics has been challenged from many perspectives during the final decades of the twentieth century.[4] Moreover, the most obvious evidence on which to base claims about direction of address—gendered pronouns or other clear referents—is scanty; Margreta de Grazia rightly points out that about five sixths of the first 126 sonnets and a slightly smaller proportion of the entire collection do not specify an addressee through a gendered pronoun.[5]

If it is puzzling that the conventional wisdom about the sonnets has been challenged only intermittently, it is even more puzzling that occasional challenges to it have had so little impact on most critics of these poems or, in some cases, even on the challengers themselves. The handful of scholars who raise questions about the bipartite division typically retreat from the most radical implications of those questions. Hilton Landry briefly questions "the myth of two groups," arguing that the sequence lacks the narrative continuity generally associated with such a structure, but proceeds implicitly to accept it by gendering the addressees even when the texts do not specify whether they are male or female.[6] One of the most perceptive students of these poems, Stephen Booth, observes with his customary skepticism that "we have no strong reason to assume the 1609 order to be either the order of their writing or the order in which Shakespeare would have wanted them read." But he also states that "there is . . . some basis for the widespread critical belief that sonnet 126 is intended to mark a division between sonnets principally concerned with a male beloved and those principally concerned with a woman."[7] Notice the judicious reservation in "some basis"; notice, too, that the statement tilts toward accepting the division. Gregory W. Bredbeck acutely notes that the procreation sonnets and Sonnet 20 often deflect erotic interpretation by concealing gender; he does not, however, explore at any length the implications of this argument for the sequence as a whole.[8] In earlier work on these poems, I myself contended that critics impose a narrative and dramatic framework on a sequence that resists those modes, yet I implicitly accepted the conventional assumptions about addressees and the plot outlined above.[9]

---

[4] The most influential recent challenge appears in Margreta de Grazia, *Shakespeare Verbatim: The Reproduction of Authenticity and the 1790 Apparatus* (Oxford: Clarendon Press, 1991); see also Peter Stallybrass, "Editing as Cultural Formation: The Sexing of Shakespeare's Sonnets," *Modern Language Quarterly* 54 (1993): 91–103.

[5] See de Grazia, "The Scandal of Shakespeare's Sonnets," *Shakespeare Survey* 46 (1993): 35–49, esp. 40–41.

[6] Hilton Landry, *Interpretations in Shakespeare's Sonnets* (Berkeley and Los Angeles: U of California P, 1963), 4–5, esp. 5.

[7] Stephen Booth, ed., *Shakespeare's Sonnets* (New Haven, CT, and London: Yale UP, 1977), 545 and 430.

[8] Gregory W. Bredbeck, *Sodomy and Interpretation: Marlowe to Milton* (Ithaca, NY, and London: Cornell UP, 1991), 167–80.

[9] Heather Dubrow, *Captive Victors: Shakespeare's Narrative Poems and Sonnets* (Ithaca, NY, and London: Cornell UP, 1987), 171–90. In a more recent book I allude to the possibility of questioning the direction of address but do not develop the point; see *Echoes of Desire:*

Finally, an extensive defense of the division into two groups and of the type of plot that results from it has recently issued from the same scholar who has offered the most trenchant evidence for attacking that division. Having previously traced Malone's division of the sonnets to an Enlightenment agenda and demonstrated that many readers before Malone did not assume that the first 126 poems were exclusively directed to a male, de Grazia writes, "This is not, however, to say that Malone got it wrong. . . . Some kind of binary division appears to be at work."[10] The primary scandal of the sonnets, her thought-provoking essay proceeds to assert, is neither the sexual preference of the sonnets' speaker nor the plot their critics have falsely assigned to them. It is rather their transgressive approach to class: praising the youth supports social distinctions, while praising the Dark Lady threatens them, and Sonnet 126 demarcates the divide between those two very different activities.

In order to interrogate conventional wisdom about the sonnets' addressees more radically than de Grazia and others have done, one must first disentangle a range of issues connected with these knotty poems. Critics have long debated the biographical background, if any, of the sequence, but the relationship between that question and the challenge of identifying addressees is more complex than Shakespeareans sometimes acknowledge. Even if historical personages corresponding to the Friend and Dark Lady existed and inspired particular sonnets, it remains possible both that other lyrics in the cycle allude to neither of them and that some of the poems they originally sparked cannot ultimately be associated with corresponding fictive characters. Thus, for example, a sonnet composed in response to a male figure might have been reshaped to allude to the woman in the sequence instead.

Another important epistemological distinction involves the issue of sequence: whether the poems now exist in the order their author intended is closely related to, but separable from, the likelihood of determining their addressees. Some argue that the arrangement of the 1609 edition closely corresponds to the author's intentions, one being to distinguish poems concerning the Friend from those about the Dark Lady. Others contend that, though some individual poems may be out of order, the basic two-part structure determined by Shakespeare survives intact and indicates the direction of address. I will assert instead that the collection published by Thorpe is imperfect in many ways and does not necessarily prove that its author intended a bipartite division. Moreover, even if Thorpe's edition mirrors Shakespeare's own design, we would not invariably know the addressees. Influenced by the resistance to narrativity that characterizes a number of sonnet sequences, the author did not arrange these sonnets in a way that tells a clear story and unmistakably signals the direction of address of each lyric.[11]

---

*English Petrarchism and Its Counterdiscourses* (Ithaca, NY, and London: Cornell UP, 1995), 122–23.

[10] De Grazia, "Scandal," 41. De Grazia's critique of Malone appears in *Shakespeare Verbatim*, 152–63.

[11] On Shakespeare's approach to narrative and dramatic elements, see Dubrow, *Captive Victors*, 171–90; and the article on which this section of the book is based, "Shakespeare's

The consequences of my assertions are extensive: many other claims about the sequence are revealed as no less unstable, and perhaps even no less self-serving, than the emotions the sequence chronicles. Other possibilities open, though they are as impossible to establish as they are intriguing to consider. For example, what if we were to admit the possibility that one of the highly erotic poems after 126 refers to the Friend? To do so is not to deny that some assumptions about the addressees of these poems remain highly probable. It is not at all likely (though conceivable) that more than one woman with dark hair and darker morals lies behind Sonnets 127–52.[12] But even this issue cannot be definitively resolved; more to the point, the addressees of a few poems in Sonnets 127–52 and of many sonnets that precede that group are far harder to determine than Shakespeareans usually admit. Often there is no way of being reasonably confident about whether a given poem involves the Friend, the Dark Lady, or some third party, and this uncertainty has many implications for the imputed narrative of the sequence as a whole.

Acknowledging and exploring such indeterminacies about plot and direction of address can illuminate the workings of this sequence and of sonnet cycles in general, notably their approaches to narrativity. Such an attack on conventional wisdom can also illuminate the workings of our own profession, explaining why otherwise incisive critics retreat from some (though by no means all) of the most transgressive consequences of their skepticism. To put it another way, the plot that Shakespeareans impose on Shakespeare's sequence reveals the plots—in the several senses of the term—that attract the academy.

## II

To support the constellation of presuppositions questioned in this essay, critics variously adduce the status of Sonnet 126, literary and biographical tenets about Shakespeare's process of composition, and influential interpretations by earlier critics. To begin with, the stanzaic irregularities of Sonnet 126 function for some as signposts of a change in addressees: this is, after all, a poem of only twelve lines, and the closural function established by that prosodic variation is intensified by an emphasis on termination, notably in the word "quietus" (l. 12) and the climactic allusions to death and loss. Such evidence is strong but by no means conclusive. Sonnet 126 is not unique in its structural irregularity; Sonnet 99 ("The forward violet thus did I chide") has fifteen lines. Indeed, given that Shakespeare's sonnets include a repeated couplet, several paired poems that may well be drafts of each other, and many other apparent irregularities, it is tricky at best to assign thematic significance to the fact that Sonnet 126 deviates from standard sonnet structure.

Even accepting that Sonnet 126 may serve special closural functions signaled by its twelve-line structure does not establish irrevocably that the poems preceding it involve the Friend and the ones succeeding it concern

---

Undramatic Monologues: Toward a Reading of the *Sonnets*," *Shakespeare Quarterly* 32 (1981): 55–68.

[12] For a similar position, cf. Booth, ed., 549.

the Dark Lady. Whether or not the poems can be clearly divided into two large groups, it is obvious that the sequence as a whole includes a number of subdivisions or clusters. Brents Stirling goes so far as to assert that most of the poems initially formed discrete groups;[13] Sonnet 126 might originally have been intended to conclude one of those groups rather than all the poems about the Friend. Certainly it would be at least as appropriate as a conclusion to the procreation sonnets. Like those poems, it focuses on Nature and emphasizes that the passage of time threatens even, or especially, the lovely youth. Several other poems might seem like equally appropriate conclusions to a series of sonnets focusing on the Friend. We might assume, for instance, that Sonnet 87 ("Farewell, thou art too dear for my possessing"), which opens with a word signaling leavetaking and concludes "Thus have I had thee as a dream doth flatter: / In sleep a king, but waking no such matter" (ll. 13–14), plays that role. And even if one grants that Sonnet 126 does establish a bipartite division, there is no reason to assume that the 1609 order reproduces that division; it remains possible that some poems intended for one group or the other slipped out of place.

Another premise sometimes lies behind the belief that we can determine the poems' direction of address and construct a plot built on that determination: namely, the presupposition that they have an immediate relationship to biographical experiences with two persons who correspond to the Friend and Dark Lady. This theory of straightforward mimeticism involves dubious assumptions about the biographical background to the sequence. Among the soundest observations on that subject is John Kerrigan's: "The text is neither fictive nor confessional. Shakespeare stands behind the first person of his sequence as Sidney had stood behind Astrophil—sometimes near the poetic 'I,' sometimes farther off, but never without some degree of rhetorical projection."[14] As this statement suggests, the sonnets probably exemplify a wide spectrum of connections to biographical events. The many readers who have sensed some such episodes behind the intensity of these lyrics are operating from a sound instinct: the immediacy and force of many sonnets hint that they are written by someone whose knowledge of their events could only be firsthand. Yet all the poems need not have the same genesis. Some may, with little mediation or correction, record an episode with a person who corresponds closely to the fictive characters we now know as the Friend or Dark Lady; others may initially have been written in response to historical people or events but were later revised in relation to this sequence or, alternatively, incorporated into this group without any revision; and yet others may well have been composed by Shakespeare with no mistress—or master—save his muse in mind.[15]

[13] This argument is explored by Brents Stirling in *The Shakespeare Sonnet Order: Poems and Groups* (Berkeley and Los Angeles: U of California P, 1968). Though I have reservations about all attempts to reorder the sequence, Stirling's is in my opinion the most responsible effort in that direction.

[14] John Kerrigan, ed., *The Sonnets and* A Lover's Complaint (Harmondsworth, UK: Penguin, 1986), 11.

[15] A few critics have touched on the possibility of multiple addressees. See, for example, C. L. Barber, "An Essay on the Sonnets" in the Laurel Shakespeare *Sonnets*, ed. Charles Jasper Sisson (New York: Dell, 1960), 7–33; Barber notes that the poems might have been written to more than one young man (8), a hypothesis that seems to me conceivable but less probable than those explored in my essay.

Conceivably, Shakespeare drafted some sonnets unconnected to the Friend and Dark Lady early in his career, perhaps even a discrete group of them, and then affixed them to his later sonnets; this could account for one or more of the groupings, such as the poems on absence.[16] The popularity of *Astrophil and Stella* when it was published in 1591 inspired a tidal wave of imitations; arguably Shakespeare responded by crafting some contributions to the genre shortly after Sidney's sequence appeared. Critics who accept the possibility of two *Lears* should surely be willing to entertain the possibility of radically revised and superimposed groups of sonnets coalescing into what we now know as Shakespeare's sonnets. If so, it remains more than possible that many poems within the sequence do refer to the same events, whether experienced biographically or not; but again, to demonstrate that many do so is not to prove that all do so. As Stephen Booth has persuasively argued, Shakespeare's sonnets both support and undermine a search for coherence.[17] Certainly the presence of Sonnets 94 ("They that have pow'r to hurt, and will do none"), 116 ("Let me not to the marriage of true minds"), and 129 ("Th' expense of spirit in a waste of shame"), a group of poems that generalizes about love and lust without referring to a particular lover or relationship, invites us to ask whether the sequence includes other, similar poems which readers have associated with the Friend and Dark Lady without adequate evidence.[18] For example, references to reputation and faults in Sonnet 121 (" 'Tis better to be vile than vile esteemed") may tempt some critics to read it in relation to events in the narrative about the Friend which they have found—or inserted—in the sequence; but those issues are general ones that do not require presupposing a commentary on a particular relationship. Such speculations suggest that we cannot determine the direction of address of some sonnets because these poems were never intended to involve the Friend or Dark Lady or, alternatively, were adapted cursorily and ambiguously in order to do so. In either case the reader would be less likely throughout the sequence to encounter clear, consistent renditions of character and of characters.

But even critics who reject the idea of mimetic correspondence with experiences outside the sonnet cycle may nonetheless attribute to it an intellectual coherence that permits, indeed encourages, assumptions about to whom the poems refer. According to this reading, whatever the biographical events behind the poems, Shakespeare the dramatist evokes coherent if fictional personages throughout this sequence. The first 126 poems involve the young man and the rest involve the woman because the lyrics paint consistent portraits. Surely this argument holds for certain poems; even the most committed skeptic might hesitate to assert that the procreation sonnets are discrete lyrics that address a cohort of handsome young men, fictive or otherwise, all of whom are reluctant to marry. Yet the assumption that the Dark Lady and Friend are marked by characteris-

[16] Dover Wilson briefly mentions the possibility that the sequence may include some sonnets not originally composed for it (18).

[17] See Booth, ed., 545; and Booth, *An Essay on Shakespeare's Sonnets* (New Haven, CT, and London: Yale UP, 1969), 1–28.

[18] These three poems are discussed from a different perspective by Carol Thomas Neely in "Detachment and Engagement in Shakespeare's Sonnets: 94, 116, and 129," *PMLA* 92 (1977): 83–95.

tics that regularly allow us to categorize a given poem as pertaining to one or the other of them depends not only on a belief in stable identities (a point to which I will return) but also on a disregard for the perils of circular reading. That is, we assume that a given poem evokes one or the other of those personages, deduce certain traits from the text, and then assign lyrics concerned with the same traits or issues to the same character. For example, though Sonnet 48 ("How careful was I, when I took my way") nowhere establishes the gender of its addressee, its emphasis on that personage's preciousness and on the topos of absence substantiates our assumptions that the poet sees the Friend as praiseworthy and that one or more episodes of absence complicate their relationship. Hence it seems more likely that other poems with those preoccupations refer to the Friend as well, and the cluster of absence sonnets in the first part of the sequence buttresses the conviction that the earlier poems in the group do indeed concern the Friend. If, however, we admit that this lyric could refer to the Dark Lady, then the argument that references to praiseworthiness or absence in other sonnets flag their addressee becomes more problematical.

Another reason many Shakespeareans have accepted the premises challenged in this essay is that these notions have been the underlying presuppositions of certain highly influential articles or books and the explicit theses of others. These studies have not, however, established a definitive case for the addressee of each poem; indeed, in some instances their analyses can be redirected to support the indeterminate readings for which I am arguing. For instance, Joel Fineman's *Shakespeare's Perjured Eye* argues that the sonnets establish two alternative worlds corresponding to two principal groups: the poems involving the young man celebrate idealized specularity, while those concerning the Dark Lady lament duplicities occasioned and represented by language's replacement of vision.[19] But just as the Lacanian model underlying Fineman's analysis assumes the interpenetration and coexistence of the Imaginary and Symbolic, Fineman, throughout the book, stresses the imbrication, conflation, and erosion of his two categories: "Yet the sequence as a whole refuses to be . . . discriminated into two distinct and isolated parts. Assuming we read them both, the two parts of the sequence cannot be kept separate from each other, for when we begin to compare them each with each the second sub-sequence retroactively undoes the first, with the latter 'forswearing' the former in a definitive revisionary way."[20] Fineman himself traces this undoing to the instability of the subjectivities attributed to the Friend and Dark Lady. To Fineman one may respond, less subtly but no less persuasively, that the structure of the sequence itself is unstable: each section may contain poems that are out of place, referring to characters or values customarily associated with the other section. Clearly one explanation does not preclude the other.

Longstanding defenses of the sequence's order, which typically carry with them presuppositions that we know about the poems' characters, recently culminated in an important and learned essay by Katherine Duncan-Jones. In it she attempts to defend the structural integrity of the

---

[19] Joel Fineman, *Shakespeare's Perjured Eye: The Invention of Poetic Subjectivity in the Sonnets* (Berkeley: U of California P, 1986); a useful overview of his complex argument appears on page 15.
[20] Fineman, 132.

sequence on the basis of the professional integrity of its publisher and the unity of its design.[21] Her points on thematic connections within the sequence are certainly well taken. But the contention that Thorpe was too reliable to publish an unauthorized edition assumes that he was quite atypical of Elizabethan publishers; Duncan-Jones admits that he was responsible for one unauthorized edition, and her effort to dismiss this publication as a prank, "a deliberate piece of mischief," has negative implications for his behavior elsewhere.[22] She cites the outbreak of plague in 1608–09 and the subsequent closing of the theaters as a reason for Shakespeare to have sold this text to Thorpe;[23] but, as G. B. Evans points out, it is also possible that an unauthorized edition would have seemed less risky to Thorpe if, because of the plague, Shakespeare had left the city. In addition, Evans questions whether, given the sexual overtones of the relationship with the young man, Shakespeare would have chosen to publish poems about it.[24]

Duncan-Jones's argument assigns to the sequence a four-part structure: she posits an introductory group of procreation sonnets, followed by 108 sonnets on friendship, the envoi in Sonnet 126, and the poems to the Dark Lady. Even if Shakespeare, like Sidney, Fulke Greville, and other writers, does take pains to construct a unit of 108 lyrics, that pattern would suggest but not prove structural unity in other respects. However, as is often the case in numerological analyses, arriving at the proper number involves some special pleading. It is not clear that the sequence does indeed contain a unit of 108 poems. Did Shakespeare really intend to include poems that seem to be versions of each other, such as Sonnets 57 ("Being your slave, what should I do but tend") and 58 ("That god forbid that made me first your slave"), in a final manuscript, as he would have had to do to achieve the number 108?

The assertion that the 1609 version is a coherent collection in the order its author intended, the argument offered by Duncan-Jones and many other critics, provides another justification for assigning the first group to the Friend and the later group to the Dark Lady. One of the principal limitations of this position should by now be clear. As many readers have noted, the 1609 version of the sonnets contains manifold imperfections, such as the repetition of a couplet in Sonnets 36 ("Let me confess that we two must be twain") and 96 ("Some say thy fault is youth, some wantonness"), the extra line of Sonnet 99, and poems so similar—especially the pair to which I referred earlier, Sonnets 57 and 58—that to some they have seemed drafts of the same lyric. One could conceivably attribute a couple of these flaws to printers' errors or attempt to justify others on aesthetic grounds by arguing that the repetition of couplets draws attention to other differences between

---

[21] Katherine Duncan-Jones, "Was the 1609 *Shake-speares Sonnets* Really Unauthorized?" *Review of English Studies* 34 (1983): 151–71. Duncan-Jones develops her thesis about the 1609 edition in her discussion of Sonnet 126 in "Filling the Unforgiving Minute: Modernizing SHAKE-SPEARES SONNETS (1609)," *Essays in Criticism* 45 (1995): 199–207, esp. 205–6. I am grateful to the author for making this second essay available to me while I was writing this article.

[22] Duncan-Jones, "Was the 1609 *Shake-speares Sonnets* Really Unauthorized?" 163.

[23] See Duncan-Jones, "Was the 1609 *Shake-speares Sonnets* Really Unauthorized?" 162.

[24] See the New Cambridge Shakespeare *Sonnets*, ed. G. B. Evans (Cambridge: Cambridge UP, 1996), 114. I thank Professor Evans for sharing his work with me prior to publication.

the sonnets in question.[25] Yet the presence of so many fault lines in the sequence has encouraged an alternative interpretation: that the 1609 edition represents not that dream of traditional textual editors, the author's final intention, but rather a set of poems in various stages of composition. If this is so, the division between poems to one addressee and those to another is not likely to be perfect.

Moreover, the belief that Thorpe's 1609 edition reproduces the poems in a coherent order is often associated with two dubious assumptions about how structural order functions in this sequence and in Petrarchism generally: the expectation that all the poems in a collection will involve a specified addressee with clearly defined characteristics and that many or most of these lyrics will participate in a discernible plot connected with that addressee. To be sure, one can make a case that certain English sequences, notably *Astrophil and Stella*, function in just that way.[26] (Even in that instance, some critics have speculated that Sidney wrote the trochaic songs before he conceived of the sequence and then inserted them within it.[27]) In many other sonnet sequences, such as Samuel Daniel's *Delia*, the lady is so vaguely defined that only the title establishes the principle that all the poems refer to a single mistress, and little plot is perceptible. Other books juxtapose sonnets that refer to a clearly specified addressee and build a plot with poems that could appear in virtually any sonnet sequence. Barnabe Barnes's extraordinarily violent *Parthenophil and Parthenophe*, for example, culminates in a rape, yet it includes many lyrics that might have been lifted from any miscellany. Similarly, Lady Mary Wroth's *Pamphilia to Amphilanthus* defines the speaker carefully and attributes a few salient characteristics to her lover, but within this cycle a large number of poems are lyric meditations unrelated to any plot line. Other cycles make no pretense of a coherent plot or a single beloved; indeed, the Scottish Petrarchan Alexander Craig addresses a large number of presumably fictional ladies in his *Amorose Songes, Sonets, and Elegies*. In short, Petrarchism offers a wide range of models for the structure of a sequence. Its norms and forms do not enjoin a poet to connect every lyric to the mistress constructed by the sequence or even to construct a single mistress; nor do they mandate a clear plot. Because English sequences approach their addressees and plots in such varied ways, an early modern reader would not have assumed that a given cycle included one mistress and a readily discerned narrative. And Shakespeare's sequence, as I have argued at length elsewhere, eschews the narrative and dramatic modes more than most contemporaneous sequences do. A few incidents and events can surely be discerned, but most of the sonnets are internalized meditations unconnected to a narrative line. Even if Duncan-Jones is right that the 1609 edition reproduces the poems in the order their author intended, his arrangement of them was likely to have been loose and at some points arbitrary—and perceived as such by many Elizabethan readers.

---

[25] For that and other arguments about this repetition, see Booth, ed., 313.

[26] Such readings of Sidney are propounded in David Kalstone, *Sidney's Poetry: Contexts and Interpretations* (Cambridge, MA: Harvard UP, 1965); and Neil L. Rudenstine, *Sidney's Poetic Development* (Cambridge, MA: Harvard UP, 1967).

[27] On the status of the songs, see, for example, William A. Ringler Jr., ed., *The Poems of Sir Philip Sidney* (Oxford: Clarendon Press, 1962), xlvi.

## III

What, then, are the consequences of questioning the assumption that we know the addressees of virtually all the sonnets and can construct on that basis a plot? To begin with, certain interpretations survive intact; as I have already indicated, I am arguing neither for a set of totally discrete poems nor for an infinite number of addressees. Shakespeare's use of masculine pronouns and repeated references to ideal beauty and youth encourage the reader to posit a single male addressee for such lyrics as the procreation group and Sonnets 22 ("My glass shall not persuade me I am old"), 42 ("That thou hast her, it is not all my grief"), 54 ("O how much more doth beauty beauteous seem"), 63 ("Against my love shall be as I am now"), and 67 ("Ah, wherefore with infection should he live"). Similarly, the gendered pronouns and references to intertwined physical and moral darkness support the conventional wisdom that many of the poems after Sonnet 126 concern the Dark Lady. (This does not, however, preclude the possibility raised above: perhaps even some of these sonnets were originally written with a different addressee, real or fictive, or with no particular addressee in mind and then incorporated into the sequence.)

Yet the questions I pose result in far fewer firm assertions and far more interpretive options. On the one hand, because of the paucity of narrative in this sequence and the possibility that some of the poems traditionally associated with the Friend or Dark Lady do not involve the personage in question, it is even harder to extract a clear plot line than many readers have admitted. On the other hand, once the direction of address is thrown into question, many alternative plot lines become credible. I do not propose these possibilities as definitive reinterpretations: the aim of this essay is hardly to substitute one set of positivistic readings for another. At the same time, these alternatives invite some intriguing and disturbing speculations about the sequence.

First, then, recognizing that some sonnets among the first 126 could refer to the Dark Lady implies much about that figure, the speaker, and the culture that contributed to constructing them. There is no overriding reason to assume that poems such as Sonnets 50 ("How heavy do I journey on the way") and 51 ("Thus can my love excuse the slow offense"), which concern an absence, describe separation from the Friend rather than from the Dark Lady. Absence is, of course, a very familiar topos in Petrarchism. Nor should one assume that the defense of an unchanged mode of writing in Sonnet 76 ("Why is my verse so barren of new pride?") alludes to creating sonnets about the Friend; if it would be tellingly appropriate to respond to his constancy, real or imputed, in a constant style, it would be tellingly ironic to react in that way to the Dark Lady's many versions of inconstancy.

But what if one extends this analysis to the more celebratory poems in the first part of the sequence? Suppose, for example, the generations of undergraduates who have assumed a female addressee for the frequently anthologized lines of Sonnet 18 ("Shall I compare thee to a summer's day?") are right and it is the Dark Lady who is celebrated as "lovely and . . . temperate" (l. 2)? The tortured and tortuous love staged in the later sonnets may be but one of several responses to her. And the image of the Dark Lady herself which emerges from the final group of sonnets—that she is attractive but duplicitous—may be one of several contradictory or at least contestatory images in the sequence. Our assumption that she is unremittingly evil would be complicated if we were to envision her as the subject of a sonnet such as 38, which nowhere definitively establishes its addressee: "How can my Muse want subject to invent / While thou dost breathe, that pour'st into my verse / Thine own sweet argument" (ll. 1–3).

Depending on the critical perspective from which one approaches them, such possibilities have a number of consequences. From a characterological viewpoint, the sequence testifies to what might be described as the Dark Lady's infinite variety. Like Cleopatra, she is a quick-change artist. This viewpoint would reinforce the duplicity frequently ascribed to her throughout the sequence. Hence the apparent contradictions among the various images of the Dark Lady might also be adduced to dismantle traditional concepts of stable character and support instead an emphasis on destabilized subjectivities.[28] These readings undermine expectations of consistency and wholeness; conceived in Lacanian mirrors, the subjectivity of the Dark Lady is further splintered in the "wilderness of mirrors" that is this sequence.

These apparent contradictions in the construction of the Dark Lady may also testify to how the subjectivities of the speaker and the poet behind him operate. Arguably desire, anger, misogyny, or some volatile admixture of all these potent chemicals prevents Shakespeare the character within the sequence, Shakespeare the poet, or both from constructing a consistent portrait of the Dark Lady. The sequence itself contains lines that buttress this possibility: "For I have sworn thee fair, and thought thee bright" (147.13), for example, might refer back to the brightness mentioned in earlier sonnets. Such contradictions not only exemplify but also clarify the workings of misogyny in the speaker, the poet, and English Renaissance culture. In Tudor and Stuart England the ideologies of gender are consistent in almost nothing save their inconsistency: the careful reader of texts in which such ideologies are expressed finds not a monolithic and hegemonic position but rather a series of contradictions within the works of a single writer and among treatises by different writers on such issues as the amount of authority the wife should have in marriage. Misogyny is often part of a never-ending cycle in which respect, admiration, and attraction generate reactive distancing, and vice versa. In no discourse is this more true than Petrarchism; witness, among a host of many other examples, Spenser's *Amoretti*, which juxtaposes with its most respectful lyrics poems so fiercely hostile toward the mistress that some critics nervously and unpersuasively attempt to assign them to an abortive earlier collection, another lady, another country. It would not be surprising if even a Dark Lady were praised in a poem such as Sonnet 18.

Although the majority of poems after Sonnet 126 are addressed to a woman, some intriguing revisionist readings are permitted by other texts in the group. The bitter denunciations of lust in Sonnet 129 are sometimes read as general but sometimes, because of its placement in the sequence,

---

[28] Such labels as "traditional" are, however, as dangerous as they are tempting in the current critical climate; in this instance it is important not to oversimplify earlier analyses of character. The role of the unconscious and the conflicts among ego, superego, and id, for example, indicate that Freud's concept of character is less unitary than casual allusions to it might suggest.

read in relation to the Dark Lady. They might, however, refer specifically to the male youth as well as to everyone. The repeated references to his "sensual fault" lend some credence to that reading. Sonnet 143 ("Lo as a careful huswife runs to catch") figures the relationship between its speaker and its addressee as that between a harried parent and her child. Whereas the phrase "play the mother's part" (l. 12), as well as the simile of the housewife in which the poem is grounded, encourage the reader to assume a female addressee, a male lover could also be the protagonist of the drama evoked in this poem. (It would hardly be Shakespeare's first or only experiment with crossdressing.) Indeed, this reading opens the possibility that covert antagonism leads to representing a male as the hapless housewife in the poem; reduced to childishness by love and neglect, the speaker on the one hand declares his affection and on the other retaliates by charging his beloved with the effeminacy so feared in his culture.[29]

The most unsettling possibilities, however, involve Sonnet 128 ("How oft when thou, my music, music play'st"), which turns on a series of conceits about music. This lyric nowhere genders its addressee, nor does the poem contain references to darkness that ally it with the Dark Lady poems. Though women often played the virginal, sixteenth-century allusions to that instrument testify that men did so as well,[30] and the young man is indirectly associated with music in an earlier poem that is clearly addressed to him, Sonnet 8 ("Music to hear, why hear'st thou music sadly"). It is conceivable that the youth is the addressee of Sonnet 128. If so, the sequence includes a poem more openly erotic than those that practitioners of gay and lesbian criticism and queer theory have sedulously examined, especially when one considers the sexual innuendos Booth has uncovered in the poem:[31]

> How oft, when thou, my music, music play'st
> Upon that blessed wood whose motion sounds
> With thy sweet fingers when thou gently sway'st
> The wiry concord that mine ear confounds,
> Do I envy those jacks that nimble leap
> To kiss the tender inward of thy hand,
> Whilst my poor lips, which should that harvest reap,
> At the wood's boldness by thee blushing stand.
> To be so tickled they would change their state
> And situation with those dancing chips,
> O'er whom [thy] fingers walk with gentle gait,
> Making dead wood more blest than living lips:
>     Since saucy jacks so happy are in this,
>     Give them [thy] fingers, me thy lips to kiss.

Some critics, notably Bruce R. Smith, discern in the cycle a linear progression from struggle against homoerotic responses to acknowledgment of them in Sonnet 20 ("A woman's face with Nature's own hand painted");[32]

---

[29] Many recent studies have traced a fear of effeminacy in early modern England; see, for example, Laura Levine, Men in women's clothing: Anti-theatricality and effeminization, 1579–1642 (Cambridge: Cambridge UP, 1994).

[30] The Oxford English Dictionary, 2d ed., prepared by J. A. Simpson and E.S.C. Weiner, 20 vols. (Oxford: Clarendon Press, 1987), 19:667.

[31] See Booth, ed., 437–41.

[32] See Smith, 245–57.

these Shakespeareans might well argue that the progression culminates in the open eroticism of Sonnet 128. Or, if one questions that sort of linear movement, then the sequence might seem to juxtapose poems that ostensibly deny or express ambivalence about homoeroticism, such as Sonnet 20, with lyrics like Sonnet 128, which openly revel in the relationship. From another perspective, accepting that poems such as Sonnet 128 refer to the male friend complicates the homosocial bonds that Eve Kosofsky Sedgwick traces in the sequence, adding other points on the spectrum she describes: desire in the sonnets includes not only relations with women serving the needs of male-male love but also expressions of that love more overtly erotic than the poems normally associated with it.[33] All these are options permitted, but by no means established, by my revisionist approach to the issue of addressees.

As even the few examples I have examined suggest, questioning conventional wisdom about the addressees of the sonnets overturns presuppositions about their story line as well, opening the possibility of episodes very different from the ones critics have seen in the sequence, though these, too, remain only speculative. For instance, if sonnets such as the absence poems and Sonnet 55 ("Not marble nor the gilded [monuments]") do concern the Dark Lady, one might posit a period of idyllic happiness with *her* followed by disillusion. One need no longer interpret the sequence in terms of a narrative movement from the idealized Petrarchism expressed in the first group of sonnets to the virulent anti-Petrarchism of the poems addressed to the Dark Lady. And should we necessarily assume that the discovery of betrayal chronologically succeeds poems that evoke a happy relationship? Surely this sequence, perhaps more than any other text in the language, demonstrates ways to disguise and deny what one knows, excuse what one abhors, embrace what or whom one rejects. This text, then, need not rest on a plot in which actions generate consistent and logical reactions. Again, my aim is neither to advocate any of these alternative readings nor to dismiss more familiar ones out of hand—indeed, I have stressed throughout this essay the difficulty of arriving at an objective and definitive plot—but to suggest that the sequence permits a reader to construct any number of narratives.

## IV

Why, then, have so many critics accepted debatable assumptions about the addressees and the plot of Shakespeare's sonnets? The attraction to such interpretations is overdetermined and requires a number of explanations. The least subtle one is not the least significant: it is easier to discuss these poems critically if one can determine to whom they refer and what story they tell. This motive, though a longstanding one, may have become more urgent in the past few decades: quite possibly the privileging of drama over lyric in Renaissance studies has fueled an interest in reading even a sonnet sequence in terms of plot and of clearly defined characters, despite the recent emphasis on subjectivity. In any event, definitively connecting some

---

[33] Eve Kosofsky Sedgwick's highly influential analysis of the sequence appears in *Between Men: English Literature and Male Homosocial Desire* (New York: Columbia UP, 1985), 28–48.

poems to the male Friend and others to the Dark Lady facilitates the projects of feminism and cultural studies in particular because the assumption that this sequence can be neatly divided into two parts allows a critic to find in them allusions to a society divided by gender and class.

Furthermore, the map of misreading that I have been describing smooths the process of interpretation in another way as well, charting a pattern very like those sometimes enacted in Petrarchism. Critics often take Thomas Wyatt's narrative in "They flee from me" as an objective account of sequential events: once the woman or women in question were loving, and now they reject the speaker. This reading is plausible; alternatively, however, perhaps Wyatt or his speaker or both, unable and unwilling to cope with behavior perceived as simultaneously loving and deceitful, chooses to resolve the problem by creating a temporal narrative. In other words, Wyatt suggests that loving hate was at first love and then hate, thus firmly separating the entwined terms of the oxymoron. Petrarch adopts a comparable strategy when sharply distinguishing the way Laura speaks in the "*in vita*" and "*in morte*" sonnets (though the specific point of division between these groups remains problematical). Similarly, rather than acknowledging the possibility that the Dark Lady has some of the positive qualities attributed to the Friend or the proposition that the Friend was always inscrutable and unreliable, many readers have adopted a plot in which a Golden Age of loyalty between the Friend and the poet is destroyed when the Dark Lady seduces the Friend. Thus critics, like poets, attempt to resolve the coexistence of contradictions: they unchain the synchrony of an oxymoron and project its respective components onto the diachrony of narrative.[34]

Arguably a more general impulse towards linearity and even teleology is also at work when literary critics so confidently impose a two-part structure on Shakespeare's sequence. *Pace* Lyotard, certain master narratives do survive; for instance, attraction to an equivalent of the Whig view of history still structures many critical narratives. Witness the assumption that the so-called Shakespearean sonnet was the ideal form toward which earlier English experiments with Petrarchan rhyme schemes were groping (an assumption, incidentally, that is reminiscent of theories of manifest destiny and, like those theories, demonstrates how models of narrativity can both justify and mask political agendas),[35] or the belief that poststructuralism is the culmination of less sophisticated modes of analysis. This impulse toward linearity and teleology, then, may also intensify critics' attraction to narratives of Fall and apocalypse—narratives, in other words, in which a seemingly fair dark snake enters the garden where the poet and Friend had been happily tending the roses and "forward violet[s]."

Critics' urge to impose a plot on the sequence, while impelled by an interest in modes of narrativity, is intensified by certain reactions to this text in particular. Stephen Booth rightly points out that the sonnets offer just enough evidence of coherence, notably in the procreation sonnets, to

---

[34] Compare my discussion of what I term "temporal displacement" in *Echoes of Desire*, esp. 111–13 and 78–79.

[35] This view of Petrarchism appears in many sources, notably J. W. Lever, *The Elizabethan Love Sonnet* (London: Methuen, 1956), 12–13.

encourage us to seek for more.[36] Peter Brooks relates the narrative drive to Lacan's concept of an "unsatisfied and unsatisfiable" desire.[37] The inconsistencies and indeterminacies of Shakespeare's lyrics increase precisely that drive in many of their readers; whereas Booth connects our wish to impose order on the sequence to the hints of order already present there, the signs of disorder provide an even greater impetus. In other words, in a sequence whose geometry is based on triangulation, the reader becomes the Rival Poet.

But narrative involves a desire to exclude as much as to order, a wish to rule out other stories that often persist, submerged and struggling, as traces of alternative genres, intertextual allusions, and so on. Critics' unacknowledged anxieties about the possible homoerotic undertones in this text may have led them to replicate one of the most common narratives our culture scripts: the regendering of guilt. That is, by imposing on the sonnets the plot I have outlined, Shakespeareans can deflect onto the Dark Lady's corruption anxieties about homoerotic corruption and betrayal. Certainly in reading these poems, critics have located evil primarily within one person rather than claiming that it is pervasive and systemic. Thus they create clear moral categories, performing the very process that Sonnet 144 ("Two loves I have of comfort and despair") itself vainly attempts to enact. And in doing so, they gender and in a sense localize transgression. I am not denying that, even if one relies only on the poems that deploy pronouns unmistakably to gender their addressee, the sequence paints a picture more critical of women than of men. But many readers collude in this process by assuming that sonnets without a clearly marked direction of address refer to the Friend if they are largely positive and to the Dark Lady if they are negative. Just as Sonnet 129 first deflects guilt about desire from the subject to the abstract force of lust and subsequently to the woman, so in reading the sequence as a whole, a number of Shakespeareans repeatedly identify a frailty whose name is woman.[38]

The gendering of evil is, then, but one example of the unfortunate consequences of transforming uncertainties about this sequence into dubious certainties. Although the sonnets have benefited from incisive, even brilliant critical analyses on occasion, too often Shakespeareans impose their own presuppositions on and script their own narratives for a sequence that offers at best ambiguous support for such interpretations. They do so in the hope that the uncertainties of the poems and the anxieties of their readers will crown themselves emplotted, resolved, assured.


[36] See Booth, *Essay*, 1–4.

[37] Peter Brooks, *Reading for the Plot: Design and Intention in Narrative* (New York: Alfred A. Knopf, 1984), 55.

[38] It is tempting to speculate that at least some of the critics attracted to this misogynistic reading impose on the sequence an allegory for developments in our own profession during the past two decades. That is, they construct the fantasy that an Edenic period of homogeneous and harmonious male faculties was shattered by the intrusion of outsiders, darkly ambitious ladies and dark-skinned ladies and men. These intruders, the myth goes, proceeded to confound the distinction between fair and foul, canonical and noncanonical, male and female, acceptable and repugnant sexual preferences.

# Shakespeare's Undramatic Monologues: Toward a Reading of the *Sonnets*

HEATHER DUBROW

> There is, it seems to us,
> At best, only a limited value
> In the knowledge derived from experience.
> The knowledge imposes a pattern, and falsifies.
> For the pattern is new in every moment
> And every moment is a new and shocking
> Valuation of all we have been.
> T.S. Eliot, "East Coker"

W E ASSUME THAT THE NON-DRAMATIC POETRY of a great playwright
will in fact be dramatic in many senses of that complex term. And we
assume that when a writer who, among his manifold gifts, is a skilled storyteller
chooses to write sonnets, at least some of them will be narrative. Those presuppositions help to explain why, despite all the other controversies about Shakespeare's *Sonnets*, certain concepts are so repeatedly and so uncritically brought
to bear on interpretations of these poems. We are regularly informed, for example,
that they are "dramas" or "stories," a view reflected in the frequency with which
critics of the *Sonnets* include the word "dramatic" in the titles of their studies
and then proceed to comment on the "plots" and the "characters" that they
find in the sequence.[1] But in literary criticism, as in so many other human activities, we are prone to see what we expect to see, and nothing else. While
Shakespeare's *Sonnets* evidently do include certain dramatic and narrative elements, in focusing on that aspect of them we have overlooked a more revealing

---

[1] See, e.g., Giorgio Melchiori, *Shakespeare's Dramatic Meditations* (Oxford: Oxford Univ.
Press, 1976); G. K. Hunter, "The Dramatic Technique of Shakespeare's Sonnets," *Essays
in Criticism*, 3 (1953), 152–64; Robert Berkelman, "The Drama in Shakespeare's Sonnets,"
*College English*, 10 (1948), 138–41. Philip Martin maintains that Shakespeare's *Sonnets* are
less dramatic than Donne's lyrics in that the speaker is less fully realized, but far more dramatic
than the sequences of other Elizabethan sonneteers (*Shakespeare's Sonnets; Self, Love and
Art* [Cambridge: Cambridge Univ. Press, 1972], pp. 138, 142–43).

---

HEATHER DUBROW, Associate Professor of English at Carleton College, is the author
of *Genre*, which will be published shortly by Methuen (as part of their Critical Idiom
Series), as well as a number of articles on sixteenth- and seventeenth-century literature.

and more surprising fact: that many of the characteristics central to other dramatic and narrative poetry, including other Renaissance sonnet sequences, are signally absent from Shakespeare's *Sonnets*.

## I

A comparison of Shakespeare's Sonnet 87 with two other works that also concern a leavetaking will highlight his approach to the genre. The famous lines of Drayton's *Idea* 61 demonstrate how a poem in what is essentially a lyric mode can become dramatic:

> Since ther's no helpe, Come let us kisse and part.
> Nay, I have done: you get no more of Me,
> And I am glad, yea glad with all my heart,
> That thus so cleanly, I my Selfe can free,
> Shake hands for ever, Cancell all our Vowes,
> And when We meet at any time againe,
> Be it not seene in either of our Browes,
> That We one jot of former Love reteyne;
> Now at the last gaspe, of Loves latest Breath,
> When his Pulse fayling, Passion speechlesse lies,
> When Faith is kneeling by his bed of Death,
> And Innocence is closing up his Eyes,
>     Now if thou would'st, when all have given him over,
>     From Death to Life, thou might'st him yet recover.[2]

Rather than describing the episode in which the lovers part, Drayton enacts it. We are asked to believe (and, thanks to his skill, the illusion is persuasive) that we are actually witnessing the speaker bidding farewell to his lady. We are as conscious of her implicit but powerful presence as that speaker is himself. And we are conscious, too, that what the poem claims to enact is a specified and unique moment in time. To be sure, Drayton briefly uses allegory to distance us from that moment—but his main reason for establishing such a distance is to create a foil against which his final appeal to the woman will seem all the more immediate.

Though Petrarch's *Canzonière* CXC is primarily concerned with rendering certain states of mind—the poet's joy at the beauty of Laura and his intense sorrow at her loss—he evokes those states by telling a story:

> Una candida cerva sopra l'erba
>     Verde m'apparve, con duo corna d'oro,
>     Fra due riviere, a l'ombra d'un alloro,
>     Levando 'l sole, a la stagione acerba.
> Era sua vista si dolce superba,
>     Ch'i'lasciai per seguirla ogni lavoro;
>     Come l'avaro che 'n cercar tesoro
>     Con diletto l'affanno disacerba.
> 'Nessun me tocchi.' al bel collo d'intorno
>     Scritto avea di diamanti e di topazi;

---

[2] The citation from Drayton is to *The Works of Michael Drayton*, ed. J. William Hebel, Kathleen Tillotson, Bernard H. Newdigate, 5 vols. (Oxford: Oxford Univ. Press, 1931–1941).

'Libera farmi al mio Cesare parve.'
Et era'l sol gia volto al mezzo giorno;
Gli occhi miei stanchi di mirar, non sazi;
Quand'io caddi ne l'acqua, et ella sparve.[3]

Petrarch's poem may be visionary and mystical, but like other narratives it is firmly anchored in time. It has a clear beginning, middle, and end: at the opening of the poem the speaker sees the deer, then he admires her, and then he loses her.

Shakespeare wears his rue with a difference:

> Farewell, thou art too dear for my possessing,
> And like enough thou know'st thy estimate.
> The charter of thy worth gives thee releasing;
> My bonds in thee are all determinate.
> For how do I hold thee but by thy granting,
> And for that riches where is my deserving?
> The cause of this fair gift in me is wanting,
> And so my patience back again is swerving.
> Thyself thou gav'st, thy own worth then not knowing,
> Or me, to whom thou gav'st, else mistaking;
> So thy great gift, upon misprision growing,
> Comes home again, on better judgment making.
>    Thus have I had thee as a dream doth flatter,
>    In sleep a king, but waking no such matter.
>                   (Sonnet 87)[4]

The opening word, "Farewell," suggests that this sonnet is going to enact a parting in much the same way that Drayton's does; and the third quatrain does in a sense tell a story. Yet Shakespeare's poem is not necessarily a rendition of a particular event that takes place at a particular moment: one cannot tell whether the parting is in the process of happening or has already occurred. For Shakespeare's primary concern is not to imitate an incident in which a lover says farewell but rather to evoke the lover's reflections on the process of parting. And Shakespeare's sonnet differs from Drayton's in another and no less significant way: while most of the assertions in Drayton's sonnet are addressed to the beloved, most of those in Shakespeare's are not. In the couplet, for example, Shakespeare's speaker seems to be brooding on his experiences rather than either enacting them or announcing their significance to the person he has loved.

The characteristics of that couplet and of the sonnet in which it figures recur throughout Shakespeare's sonnet sequence. The narrative, dramatic, and lyrical are not, of course, necessarily exclusive of each other, either in general or in Shakespeare's sonnets in particular. In his sequence as a whole, and not infrequently within a single sonnet, we do encounter instances of all three modes.[5] Sonnets 153 and 154, for example, are certainly narrative according to virtually

---

[3] The citation from Petrarch is to *Le Rime*, ed. Giosuè Carducci, Severino Ferrari (Florence: Sansoni, 1965).

[4] All citations from Shakespeare are to *Shakespeare's Sonnets*, ed. Stephen Booth (New Haven: Yale Univ. Press, 1977).

[5] Definition of *lyric*, *dramatic*, and *narrative* has, of course, long been among the most complex and most controversial problems in literary theory. The three modes have been differentiated through their "radicals of presentation," analyzed in terms of linguistic models,

any definition of that term; the entire sequence is indubitably dramatic in the sense that it vividly bodies forth the speaker himself, developing and drawing attention to the nuances of his character. Nevertheless, it is not the presence of certain narrative and dramatic elements but rather the absence of others that is most striking when we read Shakespeare's sequence and most telling when we juxtapose it with the sonnets composed by many other Renaissance poets.

## II

One of the clearest and most important indications that the majority of the *Sonnets* are in certain senses neither narrative nor dramatic is that they do not include a temporal sequence of events, as does, for example, Petrarch's "Una candida cerva sopra l'erba."[6] As we read Shakespeare's *Sonnets*, we witness tortuous shifts in the speaker's emotions and judgments, but very seldom do we encounter a chronological progression of occurrences. Instead, his monologues take place in the kind of eternal present that is usually a mark of lyric poetry.[7] Characteristically, they generalize about an event that recurs frequently rather than focusing on one instance of it: "When I consider everything that grows" (Sonnet 15, line 1); "When to the sessions of sweet silent thought / I summon up remembrance of things past" (Sonnet 30, lines 1–2). In another sense, too, the sonnet sequence that so vividly evokes the horrors of time is not itself rooted in time: Shakespeare's poems seldom refer to datable real incidents or even to incidents that occur at a specific, though symbolic, moment. Petrarch alludes to the date of his meeting with the real woman who was transformed into Laura and the date of her death, and his sequence may also have complex symbolic relationships to the calendar. Spenser's sonnets are apparently keyed to the seasons. One of Daniel's refers to a trip to Italy.[8] But in Shakespeare we find very few such references. To be sure, in one poem the speaker does suggest that he met his beloved three years before; but nowhere else does he allude to time in so specific a way.[9] And Shakespeare is no more specific about place.

---

compared to three stages in the life of a human being or the development of a society, and so on. A useful summary of the various theories may be found in Paul Hernadi, *Beyond Genre* (Ithaca: Cornell Univ. Press, 1972), especially chapters 2 and 3. This essay adopts the traditional and widely accepted contrast between the emphasis on the subjective and introspective in the lyric and the enactment of an external situation in the dramatic. For an influential encapsulation and expansion of that position, see Northrop Frye, *Anatomy of Criticism* (Princeton: Princeton Univ. Press, 1957), esp. pp. 243–337. (A few recent critics have attempted to refine or undercut the customary interpretation of the lyric as a subjective form. See, e.g., Käte Hamburger, *The Logic of Literature*, trans. by Marilynn J. Rose [Bloomington and London: Indiana Univ. Press, 1973] ).

[6] On the role of the temporal in drama, as opposed to lyric poetry, see, e.g., Jackson G. Barry, *Dramatic Structure* (Berkeley: Univ. of California Press, 1970), esp. pp. 110–25.

[7] Anne Ferry comments acutely on the role of the lyric present in the poems about time (*All in War with Time* [Cambridge: Harvard Univ. Press, 1975], pp. 3–63).

[8] See Thomas P. Roche, "The Calendrical Structure of Petrarch's *Canzonière*," *Studies in Philology*, 71 (1974), 152–72, for a useful summary of previous work on the temporal structure of Petrarch's sequence and a thought-provoking new theory.

[9] Sonnet 107 ("Not mine own fears nor the prophetic soul") is sometimes used by scholars in their attempts to date the sequence; but its allusions to events are vague and ambiguous, as is evidenced by the contradictory theories about dating that its lines have engendered.

We know that Sidney's Stella takes a ride on the Thames, while Shakespeare's *Sonnets* never mention a particular locale.

The omission of such allusions to place and time is all the more suggestive in light of Shakespeare's repeated—one is almost tempted to say frenetic—puns on "will." Like Sidney's play on "rich" or his adoption of the pseudonym "Astrophil," these puns are evidently intended to remind us that the poems in question are closely linked to autobiographical experience.[10] One would presume that the same attitudes that lead a poet to pun on, and hence draw attention to, his own name might well encourage him to refer to specific dates and places. But this Shakespeare chooses not to do.

The lack of temporal perspective in most of the *Sonnets* reflects the absence of anecdotal sonnets. With only a handful of exceptions, Shakespeare's sequence omits not only the mythological stories that so frequently grace the sequences of other sonnet writers but also non-mythological allegories like Spenser's *Amoretti* LXXV ("One day I wrote her name vpon the strand").[11] Moreover, Shakespeare seldom chooses to narrate an incident that happens to the lovers, as, say, Sidney does in *Astrophil and Stella* 41 ("Having this day my horse, my hand, my launce"). It is as uncharacteristic of Shakespeare to begin a sonnet with "One day" as it is characteristic of Spenser to do so.

A sonnet that does not narrate an anecdote may, of course, be anchored in a specific event or situation nonetheless: it can be the outgrowth of an occurrence which, though not recounted systematically, is referred to frequently and specifically in the course of the poem. Many readers have assumed that the vast majority of Shakespeare's *Sonnets* are "situational" in this sense. But in point of fact comparatively few of them are.[12] In some of Shakespeare's monologues the reflections are inspired not by a particular situation but by a general problem; thus in Sonnet 94 the speaker evokes a certain kind of personality, and Sonnet 129 is an anguished consideration of the nature of lust. Because poems like these rely so heavily on generalizations, critics regularly describe them as interesting exceptions to Shakespeare's approach elsewhere in the sequence. They are, however, merely extreme instances of their author's tendency to detach the speaker's emotions and speculations from an immediate situation.[13]

Some poems in the sequence imply that a specific incident may lie behind

---

[10] John Burrows makes a similar point about Langland's puns on "will" in *Piers Plowman* in an unpublished paper delivered at the University of Sussex Renaissance Colloquium, February 1975; I am indebted to his remarks. The puns on "will" also confound the question of the extent to which Shakespeare is using a persona.

[11] There are a few exceptions, but they are exceptions that prove the rule. The sonnets that do contain anecdotes, such as 50, 51, 153, and 154, are so weak and derivative that they may well merely be experiments with a type of sonnet in which Shakespeare quickly lost interest. That some editors have tried (though without persuasive evidence) to argue that Sonnets 153 and 154 are not even by Shakespeare reflects the fact that they are very atypical.

[12] The absence of anecdotes is briefly noted by Anton M. Prikhofter ("The Beauty of Truth" in Hilton Landry, ed., *New Essays on Shakespeare's Sonnets* [New York: AMS Press, 1976], pp. 113–14); Prikhofter goes on to argue, however, that the poems are characterized by intense "situational visualization" (p. 122).

[13] For the conventional argument that such poems are atypical in the sequence, see, e.g., Carol Thomas Neely, "Detachment and Engagement in Shakespeare's Sonnets: 94, 116, 129," *PMLA*, 92 (1977), 83–95. Attempting to distinguish those three poems from the others in the sequence, she writes, "Not actions themselves, they are about inaction. . . . The three sonnets are deliberately detached from the particulars of the relationship" (p. 83). I contend that many other sonnets in the sequence might be described in very similar terms.

the speaker's reactions but omit any discussion of details. We learn little about the "forsaking" to which Sonnet 89 alludes, for example, or the reasons for the parting described in the absence sonnets. As we read Sonnet 35 we do not know what the "sensual fault" to which it refers may be, or even whether "fault" indicates a particular lapse or a general character trait.[14] If we try to enumerate the situations on which Shakespeare's *Sonnets* are based, we find that our list is short and the events on it shadowy. The poet encourages the Friend to marry; there is a period of separation, and there are one or more quarrels; the Friend is praised by another poet; the Friend betrays the speaker with the Dark Lady. By contrast, in *Astrophil and Stella*, a sequence about two-thirds the length of Shakespeare's, the situations include a stolen kiss, Stella's illness, her ride on the Thames, an absence, a quarrel, Astrophil's triumph in a tournament, and many more.[15]

### III

If most of Shakespeare's *Sonnets* do not tell stories, neither do they enact dramas in the way that, say, Drayton's *Idea* 61 does ("Since ther's no helpe, Come let us kisse and part"). And yet the reader becomes involved in these poems. One Shakespearean has attempted to explain why: "By setting up a system of tensions between forces presented as persons, Shakespeare's sonnets engage the reader's interest in a manner akin to the dramatic."[16] It is true that some of the *Sonnets*, notably the poems addressed to Time, do operate this way. But most do not: Shakespeare's *Sonnets* embody the tension of conflicting forces, but those forces are more often internalized within the speaker than dramatized as characters.

Though the Friend and the Dark Lady dominate the speaker's thoughts, in some important respects they do not function as active participants within the *Sonnets*. The problems engendered by their behavior are frighteningly immediate, but the characters themselves are not. Except for the fact that the young man is attractive and the lady is dark, we do not know what they look like.[17] Unlike

---

[14] Writing about the interior monologue, Seymour Chatman points out that in it there is "no deference to the ignorance or expository needs of a reader or other character" (see "The Structure of Narrative Transmission," in Roger Fowler, ed., *Style and Structure in Literature* [Ithaca: Cornell Univ. Press, 1975], p. 250). In this respect, as many others, the *Sonnets* are closer to the interior monologue than most other narrative forms; they do not conform completely, however, to this or any of the other categories that Chatman and other readers have established when discussing narrative.

[15] The arguments in this section are open to one obvious objection: one could assert that, while individual sonnets do not tell a coherent story, when properly reordered the whole sequence does. My answer (though it is one that cannot be argued within the scope of this paper) is that attempts to reorder the sonnets are futile because Shakespeare never intended an order. The fact that no acceptable order has been found despite great efforts is revealing. It is also revealing that many of the sonnets seem imperfect and experimental, not members of a finished sequence but rather of a loose collection. Winifred Nowottny suggests that "paired" sonnets sometimes represent an earlier and a later version of the same poem ("Some Features of Form and Style in Sonnets 97–126," in Landry, *New Essays on Shakespeare's Sonnets*, pp. 88–107).

[16] G. K. Hunter, "Dramatic Technique," p. 154.

[17] G. K. Hunter also notes this fact but interprets it very differently, arguing that, despite the paucity of visual description in the sequence, "the brilliance of the language makes the context of [the speaker's] emotions so vivid that the reader naturally supplies from his imagination a complete dramatic situation" (p. 155).

the main characters in most sonnet sequences, they are never assigned names, even fictional ones, even in those poems that refer to them in the third rather than the second person. The epithets by which they are addressed serve, if anything, to distance us further from them. When, for example, Shakespeare opens Sonnet 56 on the command, "Sweet love, renew your force," he establishes an unresolved ambiguity about whether the poem concerns his beloved or the abstract quality of love, or both. When he directs an apostrophe to "Lascivious grace" (Sonnet 40, line 13), he initially seems as much to be brooding on the abstraction that the epithet expresses as to be talking to a person who has been reduced (or who has willingly reduced himself) to the state expressed by that oxymoron.[18] Similarly, only once (Sonnet 34, line 13) in 154 sonnets does Shakespeare allude to the movements or gestures of the beloved in a way that suggests that he is physically present and actually listening to the speaker. Contrast *Astrophil and Stella* 31, which so unequivocally sets up the fiction that Astrophil is in the presence of the moon, or *Astrophil and Stella* 47, whose "Soft, but here she comes" (line 13) so effectively signals Stella's arrival.[19]

It is a truth as significant as it is neglected that the Friend and the Dark Lady are not quoted directly within the poems. Despite all his experience in writing plays, Shakespeare chooses not to create the kind of dialogue on which such poems as *Astrophil and Stella* 54 ("Because I breathe not love to everie one") or *Idea* 24 ("I heare some say, this Man is not in love") or even *Amoretti* LXXV ("One day I wrote her name vpon the strand") are based. On those rare occasions when the words of the beloved are recorded, they are presented in a form that distances us from the statements and their speakers: the poet either uses indirect discourse to report what the beloved has said ("When my love swears that she is made of truth" [Sonnet 138, line 1]) or predicts what he or she is likely to say rather than what has actually been said ("O then vouchsafe me but this loving thought: / Had my friend's muse grown with this growing age" [Sonnet 32, lines 9–10]).

If the lovers remain shadowy in the sonnets addressed to them, so too do the other characters who occasionally appear.[20] We know surprisingly little about the Rival Poet himself, though we learn much about his impact on the speaker's emotions. When Shakespeare chooses to refer to society's reactions to his love, he characterizes it vaguely as "all tongues" (Sonnet 69, line 3) rather than evoking specific figures like the nymphs who berate Astrophil. Time is personified, of course, but it generally functions more as a threat looming over the speaker than as an active character. Even in Sonnet 19, the poet only anticipates the effects of "Devouring time" on his beloved, whereas Spenser is engaged in fighting with the waves (and Donne actually invites his "Busie old foole" into his bedroom). It is revealing, moreover, that the kinds of characters who populate other sequences and create miniature dramas by arguing with the speaker are totally

---

[18] The ambiguity in Sonnet 56 is also noted by Stephen Booth (*Shakespeare's Sonnets*, p. 230).

[19] The citation from Sidney is to *The Poems of Sir Philip Sidney*, ed. W. A. Ringler (Oxford: Oxford Univ. Press, 1962).

[20] The absence of other characters and hence other viewpoints in the *Sonnets* links them to the dramatic monologue. Robert Langbaum argues that that form reflects a belief in the relativity and insubstantiality of truth (*The Poetry of Experience* [London: Chatto and Windus, 1957], pp. 107 ff.); this belief is also characteristic of the speaker in Shakespeare's *Sonnets*. The *Sonnets* deviate from the dramatic monologue, however, in several important respects.

absent from Shakespeare's poems. The ladies who are Laura's companions, the cynical friend who berates Drayton, the court nymphs who criticize Astrophil—no figures like these appear in Shakespeare's *Sonnets*.

Nor is Shakespeare prone to replace them with internalized characters. Though the morality tradition influences his sequence in other ways, only rarely does he depict the conflicts within his speaker as allegorical personages engaged in a confrontation. Many of his sonnets concern a debate between opposing forces such as reason and passion; but very few evoke that debate through allegorical characters like those that figure so prominently in *Astrophil and Stella*.

Most of the sonnets are not narrative, then, in the sense that the speaker is not recounting a story to the reader or to any other implied audience. And they are not dramatic in the sense that we are not witnessing a confrontation that occurs at a specific place and time between a speaker and a particular listener, or even between two clearly distinguished personages within the speaker. Instead, it is the lyric mode that predominates. Some of the poems resemble an internalized meditation, others a letter, others a monologue that the beloved hears but apparently does not respond to.

The soliloquy immediately presents itself as a parallel to and an inspiration for Shakespeare's unusual approach to the sonnet, and in certain respects the comparison is an illuminating one. The speaker in Shakespeare's *Sonnets* often seems to be thinking aloud, to be at once speaking audibly and meditating. But, as the passages that I have cited suggest, in one crucial way the *Sonnets* differ from the soliloquies that are so frequently embedded in their author's plays: the soliloquy normally takes place at a unique moment and is often provoked by a clearly defined event that has preceded it, whereas most of the *Sonnets* are signally lacking in those types of particularization.

## IV

Most readers have found the differences between Shakespeare's sonnets and those of his contemporaries puzzling. Several of the most idiosyncratic qualities of Shakespeare's *Sonnets* stem from the poet's decision to shape so many of them as lyrics in the sense of subjective reflections. Thus his couplets, which fail to provide the reassuring summaries we have been told to expect at the end of a "Shakespearean sonnet," can best be understood if we remember the mode in which Shakespeare is generally writing. As long as we think of the *Sonnets* as dramas or stories, we will be conditioned to expect their couplets (like those of many other sonneteers) to be reasoned statements of objective truths: we will expect them to function rather like the chorus's commentary in a play or the narrator's judgments in a novel. When, however, we recognize that so many of the *Sonnets* are internalized monologues, we are in a position to observe that one purpose of Shakespeare's couplets is to reflect the chaos in the speaker's mind, a purpose to which a couplet that merely summarized the preceding twelve lines would prove inadequate.[21]

---

[21] For a different but not incompatible reading of Shakespeare's couplets, see Stephen Booth's valuable study, *An Essay on Shakespeare's Sonnets* (New Haven: Yale Univ. Press, 1969), pp. 130–43. Booth argues that the couplets, while not resolving all of the ambivalences presented earlier, do bring order to the poem and reassurance to its readers. I contend that such order and reassurance often serves to demonstrate the disorder in the speaker's mind and in his world. Barbara Herrnstein Smith offers an opposing reading of couplets such as the ones

Some of Shakespeare's couplets resolve difficult problems too neatly, an impression intensified by the tidiness and balance inherent in the couplet form. Thus, for instance, "Pity me then, dear friend, and I assure ye, / Ev'n that your pity is enough to cure me" (Sonnet 111, ll. 13–14) does not persuade the reader that the diseases of the heart chronicled in the previous twelve lines can be cured as readily as the speaker hopes. The jingly rhyme increases our sense that the speaker is whistling in the dark, our sense that the couplet is merely another vain attempt to solve his dilemmas.

Other couplets offer responses that seem inappropriate reactions to what has come before. Once again we are more aware of the stresses that make the speaker seek reassurance than of the reassurance that the couplet, if only by virtue of its innately epigrammatic tone, claims to provide. The quatrains of Sonnet 33, for example, draw attention to the wrongs that the poet has suffered at the hands of his beloved:

> Full many a glorious morning have I seen
> Flatter the mountain tops with sovereign eye.
> Kissing with golden face the meadows green,
> Gilding pale streams with heav'nly alchemy,
> Anon permit the basest clouds to ride
> With ugly rack on his celestial face,
> And from the forlorn world his visage hide,
> Stealing unseen to west with this disgrace.
> Ev'n so my sun one early morn did shine,
> With all triumphant splendor on my brow;
> But out alack, he was but one hour mine,
> The region cloud hath masked him from me now.
>
> (ll. 1–12)

Here Shakespeare develops the metaphor of the sun in a way that emphasizes its guilt and hence by implication that of the Friend. Thus "Flatter" (line 2) and "Gilding" (line 4) have connotations that are at the very least ambiguous: flattery can be sycophantic, and gilding can be deceptive. The sort of couplet that these quatrains lead us to expect is something like "I thought our love an everlasting day / And yet my trust thou didst, my love, betray." If we try to read the poem through with this couplet tacked on the end, we find that the uncanonical lines fit the spirit of the poem. If, on the other hand, we read the sonnet through with the couplet that Shakespeare did in fact write—"Yet him for this my love no wit disdaineth; / Suns of the world may stain when heav'n's sun staineth" (ll. 13–14)—we become uneasy. Shakespeare's speaker is trying to fool himself; he takes one conceivable moral from the metaphor (the Friend's betrayal is justified by that of the sun) and neglects the more central one that the reader has been observing (the Friend, like the sun, has been culpably deceptive).

Similarly, the many couplets that offer an unexpectedly pessimistic interpretation of the issues in the poem suggest the impingement of new facts—especially

---

I am analyzing (*Poetic Closure* [Chicago: Univ. of Chicago Press, 1968], esp. pp. 141–45, 227–29). She maintains that some of Shakespeare's couplets represent a satisfying resolution of the speaker's dilemmas; others effect closure by freely admitting to perplexity; and still others fail aesthetically because the poet is unable to solve the problem of concluding a poem that purports to represent the very process of thought.

new apprehensions and doubts—on the speaker's troubled consciousness. Sonnet 92, for instance, ends "But what's so blessèd-fair that fears no blot? / Thou mayst be false, and yet I know it not" (ll. 13–14). Just as an unexpected fear enters the speaker's mind and disturbs the peace he has been attempting to achieve, so an unexpected idea enters the couplet and disturbs its potential function as a neat summary of the preceding quatrains.

All of these couplets are a response to the fundamental paradox that confronted Shakespeare as he wrote the *Sonnets*. The sonnet is, as so many of its readers have remarked, one of the most orderly of literary forms; it is tightly structured and compact. Its couplet is the most orderly and ordering of its elements. No matter what the content of the couplet, in contrast to the syntactical and metrical complexities of the preceding quatrains it will often sound like an easily achieved truism. Frequently, too, the convictions expressed in the couplet will be so epigrammatic that they mirror and intensify the impression of assurance that the very form conveys.

The experiences evoked by Shakespeare's *Sonnets* are, however, unusually tumultuous even in a genre that specializes in psychological torment. As we have seen, in a number of ways his sonnets focus our attention on the speaker's chaotic reactions. We would no more expect a man who is wrestling with the kinds of unresolved contradictions plaguing Shakespeare's speaker to express them in the carefully structured and epigrammatically decisive lines of a couplet than the Elizabethans would have expected a madman in a play to speak in verse. Like the poet in Donne's "The Triple Fool," we assume that grief brought to numbers cannot be so fierce.

Rather than ignoring or struggling to overcome these characteristics of his form, Shakespeare exploits them. The reader comes to view the sentiments in many of the couplets not as objective summaries of the problems that the quatrains have been exploring, but rather as yet another symptom of the anguish and confusion that those problems have caused. As we have seen, those couplets that abruptly reverse the ideas in the quatrains and thus disturb the way the sonnet form generally functions reflect the process by which troubling new thoughts disturb the speaker's emotions. Such couplets are the formal equivalent of the turmoil in the lover's heart. Similarly, those couplets that seem deliberately to oversimplify experience effectively mirror the speaker's vain attempts to resolve the conflicts in his own mind: he often appears to turn to the couplet with relief, to find in its easy absolutes of hope or despair (and the straightforward syntax in which these emotions are expressed) a welcome alternative to the torturing ambivalences with which he has been wrestling (and the tortuous syntax in which he has expressed them).

Though Shakespeare's couplets often resemble soliloquies in their evocations of a mind brooding on experience, those that oversimplify complex realities differ from most Elizabethan soliloquies in the unreliability of their reflections: the speaker is lying to himself and hence to us. On first reading we may be confused or even deceived into taking the lines at face value, much as the figure delivering them is himself confused or deceived. That speaker is in a sense compounding his lies by the very act of presenting them through the vehicle of an epigrammatic couplet. For in the sonnets in question that prosodic form itself functions deceptively: we have come to expect from it, not the unreliable and subjective half-truths or untruths that we may in fact encounter, but unexceptional verities. We may therefore be seduced by the very nature of the couplet form into momentarily believing the speaker's assertions.

Shakespeare's couplets explore and often exemplify an issue with which the whole sequence is very concerned: our predilection for deceiving ourselves and others. The Dark Lady uses her artfulness to lie verbally to her lover ("When my love swears that she is made of truth, / I do believe her though I know she lies" [Sonnet 138, ll. 1–2]), while the Friend's physical appearance is itself a kind of visual lie. The behavior of the Friend and the Dark Lady is contagious in this as in so many other regards, for the speaker himself comes to use art (in many senses of that term) to twist or destroy the truth. Some of the speaker's lies are offered in the service of his lovers, for whom he undertakes the process he describes in Sonnet 35: "Myself corrupting salving thy amiss, / Excusing thy sins more than thy sins are" (ll. 7–8). But the most disturbing of the deceptions in the sequence are the speaker's self-deceptions. By shaping so many of the poems as internalized lyrics, Shakespeare provides a forum for his speaker's repeated attempts to lie to himself. Sometimes a whole poem represents his effort to impose a more comforting but fallacious interpretation on a reality that, as the reader uneasily recognizes, demands a different response. At other times the couplet undercuts the neat but false interpretation in the quatrains. Most often, however, it is the couplet itself that contains the lie. The main reason that several of the most complex sonnets in our language end with couplets that are simple or even simplistic is that the pat answers in those lines demonstrate the habits of self-deception that repeatedly lead the speaker, like his companions, to distort his perceptions, his morals, and his language. In sonnets like these, the couplet form itself becomes a symbol of our cursed rage for order, our tendency to simplify and sanitize our experience, even at the expense of truth.

V

Their emphasis on the lyrical rather than the narrative or dramatic also helps to explain another characteristic of Shakespeare's *Sonnets*: how immediately and how intensely they evoke the speaker's feelings. The reader need channel little or none of his attention to an exposition of a situation or an exploration of the beloved's psyche; he focuses instead on the poet-lover himself. For example, the impact of Sonnet 12, at first glance a comparatively impersonal poem, in fact stems not merely from its vivid depiction of time's ravages but also from its moving evocation of its speaker's sensibility:

> When I do count the clock that tells the time,
> And see the brave day sunk in hideous night,
> When I behold the violet past prime,
> And sable curls all silvered o'er with white,
> When lofty trees I see barren of leaves,
> Which erst from heat did canopy the herd,
> And summer's green all girded up in sheaves
> Borne on the bier with white and bristly beard;
> Then of thy beauty do I question make
> That thou among the wastes of time must go,
> Since sweets and beauties do themselves forsake,
> And die as fast as they see others grow,
>     And nothing 'gainst time's scythe can make defense
>     Save breed to brave him when he takes thee hence.

In one sense this sonnet is a carefully documented argument. The quatrains, which present a series of facts marshaled to support the thesis in the sestet, function as part of a syllogism (all sweets and beauties die; you yourself are a sweet and beauty; therefore you will die). But in presenting this case the poem repeatedly directs our attention to the mind brooding on it: like Marvell's "To His Coy Mistress," this lyric is as much concerned with the speaker's thoughts about death as with ways of combatting that inevitable but unendurable fact. The first five lines contain no fewer than four verbs referring to the speaker's processes of cognition ("do count" . . . "see" . . . "behold" . . . "see"), three of which are preceded by the personal pronoun "I." The anaphora in lines one and three ("When I") further heightens the emphasis on the speaker's sensibility. "Then of thy beauty do I question make" (l. 9), which follows these two quatrains, contains in microcosm the characteristics that we have been noting, for one may gloss those words in two ways: (1) I ask you a question ("thy beauty" functioning as synecdoche in this interpretation) or (2) in my own mind I raise a question about your beauty. Even while communicating with the beloved, then, the speaker also seems to be communing with himself. As he considers the beloved's behavior, therefore, the reader is also led to concentrate on how that behavior affects the speaker.[22]

While a thorough affective study of the *Sonnets* would demand a separate essay, one important truth about the reader's responses is clear: the primary effect of the lyrical mode of these poems is to intensify our identification with the speaker.[23] And one reason our identification becomes so deep is that these sonnets are far more universal than those by any other English poet (with perhaps the interesting exception of Wyatt). As we have observed, they are not linked to particular dates or seasons or places. More important, because the events and situations to which Shakespeare alludes are presented only sketchily, we can readily relate the *Sonnets* to our own lives; we are not conscious of local details that do not conform to our own experiences.

Above all, we identify closely with the speaker because the emotions and reactions we experience when reading the poems are very similar to the emotions and reactions the poems are about. Like the speaker, we are confused by ambiguities in language and in the situations language is exploring. When we read Spenser's *Amoretti* VIII ("More then most faire, full of the liuing fire") we have few doubts about the judgments being passed on the lady; when we read Sonnet 94, however, we have, and I suspect are meant to have, few certainties. We are forced to keep thinking about the issues being raised, to keep re-examining the charged and ambiguous words of the poem.

Like Shakespeare's speaker, his readers try to find oases of order and stability in the tumultuous world of the *Sonnets*. The speaker reaches out for the overly simple answers expressed in his couplets in a way that is not unlike the way we reach out for a reordering of the *Sonnets* that would lessen their complexities and explain their ambiguities. If it is true that the *Sonnets* are the record of

---

[22] The line also exemplifies a characteristic that I argue is central to the sonnet: even the first of the glosses on it that I suggest describes what is apparently a repeated process of asking the Friend a question. The sonnet does not set up a scene or recount a particular situation.

[23] Some recent studies of the *Sonnets* use the techniques of affective criticism and in so doing note similarities between reader and speaker. See Booth, *An Essay on Shakespeare's Sonnets*, esp. pp. 110–15; and Roger Fowler, "Language and the Reader," in Fowler, ed., *Style and Structure*, pp. 79–122.

meditations, it is equally true that they encourage meditation in their reader far more than most poetry does. Since we are not offered neat answers, we, like the speaker, keep brooding on the questions that have been raised.

## VI

The nature of Shakespeare's *Sonnets* reflects the nature of the experience they evoke. Most of them are lyric rather than narrative or dramatic because they concern a world in which narrative and dramatic modes would be inappropriate. One reason so few of these poems reflect a chronological sequence of events is that their speaker is trapped in brooding rather than acting or even being acted on. His mind is tormented with calamities that the future may bring (his beloved will betray him, Time will destroy even this most precious of mortals) or that the present, unbeknownst to him, may already hold (his two friends may have already been unfaithful to him, the beloved may be morally stained). And these calamities are rendered more painful by the fact that the speaker is powerless, whether to prevent those disasters that the future may hold or to be certain that those the present may contain have not in fact come to pass:

> Yet eyes this cunning want to grace their art;
> They draw but what they see, know not the heart.
>                      (Sonnet 24, ll. 13–14)

> And even thence thou wilt be stol'n, I fear.
>                      (Sonnet 48, l. 13)

In dramas, including the miniature version of drama that a sonnet can embody, characters often commit definite actions; in narratives, even fourteen-line narratives, usually definite events occur. But, as the passages above suggest, the dominant mood of Shakespeare's *Sonnets* is fearful anticipation and troubling suspicion, not clear-cut events. Narrative and dramatic modes would not have been as suited to evoking such a milieu.

Just as Shakespeare's decision to omit certain narrative and dramatic elements from his *Sonnets* aptly expresses his speaker's painful inaction, so it expresses the uncertainties suffered by that speaker and by the reader who is so intimately involved with him. If presented within the intense and concentrated form of the sonnet, both the narrative and the dramatic modes tend to suggest moral and epistemological certainties. When sonnet writers use mythological allegories, for example, they generally do so in order to make some simple but significant point about love; Cupid's tricks may remind us that love is deceptive, and Venus' fickleness that women are untrustworthy. Similarly, in narrating an event involving a lover and his mistress, sonneteers usually establish some important facts about the participants, such as the lady's unremitting and unremorseful chastity. And when sonnets imitate a dialogue between opponents, the two figures generally argue neatly antithetical positions. A victory for one position or the other, or possibly a synthesis of both, is achieved by the end of the sonnet. Even if the poet-lover himself remains trapped in his moral dilemma, a sequence relying extensively on narrative and dramatic modes can establish important verities. Thus *Astrophil and Stella* as a whole documents truths about Neoplatonism that Astrophil can only imperfectly grasp.

In so frequently avoiding the narrative and dramatic in his *Sonnets*, Shakespeare declines to provide the kinds of ethical truths and moral certainties that those modes can generate. He is achieving in formal terms the types of moral confusion he is exploring thematically. Just as the experience of the reader mirrors that of the speaker in these poems, so form mirrors content to an extent unusual in even the greatest art.

THOMAS M. GREENE

# Anti-hermeneutics: The Case of Shakespeare's Sonnet 129

A scholarly contention has recently re-arisen over the editing of Shakespeare's *Sonnets* that focuses conveniently a complex of perennial problems, not only affecting the editing of Shakespeare or any other author but also adumbrating vaster questions of historical understanding. In his useful, important, and exhaustive edition with commentary on the *Sonnets,* Stephen Booth takes vigorous issue with a well-known essay by Robert Graves and Laura Riding, "A Study in Original Punctuation and Spelling." This essay, published in its original form over fifty years ago, argues against the modernization of Shakespeare by comparing the original and re-edited texts of a single sonnet, 129, "Th'expense of Spirit in a waste of shame." By explicating the allegedly richer, more open, more polysemous quarto version and by showing the reductive flatness imposed by modernization, Graves and Riding call into question what they call the "perversely stupid" habits of most modern editors. Professor Booth, no mean polemicist himself, labels this essay "an exercise in irresponsible editorial restraint" and devotes more than five large pages to disposing of its arguments. His basic position is that "an editor distorts the sonnet more for a modern reader by maintaining the 1609 text than he would if he modernized its spelling and punctuation."[1]

No one can deny the enduring importance of this contention between, on the one hand, two practicing poets writing a long time ago as radical critics beyond the pale of the scholarly guild and on the other hand a gifted contemporary member of the guild, not lacking in professional independence and even irreverence, but in this dispute adopting something close to a hard-line conservative position. But in describing Booth as the conservative one may already falsify the issue, since Graves and Riding would argue that they are the true conservatives, preserving Shakespeare's original words and meanings against the tendentious contaminators of the intervening centuries. Perhaps one useful step toward resolving the quarrel would be to ask which side has the better right to be called conservative in the best, most positive sense.

Clearly this inexhaustible question will not be settled simply by an appeal to Sonnet 129, but a glance at the two versions competing for our attention could be instructive. Booth provides both the quarto text and, facing it throughout, a compromise modernization that represents what he calls a "mid-point" between the punctuation and spelling of the original and modern directive adaptations.

Th'expence of Spirit in a waste of shame
Is lust in action, and till action, lust                                     2
Is periurd, murdrous, blouddy full of blame,
Sauage, extreame, rude, cruell, not to trust,                        4
Inioy'd no sooner but dispised straight,
Past reason hunted, and no sooner had                               6
Past reason hated as a swollowed bayt,
On purpose layd to make the taker mad.                             8
Made In pursut and in possession so,
Had, having, and in quest, to have extreame,                     10
A blisse in proofe and proud and very wo,
Before a ioy proposd behind a dreame,                               12
    All this the world well knowes yet none knowes well,
    To shun the heaven that leads men to this hell.               14


Th'expense of spirit in a waste of shame
Is lust in action, and till action lust                                     2
Is perjured, murd'rous, bloody, full of blame,
Savage, extreme, rude, cruel, not to trust,                        4
Enjoyed no sooner but despisèd straight,
Past reason hunted, and no sooner had,                             6
Past reason hated as a swallowed bait,
On purpose laid to make the taker mad;                            8
Mad in pursuit, and in possession so,
Had, having, and in quest to have, extreme,                      10

A bliss in proof, and proved, a very woe,
Before, a joy proposed, behind, a dream.                          12
   All this the world well knows, yet none knows well
   To shun the heav'n that leads men to this hell.        14

What are the main differences? Booth supplies a comma after
"blouddy" in line 3 and another at the end of line 6 where the
quarto has nothing; at the end of line 8 he substitutes a semicolon
for the quarto's period; together with virtually all editors he emends
the first word of line 9 from "Made" to "Mad," adds a comma after
"pursut" in line 9, and shifts the third comma in line 10. In lines
11 and 12 the surgery is radical: in 11 two commas are added and
"a" is substituted for "and"; in 12 three commas are added and a
period at the end replaces the quarto's only comma. Finally in line
13, a comma is shifted from the end to the middle. The spelling is
modernized, with apostrophes inserted in "murdrous" and
"heaven." If this text does represent a midpoint in editorial tact,
we're left to wonder what further changes are possible, but in fact
the text from *The Oxford Book of English Verse* quoted by Graves and
Riding is still more freely repunctuated.

   This is not the occasion to analyze thoroughly the semantic
transformations, some subtle and some obtrusive, effected by the
modern version. But if one stands back and contemplates the two
texts as a set, a few impressions emerge immediately. The revised
version is undeniably more accessible. Assuming with Booth that
the Jacobean reader found few obstacles to reading the poem and
that the modern reader should be assisted to enjoy a similar facility
so far as possible, then unquestionably the revised version does
extend us that assistance. It smoothes over almost all the superficial
perplexities in this poem of anguish and despair, this terrible sonnet. For example it attaches the third quatrain to the first two, thus
allowing all three to form one coherent sentence, rather than attaching the third quatrain to the couplet as the quarto does, a little
mysteriously. The new version helps us to understand the first word
of line 9, which here simply echoes the last word of the previous
line—"mad"; in the quarto version one's eye has to move further
back in line 8 to the verb "to make" and then understand "Made" in

the next line as an altered form of it. "Mad" clearly assists the
reader, as does the substitution of "a" for "and"; the line in its old
version *could* mean, as Graves and Riding point out, that lust is
both bliss and woe at once, both "in proof" and "provd," during its
gratification and afterwards. But that meaning has to be worked for.
The revised line 12 imposes a reassuring tidiness on the puzzling
original, where we have to struggle to see how lust could be a joy
which is "proposd," envisioned, behind a dream. Again the original
*could* make sense, but not easily. Throughout the modern version
supplies us with the *facilior lectio,* and if that is what it takes for our
reading to approach the Jacobeans', then undoubtedly the quarto
text can only be regarded as unsuitable. "In 129," writes Booth,
"modern punctuation gains 'sheer facility in reading' and denies a
modern reader nothing that Shakespeare's contemporaries would
have perceived."[2]

Surely for better or worse the modernization does more than
that. It really acts as a shield for the modern reader, a shield extended to protect him from the problematic contingencies of the
original. It protects him from worrying whether the punctuation in
front of him corresponds to Shakespeare's actual intent or only his
compositor's—whether in fact it corresponds to any knowledgeable
intent rather than an ignorant man's caprice. The altered text does
certainly correspond to a knowledgeable intent, its editor's, and in
this certainty we take comfort. We're protected as well from the
strenuous effort of groping unassisted for those shifting, floating,
ambiguous relations of clause to clause, phrase to phrase, that constitute one of the outstanding rhetorical features of the *Sonnets* and
which Booth himself stresses. Thus in the altered text we don't have
to grope for the elusive, possibly nonexistent connection between
the third quatrain and the couplet that would justify their separation by a mere comma after line 12. But should we really have this
protection? Do we truly want it? Don't we ultimately want, or
shouldn't we want, the actual mysterious artifact history has handed
down to us with all its built-in puzzlements and uncertainties?
Some of these surely the Jacobean reader wrestled with also. What
*did* he do with that "Made" in line 9? Why should we be spared his

perplexities if his experience is the norm we're expected to approach?

Most decisively and significantly the altered text shields us from that curious Renaissance sense of grammar that fails to isolate a self-contained sentence from its successor. Take one of the most assertive and distinct and self-enclosed affirmations in the *Sonnets:* "Let me not to the marriage of true mindes / Admit impediments." That affirmation is denied in the quarto the full stop it deserves according to our logic: ". . . Admit impediments, love is not love . . ." Here at least the practice is too common to blame only on the compositor, and even if it were the compositor's alone, we have no reason to believe that it troubled the Jacobean reader. We are forced to recognize that the sense of syntactic closure, the sense of declarative completeness, the very status of the affirmation during the Jacobean period violate our grammar and our logic. This troubling recognition would also be spared us if we confined our reading to the altered text. Even if it were true that modern punctuation denies us nothing a Jacobean would have *perceived,* it does deny us something crucial about the presuppositions he brought to the printed page: it denies us something about his mind-set. Modernization in this respect is less conservative because it fails to preserve an important element of Shakespeare's semiotic world. It not only conceals the mysteries, the contingencies, the authentic riddles truly present for us in the original; it conceals those offenses to our logic that historical distance will always impose.

That distance makes itself felt equally in the puzzles posed by individual words. In Sonnet 129 the opening phrase immediately presents a kind of hermeneutic hurdle. The expression "expence of Spirit" sustains the fundamental metaphor of the sequence linking economics with emotion and sexuality. The constant concern with husbandry, with cost-accounting, with thrift and profligacy, with a friendship too dear for one's possessing, with bonds and terms and leases—this repetitive series of analogies organizes the *Sonnets,* and there is nothing a priori in this figural pattern that is necessarily inaccessible to a twentieth-century reader. The metaphor begins to lose us only when the economic implications of "expence" are taken literally at the physiological level. The sexual act is really impoverishing only if one holds the medieval and Renaissance belief that it shortens a man's life. If, in place of the restorative, therapeutic release our post-Freudian society perceives, one attributes to sex a literal expenditure of vitality, then the struggle between the sexes takes on a crude economic reality, and we begin to understand the linkage made by the Wyf of Bath. She ends her tale by praying for "housebondes meeke, yonge, and fressh abedde" while calling down a plague on "olde and angry niggardes of dispence."[3] In Sonnets 1–126 of Shakespeare's sequence, the bourgeois poet speaks for the values of husbandry, as befits his class, in order prudently to correct the failures of this art assigned to that social class of "unthrifts" which includes the friend. It is true that the conduct associated with good husbandry shifts radically; if in Sonnets 1–17 it means marriage, and solitude is "unprovident," by Sonnet 95 ("They that haue powre to hurt . . .") only the solitary can "husband natures ritches from expence," with a stinginess not calculated to please the Wyf of Bath. In Sonnet 129 the young man's profligacy is less at issue than, one presumes, the bourgeois speaker's among others. The phrase "th'expence of Spirit" means several things, including the implication that the speaker has been *unclassed* by lust, that he is now guilty of that aristocratic waste he had attempted in so many preceding poems to moderate. In yielding to lust he is yielding to a literally self-destructive extravagance, which heretofore he has followed tradition in charging to his social superiors.[4] This biological as well as sociological undoing of the self, implicit in Shakespeare's word "expence," remains an abstraction for us even if we catch its resonance. We might begin to recapture that reference to personal ontology by taking seriously the lost implications of such words as "dissolute" and "dissipated."

Modernized spelling also helps to conceal the different status of the word itself in a prelexicographical culture. The quarto calls attention to the word "Spirit" by capitalizing it, a stress modern editors tend to drop. The word is not easily defined in any case. Glosses for "Spirit" suggested by Booth and other editors include "physical vigor," "mental energy," "spiritual essence," "life force," "bodily fluid," "penis erectus," and "the subtle vapor supposed to be contained in the heart and needed for generation." This gives seven distinct glosses which the modern reader experiences as a supersaturated plethora of competing meanings. But it is unlikely that the prelexicographical reader felt this kind of division and subdivision; it is more likely that he or she read the word "Spirit" as a multifaceted unity we can only try to imagine. The polyvalent word before the era of dictionaries could not simply be felt as the sum of an indefinite series of parallel definitions; it must have been apprehended as a veined monolith. It was not yet reducible to a vertical list of semidiscrete equivalents. It must have remained somehow a simultaneous whole which nonetheless presented multiple aspects to be perceived as context indicated. Not only do the lost meanings of a word elude us but the very process of their fusion within a single signifier.

One peculiarly elusive word appears at the openings of lines 2 and 3. One of the most deceptive signifiers in the code of any remote text is the copula: deceptive because to the naked eye it looks to be the most unchanging and the most transparent of all parts of speech. But in fact the copula, underlying implicitly or explicitly most metaphorization and predication, is the part of speech most sensitive to historically shifting intuitions of relationship and reality. It is rooted in each culture's, each era's metaphysical and epistemological assumptions—not necessarily the assumptions spelt out discursively but those silently shared and invoked in poetry as in ordinary speech. Fully to understand the force of a copula in a given text is to understand a good deal of the text and the semiotic universe that nourished it. Shakespeare's Sonnet 129 is largely controlled by those two copulas appearing at the opening of the second and third lines. The second of these is the more important, since so much of what follows depends on it; it is also the more mysterious. To begin to understand the force of "is" in line 3, we have to decide whether its subject, "lust," the last word in line 2, is passion working within a given individual; or rather the lustful individual himself; or rather a partially allegorized Lust, a sort of personification out of Spenser, or rather the experience of gratification. If we read "this hell," the last words of the sonnet, to summarize all that has been predicated about lust, then we have to extend the meaning of that word to the object of male desire, since the word "hell" in subsequent sonnets will clearly acquire a specific anatomical reference.[5] "Lust" thus has four or five potential meanings that fade in and out or reinforce each other a little confusingly as the reader moves through the series of participles, nouns, and clauses that maintain the predication apparently through line 12. All the rich, disturbing intricacy of meaning hangs upon that "is." Is lust "murdrous" because it destroys the individual who feels it, or is he led to feel murderous toward the person he desires? Or toward himself? Is lust "cruell" toward other feelings and traits, virtues and vices, in a kind of shadowy psychomachia, or toward human beings? Are we dimly invited to half-imagine some hypostasized embodiment, some furious naked "salvage man" spotted with gore, both hunted and hated? How does that potential predication jibe with lust as bliss and woe in line 11? There the "salvage man" disappears and lust "is" the feelings stemming from the end of its quest. Is it possible for so many alternative predications to be jammed into one uncertain copula? As we read we have to keep revision or recombining our notions of just how the signifier "lust is," can be something. We strain to grasp the mysterious equations implied in that deceptively innocent bridge. Only if we are puzzled by it will we begin to unravel its secrets. Booth's argument against distortion obscures the need for puzzlement. We need to register the actual warping, which from our perspective is there, before we can set out to deal with it. The distortion in the case of the copula is particularly insidious because modernization leaves it untouched.

"No editor," Booth writes, "is likely to succeed perfectly in accommodating a modern reader and a Renaissance text to one another, but that is no reason to do nothing."[6] The question is what one *can* do if one measures the full distance between the two. To do what Booth and most editors do risks a sham accommodation with the past which in fact increases our estrangement from it. How does the editor avoid that trap? To begin to answer this question satisfactorily one really needs a theory of understanding; one has to ask how a reader would evade the trap. One has to bracket the editorial problem and consider the larger problems of hermeneutic theory; one has to reflect on the process of understanding any remote text. The growing body of hermeneutic speculation is by no means irrelevant to the practical decisions of editors, just as the consequences of their decisions are not irrelevant to theory. The crucial question focused by Booth's polemic is not whether we want original or altered texts—both are necessary for different purposes—but rather how and to what degree a modern reader's experience might resemble that of its first readers.

No linguist would dissent from Sapir's formulation.

> Language moves down time in a current of its own making. It has a drift. . . . Nothing is perfectly static. Every word, every grammatical element, every locution, every sound and accent is a slowly changing configuration, moulded by the invisible and impersonal drift that is the life of language.[7]

This drift was first discovered for the modern world by Dante and the philologists of the Italian Renaissance. Lorenzo Valla insisted on the central dilemma of anachronistic reading with all the energy of his ferocious intelligence. Changing referents require changing terms: *nova res novum vocabulum flagitat.* But referents and words change at varying rates of speed. Language ideally requires a continuity which neither words nor things possess.

The fact of historical estrangement, historical solitude, is doubtless most fully grasped by those like Valla who spend their careers contending with it. The pathos of estrangement has never been evoked more beautifully than by one of the heroes of modern philology, Wilamowitz.

> The tradition yields us only ruins. The more closely we test and examine them, the more clearly we see how ruinous they are; and out of ruins no whole can be built. The tradition is dead; our task is to revivify life that has passed away. We know that ghosts cannot speak until they have drunk blood; and the spirits which we evoke demand the blood of our hearts. We give it to them gladly; but if they then abide our question, something from us has entered into them.[8]

A little of ourselves will always enter into the ghosts we force to speak. If, as Heidegger suggests, we are what we understand to be, then what we understand to be will already be a part of us. The conversation with our classics will always be partial; we can never altogether escape interpretive anachronism. "Which of your Hesterdays Mean Ye to Morra?": that Joycean song haunts the historian of meanings. It haunted Theodore Adorno: "Nothing more is given to philosophy than fleeting, disappearing traces in the riddle-figures of that which exists and their astonishing entwinings."[9] We can love from the past only that which we have begun by misunderstanding and continue to understand gropingly. Perhaps this is why we love the shard, the ruin, the blurred hieroglyph as we love those broken, discolored, weather-beaten statues, hieratic and withdrawn, standing at the portal of a cathedral.

One can approach the central hermeneutic problem through the experience of the classroom. The teacher is compelled by his role to perform a kind of activity analogous to textual modernization. He is obliged to translate, to find contemporary equivalents and glosses for his students in order to make a remote text "accessible." He can only present a literary work to them in their terms or in terms they can follow. In doing this the teacher has literally no choice. But if he is at all self-conscious, he knows that his glosses and his explanations are subtly or palpably inaccurate. How will he gloss the word "Spirit" at the opening of Sonnet 129? He has no means of conveying the different feeling for syntactic closure of the English Renaissance. And what happens in the classroom is only a heightened imitation of what happens to the solitary reader in his study; he too inevitably translates into his own dialect. He appropriates, anachronizes, no matter how deep his historical consciousness. If we read Sonnet 129 in its quarto version, we try to organize its apparent disorder and soften its offences to our mind set. To begin to read any unfamiliar text is to try to make it less strange, make it new. In Norman N. Holland's Freudian vocabulary, the act of reading involves " a kind of fusion or introjection based on oral wishes to incorporate."[10]

The act of appropriation has been described more than once in hermeneutic theory. Hans-Georg Gadamer calls it *Aneignung,* and Paul Ricoeur uses the French word *appropriation.* In the thought of each it has a positive resonance; ideally for each it leads to self-knowledge. For Ricoeur appropriation occurs when "the interpretation of a text is completed by the self-interpretation of a subject who henceforth understands himself better or differently or even begins to understand himself."[11] Gadamer quotes with approval Hegel's statement that *Aneignung*—appropriation or assimilation—"is the fundamental fact of being alive." But his own hermeneutics invests the term with a somewhat different significance. Gadamer's analysis of the entire process of understanding is very rich and sometimes profound. His perception of its historicity, its "situatedness," his critique of nineteenth-century historicism, his analysis of the mutual questioning between reader and text, his quest for a dialogue across time—these and other contributions to hermeneutic thought are welcome and valuable. But other elements of his theory raise doubts about its viability as a whole system.

According to Gadamer, understanding begins when something other, something outside addresses us. Something, such as a text from the past, asserts its own validity, which is distant from our own. In responding to this stimulus we are led properly to an awareness of our own prejudices and can correct our own preunderstandings through a circular process which is not vicious but productive. The proper goal of the hermeneutic encounter for Gadamer is a blending or fusion of horizons, a *horizontverschmelzung*. This occurs when the interpreter widens his own horizon of experience to include that of the text, reaches an intuitive understanding of the questions the text poses and answers through the common medium of language; he thus enlarges his own personal horizon, perceives it afresh, and gains insight into both worlds now blended into one. This experience is possible because both interpreter and text belong to a single continuous tradition.

> Historical consciousness is aware of its own otherness and hence distinguishes the horizon of tradition from its own. On the other hand, it is itself . . . only something laid over a continuing tradition, and hence it immediately recombines what it has distinguished in order, in the unity of the historical horizon that it thus acquires, to become again one with itself.[12]

This act of combining followed by a reassuring return to selfhood is so smooth because the tradition for Gadamer is in fact so "continuing"; it seems to be free of all revolts, gaps, leaps, and disjunctures. The concept of tradition becomes an instrument to tame, sweeten, and abstract history, which now appears purely unbroken and unalienating. It is true that Gadamer speaks of a tension between the two horizons. But functionally this tension counts for less than the blending mediation. Distance in time, Gadamer writes, is "not a yawning abyss, but is filled with the continuity of custom and tradition, in the light of which all that is handed down presents itself to us." Elsewhere he speaks of tradition as "an unbroken stream."[13] But tradition as we know it may not be a healing, sacred river but a polluting Love Canal which carries dangerous flotsam. Tradition as a stream has many tributaries, falls, and blockages. It runs less smoothly than this account suggests, and the history of interpretation as we know it reveals the defenses interpreters have had to raise against the threat of tradition. What if the tension between horizons proves to be intolerable? Allegoresis developed partly as one defense against unwelcome meanings suspected in past texts; we in our day have abandoned allegoresis for a more economical defense, ironization. If a given text, say More's *Utopia*, asserts too emphatically its estrangement from us, we shield ourselves by reading it ironically. Frank Kermode has recently shown the affinities of interpretation not with a fresh openness but with an enclosing institutionalism, with a group of insiders reluctant to open their gateway and reveal their arcane knowledge.[14] Graves and Riding, we remember, wrote very consciously as outsiders against one form of institutional protectionism.

The actual status of the original text emerges from Gadamer's formulation a little blurred.

> The true historical object is not an object at all, but the unity of the one [the object] and the other [true historical thinking taking account of its own historicality], a relationship in which exist both the reality of history and the reality of historical understanding.[15]

If the true object is not an object, then it is difficult to see how it can form half of a higher unity. What seems to emerge from this sentence as actually real is a historical understanding lacking a solid thing to understand. For Gadamer the text has no existence independent of the tradition in which it is understood; in effect he denies the text an original historical situatedness such as he claims for the interpreter. This denial calls into question the equality of the dialogue as well as the tension between horizons. Essentially the text is robbed of its own particular horizon. The supposed dialogue lacks symmetry because only the interpreter's governing assumptions are called into play, not those of the text. The context of each work is not its original, living semiotic matrix but rather a series of posthumous readings. Gadamer in his own way wants to protect us from our solitude. The resulting concept of appropriation fails to isolate its potential self-deception. His account of understanding blurs a little the central problem of interpretation: language changes, modes of experience change, texts become estranged, and yet the contact with texts in their authentic otherness would provide precious knowledge and self-knowledge, would save us from hermeneutic narcissism.

My own plea would be for a moment in the process of understanding which no hermeneutics has authorized. I would ask for a moment which deliberately tries to frustrate appropriation, which tries to restore the work to its own world of meanings perceived in all their distant strangeness. Simply to draw the work to ourselves, wilfully, voraciously, is to dim that clarification which contact with otherness does truly bring. Let us for a moment refuse to appropriate; let us try, however unsuccessfully, to return the work to its own mysterious alienation. Instead of clutching it too quickly, we should recognize its isolation and vulnerability, recognize what deceives our expectations, offends our proprieties, refuses dialogue, will not abide our questions. We need to measure without blinking the pathos of estrangement, the ruptures of history, the blockages of tradition.[16] It is true that this act of distancing the work is itself subject to the distortions of our historical moment. But if our distortions are to be progressively corrected, they will not be affected by a bland tradition but by perceived interuptions of tradition. Let us try for a moment to overcome that force which Heidegger calls "averageness" (*Durchschnittlichkeit*) and which, he says, smoothly suppresses every kind of spiritual priority. "Overnight," he writes, "everything that is primordial gets glossed over as something that has long been well known. . . . Every secret loses its force."[17] Let us try to recover that sense of the work's forceful secrecy. Let us for a moment refuse to understand.

The response to that moment can take one of two directions. One alternative would be to find a kind of freedom in this impasse, call the rupture radical and total, and play with the flotsam of the past as context-free, neutral counters to be juggled at will. This response would free the interpreter from any responsibility to a vestige of original meaning, which, according to Jacques Derrida, will undergo a loss inherent in the character of all utterances. One can then appropriate with a vengeance, liberated from all constraints; one might even hope with Derrida to take a kind of Nietzschean joy in an endless innocent game of free associations. The one thing excluded from such play would of course be the stimulus of contact as well as the risk; there could be no dangerous impact which would challenge and conceivably clarify. The work interpreted would be an ink-blot test in which the interpreter would reveal over and over only his own obsessions without understanding them, lacking any transcendental key to make sense of his private musings. Derrida's own discussions of texts by Plato, Descartes, Leibniz, Rousseau, Hegel, and others do not in fact play with them freely and "innocently," but tend rather to subject these texts to precise and often brilliant analysis which assumes personal time-bound authorship.[18] Everyone doubtless has a right to his own avocations, but some will be moved to ask, as Shakespeare asks his friend: "Why dost thou spend, upon thy selfe thy beauties legacy?" For some, the pleasure of the "profitless usurer" quickly loses its charm.

The alternative to this hermeneutic play with free associations would be much more austere. This course would try to avoid that self-indulgence as it avoided the opposite mirror indulgence that denies the work's estrangement. This hermeneutic would accept estrangement as a given and then search out patiently some bridge, some passage, some common term which might help to mitigate it. On this basis one would suspect all modernized versions and easy assimilations, one would settle for less than full understanding, but one would accept a responsibility for a partial interpretive correspondence to an intrinsic meaning or complex of meanings. One would think not of appropriating but of working out a reading appropriate to those intrinsic meanings. One would conceive of a text coming to us bearing its own intentionality—not the intentionality of its creator but simply its own patent design for a certain kind of use. A chair exists to be sat on; a text exists to be read and read *appropriately,* within certain limits of potential response. It carries with it coded directions or provocations to the mind, and certain types of mental responses befit a given text more closely than others. The task of the reader is to ascertain the experience or the activity most perfectly corresponding to the text's coded instigations. In the case of a remote text—and no formula can specify how remote is "remote"—the directions or instigations will always be blurred, but one accepts a need to begin deciphering them. In the case of a mathematical equation one can think of the directions to the mind as *commands* to perform certain operations; in the case of a poem one can think of the directions rather as *orientations.* To interpret, Ricoeur writes suggestively, is to set out toward the *orient* of the text. To think of interpreting as an appropriate response to coded but blurred directions is not to limit the potential wealth of suggestion of a literary work, but it is to rule out the expense of spirit in self-indulgent anachronism. The wealth of significance has to stem from the work's concrete historical situation as we can best divine it.[19] If it does this, then we may gain a small accretion of self-knowledge. In the case of Shakespeare's sonnets, this would include—what can be gathered from most Renaissance poems—the limiting regularity, the hypertrophy of logic in our assumptions about words and syntax; in the case of Sonnet 129, this might include an altered view of the pallid, therapeutic sexuality of our post-Freudian era, Eliot's "natural, life-giving, cheery automatism,"[20] which is not of course to be found in Freud. But these crude indications of acquired self-consciousness badly approximate the gradual, profound growth of understanding whereby we slowly and fumblingly come to situate ourselves in history.[21]

The first, simple, and difficult act of reading is to see the remote text as truly remote. To begin to measure its removal from us, to intuit its privacy and specificity, to make out the density of its aura, one has to restore it to its original silence. The text comes to us as a shard, out of its own quietude and distance; by disencumbering it of its secular impediments, by stripping it of its false modernity, we release it to withdraw from us back into its own universe of meanings, cruelly and beautifully back where we can gauge its strangeness. In that strangeness begins true knowledge, the true partial knowledge that history allows us. We can begin to read only after granting the text the seclusion and the particularity of its unique inflection.

## NOTES

1. The essay by Graves and Riding first appeared under the title "William Shakespeare and E. E. Cummings" in *A Survey of Modernist Poetry* (London: Heinemann, 1927) and in revised form was later included in Graves's *The Common Asphodel* (London: Hamilton, 1949) under the title "A Study in Original Punctuation and Spelling." The reply to Graves and Riding appears on pp. 447–52 of *Shakespeare's Sonnets*, edited with analytic commentary by Stephen Booth (New Haven: Yale University Press, 1980). The passages quoted appear on p. 447.

2. Booth, *Sonnets*, p. 450. Booth explains and defends his editorial policy on p. ix of his preface as follows:

> My primary purpose in the present edition is to provide a text that will give a modern reader as much as I can resurrect of a Renaissance reader's experience of the 1609 Quarto; it is, after all, the sonnets we have and not some hypothetical originals that we value. I have adopted no editorial principle beyond that of trying to adapt a modern reader—with his assumptions about idiom, spelling, and punctuation—and the 1609 text to one another. . . . Both my text and my commentary are determined by what I think a Renaissance reader would have thought as he moved from line to line and sonnet to sonnet in the Quarto. I make no major substantial emendations and few minor ones. It might therefore seem reasonable to reprint the Quarto text alone and simply comment on that, but the effects of almost four centuries are such that a modern reader faced with the

Quarto text sees something that is effectively very different from what a seventeenth-century reader saw.

In modernizing spelling and punctuation I have taken each poem individually and tried to find a mid-point between following the punctuation and spelling of the Quarto text (which modern readers, accustomed to logically and semantically directive punctuation and spelling, are inclined to misinterpret) and modern directive spelling and punctuation (which often pays for its clarity by sacrificing a considerable amount of a poem's substance and energy). In each case I have tried to find the least distorting available compromise. Sometimes no compromise is satisfactory, and I describe the probable operation of a line or quatrain in a note.

3. Lines 1258–63. See also "The Shipman's Tale," 7.170 ff.

4. The considerable reality behind the nobility's reputation for extravagance is detailed in chapter 10 of Lawrence Stone's *Crisis of the Aristocracy, 1558–1641* (Oxford: Oxford University Press, Clarendon Press, 1965).

5. See, e.g., Sonnet 144, line 12.

6. Booth, *Sonnets*, p. 448.

7. Edward Sapir, *Language* (New York: Harcourt, Brace and World, 1949), pp. 150, 171.

8. Ulrich von Wilamowitz-Moellendorff, *Greek Historical Writing and Apollo*, trans. G. Murray (Oxford: Oxford University Press, Clarendon Press, 1908), p. 26.

9. T. W. Adorno, *Moments Musicaux* (1930), quoted by Susan Buck-Morss, *The Origins of Negative Dialectics* (New York: The Free Press, 1977), p. 52.

10. Norman N. Holland, *The Dynamics of Literary Response* (New York: Norton, 1975), p. 104.

11. French text in Paul Ricoeur, "Qu'est-ce-qu'un texte?" in *Hermeneutik und Dialektik*, ed. R. Bubner et al. (Tübingen: Mohr, 1970), 2:194–95.

12. Hans-Georg Gadamer, *Truth and Method* (New York: Seabury, 1975), p. 273. German text in Gadamer, *Wahrheit und Methode* (Tübingen: Mohr, 1960), p. 290:

Das historische Bewusstsein ist sich seiner eigenen Andersheit bewusst und hebt daher den Horizont der Überlieferung von dem eigenen Horizont ab. Andererseits aber ist es selbst nur... wie eine Überlagerung über einer fortwirkenden Tradition, und daher nimmt es das voneinander Abgehobene sogleich wieder zusammen, um in der

Einheit des geschichtlichen Horizontes, den es sich so erwirbt, sich
mit sich selbst zu vermitteln.

13. Gadamer, *Truth and Method,* pp. 264–65, 262.

14. Frank Kermode, *The Genesis of Secrecy: On the Interpretation of Narrative* (Cambridge: Harvard University Press, 1979).

15. *Truth and Method,* p. 267. German text in *Wahrheit und Methode.*
p. 283: "Der wahre historische Gegenstand ist kein Gegenstand, sondern
die Einheit dieses Einen und Anderen, ein Verhältnis, in dem die
Wirklichkeit der Geschichte ebenso wie die Wirklichkeit des geschichtlichen Verstehens besteht."

16. Maurice Blanchot evokes the danger to the literary work judged to
be good; it is likely to be "made useful" and exploited. The work judged
to be bad on the other hand is preserved by its lack of esteem: ". . . set aside,
relegated to the inferno by libraries, burned, forgotten: but this exile, this
disappearance into the heat of the fire or the tepidness of oblivion, *prolongs
in a certain way the just distance of the work.* . . . The work does not endure;
it is" (my italics). French text in *L'espace littéraire* (Paris: Gallimard, 1955),
p. 270.

17. Martin Heidegger, *Being and Time,* trans. J. Macquarrie and E.
Robinson (New York: Harper and Row, 1962), p. 165.

18. "This structuralist thematic of broken immediacy is therefore the
saddened, *negative,* nostalgic, guilty Rousseauistic side of the thinking of
play, whose other side would be the Nietzschean *affirmation,* that is the
joyous affirmation of the play of the world and of the innocence of becoming, the affirmation of a world of signs without fault, without truth, and
without origin which is offered to an active interpretation" (Jacques Derrida, *Writing and Difference,* trans. A. Bass [Chicago: University of Chicago
Press, 1978], p. 272; French text in *L'écriture et la différence* [Paris: Seuil,
1967], p. 427). The very allusions to Rousseau and Nietzsche in the
sentence quoted imply a knowable, traceable continuity, an identifiable
determinacy inherent in the ideas of these two thinkers and resistant to the
misunderstandings of history. The "immediacy" of their work would
appear not to have been broken. It is unclear finally just how much
Derrida concedes to history.

19. It is true, as Stanley Fish has argued, that interpretation is guided
by context, but to deny the text (with Fish) *any* priority to interpretation
is to be excessively rigid. The literary text when read as literature is
precisely of that kind which invites a series of circular adjustments between itself and its interpretive context. This series never ends; it never
fully succeeds; but a fitting interpretive context possesses a flexible capacity for revision which Fish is unwilling to recognize. The fact is that

interpreters can meaningfully discuss a text, persuade one another, and revise their interpretations without surrendering an entire "set of interpretive assumptions." Revised interpretations within a single "context" are possible because a prior text does exist. See Stanley Fish, "Normal Circumstances, Literal Language, Direct Speech Acts, the Ordinary, the Everyday, the Obvious, What Goes without Saying, and Other Special Cases," *Critical Inquiry* 4 (1978), 625–44.

20. T. S. Eliot, *Selected Essays* (London: Faber and Faber, 1956), p. 429.

21. Wolfgang Iser writes suggestively of the reading process: "The production of the meaning of literary texts . . . does not merely entail the discovery of the unformulated . . .; it also entails the possibility that we may formulate ourselves and so discover what had previously seemed to elude our consciousness," (*The Implied Reader* [Baltimore: Johns Hopkins Press, 1974], p. 294). But I would not agree that "the convergence of text and reader brings the literary work into existence" (p. 275). To split the text and the work is to court a potentially narcissistic subjectivism.

# LOVES OF COMFORT AND DESPAIR: A READING OF SHAKESPEARE'S SONNET 138

BY EDWARD A. SNOW

> Lying holds an honorable place in love; it is a detour that leads us to truth by the back door.
> (Montaigne, *On Some Verses of Virgil*)

Sonnet 138 ("When my love sweares that she is made of truth") is one of those sonnets that seem to have served as touchstones for Shakespeare's dramatic imagination.[1] Its paradoxes and its elusiveness of tone locate a crucial threshold within the world of the plays: on the one side *Hamlet, Troilus and Cressida,* and *Othello,* with their disgust with sexuality, their distrust of women, and their cynical, disillusioned, and/or subjectively isolated male protagonists; on the other *Antony and Cleopatra,* with its intermingling of male and female selves, its acceptance of the realities of sexual relatedness, and its chastened yet visionary reaffirmation of the romantic idealism of *Romeo and Juliet.* This is one case, then, where a close reading should open on the largest Shakespearean horizons, and on the basic forces that contend there.

There is another reason for paying close attention to how the poem works. For in addition to locating the threshold that separates *Othello* from *Antony and Cleopatra,* the sonnet passes over it, to achieve something of an epiphany. We come upon it, within either the sonnet sequence or Shakespeare's work as a whole, not as a field of conflicts but as a moment of repose. The grounds for cynicism and despair in Shakespeare's romantic vision are the stuff of the poem, but it manages to transform them into something workable, even strangely affirmative and idealistic. And this transformation is accomplished through the minutest semantic and syntactic adjustments. Indeed, if one can generalize from the sonnet, then no more separates what is most negative from what is most positive in Shakespeare than a subtle distinction in tone.

The following line-by-line commentary is largely an attempt to make this distinction palpable.[2] The differences between the versions of the sonnet published in the 1599 *Passionate Pilgrim* and

462

ELH  Vol. 47  Pp. 462-483
0013-8304/80/0473-0462 $01.00    © 1980 by The Johns Hopkins University Press

the 1609 Quarto will be accorded a place of central importance, for they unfailingly bring the special quality of the latter into focus, and illuminate the nature of the "crossing" that is its achievement. The earlier version still hesitates at the threshold in question, and in the end relapses into metaphors that evoke the repressive, claustrophobic atmosphere of *Othello* ("Since that our faultes in love thus smother'd be"); while the 1609 version passes over into the lucid, accommodating, fully manifest space of *Antony and Cleopatra* ("And in our faultes by lies we flattered be"). Obviously, then, the assumption will be that 1599 is an early Shakespearean version, and not an imperfectly remembered transcript; the ensuing discussion will hopefully become in turn an argument for the validity of that assumption, or at least for its fruitfulness as a working hypothesis.[3]

ll. 1-2:  When my love sweares that she is made of truth,
I do beleeve her though I know she lyes,[4]

In the mouth of Hamlet, Troilus, or Othello, these lines might easily express cynicism or desperate confusion; yet the tone they establish here—and the sonnet as a whole manages to sustain—is gentle, resolved, lovingly acceptant. The note of affection tends to come through even more strongly, in fact, in "though I know she lyes" than in "I do beleeve her." The intimate, almost complacent tone is simultaneously a seduction and a provocation: what should be a logical contradiction is presented as if it were matter-of-factly intelligible; what seems an obvious piece of self-deception communicates lucidity and peace of mind.[5]

Yet beneath the sonnet's apparent offhandedness, fine and crucial distinctions are continually being made. The mistress swears that she is *made of truth*, not that she is "true" or "telling the truth"; and the speaker believes *her*, not her vows or her lies. The continuing life of a relationship can depend on, may even consist in the recognition of the gap between what one is and what one says, or what one says and what one means in the saying of it. And—as if really to take her at her word, more literally even than she intends—if she is *made* of truth, even her lies must be true, or manifest her truth; such lies, properly understood, may elicit belief rather than undermine it. Enobarbus obscurely makes this case for Cleopatra's "passions" (the word is used with metaphysical tact, alluding as it does to both the actor and the man of conviction) in one of *Antony and Cleopatra*'s many reminiscences of Sonnet 138:

*Edward A. Snow*                                                463

| Enobarbus: | Cleopatra, catching but the least noise of this, dies instantly; I have seen her die twenty times upon far poorer moment. I do think there is mettle in death, which commits some loving act upon her, she hath such a celerity in dying. |
| Antony: | She is cunning past man's thought. |
| Enobarbus: | Alack, sir, no, her passions are made of nothing but the finest part of pure love. We cannot call her winds and waters sighs and tears; they are greater storms and tempests than almanacs can report. This cannot be cunning in her; if it be, she makes a show'r of rain as well as Jove. |
| | (1.2.137-48) |

In answer to the question of whether Cleopatra's "deaths" are spontaneous reactions to the prospect of Antony's absence or calculated deceptions designed to keep him in Egypt, Enobarbus replies that such distinctions do not apply in her case—and that love, whose essence is the stuff of her passions, is not the best place to try to make them. It is this capacity to defeat the mind's attempts to distinguish spontaneity from calculation, truth from pretense, that *is* her truth—the truth that elicits Antony's love, in spite of his frustrations ("But that your royalty / Holds idleness your subject, I should take you / For idleness itself" [1.3.91-93]), and Enobarbus's belief, in spite of his ironical defenses. The speaker of Sonnet 138 is both Antony and Enobarbus in this respect: for him belief *is* a matter of love, or at least presupposes it (the introductory "my love" suggests that the issues of the sonnet have been settled long in advance), and it has to do with the person of his beloved rather than her professions. The antithetical situation is dramatized in *Othello,* where we witness the disastrous consequences (and in a sense the substancelessness) of a love anxiously, idealistically predicated on belief ("My life upon her faith!" [1.3.294]).

The paradoxes of Sonnet 138 are even more directly recalled near the end of *Antony and Cleopatra,* in a piece of comic dialogue that once again seems to be concerned with the integrity of Cleopatra and her many "deaths":

| Cleopatra: | Remember'st thou any that have died on't? |
| Clown: | Very many, men and women too. I heard of one of them no longer than yesterday, a very honest woman—but something given to lie, as a woman should not do but in way of honesty—how she died of the biting of it, what pain she felt. |
| | (5.2.249-54) |

*A Reading of Shakespeare's Sonnet 138*

The speaker of the sonnet may similarly choose to believe that his mistress lies "in way of honesty": "When she swears her truth to me, and lies in doing so, that very lie proves her truth, since it demonstrates that she loves me enough to keep the truth from me, cares enough about preserving our relationship, and protecting my feelings, to conceal her infidelities within it." "I do beleeve" suggests something closer to a pledge or an enactment than a passive acceptance (it answers to her vows in a marriage of similarly devious minds), as if her truth were contingent on his investment in it. Although the folly of Troilus's self-willed delusion is not far off the horizon, there is a peculiar clarity and ethical strength about such a train of thought. Its positives come into focus when we realize that such a piece of casuistry is exactly what a non-tragic Othello would have to become capable of, regardless of Desdemona's actual "guilt" or "innocence" (the play goes to painful lengths to show that no objective proof—whatever that might consist in—would restore his faith). We are actually closer to a more complaisant version of Juliet's passionate realism:

> Dost thou love me? I know thou wilt say "Ay,"
> And I will take thy word; yet if thou swear'st,
> Thou may prove false: at lovers' perjuries
> They say Jove laughs.

> (2.2.90-94)

In Sonnet 138 the laughter of the gods has been internalized (cf. Hubler's description of its tone as "amused contentment"),[6] not without a tendency to look on truth askance and strangely, but miraculously without cynicism or disillusionment.

There is yet another, entirely different side to the issue of lies and the belief in them in the sonnet, as the passage from *Romeo and Juliet* suggests: it has to do not with infidelity but with the burden of experience, and not with calculated deception but with the passionate untruths of love itself. The lover's vows in *As You Like It* that so closely echo those of Sonnet 138—"It is to be all made of faith and service / And so am I for Phoebe" (5.2.89-90)—are elicited by the exuberance of being in love, not by an accusation of infidelity. Rosalind's skepticism about such vows is based on a general knowledge of how the world goes ("Say 'a day,' without the 'ever.' No, no, Orlando, men are April when they woo, December when they wed; maids are May when they are maids, but the sky changes when they are wives" [4.1.146-49]); and what makes her such a positive force in the play is her ability to give herself to love in spite

*Edward A. Snow* 465

of her "knowledge" (as if she were Mercutio and Juliet in one). The Player Queen swears that she will never wed a second time in response to her husband's insecurities, not his accusations, and only the most inveterate cynic would suggest that she is not sincere when she does so. Yet her vows reinforce the Player King's obsession with accident and mutability, in another close reminiscence of Sonnet 138 ("I do believe you think what now you speak, / But what we do determine, oft we break" [*Ham.*, 3.2.186-87]), and even Gertrude catches the note of insecurity that haunts such vows ("The lady doth protest too much, methinks" [3.2.230]). We ourselves probably believe Sonnet 116 ("Love's not Time's fool") though we "know" better—indeed, the strength of our belief is probably directly proportionate to our experience that all it denies is true. Perhaps closest of all to the speaker's attitude toward his mistress's oaths in this respect is Cleopatra's response to the oaths she is forever intent on drawing out of Antony:

Antony:               Let Rome in Tiber melt, and the wide arch
                        Of the rang'd empire fall! Here is my space,
                        Kingdoms are clay; our dungy earth alike
                        Feeds beast as man; the nobleness of life
                        Is to do thus—when such a mutual pair
                        And such a twain can do't, in which I bind,
                        On pain of punishment, the world to weet
                        We stand up peerless.
Cleopatra:                        Excellent falsehood!
                        Why did he marry Fulvia and not love her?
                        I'll seem the fool I am not. Antony
                        Will be himself.
Antony:                       But stirred by Cleopatra.

                                      (1.1.33-43)

Cleopatra knows the untrustworthiness of Antony's vows as guarantors of the future from her own experience with him as well as from her knowledge of his past ("Why should I think you can be mine, and true / (though you in swearing shake the throned gods), / Who have been false to Fulvia? [2.3.27-29]). Yet beneath the apparent cynicism of "Excellent falsehood!" there is genuine acceptance on the part of someone for whom the distinction between common lies and ennobling, passionately embodied fictions is more important than the Roman-minded difference between truth and falsity.[7]

Thus it may be that the speaker of Sonnet 138 "knows" that his mistress lies not because he possesses empirical evidence of actual infidelities (the example of *Othello* should put us on the alert here), but because of what his own experience (or "age," as he euphemistically puts it) in love tells him about the nature of lover's vows: "When she pledges her truth to me, I believe that she is sincere, and that the love she expresses for me is real; yet I know from experience that such vows are by their very nature lies—especially in the case of the two of us, who are both too 'old' in love to be made of truth."

From this point of view, what threatens the relationship is the speaker's own self-doubt and its potential for cynicism and disillusionment rather than his mistress's potential for actual betrayal. Here again, the dialectic between *Othello* and *Antony and Cleopatra* clarifies what is at stake in the sonnet. In *Othello*, a preoccupation with past and future loves, with mutability, with a series of betrayals in which the present love is inextricably implicated, is merely the necessary obverse of the brittle idealism that must disavow it; suppressed from within, it returns in the external world as a paranoid, persecutory, randomly embodied voice preying on the insecurities that are its real substance:

> Look to her, Moor, if thou hast eyes to see;
> She has deceived her father, and may thee.
>
> (1.3.292-93)

> It cannot be that Desdemona should long continue her love to the Moor—put money in thy purse—nor he his to her. It was a violent commencement, and thou shalt see an answerable sequestration—put money in thy purse. These Moors are changeable in their wills—fill thy purse with money. The food that to him now is as luscious as locusts shall be to him shortly as acerbe as the coloquintida. She must change for youth: when she is sated with his body, she will find the error of her choice. She must have change, she must; therefore put money in thy purse.
>
> (1.3.341-52)

In all such passages we hear Othello's own inner voice as well as that of the hostile elements in his external world.

In Cleopatra, however, the life force is able to triumph over what experience "knows," and achieve in the process a heightened, all-inclusive lucidity. Her first scene with Charmian is a perfect gloss on Sonnet 138's "And age in love, loves not t'have years told":

Cleopatra:                     Who's born that day
            When I forget to send to Antony,
            Shall die a beggar. Ink and paper, Charmian.

*Edward A. Snow*                                                467

|            | Welcome, my good Alexas. Did I, Charmian, |
|------------|-------------------------------------------|
|            | Ever love Caesar so?                      |
| Charmian:  | O, that brave Caesar!                     |
| Cleopatra: | Be choked with such another emphasis!     |
|            | Say, "the brave Antony."                  |
| Charmian:  | The valiant Caesar!                       |
| Cleopatra: | By Isis, I will give thee bloody teeth    |
|            | If thou with Caesar paragon again         |
|            | My man of men.                            |
| Charmian:  | By your most gracious pardon,             |
|            | I sing but after you.                     |
| Cleopatra: | My salad days,                            |
|            | When I was green in judgment, cold in blood, |
|            | To say as I said then. But come, away,    |
|            | Get me ink and paper.                     |
|            | He shall have every day a several greeting, |
|            | Or I'll unpeople Egypt.                    |

                                              (1.5.64-78)

What is being celebrated in this passage is Cleopatra's capacity to be rich in memory yet young in love, to will through her passions (and her sense of humor) a present enhanced rather than burdened by the past. Although the speaker of Sonnet 138 gently, wryly acquiesces where Cleopatra passionately transcends, it is *Antony and Cleopatra*'s mood of time-bound acceptance rather than *Othello*'s mixture of cynicism and despair that his attitude ultimately resembles.

The troubled feelings about sexuality that are in a sense the crux of the sonnet come to the fore in the puns of line 2. In the absence of the preposition and its object, "she lyes" can imply either "lies to me" or "lies with me" (for the latter, after all, are the lies the speaker *knows*). These alternatives tend to imply and become equivalent to each other (with "lies with other men" merely an internal, wholly subjective middle term—just as the fantasy of an adulterous liaison that Desdemona lies to him about serves to mediate Othello's own repressed sense of what lying with her involves for him)—as if what the speaker had to overcome were not his awareness of her promiscuity but his own "knowledge" of her sexually.[8] The attitude that sex itself is illicit and corrupting, and that to have intercourse with a woman is to know her for a whore and a liar, is a demon upon which the critical force of much of Shakespeare's canon is brought to bear. The 1609 version of the sonnet manages to sustain throughout the gentle ascendancy of "I do beleeve her" over "I know she lyes" (the lies of line 2 have, in fact,

468                    *A Reading of Shakespeare's Sonnet 138*

by line 14 been converted into the grounding, consoling truth of the relationship). In doing so, it achieves a triumph similar to that of *Antony and Cleopatra* over the darkest, most compulsive forces in Shakespeare's world.[9]

ll. 3-4:    That she might thinke me some untuterd youth,
             Unlearned in the world's false subtilties.

Here the two versions begin to diverge: 1599 reads "unskillful" instead of "unlearned" and "forgeries" instead of "subtilties." "Unlearned" implies a more benign attitude toward an ironically-regarded self-image than "unskillful"; sexual inexperience becomes a matter of innocence rather than awkwardness or incompetence. The substitution of "subtilties" for "forgeries" shifts the issue of true versus false toward the more ethically neutral (or elusive) one of simple versus complex, and opens the possibility of an epicurean rather than a puritanical consideration of "lies." (Forgeries are always strongly negative in Shakespeare, as in Adonis's "Love is all truth, Lust full of forged lies" [*Ven.*, 804]; subtleties more often call for aesthetic appreciation, as in Berowne's "Subtle as Sphinx, sweet and musical / As bright Apollo's lute" [*LLL.*, 4.3.339-40], or Prospero's "You do yet taste / Some subtleties o' th' isle" [*Tmp.*, 5.1.123-24].

The musical patterns established in the first three lines clearly demand "subtilties" rather than "forgeries" (note especially the interplay of t's, l's, d's, and s's that keeps the verse on the tip of the tongue, and the fluid elision of "false" into "subtilties")—a fact that might seem to argue for 1599 as an imperfect transcription rather than an early version of 1609. Yet the very thing that makes the variants in 1609 compelling when considered as authorial revisions is that they seem not so much to change the original into something else as bring to light what has been there, half-suppressed, all along—as if the poet were finally realizing the affirmative core of his situation and relinquishing his defenses against it.[10] That revisions which make for a more complex, humane breadth of vision should also make for a more beautiful, logically coherent poem is symptomatic of the level at which the poem's affirmations reside. For once aesthetic value inheres naturally in the unembellished texture of human realization, instead of becoming something created and imposed in its despair.

The grammatical and syntactical ambiguities of ll. 3-4 reflect the complicated intersubjectivity of the relationship they describe.

*Edward A. Snow*                        469

"That she might thinke me" can express an intent on the part of the speaker either to deceive his mistress or to grant her wish, cooperate in her own self-deceptions. The latter possibility is made more plausible by the syntactical ambiguity which allows "That" to modify either "I do believe her" or "she lyes." The more esoteric argument would thus run: "My love lies to me by way of ridiculously exaggerated lovers' vows not primarily in order to deceive me but in order to believe that she is in love with someone young and foolish enough to believe them; and understanding these motives, I willingly assent to them, so that she might allow herself the naive enthusiasm of a Juliet, and feel young in love herself. In doing so I enter into complicity with an image of myself that it flatters me to see held by her. And there is something of truth in all this: I don't merely pretend, I *do believe* her." As an explanation of a beloved's actual infidelities, the casuistry of this may be painful to reflect upon. Yet the calm, lucid tone, the strength and ease of address, create the opposite effect from the lonely, desperate rationalizations of Sonnet 42 ("Loving offendors thus will I excuse yee, / Thou dost love her, because thou knowst I love her, / And for my sake even so doth she abuse me, / Suffring my friend for my sake to approove her"). The speaker's convoluted reasonings and quixotic generosity on the question of intent arrive at a truth, a reality, that may be closed to a more "realistic" view of things; they communicate to us not an isolated consciousness but a relationship, a mutuality, in which (I think) we believe.

ll. 5-6:  Thus vainely thinking that she thinkes me young,
Although she knowes my days are past the best,

Line 7 will establish that it is the speaker who is doing the "thinking" here; but when we reach the end of line six we are still not sure whether it is his or his mistress's state of mind that is being described. Somewhere in the course of the first six lines we lose our sense of which side of the relationship we are on, and enter an area of radical intersubjectivity. The rest of the sonnet draws back into a simpler, externally situated mutuality ("On both sides thus," "I lye with her, and she with me"), but without really annulling what has gone before. The "I," "she," and "we" take their special resonance from their situation within the (prior?) intersubjective field, while the vertiginous mix of consciousnesses gains a merciful embodiment in the flawed unions of two separate, physical selves.

The whole poem thus hinges on the change from 1599's "Although *I* know my yeares be past the best" to 1609's "Although *she* knowes my days are past the best." The 1599 version stresses the gulf between what she thinks and what he knows, and between what he gives her to know of him and what he knows to be true of himself. The radical dialectic of selves set in motion in the first five lines comes unhappily to rest in the isolated, divided subjectivity of the speaker, with the mistress a distant object of concern outside the poem's actual field of consciousness.

But the 1609 version reaffirms the essentially intersubjective nature of that field. The substitution of "she" allows the secondary train of thought that takes the mistress rather than the speaker as the subject of predication to extend more plausibly through line 6: "She may think (such is the power of her vanity) that she thinks me young (and that I believe her), but she really knows full well how old I am (and that I know she lies)." And at the primary level of discourse, it transforms the speaker's preoccupation with what goes on in the mind of his mistress from what isolates him to what saves him from solipsism. In place of 1599's "I thus self-conceitedly hold on to the thought that I have made her think I am young, even though that thought is in vain, since here inside my thoughts I know how old I really am (to think of her thinking of me as a youth only intensifies my cynical awareness of myself as old, and vain)," 1609 gives us something closer to "I thus flatter myself with the thought that she thinks me young (and believes that I believe), yet that thought is a mere vanity on my part, since I know that she knows quite well how "old" I am (and thus knows that I know)." It is the difference between "I may be able to deceive her but I can't deceive myself," and "I might be able to deceive myself if I weren't aware of how well she knows me, how obvious the truth of me is to her." In the former version, "knowledge" is just the furthest extension, and the ultimate despair, of the speaker's "thinking"; in the latter, it refers to the experiential, time-bound actuality of their relationship together (on the one hand, Othello's "By heaven I'll know thy thoughts" [3.3.161]; on the other, Cleopatra's "Not know me yet?" [3.3.161]). With the change in 1609, the mistress enters constitutively into the speaker's subjectivity: his consciousness of her perspective on him mediates his own reflection on himself ("she knows" condenses "I know that she knows," and carries the force of a *self*-realization.) The speaker gains a saving distance from himself and moves emotionally nearer his mistress, as the note of self-contempt in 1599 becomes something closer to self-

*Edward A. Snow*                                                                471

bemusement in 1609, and the implied contempt for the mistress (for being fooled by him) shifts toward an affectionate, if similarly bemused respect (for seeing through him). The earlier version makes us feel the impossibility of the relationship; the later one, its fittingness, its inevitability.

Throughout the first six lines of the sonnet, the wordplay on "think" and "know" works to undermine the psychological and epistemological distinction they appear to define. In every instance, both can be paraphrased as "believe": "think" in the weak sense (supposition, conjecture, delusion), "know" in the strong sense (assurance, conviction). What establishes the difference between "strong" and "weak" belief, meanwhile, is left entirely unexplained—as if it were the assumption, or the achievement, upon which the poem as a whole is founded. The one actual use of "believe" is self-consciously, challengingly paradoxical—the poem insists on *"do* believe" where logic would seem to demand *"pretend to* believe."[11] In place of a rational, clearly demarcated hierarchy where thought leads to knowledge and knowledge to belief (or a religious order where belief dictates knowledge and knowledge contains thought), the sonnet establishes an emotional continuum where everything is ultimately a matter of "belief," and the distance between suspicion and trust a matter of quantities that cannot be rationally measured or sustained. In this respect its language works to the same ends as the remarkably similar wordplay of *Othello*:[12]

Othello:         What dost thou say?
Iago:             Nothing, my lord; or if—I *know* not what.
Othello:         Was not that Cassio parted from my wife?
Iago:             Cassio, my lord? No, sure, I cannot *think* it,
                    That he would steal away so guilty-like,
                    Seeing your coming.
Othello:                        I *do believe* 'twas he.
                             (3.3.35-40; italics added)

Othello:         Honest? ay, honest.
Iago:                    My lord, for all I *know*.
Othello:         What dost thou *think*?
Iago:                      *Think*, my lord?
Othello:         *Think*, my lord? By heaven, thou echo'st me,
                    As if there were some monster in thy *thought*
                    Too hideous to be shown. . . .
                    . . . If thou dost love me,
                    Show me thy *thought*.
Iago:                    My lord, you *know* I love you.

Othello:                                                I *think* thou dost;
                    And for I *know* thou'rt full of love and honesty,
                    . . .

Iago:                                                For Michael Cassio,
                    I dare be *sworn* I *think* that he is honest.
Othello:            I *think* so too.

(3.3.104-26; italics added)

Yet the speaker of the sonnet resides comfortably in the language that destroys Othello's faith; his paradoxes convey not confusion but an almost Montaignian lucidity and composure. The discoveries upon which all of Shakespeare's tragic protagonists come to grief—the opacity of the self, the otherness of others, the absence of immediate relation, either with the self or the other—are the givens of the sonnet's world, the conditions for "belief" rather than impediments to it.

ll. 7-8:    Simply I credit her false speaking tongue,
            On both sides thus is simple truth supprest:

Again, the language expresses an ambivalence while giving the feel of having resolved it. "Simply" can mean "naively" or "foolishly" (thus paralleling "vainely" in line 5), but also "straightforwardly," "candidly," "absolutely," "without reserve" (in which case "Simply I credit" will be heard to parallel and clarify "I do believe" in line 2).[13] Similarly, the "simple truth" can be suppressed in favor of either multiple lies or a more complex truth.[14] Contradictory perspectives are acknowledged, yet tonally it is the positive meanings that achieve priority: the feel of the line conveys not cynicism or inner division but an ethically-invested clarity.

The affirmative thrust of the line becomes characteristically more emphatic in comparison to the 1599 version. In "I smiling, credit her false speaking toung," the speaker is cut off from the mistress and his act of "crediting" her by the smiles he interposes between them ("outfacing" in line 8 reinforces the hypocritical, defensive quality of these smiles). It is the world of *Hamlet* and *Othello* that is evoked: intentionality is hidden behind its actions; the truth is what remains within, passing show, the false what is given to the other to know. The prevailing mood here *is* one of cynicism and self-contempt; to the degree that the speaker is claiming to control or be satisfied with his situation, his despair and impotence within it become only the more painfully apparent. In the 1609 version, however, the "I" is grammatically, syntactically, and metrically im-

*Edward A. Snow*                                                            473

plicated in its predicates by its middle place in the strongly linked unit "Símply I crédit"; the forward thrust of the line moves the speaker toward the mistress and into the relationship between them. The self here actively invests itself in, relinquishes itself to its act of crediting and the paradoxical bond it thereby creates.

In the 1599 version, the two sides of the relationship are doubly isolated from each other, she behind her lies and he behind his smiles. But 1609's "On both sides thus is simple truth supprest" implies, and achieves, a mutuality; the two lovers cooperate in creating and sustaining what lies between them, and they are but its opposite aspects, its two "sides" (or so at least the quixotic generosity of the poem would have it). The speaker takes what is given, and, without illusion (it *is* a "false speaking" tongue, though again it is the tongue itself and not what it says that he credits), defines it, simply credits it, as the truth that is between them. Whatever he perceives of her (and of himself as well) he chooses to take as existing on the surface of the relationship, as tacitly given him to know rather than withheld from him in a place his understanding violates. Lucidity is taken to its limits in such a gesture, but it leaves it object intact—even becomes, *contra* Eliot, a source of indiscriminate forgiveness, a place of rest.

Again, it is the world of *Antony and Cleopatra* into which we have moved. The beautiful reconciliation scene between Antony and Cleopatra after the defeat at Actium ("Forgive my fearful sails") might be but a dramatic fleshing out of the mood and ethos of Sonnet 138. The tacit agreement to suppress the issue of Cleopatra's motives in running from the battle (and there may not be a more striking instance in Shakespeare of a situation in which the "simple truth" may be utterly problematical, or perhaps not even exist) involves an acknowledgment on both sides of their irrevocable investment in their relationship, their need for it to continue, apart from and beyond all other considerations.

ll. 9-12:    But wherefore sayes she not she is unjust?
             And wherefore say not I that I am old?
             O loves best habit is in seeming trust,
             And age in love loves not t'have yeares told.

The discourse of the sonnet operates not unlike that of myth as analyzed by Levi-Strauss: as a strategy for making the unthinkable thinkable, the unworkable workable (the poem thus serves the relationship it describes in the way that myth serves culture). The difficult issue of the mistress's infidelity is silently displaced by the more manageable one of her failure to tell the truth about it. Likewise, the potentially humiliating lack of correspondence between her lies and his silence, her "injustice" and his "age," is transformed into an equivalence, and an implication of reciprocal awareness. In the 1599 version, line 11 answers line 9, and line 12 line 10; but in 1609 both answers apply equally to both questions: line 12, for instance, "And age in love loves not t'have yeares told," may explain that she lies to him out of concern for his feelings as well as that he remains silent in order to keep his age a secret. Finally, the focus is shifted from the lies that are *told* to the truths that are *not spoken,* from his smiles and her false-speaking tongue to the tacit realm they share by means of their silences (a process that remains incomplete in the 1599 version, where in spite of the forced similarity between her lies about her "youth" and his silence about his "age," it is still a matter of what she says versus what he keeps to himself).

The euphemisms of lines 9 and 10 acquire an unwonted precision and richness of suggestion in the context created for them by the complexity of the octet (and the relationship it describes). "Unjust" leaves the exact nature of the mistress's fault appropriately unstated and open to question,[15] and displaces the language of "true versus false" with a more subtle and humane ethical vocabulary. "Old" may refer us in a relatively straightforward manner to subjectively isolated male anxieties about performance and sexual desirability (as in Othello's "the young affects in me defunct" [1.3.263-64]), but it may, just as easily, recalling the example from *Antony and Cleopatra* mentioned earlier, allude to a reluctance on both sides to have past affairs recalled (and past "injustices" within the present relationship: "age in love" can be taken to refer either to someone in love who is past his prime, or, more wonderfully, to a love of long standing).[16]

The word-play of line 11 once again condenses the cynical view of the relationship with its benign opposite (although it is difficult to hear the *tone* of the line as other than poignant and heartfelt). The image of clothing evoked by "habit" is itself two-sided. Booth remarks that "Shakespeare customarily associates clothes with deceit, concealment, and pretense—with trying to seem other than one actually is";[17] but this ignores Cleopatra's "Give me my robe, put on my crown, I have / Immortal longings in me" (5.2.280-81), and all the merciful gestures of clothing and covering that counterbalance the obsessions with *both* disguising *and* stripping bare in *King Lear*. The line can just as easily express an altruistic concern with protecting and enhancing the relationship as it can a self-serving strategy of concealment within it. The difference between the two versions again underscores the thrust in 1609 toward psychic health. In 1599's "O, Love's best habit's in a soothing toung," the "Love" referred to is an individual posture, and its personification as part-object reinforces the sense of unhappy investment in it; but 1609's "O loves best habit is in seeming trust" refers primarily to the whole, inclusive relationship.

The same ambiguity extends to the non-metaphorical connotations of "habit": either "habitual," with the negative suggestions of tiredness or jadedness, or "habituation," *"habitus"*—in the latter case again expressing concern for the continuation and well-being of the relationship. "Seeming trust" can mean either "appearance of trust" or "trust in appearances" (the trust itself an appearance to be trusted). Even if the former, the emphasis only *may* be on the falseness, the pretense of trust; it may just as plausibly be on the importance of trust *appearing,* manifesting itself in the relationship, quite apart from all private, subjective considerations (as in the similarly elusive yet genuinely committed ethos stated at the end of Andrew Marvell's "Mourning": "I yet my silent judgment keep, / Disputing not what they believe; / Yet sure as oft as women weep, / It is to be supposed they grieve"). "Seeming trust" may be love's "best" habit not just because it is the most practical and serviceable strategy available, but because it represents an *ideal* of magnanimity, is the truest and most faithful form that love is capable of assuming. Indeed, that the poem offers us a form of love that might be "best" in both of the supposedly antithetical senses of the word is the very heart of its affirmative strength.[18]

ll. 13-14:    Therefore I lye with her, and she with me,
            And in our faultes by lyes we flattered be.

Booth's comments on this final couplet are especially acute:

> The complementary actions announced in line 13, their presentation in urgently parallel constructions (*I lie with her* and *she with me*), and the fact that each of the two clauses asserts the same necessarily cooperative action, all prepare the way for line 14, a line that sums up the speaker's grounds for cynicism, bitterness, and despair, and also one in which the unity of the two lying lovers, whose syntactic independence wanes as the poem

progresses, reaches a compensating completion in the trium-
phantly mutual pronouns, *our* and *we*.[19]

I would only want to argue that the speaker's grounds for cynicism, bitterness, and despair are not only summed up but *transformed* in the couplet: they become the very substance of its
triumph. The final couplet of 1599 gives an especially compelling
version of the negativity that is largely overcome in 1609. "Therefore I'le lye with Love, and love with me" absents the mistress and
isolates the speaker with an abstraction in which he seems to have
little real conviction. "Therefore" seems to deduce a plan of action
to be projected into the future, with the "I" characteristically behind its gestures, willing them and at a distance from them. In 1609,
conversely, the mistress becomes fully present in the poem (the
word "love" disappears into the immanent texture of the relationship), while the poem achieves a sense of presentness that is itself a
value, on both the aesthetic and existential planes (by now inextricably fused in the poem). Its "lies" take place here, now, in the
openness of the poem, rather than in an imagined future projected
out of the speaker's loneliness. Unlike the speaker of 1599, who
confides to his audience almost like Iago in his asides, the speaker
of 1609 accepts his manifestness within the space of the relationship (and the poem) that discloses him. His "Therefore" introduces
neither purpose nor logical conclusion; it merely recapitulates,
and settles into, the situation unfolded in the previous lines, con-
firming in the process the lucidity and openness to a perspective
from beyond the self that have been achieved there.

The intricate differences between the final lines of the two versions make the most compelling argument for a Shakespearean revision. The language of 1599 ("Since that our faultes in love thus
smother'd be") works subliminally to evoke the negative feelings
supposedly suppressed within the "ill rest" it describes.
"Smother'd" is violently overdetermined—it carries much the same
psychic charge as Othello's smothering of Desdemona.[20] On the
one hand, it conveys the speaker's sense of being isolated "in" love
and constricted "by" it; on the other, it makes his own embraces
into sardonic, self-contemptuous acts of aggression both on the
mistress, on "Love," and on himself "in" love. The implied
equivalence between "lye[s]" and "love" is dark and perverse; it
combines with the syntactical ambiguity of "faultes in love" to
undermine any sense of conviction in the virtue or the workability
of the arrangement apparently embraced in these final lines.

*Edward A. Snow*                                                    477


239

"Faultes" may be incurred *in* love (may, indeed, be the fault *of* love, in both senses of the preposition), and thus be what must be suppressed by the very lies (sexual or epistemological) that manifest love's imperfection. Or love may exist to cover over faults that are intrinsic to prior, separate selves—yet those faults manifest themselves in love as lies (again, both sexual and epistemological), and those lies define what "Love" is between the lovers at least to the degree that they mar it. Either way, sexual guilt and a strong sense of original sin reinforce a hopeless circularity, in which one's acts of covering both expose and immerse the self in what they attempt to suppress (thus a mode of coping that is at the same time an "outfacing" and "smothering").

The deft changes in 1609 lift the burden of introverted guilt and shame that weighs so heavily upon the lovers in the 1599 version, and create instead the sense of an actual physical space in which the relationship can breathe. Indeed, one of the things that makes the prepositional structure of 1609 seem so natural and intuitively satisfying (even though it is more difficult grammatically than 1599's version) is its subliminal evocation of the lovers' carnal situation: when we hear "*in* our faults *by* lyes" we think of the speaker and his mistress lying *in* bed *beside* each other (whereas the speaker of 1599 remains locked within his own dark embraces). The physical reality of the relationship grounds a difficult syntax, just as the sexual connotations of "lyes" subsume the falsehoods that are the word's primary referent at the beginning of the sonnet. That the faults of the speaker and his mistress subliminally correspond to the bed in which they make love (especially given that the end result is now flattery instead of smothering) suggests how profoundly self-forgiving and acceptant the poem has become. The faults of 1609 are less objects of conscience/consciousness than ontological givens—preconditions "in" which relation (even if "lying" is its mode) and being (even if "flattery" is its attribute) are sustained.

Whatever connotations of moral culpability that remain are further lightened by the alliteration with "flattered"—a word whose appearance in the place of "smother'd" comes as a final clinching grace bestowed on poem and relationship alike. It facilitates the current running from "she," "me," and "we" into the final "be," and brilliantly condenses the key musical elements of the entire final couplet—thus acquiring a purely intuitive feeling of rightness as the culmination of the poem's discourse. And at the explicitly discursive level, it preserves the wry, delicate balance of the sonnet's ethos at the very moment the speaker appears to pass final judgment on the relationship. "Flattered" is, like the ordinary language of the sonnet as a whole, a transparent but semantically dense term whose secondary reverberations tend to counteract its superficially apparent meaning. It may denote a state of delusion—although even at this level ambiguities arise, depending on whether one thinks of the lovers as narcissistically deluded by their own and each other's deceits, or as ethically moved by the demonstration of love they choose to discern in each other's consent to "lye" together—but the speaker's use of it conveys not only a generous, good-natured lucidity, but something like tenderness and humility. And the connotative state it evokes is primarily one of pleasure and gratification rather than moral blindness, manifest reality rather than groundless illusion (the image of the two lovers "lying" together interacts beautifully with the caresses that are etymologically implicit in the word).

Finally, to the degree that it remains a matter of "faults," "flattered" locates them in the realm of the natural, the humanly inevitable, rather than in that of the morally corrupt. The sonnet leaves us with the impression of the two lovers no longer laboring under but resting upon, even buoyed up by the deceptions they practice on each other, and of an author finally acquiescing to what is acceptant and sustaining in his vision (whereas with the intrusive "smother'd" of 1599, all his withheld frustrations get the better of him).

Sonnet 138 thus takes its place in the sequence as the "realistic" opposite of the high-minded Sonnet 116 ("Let me not to the marriage of true mindes / Admit impediments"), but in doing so it brings about a subtle realignment of values. Rather than expressing a cynicism that complements the despair of Sonnet 129 ("Th' expence of Spirit in a waste of shame") and opposes the idealism of Sonnet 116, it sets against both an idealism of its own—against sexual disgust ("Injoyd no sooner but dispised straight") an acceptance of the sustaining, ongoing force of "lyes"; against a mode of affirmation that must be desperately, distantly asserted ("Love is not love / Which alters when it alteration findes") another one that can be realized, and comfortably inhabited. Sonnet 116 can only maintain its values through a series of denials and disavowals, and thus for all practical purposes creates Sonnet 129, as its necessary

*Edward A. Snow* 479

obverse; Sonnet 138, "admitting" everything, settles into a relationship that really does "bear it out," in a present for which apocalyptic metaphors have become entirely inappropriate.

*George Mason University*

## Sonnet 138

### 1599 (*PP*)

When my Love sweares that she is made of truth,
I do beleeve her (though I know she lies)
That she might thinke me som untutor'd youth,
Unskillful in the worlds false forgeries.
Thus vainly thinking that she thinkes me young,
Although I know my yeares be past the best:
I smiling, credit her false speaking toung,
Outfacing faults in love, with loves ill rest.
But wherefore sayes my love that she is young?
And wherefore say not I, that I am old:
O, Loves best habit's in a soothing toung,
And age in love, loves not to have yeares told.
   Therefore I'le lye with Love, and love with me,
   Since that our faultes in love thus smother'd be.

### 1609 (*Q*)

When my love sweares that she is made of truth,
I do beleeve her though I know she lyes,
That she might thinke me some untuterd youth,
Unlearned in the worlds false subtilties.
Thus vainely thinking that she thinkes me young,
Although she knowes my days are past the best,
Simply I credit her false speaking tongue,
On both sides thus is simple truth supprest:
But wherefore sayes she not she is unjust?
And wherefore say not I that I am old?
O loves best habit is in seeming trust,
And age in love, loves not t'have yeares told.
   Therefore I lye with her, and she with me,
   And in our faults by lyes we flattered be.

### FOOTNOTES

[1] For the classic discussion of how the themes and language of the Sonnets find their way into the plays, see William Empson's analysis of Sonnet 94, "They That Have Power," in *Some Versions of Pastoral*.

[2] I have chosen to approach the poem by way of a line-by-line commentary because it seems to me the only way to respect the way its meanings build. The sonnet is largely made up of discrete, self-sufficient units of discourse that are connected and retrospectively qualified by a series of logical connectives ("That . . . Thus . . .

Although . . . thus . . . Therefore"). Meanings accumulate which the logical structure of the poem subsequently rejects, but not until they have made their presence felt. "When my love sweares that she is made of truth, / I do beleeve her though I know she lyes," for instance, is a self-contained paradox that opens on the most complex issues of love and fidelity, and suggests a similarly complex attitude toward them; but the subsequent conjunction appears to negate the humanly complex aspects of the paradox by revealing it to be a mere purposeful façade. Only a line-by-line reading can do justice to the meanings that accumulate in the interstices of the strictly logical, discursive backbone of the poem, and reveal the larger structure which absorbs and unifies rather than retroactively cancels these meanings.

[3] The arguments for both hypotheses are summarized by Hyder Rollins in his *New Variorum Edition of Shakespeare: The Sonnets,* (Philadelphia, 1944), I, 354; see also Stephen Booth, *Shakespeare's Sonnets* (New Haven, 1977), pp. 476-81. Historical and bibliographical considerations of the 1599 text have not been able to settle the issue either way. It should be emphasized that the present discussion takes place entirely within the hermeneutic circle; it attempts merely to present the strongest case that can be made for the authenticity of the 1599 text at a strictly heuristic level.

[4] Quotations from the Sonnets are from the *New Variorum*. Quotations from the plays and longer poems are from *The Riverside Shakespeare,* ed. G. Blakemore Evans (Boston, 1974).

[5] Not all critics would agree with this description of the sonnet's mood. More often than not, it has been regarded as jaded, cynical, or despairing—an account, I will later argue, that fits the 1599 but *not* the 1609 version of the poem. Patrick Crutwell, for instance, finds it "perhaps the most terrible poem of the whole sequence [to the mistress] . . . the most terrible, and also the nakedest, since it confesses things that are not easily confessed," and speaks at length of the "grim seriousness" of the pun on "lyes" (*The Shakespearean Moment* [London, 1954], pp. 13-14). James Winny's disdainful commentary is the most formidable for being the less melodramatic; whereas Crutwell misses the tone of the sonnet altogether, he offers a grotesque, spiteful caricature of it:

> The sonnet is an enjoyable *jeu d'esprit;* a witty variation on the main theme of the sequence too shallow in feeling to be closely associated with its neighbors. The disdainful mistress has declined into a complaisant courtesan, prepared to accept a middle-aged lover on her own fickle terms; and the speaker reveals himself as a limp *roué* who would be glad to be thought young, and who adapts himself unprotestingly to the false relationship which both find congenial. The situation has a logical place in the development of the sequence, as it moves away from Petrarchan orthodoxy towards a cynically realistic presentation of love as this tired, insincere liaison of partners too indifferent even to lie convincingly to each other. But Shakespeare treats the situation wryly, and without inviting his reader to become emotionally involved, as he does in the charged writing of Sonnet 129. For the moment, lust remains a subject only for mockery (*The Master-Mistress: A Study of Shakespeare's Sonnets* [London, 1968], p. 101).

The present essay is offered as an extended argument against this view of the sonnet.

[6] Edward Hubler, *The Sense of Shakespeare's Sonnets* (Princeton, 1952), p. 45.

[7] Cleopatra's "I'll seem the fool I am not. Antony / Will be himself" might seem to place her in the same relation to Antony that Iago is to Othello. But her profession of seeming is not meant to be taken at face value, as an isolated aside; Antony is *supposed* to hear it, and he responds by folding it back into the dialectic of selves in which their relationship consists. Everything that is hidden in *Othello* is manifest in *Antony and Cleopatra*. Cleopatra is fully invested in the appearances others know

*Edward A. Snow*                                                               481

her by; the folly she here calls her pretense (in order to goad Antony) she just as often admits to be her reality—e.g., "Your honor calls you hence, / Therefore be deaf to my unpitied folly" (1.3.97-98); "Wishers were ever fools" (4.14.37).

[8] This reading is reinforced by the pun, noted by Booth (*Shakespeare's Sonnets*, p. 477), on "maid" of truth.

[9] Sonnet 138's acceptance of "lyes" is comparable to *Antony and Cleopatra's* celebration of the generative force of the "slime" that in *Othello* "sticks on filthy deeds":

> By the fire
> That quickens Nilus' slime, I go from hence
> Thy soldier . . .
>
> (1.3.68-70)

> The higher Nilus swells,
> The more it promises; as it ebbs, the seedsman
> Upon the slime and ooze scatters his grain,
> And shortly comes to harvest.
>
> (2.7.20-23)

[10] It scarcely matters that the 1599 version may have been written in the midst of the relationship, and the 1609 revisions not made until years later, long after it was over. In poetry as well as life the achievement of the present is more often than not a retrospective process—a matter of casting out remorse, of accepting *past* selves.

[11] Gerald Willen and Victor Reed (*A Casebook on Shakespeare's Sonnets* [New York, 1964], p. 140) gloss "believe" by claiming that it "clearly means 'pretend to believe,'" although they are driven to admit that "we know of no other instance of this usage in Elizabethan English."

[12] For a discusssion of the interplay between "think" and "know" in *Othello*, see Paul A. Jorgensen, " 'Perplexed in the Extreme': The Role of Thought in *Othello*," *SQ*, 15 (1964), 265-75.

[13] W. G. Ingram's and Theodor Redpath's gloss of "Simply" as "In assumed simplicity" (*Shakespeare's Sonnets* [London, 1964], p. 318) is an instance of the editorial tendency to come to terms with Sonnet 138's difficult claims by making its key words mean the opposite of what they say, and asserting pretense where it claims authenticity.

[14] Sonnet 138 thus inverts the stress placed on the dialectic in the much "simpler" Sonnet 66: "And simple-Truth miscalde Simplicitie."

[15] The usual glosses of "unjust" as "unfaithful in love," "deceitful," or "a liar" again reveal an editorial impatience with the moral complexity of the poem's outlook.

[16] Philip Martin, in *Shakespeare's Sonnets: Self, Love, and Art* (Cambridge, 1972), pp. 53-54, finds this line to hint at "the lover's self-dramatization and self-pity." But as usual with this sonnet, the closer one attends to matters of tone, the more a negative impression tends to yield to its opposite—here a wryly humorous, self-effacing concern for the well-being of the relationship itself.

[17] *Shakespeare's Sonnets*, p. 480.

[18] The ambiguity of "best" is noted by Booth, p. 480.

[19] Booth, p. 481.

[20] F's stage direction has Othello "smother" Desdemona; in Q he "stifles" her. I hope the reader who feels this comparison to be based on no more than a verbal accident will still agree that what follows applies to *Othello* as well as to the 1599 version of Sonnet 138. My own feeling is that there are very few "verbal accidents" in Shakespeare. "Smother" is certainly a key word in his imagination: it almost

482                              *A Reading of Shakespeare's Sonnet 138*

always carries connotations of a brooding, involuted consciousness, and usually appears in a context of repression heavy with a sense of sexual impotence and impending violence. The word sets the dominant tone of *The Rape of Lucrece:*

> Men's faults do seldom to themselves appear,
> Their own transgressions partially they smother:
> This guilt would seem death-worthy in thy brother.
>   O how are they wrapp'd up in infamies
>   That from their own misdeeds askaunce their eyes!
>
> (633-37)

> "With rotten damps ravish the morning air;
> Let their exhal'd unwholesome breaths make sick
> The life of purity, the supreme fair,
> Ere he arrive his weary noontide prick,
> And let thy musty vapors march so thick
>   That in their smoky ranks his smoth'red light
>   May set at noon, and make perpetual night."
>
> (778-84)

I would argue that such words carry their own memory in Shakespeare, and that as a result these two passages, as well as the final couplet of the 1599 version of Sonnet 138, are keys to the imagination that seizes on the aptness of smothering Desdemona in her wedding bed.

*Edward A. Snow*                                                   483

# The narrative poems

The poems of Shakespeare have great ability and moments of genius, but we need not labour to praise them, since we must rejoice that he went back to the theatre – recognising perhaps that they were in some way inadequate for him. Nonetheless, they saved his career at the one crucial time, and they record (though mainly in the *Sonnets*) an experience so formative that the plays echo it for the rest of his life. No other playwright known to us worked regularly for the public theatres both before and after their long shutdown because of the plague in 1592–4, after which new companies of actors had to be formed; to survive it was an achievement. At this time a patron was essential for him, whereas afterwards (apart from one graceful kindness) he seems to avoid writing for patrons. His early life is obscure but two facts stand out like rocks: he dedicated to the Earl of Southampton (b. October 1573) both *Venus and Adonis* (1593) and *The Rape of Lucrece* (1594), sounding much more intimate on the second occasion. Our first record of Shakespeare as a member of the Lord Chamberlain's Company, in which he stayed for the rest of his working life – indeed our first record of it performing at a London theatre – is dated just after the Earl's coming of age. The Earl became liable to a heavy fine for rejecting a marriage arranged during his minority, so perhaps did not pay very much, but would help to get the company launched. By writing for a patron, Shakespeare met the crisis in an accepted manner, as a modern author might apply for "relief"; the playwright Marlowe, born in the same year, was also at this time writing a mythological narrative poem, though it happened to be interrupted by his murder; maybe they pretended to one another that this was a tiresome chore. Shakespeare's metre had been made the fashionable one for the purpose by Lodge in 1589; and may I at once refer anybody who wants further information of this scholarly kind to the excellent New Cambridge edition of the

*Poems* by J. C. Maxwell (1966). I want in this essay to concentrate on what may be called the human or experiential reality of
the poems, presenting such evidence as I have about that with
decent care.

Taking this line of approach, it is a startling initial fact that
*Venus and Adonis*, his first publication, appears in the Stationers'
Register as licensed by the Archbishop of Canterbury in person.
The poem soon made its impact, and libidinous undergraduates
are said to have slept with it under their pillows. To have bearded
and won over the "little black husband" of Elizabeth, a particularly grim member of her Court, argues that the Bard was in great
nerve and good spirits. Shakespeare was not yet thirty, and few
of the people who had enjoyed his plays would remember his
name, but that is a time when authors need to make contacts.
One can glean a little from the Register itself about the conditions of his problem. The *Dictionary of National Biography*
reports that John Whitgift (1530–1604) accepted the theories of
Calvin throughout his career, sometimes to the annoyance of the
Queen, but denied their application to Church Government, so
that he was free to persecute Calvinists as well as Papists, bringing them ruin by repeated fines; at this work he showed "brutal
insolence in examining prisoners, and invariably argued for the
severest penalties". Having a private fortune, he maintained a
troop in his own livery, and this was what arrested Essex and his
followers during their attempt at rebellion. Soon after his
appointment in 1583 he secured a tightening-up of the licensing
system: for example, the ballads on separate sheets had now to
be approved; and, unlike his predecessor, he would license a few
books under his own name every year. Nearly all of them were
pamphlets on current theological controversies, for which his
decision would anyway be needed, but he also showed a credit-
able interest in the advancement of learning; for example, he
licensed books purporting to teach the Welsh language and the
history of China. The Bishop of London, who was another established licensing authority, also adopted the custom of giving his
own name to a few books each year; most of them dealt with
political news from Western Europe. He worked closely with the
Archbishop but seems to have had no literary leanings, though
he had of course social ones.

Thus in February 1591, the Archbishop and the Bishop
together licensed the rather perfunctory translation of the
*Orlando Furioso* by Sir John Harrington. The Queen (so people

said at the time) had found her maids of honour giggling over his translation of a sexy canto, and had ordered him to go and stay in his country house till he had translated the whole epic. Both his parents had been with her during her imprisonment in the Tower, when she was almost without hope, and she had made him her godson. It was agreed that the English badly needed raising to the cultural level of the Italians somehow, and yet admittedly, on the moral side, such a poem needed thorough sanctification by the Church of England. Thus the occasion had every claim upon the assistance of the hierarchy. I count about 180 entries in the Register for 1590, 40 of them by the Bishop and 8 by the Archbishop; these proportions are fairly steady for the next few years. In 1592 the Archbishop licenses a book of love poems, though in Latin – the *Amintae Gaudia* of Thomas Watson (1557?–92). Watson was a classical scholar of good family, and he had just died; he had assisted the poverty of better poets, and his verses were sure not to excite desire. The Archbishop entered the fatal year 1593 by licensing Hooker's *Ecclesiastical Polity* and on 9 April he licensed Churchyard's *Challenge*. The book is a final miscellany by a sturdy, loyal old chap, then about seventy-three, who died soon after; it calls the Queen a phoenix on several occasions. Nobody could blame the Archbishop, but he was perhaps starting to go a little out of his way, as Churchyard had no social claims. Within three weeks he had licensed the indecent *Venus and Adonis*. There is no immediate sign of trouble; it is the only year he reaches double figures, ending in September with Nashe – *Christ's Tears over Jerusalem* and *The Unfortunate Traveller* (Nashe had defended the Anglican hierarchy in comic pamphlets, and the first of these books is a work of penitence). But in the following year, 1594, only one publication is licensed by the Archbishop himself: "The Table of Ten Commandments, with the Pictures of Moses and Aaron". A poster, no doubt, for display in all churches; the Queen felt she had to let him keep up appearances so far. In the following year he appears to be forgiven, signing for works of theological controversy at a merry pace, but never again does he license anything even appearing to be a work of literature.

When the poem became notorious, somebody would look it up in the Register hoping to find an irregularity; and, when the truth got about, the Queen evidently told the Archbishop that he must stop making a fool of himself for at least a year. We may be sure he said, as a number of modern critics would say, that these randy students were the ones who had got the poem wrong; probably he could also claim that the author had told him so. A letter from Southampton would be needed for Shakespeare to get an interview, but it would cut little ice with the Archbishop, and Shakespeare would then have to rely on his own eloquence. The apology of Chettle shows that he was socially adroit.[1] He would be found to share the anxieties of the Archbishop about the petulant Earl, regarding him with grave pity. His own little poem, designed as a warning for the young man, carried a peculiarly high and severe moral allegory; and might he perhaps illustrate the point by quotation? (He would read from the final curse of Venus, saying that all loves on earth will in future be upset by parents arranging marriages and suchlike.) Whitgift had almost certainly ruined Shakespeare's father, whether the father was a Papist or a Puritan; it gives a welcome feeling of reality to see an author of revenge plays actually taking a quiet civil revenge. I doubt whether he felt this as a duty, but it might seem an excuse for letting himself be pushed forward by the giggling Southampton. He would enjoy the scene chiefly as a test of skill.

C. S. Lewis found the poem disgusting, mainly because Venus sweats, and J. C. Maxwell writes very sensibly here (his edition, p. xii): Shakespeare, he finds, is "exploiting . . . the sheer comedy of sexuality" in lines 230–40, where we meet the "sweet bottom-grass" of the erotic landscape. This explanation is rather too disinfectant; there is a joke, sure enough, based on evasion of a censorship, but a young man who felt prepared to take this Venus on would find the description positively exciting. We recognise Venus as divine because she is free not merely from bodily shame but even from social precaution; that Adonis is snubbing her just cannot enter her mind. But also the modern conventions about sweat are sharply different from the Elizabethan ones. Many love poems of the time regard the sweat of a lady as somehow a proof of her elegance and refinement; the smell is not recommended as an excitement for our lower nature, the only way it could be praised in a modern novel. In this book we find the sweat of the chaste Lucrece while she is peacefully asleep singled

---

[1] Chettle had published the dying pamphlet of Greene, which contained various libels on authors – some of them justified, says Chettle (December 1592); but he has now met Shakespeare and found "his demeanour no less excellent than the quality he professes. Besides, divers of worship have reported his uprightness of dealing, which argues his honesty, and his facetious grace in writing, which approves his art."

out for praise; one hand is

> On the green coverlet; whose perfect white
> Showed like an April daisy on the grass,
> With pearly sweat resembling dew of night.      (lines 394–6)

I do not know that any poet before Andrew Marvell praised the smell of the sweat of male farmhands, but I expect someone did. Spenser would have blamed Lewis here for being "nice", meaning squeamish and proud of it, an unsoldierly trait. And indeed the impressiveness, the final solidity, of *Venus and Adonis* does turn upon not being "nice", partly from its firm show of acquaintance with country sport, partly from not even caring whether you find the details funny or not. And then, in his own mind, the story would have some bearing on his marriage to a woman of twenty-six when he was eighteen. No doubt it all took a bit of nerve.

At the end of the poem (line 1,166) the corpse of Adonis is "melted like a vapour" and a flower springs up from his blood; Venus plucks it, saying that it smells like Adonis, though not as nice, and that the sap dripping from the break is like the tears that he shed too readily:

> . . . this was thy father's guise –
>
> . . .
>
> For every little grief to wet his eyes;
> To grow unto himself was his desire,
> And so 'tis thine; but know, it is as good
> To wither in my breast as in his blood.      (lines 1,177–82)

The earlier Sonnets frequently blame the man addressed for trying to live to himself like a flower, and for resisting a marriage; the personal application was easy enough to recognise. But people in the know were meant to regard this as only incidental to the structure. The poem recounts a Myth of Origin, like "how the Elephant got its Trunk", a form that scholars, both in Shakespeare's time and our own, revere to a rather surprising degree. (The genuinely ancient examples are believed to have been designed to support the practice of some already existing ritual or custom.) Shakespeare meant his poem to be classically respectable, unlike the plays which he could make a living from, and the motto on his title page boasts of it; but he is not hampered by the form, spurred by it rather. The terrible prophecy of Venus, at the end, at least seems to tell a general truth and thereby give the poem a universal "significance". Also, I have come to think, he extracted from the Myth of Origin a new literary device, very important in the seventeenth century, though hardly ever employed by himself in its pure form except for *The Phoenix and the Turtle*.

The central trope of John Donne, the only bit of metaphysics in Metaphysical Poetry, runs as follows: A ruler or mistress or saint is being praised, for Justice, Beauty, Holiness, or what not, and this is done by saying "You are the Platonic Idea, in person, of Justice or what not"; in the same way, Venus had always been Love walking about in person. Elizabeth Drury has to hold this position in the *Anniversaries*, or they are mere nonsense. Only Jesus Christ (an individual who was also the Logos) had ever deserved such praise, but the literary acceptance of classical deities meant that it could be used without feeling blasphemous. It has become an arid formula when Donne writes to the Countess of Bedford:

> Your (or You) Virtue two vast uses serves;
> It ransoms one sex, and one Court preserves.

The two words in parenthesis have to mean "or perhaps Virtue *is* you", but probably poor Donne is just hammering out the formula to try and get some of his wife's grocery bills paid. When I was a student, people thought that he had imported this trick from Spain, but Edward Wilson kindly tells me that there is at least no prominent use of it in sixteenth-century Spanish poetry. Some recent critic has named the trick "inverted Platonism", and it certainly needs to be distinguished from Platonism. It is rather silly, though there were some splendid uses of it, so perhaps I will not seem too patriotic when claiming it as a home product.

No one will be surprised that Shakespeare could see the dramatic or "quibbling" possibilities of his story, as when saying of Venus:

> She's Love, she loves, and yet she is not loved.     (line 610)

or when the irritated Adonis, like C. S. Lewis, says that what she calls love is really "sweating Lust" (line 794). But Venus at line 12 is already saying it about Adonis, who is merely human – at any rate, till after he is dead. In the full "metaphysical" trope, it is standard to say that the death of the individual entails a universal absence of the abstraction – after Punctuality Smith has died, nobody can ever catch a train again. But why should this be true

of Adonis, unless because Venus will go off in a huff? Her pre-
sentiment of his death, she says, cannot be true because the
consequences of it would be too awful:

> "O Jove," quoth she, "how much a fool was I
> To be of such a weak and silly mind
> To wail his death who lives, and must not die
> Till mutual overthrow of mortal kind!
> > For he being dead, with him is beauty slain,
> > And, beauty dead, black chaos comes again."
>
> (lines 1,015–20)

She already expects the race of man to destroy itself; and the last
two hundred lines of the poem, after she has found him dead, are
loaded with her despairing insistence that there is no love left in
the world. The conception is not a minor decoration in the poem.

Shakespeare did not need to invent it here because he had
already used it superbly in *Titus Andronicus* (V.ii), published in
1594 to help launch the Company but probably written about
1590. The Empress Tamora, who has done great wrong to Titus,
believes him to be in consequence so mad that he can be tricked
into facilitating the murder of his surviving son Lucius. She therefore visits him disguised as Revenge-in-Person, bringing her two
sons disguised as Rape and Murder. An Elizabethan spectator
was of course thoroughly accustomed to allegorical pageants and
charades; he too could if necessary have disguised himself as
Revenge. Titus cannot help behaving queerly, but uses this
weakness to further his revenge, like Hieronymo in *The Spanish
Tragedy* of Kyd, and the eventual Hamlet of Shakespeare. He
plays up to her with eerie glee and magnificent rhetoric:

> (To Demetrius) Look round about the wicked streets of
> > Rome,
> > And when thou find'st a man that's like
> > thyself,
> Good Murder, stab him; he's a murderer.

After a good deal of this, she is so certain he is mad that he can
easily deceive her into eating her two sons, disguised as a pie. It
is wild but not irrelevant, indeed flatly true, because the practical
trouble with revenge is that it does not finish, but produces blood
feuds. Shakespeare is always prepared to think, "Why are we
interested in the story?" and then say the reason why on the
stage. The poem about Venus offered a very different opportunity for the technique, but one can see that his mind would take

to it readily. I do not know that anybody else was already using it so early.

We need not doubt that Shakespeare considered the end of the poem dignified, and half believed what he told the Archbishop. But the dedication of it already envisages that a "graver labour" will come next, so there was no change of plan before setting out on *The Rape of Lucrece*. This too is a Myth of Origin; to insist upon it, the death of Lucrece causes an absurd change in human blood (line 1,750). A hero did not need to be a god before such things could happen; one could easily have a historical Myth of Origin (for example, *Macbeth* is about how the Scots, thanks to the Stuarts, took to civilised hereditary rule instead of tribal warfare). The story of Lucrece was an exciting and dangerous example because it explained how Rome threw off her kings and thus acquired an almost superhuman virtue; though somewhat obscurely, this gave its justifying importance to the heroine's choice of suicide. Both the Bible (I Sam. 12:12–25) and the classics (in practice, Plutarch) disapproved of royalty; the institution could only be defended as a necessity for our fallen natures. Also Brutus had a mysterious importance for a patriot and a dramatist. No other great period of drama, anywhere in the world, had so much interest in madmen as the Elizabethan one. This apparently derived from the Hamlet of Kyd, whose story came from a twelfth-century historian of Denmark, "the Saxon who knew Latin". But the story had classical authority from Livy's brief remarks on Lucius Junius Brutus, who pretended imbecility in order to be safe till he could take revenge; indeed, Saxo has been suspected of imitating Livy to provide elegance for his savage material, so that Hamlet, whose basic trouble in the fairy tale was that he could not tell a lie, was truthful as ever when he said "I am more an antique Roman than a Dane." The Brutus who killed Caesar was his bastard, as Shakespeare remarks in *Henry VI, Part Two* (IV.i), though he kept it out of *Caesar*; and a more antique Brutus, a parricide as usual, had been the first to civilise Britain; hence the name. Now, it was Brutus who plucked the dagger from Lucrece's body and championed the expulsion of the kings. He had pretended imbecility up to that very moment . . .

> Burying in Lucrece' wound his folly's show.
> He with the Romans was esteemèd so
> As seely jeering idiots are with kings,
> For sportive words and utt'ring foolish things;

> But now he lays that shallow habit by
> Wherein deep policy did him disguise . . .          (lines 1,810–15)

The Romans take an oath, and the last line of the poem says that the Tarquins were banished forever.

J. C. Maxwell says in his note:

It is curious that Shakespeare makes no mention here (though the Argument concludes with it) of the historical importance of this, as involving the abolition of the monarchy (unless "everlasting" glances at it); this tells heavily against the view . . . that the popularity of the poem owed much to its bearing on political issues.

It is curious that the scholars of our age, though geared up as never before, are unable to imagine living under a censorship or making an effort to avoid trouble with Thought Police; these unpleasant features of current experience were also familiar in most historical periods, so that the disability must regularly prevent scholars from understanding what they read.

Southampton, who seemed fated to irritate the Queen, might well be inclined to cool thoughts about royalty; and Shakespeare would be wise to hesitate as to how far one might go. Though never very republican, you would think, he was certainly interested in Brutus; he had already, in *Titus Andronicus*, written better than any other Elizabethan the part of the half-genuine madman. Yet both themes are subdued to the decorum of his poem.

The resulting work is hard to read straight through, but one should realise that Shakespeare has made it static by deliberate choice. Francis Berry pointed out in *The Shakespeare Inset* that, although both these poems contain a high proportion of dialogue, the reader does not remember them so, because all the harangues might just as well be soliloquies. Indeed the silent colloquy between Lucrece and the low-class messenger, blushing together at cross-purposes (line 1,339), stands out because it is as near as we get to any contact between two minds. In a play the audience wants the story to go forward, but here the Bard could practise rhetoric like five-finger exercises on the piano. Also, the rhetoric works mainly by calling up parallel cases, so that here again the figure of myth becomes a sort of generalisation. Even this perhaps hardly excuses the long stretch of looking at tapestries of the Fall of Troy, which one may suspect was written later as a substitute for dangerous thoughts about royalty; Lucrece when appealing to Tarquin flatters his assumptions by recalling the virtues of royalty, and the highly formal structure of the work demands that she should recognise the inadequacy of such ideals after her appeal has failed. It would be sensible to have an unpublished version suited to the patron, who contributed a great deal more than the buyers would; and besides, it would give the welcome feeling of conspiracy. But anyhow the poem needs here a feeling of grim delay – she has already decided upon suicide, but has to wait for the arrival of the proper witnesses.

Whether she was right to kill herself has long been discussed, and Shakespeare was probably not so absurd as we think to let her review the Christian objection to suicide – its origins are hard to trace. St Augustine, caddish as usual, had written "if adulterous, why praised? if chaste, why killed?"; and one might suspect that the romantic rhetoric of Shakespeare is used only to evade this old dilemma. But he is interested in the details of the case, and probably had in mind a solution, though he did not care to express it grossly. Livy already has Tarquin force her by an inherently social threat; if she rejects him, he will stab both her and a male servant in the same bed and claim afterwards that he had been righteously indignant at finding them there (line 670). It is assumed that her reputation has a political importance for her aristocratic family, which she puts before everything else; he gags her with her bedclothes, but not because she is expected to resist. Immediately after the rape, and till her death, she speaks of herself as guilty, and Shakespeare concurs. However, just before she stabs herself the assembled lords protest that she is still innocent, and she does not deny this, but brushes it aside as unimportant beside a social consequence:

> "No, no!" quoth she, "no dame hereafter living
> By my excuse shall claim excuse's giving."    (lines 1,714–15)

Coleridge in a famous passage derided Beaumont and Fletcher because the ladies in their plays regard chastity as a costly trinket which they are liable to mislay, and it is not obvious why Shakespeare is different here. When Tarquin slinks from her bed, he says, "She bears the load of lust he left behind"; "She desperate with her nails her flesh doth tear"; she "there remains a hopeless castaway" (lines 734, 739, 744). Perhaps, he reflects, the instability of women is an excuse for her: they have "waxen minds . . . Then call them not the authors of their ill" (lines 1,240–4). Just before killing herself, she speaks to her husband and the

assembled lords of her "gross blood" and its "accessory yield-
ings" (lines 1,655, 1,658); one could hardly ask her to be much
plainer. She was no virgin, having several children; and it is a
basic fact about the young Shakespeare that he considers young
men in general overwhelmingly desirable to women, let alone
brave young lords. Thus she took an involuntary pleasure in the
rape, though she would have resisted it in any way possible; that
is why she felt guilty, and why some of her blood turned black,
making a precedent for all future corrupted blood (line 1,750).
The reader perhaps is also guilty, having taken a sexual pleasure
in these descriptions of sexual wrong – as much at least as the
"homely villain" who wondered how she was making him blush.
But we are not told that she would have killed herself for this
private shame; she considers the suicide useful for public
reasons. St Augustine would conclude that she deserved death
for enjoying the rape and Hell for her suicide afterwards; but the
dramatist is sure that all her reactions, in this tricky situation, do
her the greatest credit and are enough to explain the permanent
majesty of Rome.

The Passionate Pilgrim (1599) is a cheat, by a pirate who is very
appreciative of the work of Shakespeare. It starts with two
genuine sonnets (138 and 144 in Sonnets) each of them implying
plenty of story and giving a smart crack at the end; and the third
item, a sonnet extracted from Love's Labour's Lost, follows
quite naturally. Paging ahead in the bookshop, one found poems
that might easily be Shakespeare's, though most of them are now
generally considered not to be; it would be sensible to buy at
once. What we learn from this is that Shakespeare had become
news, a personality exciting curiosity, and there are other signs of
it. In the previous year, for the first time, a play had been printed
with his name on the title page ("Love's Labour's Lost, as it was
presented before her Highness this last Christmas"), and the
absurd Palladis Tamia by Meres had at least treated his work as
deserving scholarly attention. The Shakespeare Allusion Book
finds many more references to Falstaff than to any other character (Hamlet comes second, with the others far behind him). Thus
in 1598 his reputation so to speak came to the boil; this was why
his public was willing to trust him through his tragic period,
though they did not like it so much.

The editor would have printed more sonnets if he could, and
yet the ones chosen are well suited to his purpose – how could
that happen? Dover Wilson in his Introduction to the Sonnets of

*Shakespeare* thought that the Dark Woman (he will not call her a lady) had allowed a publisher two specimens with a view to raising the price of her whole collection. But this ignores the state of the market; she would have succeeded in publishing her collection and would not have needed to offer bait. I think that a visitor was left to wait in a room where a cabinet had been left unlocked – rather carelessly, but the secret poems were about five years old; he saw at once that they would sell, but did not know how much time was available. Thumbing through the notebook (the poems cannot have been on separate sheets, or he could have taken more without being noticed), he chose two with saucy last couplets for hurried copying. In one of the variants, the 1609 edition has a simple misprint, but as a rule it has slightly the better text – either because the thief miscopied or because Shakespeare had second thoughts. I think that one of these cases allows us to decide the alternative:

> I smiling credit her false-speaking tongue,
> Outfacing faults in love with love's ill rest.

In 1609 the second line has become:

> On both sides thus is simple truth supprest.

J. C. Maxwell gives an admirable gloss for the pirate version: "With (the help of) the ill-grounded sense of security that is characteristic of love", and plainly this is more like Shakespeare. But it is rather out of place; the poem has very little to do with his private experience or sensibility, commenting with sad good-humour on almost universal departures from truth. The duller line is more good-mannered in a way, and he would not give his first draft of a sonnet to his "private friends" (as Meres wrote), or even, one would think, to the Dark Lady. Poets of our own time have been known to add in the desired obscurity when they rewrite, but Shakespeare is more likely to have removed it. So probably he was the one who left the cabinet unlocked.

This publication also refutes the Herbert Theory of the Sonnets, for a reason that its supporters have been too high-minded to observe. William Herbert, later Earl of Pembroke, became eighteen in April 1598, and was hardly allowed to come to London earlier, as he was a sickly lad, addicted to headaches (Dover Wilson, *op. cit.*, p. 66); though later, I don't deny, an honest man and a useful patron, who deserved to have the First Folio dedicated to him in 1623. But this would mean that the sonnet about letting Shakespeare's boy patron borrow his mistress, when the pirate got it into print, would be hot news. The Elizabethans would call the incident thorough toad-eating, and it would be sure to get mentioned in some of the letters of gossip. I am not saying that Shakespeare would not have done it, though I think it was outside his mode of life at this date, but that he could not have hushed it up, in these circumstances. Consider what moral Ben Jonson would find to say (whereas, in 1594, moral Ben Jonson had not yet poked his nose above the boards). The first soliloquy of Prince Hal, assuring the audience that he will betray Falstaff, has close verbal echoes of the first of the pathetic sonnets ("Full many a glorious morning") trying to defend the patron for a betrayal of Shakespeare. But this does not mean that they were written at the same time; the implications would be horrible. The joke of Falstaff largely turns on the repeated bite of his self-defence, and Shakespeare may well be drawing a good deal upon his own humiliations when the servant of a patron, in his twenties. But he would need to use these memories in the assurance of secrecy, feeling them distant, feeling that they could be laughed over.

The reader should be warned of a slight change of idiom in the couplet:

> The truth I shall not know, but live in doubt
> Till my bad angel fire my good one out.

The Variorum edition gives a list of references to periodicals, mainly Victorian, and till I looked them up I imagined they proved that the Dark Lady is accused of having gonorrhea. They merely show that the phrase *fire out* was then used as we use *fire*, to mean "dismiss a person from a job"; it did not then, as now, inevitably suggest firing something from a gun. Shakespeare need only be saying: "I will not know whether the Dark Lady has seduced the Patron till she gets bored and dismisses him; then no doubt both will come round to me with indignant stories." We may be sure he did realise that an explosive insult was in the background, because he had a complex verbal awareness, as when he left his wife his second-best bed; but if the Dark Lady had really caught the disease we would hear more about it in his personal poems. A laboured epigram by Edward Guilpin, published in 1598, is I think simply a crude imitation of Shakespeare's joke here; he must have been one of the "private friends" who were allowed (says Meres) to read some of the "sugared Sonnets". It would be pretty sad to believe that Shakespeare copied the merry thought from Guilpin as soon as he read his book, and had it stolen at once.

One has to try to make sense of these dates; it is fundamental to the understanding of Shakespeare's development, I think, that the relations with a patron come in 1592–5, when a patron was needed. Leslie Hotson, indeed, has put the *Sonnets* five years earlier, in an entertaining recent book that proposed a new addressee for them (*Mr. W. H.*, 1964); he laughs at the scholars for viewing Shakespeare as Little Dopey, shambling along in the rear of Marlowe and the rest, "a remarkably late developer". But his development really is unusual; usually the lyrical power comes earlier than the constructive one. Reading through the plays in the generally accepted order – *The Comedy of Errors*, the three parts of *Henry VI*, *The Taming of the Shrew*, *Titus Andronicus* – you get hardly a breath of poetry so far, though plenty of vigorous rhetoric, and a clear mind at work making the best of the plots. A little poetry comes in with *Richard III*, so that he was just beginning to be a poet, aged twenty-seven or so, when the plague forced him to rely on it for survival. After two years, when the theatres open again, he seems essentially a poetic dramatist. Another contrast, though more trivial, is perhaps more striking. Bernard Shaw remarked that Shakespeare must have suffered torture if he ever read over his comedies after he had grown up – assuming, I think, that any adult feels an obscure personal shame when he hears another man boast of being a gentleman. Probably the boasting of lads together is much the same in all classes, but it is true that an entry of three young lords, swanking by making jokes that are assumed to be top-class, occurs in all his comedies between 1594 and 1598, whereas the characters in the early comedies are mostly traders, and the lords in *Henry VI* simply murderers. One might perhaps blame Shakespeare for choosing to write about aristocrats, but not, having chosen to, for doing some fieldwork on how they actually talked. It is not what is now called snobbery, because he could not pretend to be anything but the servant of his Earl. Probably he would be allowed to hand around drinks at a party given by the Earl for young men of standing – listening with all his ears, though, as one gathers from the plays, much more free to make jokes himself than a modern servant is. In private he seems to have scolded his lord unreasonably, as privileged servants often do. C. S. Lewis, in *English Literature in the Sixteenth Century*

(1954), spoke of "the self-abnegation, the 'naughting'," of the sonnets, more like a parent than a lover: "In certain senses of the word 'love', Shakespeare is not so much our best as our only love-poet" (p. 505). This is noble, but it is perhaps only the other side of a feeling that the gratitude is over-strained. And yet, a number of the sonnets thank the patron because

> thou . . . dost advance
> As far as learning my rude ignorance.                    (Sonnet 78)

The actual teaching of the Earl can hardly have been more than a few social tips, but as a window upon the great world Shakespeare had been feeling the need of him badly. The feelings seem better grounded if you realise that the childish patron was giving far more than he knew. And, unless you redate the plays as a whole, remembering that the evidence is quite an elaborate structure, there is only one plausible time for fitting in this bit of education.

*A Lover's Complaint* was printed at the end of the sonnets in 1609, but many critics have denied that Shakespeare wrote it – chiefly on grounds of vocabulary and imagery, but also by calling lines bad when they are simply dramatic, imagined as by another speaker (e.g. lines 106–11). Much of it, he would consider, had needed correcting before it was published, as indeed do many of the sonnets themselves; he forces the words into his rhyme scheme and general intention so hurriedly that our textual notes sometimes only amount to lame excuses (e.g. around line 235). But at least Kenneth Muir has now proved Shakespeare's authorship, by "clusters" (*William Shakespeare 1564–1964*, ed. E. A. Bloom); the principle is that if an author happens to use one word of a cluster his mind drags in most of the others soon after, and this process is not conscious or noticeable enough for an admirer to imitate it, nor is it affected, as imagery in general can be, by a change of subject matter or recent experience. I think the poem is evidently by Shakespeare on psychological grounds, and a kind of echo of the sonnets (this of course is why they were kept together, and eventually pirated together); but I am confronted by an agreement among the scholars (Maxwell's edition, p. xxxv) that it must have been written after 1600. Similar arguments have been used to maintain that the sonnets themselves were written late; the explanation, I think, is that Shakespeare often first tried out a novelty of style in his private poetry. I only ask for two years; the poem was written in 1598, with tranquillity, looking back with tender humour at his relations with Southampton, and just after killing off Falstaff. There would be no intention of publication; perhaps he wrote it in the evenings of a solitary journey. It would at any rate be a change, after seeing himself as Falstaff, to become the traditional forsaken damsel (forsaken, because by 1596 the Earl had become absorbed in his dangerous life; we need not look for a specific ground of quarrel, though we may expect that Shakespeare did, at the time). Shakespeare, like other authors, often used poetry to scold himself out of a bad state of mind, and took for granted that no one would realise he was doing it. He knew it was a delusion that the Earl had betrayed him, and writing about Falstaff had aggravated the sentiment, so he wrote a parody. Or perhaps he merely felt it was delightful to carry the belief to a wild extreme. These conjectures have the merit of explaining why the poem was written at all, though (fairly clearly) not intended for publication. Most people find that working for a repertory company is exhausting in itself, especially if they have part responsibility for the management; a man who also gives the company two masterpieces a year, as regular as clockwork, with a good deal of reading behind them, is not looking around for something to do. It is thus in order to suppose an internal reason for undertaking this quite lengthy bit of work, since there is no external one.

The first ten verses set the scene, and the rest is all spoken by the ruined girl; as many critics have remarked, the best and most Shakespearean lines express reproach:

> Thus merely with the garment of a Grace,
> The naked and concealèd fiend he covered . . .    (lines 316–17)

> O father, what a hell of witchcraft lies
> In the small orb of one particular tear!    (lines 288–9)

All the same, the girl firmly asserts in the last words of the poem that she would have him ruin her again if she got the chance:

> O, all that borrowed motion, seeming owed,
> Would yet again betray the fore-betrayed
> And new-pervert a reconcilèd maid!    (lines 327–9)

No other author would do this; one man would bewail the seduction and another treat it jovially, but not both at once. Indeed, rather few male poets seem convinced that young men in general are irresistible to women. A reader of novels will rightly feel baffled at not knowing the social arrangements of this village, where many people write sonnets expounding the suitability of the rich jewels that they are presenting to the young man (line 210); is it in Arcadia or Warwickshire? is he the son of a labourer, or the heir to a hundred acres, say?

> He had the dialect and different skill,
> Catching all passions in his craft of will,
>
> That he did in the general bosom reign
> Of young, of old, and sexes both enchanted,
> To dwell with them in thoughts, or to remain
> In personal duty, following where he haunted.  (lines 125–30)

The magical picture only applies to one person, who had been already an Earl when still a child; no wonder, after puzzling their heads, they decided that he was the one who was clever, and not just his horse (lines 114–19). In all the undramatic poems Shakespeare is deliberately holding back the power to be funny, which was considered when he wrote *A Lover's Complaint* to be much his greatest power; but he knew a joke when he saw one, even if he had just written it down himself. But perhaps when I say "funny" I would be more intelligible to young people (who have such grim ideas now of what makes a joke) if I said "charming". The chief merit of A. L. Rowse's account, on the other hand (*William Shakespeare*, 1964), was its powerful presentation of Southampton as a typical neurotic invert, intolerably disagreeable, who could only regard the Queen as a personal rival. Under James, after he had unexpectedly won back his life, he played a considerable part in founding the English colonies in America, and the only picture that conveys his charm shows him as an elder statesman. (It is in C. C. Stopes's *Life*, p. 449.) But we have a glimpse of him when twenty in the Valentine of the *Two Gentlemen of Verona*. This figure is bustling along, with a rope ladder hidden under his cloak, to abduct the daughter of the Duke of Milan, but the Duke accosts him and asks his advice – how is one to abduct a lady who is kept locked up in a high bedroom? Why, with a rope ladder, of course, equipped with grappling irons but light enough to carry under one's cloak; Valentine feels he is cleverly secret because he just manages to restrain himself from offering to share the use of his rope ladder with the outraged father, but so far from that, he and his cloak are farcically transparent. The brash informative practicality of this does not feel to me neurotic at all, and I expect that many of his servants were in love with him when he was twenty, not only Shakespeare. Plainly he seemed very young to Shakespeare, who was not only ten years older but had had a harder time. The Bard could not be considered low; as heir to an ex-mayor of Stratford he would become entitled to gentility. But the social ladder was long and steep, and the expense of the clothes the Earl wore all the time would alone be enough to make him seem legendary – though he did not seem another breed from common men, the title being a recent creation.

A grave change in the whole tone of Shakespeare's writing arrives at the time of *Hamlet* (1600), the first major tragedy, and here it would be fussy to suppose that he was even remembering his relations with the patron. Critics since A. C. Bradley have pretty well agreed that "sex-horror" is prominent all through the tragic period (perhaps burning itself out in the unfinished *Timon of Athens*, before *Antony and Cleopatra*). I do not understand this change, though I expect there is a simple answer if we knew it. The reason why *The Lover's Complaint* must have been written before it is simply that otherwise it would have been much grimmer. The change I think is prominent even in the parallels to *Hamlet* which give Kenneth Muir his main evidence; *The Lover's Complaint* is regularly less fierce than the echoes of it which convey the doom of Ophelia. We have no nondramatic poems to guide us after the tragic period has set in.

Only one remains to be considered, and it is short; but it has come to seem the only very good poem in the book, exquisite, baffling, and exalted: *The Phoenix and the Turtle*.[2] It is much better, I think, if viewed less portentously than has become usual. The occasion for Shakespeare's agreeing to write this bit of praise, in late 1598 or early 1599, was a humane and domestic one, though socially rather smart. I have no impulse to deny that vast and fundamental meanings derive or arise from the poem, such as were adumbrated when C. S. Lewis said that reading it

---

[2] There has been a recent move in favour of saying *The Phoenix and Turtle* instead of *The Phoenix and the Turtle*. It is true that the title pages of Chester speak of "The Phoenix and Turtle", and Shakespeare's poem as first printed has no title. But his way of regarding this pair has long been recognised as slightly different from Chester's. A social column will report the presence at a party of "The Earl and Countess of X" because they are expected to go together, and that is how Chester feels about his Phoenix and Turtle, but Shakespeare, whatever else he feels, always regards their co-presence with a touch of surprise. A critic may write about a poem: "The familiar lion and unicorn serve to emphasize the wholly conventional character of the imagery", but they become "the lion and *the* unicorn" when they are fighting for the

was like entering the secret origins of creation, or at least of the creation of the heroines of Shakespeare's plays. But it does not tell Queen Elizabeth to produce an heir by the Earl of Essex, nor even mutter about the marital secrets of the Countess of Bedford. If Shakespeare had been prone to say things like that, he would not have stayed afloat for at all long upon the smoking waters of the Court. It may be hoped that such theories are going out of fashion, but what we are regularly told now, though it sounds more modest, is quite as damaging to the poem. J. C. Maxwell takes it for granted when he remarks that Shakespeare's poem "contradicts the personal allegory of Chester's poem", so that "our interpretation must be from within the poem itself". He seems to feel that this makes it pure. But Shakespeare would have been abominably rude if he had behaved like that, after agreeing to take part in the social event of offering a volume of congratulation to Sir John Salisbury. The whole book was about the birth of a new phoenix from the ashes of the old one, a story that every reader had been taught at school, and here it was somehow in praise of Salisbury's marriage; but Shakespeare is presumed to say: "No, of course, the new Phoenix wasn't born. When you burned the old one you simply killed it, as anybody could have told you you would." But, even if he had tried to offer this rudeness, it would not get printed. The immense indulgences nowadays offered to the avant-garde are not in question here. Salisbury was a forthright and decisive man, brought up to advance the glory of his house, and we know he made Ben Jonson rewrite one of the poems for his book; he would no more have allowed Shakespeare to palm off on him a subjective poem than a seditious one.

Verses by Shakespeare, Marston, Chapman, and Jonson, and also by an anonymous poet who seems to be Jonson again (probably one of his team had backed out from fear of ridicule) are added at the end of a long allegorical poem, *Love's Martyr*, by

crown. Shakespeare's poem really is a bit like "The Walrus and the Carpenter", and cannot be properly appreciated unless that is seen. Looking now for evidence to support the traditional preference (though it is apparently no older than a Boston edition of 1805), I find the poem grants it repeatedly:

> Phoenix and *the* turtle fled . . . *this* turtle and his queen . . . *the* turtle saw his right . . . it made this threne, To the phoenix and *the* dove . . . And *the* turtle's loyal breast To eternity doth rest.

In effect, *The Phoenix and the Turtle* emerges as a habitual rhythm of Shakespeare's poem, and an illogical pedantry ought not to be allowed to destroy so natural a title.

Robert Chester (unregistered, 1601); a separate title page assures us that these too are "never before extant, and (now first) consecrated to the love and merit of the thrice-noble knight, Sir John Salisbury." The book appeared at the height of the War of the Theatres, when several of the contributors were quarrelling, and soon after the execution of Essex, when it was very dangerous to print a riddle that might arouse the suspicions of the Queen. Surely it is natural to expect that the poems were written earlier.

The introduction to an edition by Carleton Brown (1914) of *Poems by Sir John Salusbury and Robert Chester* (Early English Text Society, 113) is a mine of information and entertainment about these characters, and ought I think to have settled the question. Salisbury (we may use the ordinary spelling because Chester's book does) was squire of Lleweny in north Wales, and had married in 1586 at the age of twenty an illegitimate but recognised daughter of the King of Man (or Earl of Derby); some verses written for the wedding already call her a royal bird. In 1595 he came to London as a law student and was made squire of the body to the Queen; he was her cousin, and a determined Anglican (having got the estate when his Papist brother was executed for the Babington Plot), and had a standing quarrel in Denbighshire with supporters of the Essex faction. This last would be no help until the execution of Essex, early in 1601, but in June of that year he was knighted by the Queen herself. By October he is back home being elected to Parliament as Knight of the Shire, with scandalous disorders, so he must have moved fast. Clearly, the poem was hurried out to celebrate the knighthood, unregistered to save time and because the Queen would not suspect a man she was rewarding for his loyalty; but the writing would have been done beforehand, to wait for the occasion. A line from Jonson's "Epode" here is quoted in *England's Parnassus* (1600) showing that at least some of these poems were ready about two years before publication. Also an autograph copy of Jonson's "Enthusiastic Ode" survives, inscribed to the Countess of Bedford. The squire would show round all the poems at Court, as soon as they were ready; and the ever-helpful Countess might be expected to want her own copy of Jonson's contribution, as it was not yet to be available in print. In this poem he was evidently struggling to be as jolly about the Phoenix as the Turtle demanded. Clumsy as Jonson was, he would not have given it to the Countess as direct praise of her own charms; or at least, she would not have kept it, if he had.

In 1597 the squire had printed some poems at the end of *Sinetes Passion* by Robert Parry, who calls him "the Patron"; they make very elaborate anagrams (in easy singing lines) on the names of three adored ladies, one of them his wife's sister. While very pugnacious, he was what a later age called "a martyr to the fair", attentive to the ladies, so it had seemed all right at the time of the wedding to make him a sacrifice as Turtle beside the semi-royal bride as Phoenix. In 1598 he would be a very useful patron for the young Ben Jonson, who was in desperate need of one, and he seems to have told Jonson to whip up a chorus of London poets. Shakespeare's company was giving Jonson a production, and it would be consistent to help him here too – assuming that Shakespeare had no objections to the general plan. So far from that, Shakespeare was amused or charmed both by the squire and his poet – as is clear once you admit that he wrote his tribute, not while Hamlet was saying he couldn't bear to think what his mum did in bed, but while Henry the Fifth was saying:

> Though it appear a little out of fashion
> There is much care and valour in this Welshman.

Shakespeare made it part of his business to keep an eye on these pushful Welsh cousins of the Queen, and he recommended them to his audiences without hiding their absurdity.

Chester, says Brown, was probably the resident chaplain in the big house at Lleweny, anyway a dependent who praised the family by an allegory at the time of the grand wedding. Later he was induced to add a lot of tedious padding (Nature takes the Phoenix on a grand tour), but the basic allegory is quite short and readable, though radically absurd. A marriage does indeed require mutual accommodation, and love may genuinely receive "a mystical reinforcement" on the birth of a child; but to praise a grand marriage by calling it a martyrdom is a gaffe, all the more absurd because sure to be suspected of being true. Chester evidently came to feel this during the years while he was adding the encyclopedia verses, and when at last he had to tell the London poets what the whole thing meant, so that they could reinforce it, he said it meant "married chastity". This idea had not been prominent when he began, though the intention was already high and pure. When Nature at last leads the Phoenix to the Turtle, she asks whether he has been chaste, and, on being reassured, explains that for her to produce issue requires burning alive; both birds at once collect twigs, so there is no long period of married chastity. (This of course is *why* you sometimes see birds carrying about twigs.) The main poem by Ben Jonson puzzles about his set theme, in a plain-man way; it seems a new idea to him. Trying to isolate the ideal, he appears to describe a man who spares his wife the act of sex in order not to offend her delicacy. We should welcome any sign of readiness among men of that age to treat their wives more considerately, especially if it meant spacing out the childbirths; but the refined thoughts expressed by Jonson here are remote from his tastes and convictions as otherwise known. He is not a hypocrite, because he is writing to a set theme; but his modern admirers should not praise him for his nobility. Rather out of the side of his mouth, he lets drop that one need not praise a husband who chose this course merely to hide impotence:

> We do not number here
> Such spirits as are only continent
> Because lust's means are spent.

Oddly enough Shakespeare manages to work the same reflection into his mood of total praise; the reproduction of the Phoenix, he surmises, has only failed because of the married chastity of the couple:

> . . . 'Twas not their infirmity.

Various modern critics have explained that Shakespeare could not bear the thought of reproduction when he wrote the poem; but nobody has yet ascribed quite so much delicacy to Ben Jonson.

*The Mutual Flame* by G. Wilson Knight (1955) shows that the Phoenix legend had often been used to symbolise a love denied bodily consummation, because that would be adulterous or homosexual or politically disruptive, so that the love is driven to more spiritual courses. He suggests that the poem may be about the squire's love for his wife's sister, which would at least avoid absurdity. One should remember here an epigram of C. S. Lewis, that Spenser was the first poet to have the nerve to say it is convenient for a man to be in love with his own wife. There had been a change of feeling since the Middle Ages, a thing so general that poor Chester, in the backwoods, around 1587, was running

Spenser close for the priority. Salisbury of course really did consider himself ready for heroic self-sacrifice whenever that became necessary; the idea was basic to his status, and had to be expressed firmly in his book; but otherwise he wanted the book to be as jolly as possible, and his pride in his wife had better be expressed in a firmly sexy manner – that was a point where he could take over from his chaplain. His marriage had produced four children in the first four years, six in the next ten (no twins), and one of his bastards had been baptised in the parish church in 1597. No wonder Jonson argued about what Chester could have meant. The Phoenix herself will not have come to London, with all those ailing children, but a few vigorous comments survive from her and she apparently lived to be seventy-five.[3] Shakespeare might genuinely have supposed it to be an ideal though perhaps barbaric marriage.

The Wilson Knight thesis does have a secondary truth; what keeps the long absurd poem sweet is Chester's love for his master. This kind of love was avowable and not usually tormented, but when Chester comes to present himself as the Pelican, who gazes upon the burning, he positively claims a share in the honours of sacrifice; both the Phoenix and the Turtle become the "young ones" of this Pelican and feed their "hungry fancies" on her breast. He has been under-rated, I think; so long as he is praising his dear lion (the coat-of-arms of Salisbury was a white lion) he has any amount of limpid depth. And why should not his absurdity (though he fears it) express something profound? If anything seems wrong with his poem, he says as he lumbers toward the end, abandoning for a moment the disguise of the Pelican,

> tis lameness of the mind
> That had no better skill; yet let it pass,
> For burdenous loads are set upon an ass.

This is the royal generosity of the Shakespearean clown, and Shakespeare was quite right to salute it.

---

[3] Brown, *op. cit.*, p. xxvi. Chester's poem says that the Phoenix had been anxious before meeting the Turtle, being of ripe age and fearing to have no offspring. No doubt it was often a tricky business to find a good enough marriage for the bastard daughter of an Earl. I expect she was twenty-five when the elder brother of young John was hanged, so that he inherited the estate and became free to marry her in what would be considered the nick of time. It does not mean that she was the Queen, who would be sixty-five.

Once the general tone has been grasped, of slightly fuddled good-humour, the dramatic placing of the piece by Shakespeare can be seen as reasonably good. The two first additional poems are subscribed "Vatum Chorus" (all the poets) and praise the virtues of Salisbury only, not his wife or family; then two poems subscribed "Ignoto" (Unknown, by the starving but invincible Ben Jonson again of course), without pretending not to know the Phoenix legend (which would be too absurd) manage to direct our attention onto the sacrifice of the old Phoenix, not presenting it as repaid by the birth of a new one. Such is the purpose of the phrasing:

> One Phoenix born, another Phoenix burn.

The build-up is only rough, but it is an intentional preparation for what Shakespeare is going to do. Shakespeare then presents himself as one of the spectators after the burning, among the non-predatory birds who are the voice of Reason, and they fall into despair because the result of the experiment is delayed. I gather from J. C. Maxwell's edition that it was traditional to allow a period of dramatic suspense. Shakespeare ingeniously fits in the set theme of "married chastity" as an excuse for the failure of the experiment. But what follows his noble resignation, what holds the opposite page, is the astonishment of a birth from the ashes. It begins:

> O twas a moving epicidium!
> Can Fire? Can Time? Can blackest Fate consume
> So rare Creation? No, tis thwart to sense;
> Corruption quakes to touch such excellence.

The recent scholarly edition of Marston's *Poems* (1961, ed. Davenport) says firmly that this word *epicidium* (poem about death) means the poem by Shakespeare just concluded. Marston snatches a moment to compliment Shakespeare, as he bounds onto the stage to describe the event in an entirely different literary style; and his only objection is that the forecast in Shakespeare's poem has, astoundingly, turned out wrong:

> Let me stand numbed with wonder; never came
> So strong amazement on astonished eye
> As this, this measureless pure rarity.

I consider that very good poetry. The subsequent poems all deal with Salisbury's domestic life, wife or child being mentioned every time, so that Shakespeare's poem acts as a watershed. Anyhow, he could not have intended to spoil the show because of his neuroses; that would be quite outside his habits and training. He was acting as a good trouper when he left the climax to Marston, and he seems to have remembered Marston's bit long afterwards for the last scene of *The Winter's Tale*.

Having thus restored the poem to decency, one may consider its use of "inverted Platonism". It says that, because these two ideal lovers are dead, there will never be real lovers again, anywhere:

> Truth may seem, but cannot be;
> Beauty brag, but 'tis not she;
> Truth and Beauty buried be.

However, the next and final verse abandons this high extremity of nonsense:

> To this urn let those repair
> That are either true or fair;
> For these dead birds sigh a prayer.

I suppose the reason why Shakespeare can afford to be lax about it in this curious way, which allows him a graceful ending to the poem, is that he is working in an accepted mode. All the poets in the book seem in command of the trick, even Robert Chester; he uses it when the Pelican rejoices that the Turtle chose to burn alive, though the Phoenix tried to spare him (the experience turned out to be a pleasure, according to the Pelican's eye-witness account). Otherwise, he says:

> Love had been murdered in the infancy;
> Without these two, no love at all can be.

It is clear then that Chester was writing another Myth of Origin. But can he have had the whole machine ready in 1587, a homely author, remotely secluded? This seemed to me a great puzzle, and I am glad to have it removed by W. H. Matchett's book on the poem (1965). He explains that Chester added the Pelican section, at the end of his first draft, when the squire took him to London to negotiate with the poets (the squire would not himself have demanded to be praised for married chastity). In a way, Chester must have known the idea from the start because it is inherent in this use of myth, but he had become uneasy about the absurdity of his whole plan; so that it would be a great relief when the smart poets, though they did laugh at him as he had expected, told him that his absurdity had become the height of fashion. He was inspired to add what is the most eloquent and personal section of the whole work.

Matchett has a very welcome energy of logic and research; what other critics limply assume, he follows up.[4] I hope his book will drive out of people's minds the main idea which he champions, that Shakespeare was writing about the loves of Elizabeth and Essex; when he says that Shakespeare refers to the Queen as already dead in order to rebuke her for not having followed his previous advice, whereas in fact the exasperated and appalling old woman had become dangerous to anybody who had to approach her, surely this is enough to act as a purge. But I think he is right (for instance) in saying that Jonson became frightened on hearing that the poems would appear during 1601, when they were likely to be supposed to be about Essex; he made some baffling remarks in his plays of that year, hoping to offset the publication. Matchett also gets his teeth into "inverted Platonism", as one might expect, and it is a great comfort to find a critic who is prepared to attend to the words. Somehow he contrives to denounce Marston and not Shakespeare for using this trope:

Against Shakespeare's materialistic basis for negative judgment, he asserts a pseudo-Platonic basis for positive judgment. As an exposition of Platonic abstractions, Marston's poem is an awkward melange; as a compliment to an allegorized individual – claiming that this person is himself the Idea upon which all else depends – his poem further degrades the very idealism it pretends to express.

Marston says he had been wondering why all the young girls were so ugly and stupid nowadays till he saw the new Phoenix, and then he realised that Nature had just been saving up, so as to give her everything. The eldest Salisbury child, a daughter, would be about twelve when this was written for her, and it seems well enough calculated for her age-group; she would think it rather fun. If anything, I should call it Science Fiction not Platonism; it does not deserve to be rebuked as false philosophy, because it scarcely even pretends to be philosophy. But somebody else

---

[4] He remarks that a scribe may write the name of the author after copying a poem without intending a signature, and this would destroy a good deal of the edifice of Carleton Brown. But if you wrote a name with set formal flourishes, surely that implied it was your signature.

deserves the rebuke; why do modern critics invariably write down that the trope is neoplatonic? Its effects, very various, are nearly always broader and more imaginative than would be gathered from this docketing.

Elizabethan jokes are notoriously confusing, but it would be wrong to think that the Welsh squire was being fooled by the city slickers. He wanted his book as jolly as was compatible with having it sustain the glory of his house, and he rejected the first draft of Ben Jonson's "Invocation"; at least, there is no other reason why this much more solemn version in Jonson's handwriting should have got kept among the Salisbury papers. And he must rather have strained the goodwill of his chaplain when he inserted his own "Cantos" at the end of the allegory, celebrating his delight in the beauty of the Phoenix in a very unsacrificial manner (only the first is announced as written by the Turtle, but they all have his very recognisable facility and ingenuity, and the printer might well get confused among the stage directions and acknowledgements). The celebration of his knighthood positively required family jollity; indeed, one can understand that Shakespeare, though willing to assist, felt he would avoid strain if he joined them only in their darkest hour. Even so, what he was joining was a kind of domestic game.

An important idea is at work in such love poetry, though admittedly one that was ridiculous in the eyes of the world; it forbade a husband to claim marital rights through his legal superiority, and such is the point of Shakespeare's ninth verse. We know that Chapman thought the affair funny, though in a grave pedantic manner, because he headed his piece (which praised the knight who has learned his virtues by serving his lady) "Peristeros, or the male Turtle". He has had to invent a masculine form for the word, since the Greeks considered all doves female; however monogamous they may be, the creatures do not know which sex they are, but try out the alternatives (Sir Julian Huxley, in *Essays of a Biologist*, reports this of various water birds). A female Phoenix had been invented by the Renaissance to gratify a taste for Amazons – till then its secret sex had been "known to God alone"; but a Turtle wearing the trousers does seem to have been a real novelty, not only for a classicist. It proved the grandeur of the Lion, as his poet almost says in the *Epistle Dedicatory*, that he was safe from ridicule even when presented as a Turtle. The Latin "Tur tur" no doubt gave to the cooing of the pets of Venus, in the minds of the poets, a deeper note of sultry passion; to make them into symbols of chastity thus put an extra strain upon the gravity of the reader – it had been the charm of the silly creatures that no frustration attended their single-minded desires. Shakespeare's poem is a wide valley brimful of an unspecified sorrow, but one should also feel, before hearing any explanation, the gaiety inherent in its effects of sound. As the anthem of the birds reaches its severest exultation their tweeting modulates into the arch baby-talk of a dandling nurse; as we soar heavenward between the Co-supremes, we mysteriously almost graze the Cow that jumped over the Moon;

> To themselves yet either neither,
> Simple were so well compounded.

It does seem rather odd, in a way, that he went straight on from this to his great tragic period.

# Love as Trompe-l'oeil : Taxonomies of Desire in *Venus and Adonis*

## Catherine Belsey

### I

THE PAINTER ZEUXIS EXCELLED IN THE ART OF TROMPE-L'OEIL, a mode of painting that is capable of deceiving the eye by its simulation of nature. Zeuxis portrayed grapes with such success that birds flew toward his picture. His younger rival, Parrhasius, however, challenged Zeuxis to a competition to decide which painter's work was more true to life. Parrhasius won—by depicting a curtain so convincing that Zeuxis begged him to draw it and reveal the picture behind.[1] Jacques Lacan, in his seminar "Of the Gaze as *Objet Petit a*," makes a distinction between the two pictures: only the curtain that Parrhasius painted is a true trompe-l'oeil, because its effect depends on what is missing, the absence of a secret concealed behind the paint. For Lacan it is not deception alone that defines the trompe-l'oeil: on the contrary, its determining characteristic is the promise of a presence that it fails to deliver. Trompe-l'oeil tantalizes.

At a critical moment in Shakespeare's *Venus and Adonis*, when the goddess has succeeded in maneuvering her reluctant suitor into a promising physical position, but without the consequence she seeks, the text compares Adonis to the painting by Zeuxis:

> Even so poor birds deceiv'd with painted grapes
> Do surfeit by the eye and pine the maw;
> Even so she languisheth in her mishaps,
> As those poor birds that helpless berries saw.
>    The warm effects which she in him finds missing
>    She seeks to kindle with continual kissing.
>                   (ll. 601–6)[2]

But in Shakespeare's poem the grapes also represent a trompe-l'oeil in accordance with Lacan's definition. Deceptively promising oral gratification, the enticing picture of the grapes yields no pleasure for the stomach. In the same way, despite her best efforts, Venus finds that the provocative outward image of Adonis conceals nothing to her purpose: his beauty

---

This essay was written at the Folger Shakespeare Library. It owes a great deal to the stimulus of that environment and to the intellectual generosity of the readers and the staff.

[1] Pliny, *Natural History*, trans. H. Rackham, Loeb Classical Library, 10 vols. (Cambridge, MA: Harvard UP, 1938–63), Bk. 35, sec. 36.

[2] Quotations of *Venus and Adonis* follow the Arden Shakespeare edition of *The Poems*, ed. F. T. Prince (London: Methuen, 1960), 1–62.

evokes a longing, which remains unsatisfied, for his desire—or for its phallic signifier.

In painting, deceit gives pleasure. "What is it," Lacan asks, "that attracts and satisfies us in *trompe-l'oeil*? When is it that it captures our attention and delights us?" He proposes that the trompe-l'oeil pleases by presenting the appearance of a three-dimensional object which we go on to recognize as exactly that: no more than an appearance, painted in two dimensions. In order to enjoy the trompe-l'oeil, we have to be convinced by it in the first instance and then to shift our gaze so that, seeing the object resolve itself into lines on a canvas, we are no longer convinced; we have to be deceived— and then to acknowledge our own deception. The gap between these two moments is the place, Lacan affirms, of the *objet a*, the lost object in the inextricable real, the cause of desire.[3] That which delights in art—the civilizing, sublimated product of the drive—is experienced in psychosexual life as a lack, the -φ (minus *phi*), a source of indestructible longing.

The type of the desiring subject according to classical myth was Tantalus in the underworld, unable to reach the fruit that would allay his insatiable thirst. Shakespeare's Venus outdoes Tantalus in frustration, however, when she holds Adonis in her arms but can elicit no response. "That worse than Tantalus' is her annoy, / To clip Elizium and to lack her joy" (ll. 599–600). The desire of Adonis is not subject to her control: love cannot be commanded. The third dimension she wants is missing, and the absence she encounters serves only to intensify her longing.

In the event, nothing very much happens in this narrative of desire. Tantal-ized as she is, Venus cajoles and entreats. Adonis resists, rejects, and finally escapes her; he is killed by the boar, and Venus laments. The poem, exceptionally popular in its own period,[4] prompts in the reader a desire for action that it fails to gratify. Meanwhile, the critical tradition in its turn, tantalized by the poem's lack of closure, has sought to make something happen, at least at the thematic level, by locating a moral center that would furnish the work with a final meaning, a conclusion, a definitive statement. It is possible, however, to read the text itself as a kind of trompe-l'oeil, moving undecidably between modes of address and sustaining the desire of the reader in the process. I propose that it is precisely in its lack of closure that Shakespeare's poem may be read as marking a specific moment in the cultural history of love. A literary trompe-l'oeil, a text of and about desire, *Venus and Adonis* promises a definitive account of love but at the same time withholds the finality that such a promise might lead us to expect. Instead, it tantalizes and, in so doing, throws into relief the difference between its historical moment and our own.

## II

*Venus and Adonis* is a poetic record of the originating moment of desire. In Shakespeare's narrative poem the goddess of love, traditional object of all men's admiration, unexpectedly appears as a desiring subject, herself at the mercy of an intractable passion. Led by experience to expect the

---

[3] Jacques Lacan, *The Four Fundamental Concepts of Psycho-analysis*, ed. Jacques-Alain Miller, trans. Alan Sheridan (New York and London: W. W. Norton, 1977), 112.

[4] There were sixteen editions by 1640.

devotion of others and accustomed to master, imprison, and enslave her lovers (ll. 101–12), Venus is here reduced to the role of suitor (l. 6), overpowered by another's beauty and subject in her turn to indifference and disdain. The protagonist of the story thus comes to represent what the text identifies as a personification of desire itself, which is by definition unsatisfied: "She's love, she loves, and yet she is not lov'd" (l. 610). Lost, ironically, in the emotion she herself traditionally promotes, a subjection that "makes young men thrall, and old men dote" (l. 837), the queen of love has now become love's helpless victim, in her "own law forlorn" (l. 251). The goddess of love stoops—and fails to conquer.

Because she cannot command the desire of Adonis, or even protect his life, Venus finally delivers, over his mutilated body, a curse on the emotion that subjects her, condemning love itself to perpetual dissatisfaction and despair:

> "Since thou art dead, lo here I prophesy,
> Sorrow on love hereafter shall attend:
> It shall be waited on with jealousy,
> Find sweet beginning, but unsavoury end;
>   Ne'er settled equally, but high or low,
>   That all love's pleasure shall not match his woe."
>                                                 (ll. 1135–40)

Though Venus has been unable to prevail upon her unwilling lover, she has authority, nevertheless, as the personification of love, to define the condition she both represents and shares. The goddess's words thus summarize her own story and at the same time "explain" proleptically the tragic endings of those romances that constituted the classic love stories of Shakespeare's period: Troilus and Cressida, Pyramus and Thisbe, Dido and Aeneas. As a result of Love's distress, suffering and loss have become the destiny of lovers.

All myth can be read as explanatory, a record of how things came to be the way they are: a sexual relation between the sky and the earth generates life; the story of the Fall explains the presence of evil in the world. *Venus and Adonis* is also a myth of origins. In this respect it is, of course, true to its source. Ovid's *Metamorphoses* records the origins of things and accounts in the process for their present character.[5] The long narrative poem begins with the creation of the world, Jupiter's disappointment in the human beings he has made, and the consequent flood, from which only Deucalion and Pyrrha are saved. Under divine instruction, the couple throw stones over their shoulders and thereby generate a new race of human beings. The "stoniness" of their origins explains the hardy nature of the Romans as well as their capacity for work.[6] More specific in its reference, the story of Daphne, which follows that of Deucalion and Pyrrha, accounts for the sacred character of the laurel. There was a time when Apollo was happy to wreathe his forehead with the leaves of any tree, but when Daphne eludes him, he feels a special warmth for the laurel she becomes and declares that

[5] Leonard Barkan, *The Gods Made Flesh: Metamorphosis and the Pursuit of Paganism* (New Haven, CT, and London: Yale UP, 1986), 19, 27, and passim.

[6] Ovid, *Metamorphoses*, trans. Frank Justus Miller, Loeb Classical Library, 2 vols., rev. ed. (Cambridge, MA: Harvard UP, 1984), Bk. 1, ll. 414–15.

from now on it will be the source of garlands for him and, ironically, for Roman generals returning in triumph.[7] Later in Book 1, Argus asks how the reed pipe came to be invented, and Mercury responds by telling him the story of Pan and Syrinx.[8] An assembly of classical narratives, the *Metamorphoses* retains the mythic character of much of the material it so elegantly rewrites.

The stories from this familiar grammar-school text[9] which were most widely reproduced, elaborated, and imitated in the Renaissance concern the quest for a prohibited sexual pleasure either frustrated or compensated by metamorphosis: Daphne and Syrinx saved from rape in the nick of time; Narcissus unable to satisfy the erotic impulse his own image arouses and transformed into a flower. If desire is a quest for presence, for the full (imaginary, impossible) presence of the beloved to the lover, and to the degree that its perpetuation is an effect of presence deferred, these Ovidian narratives surely constitute perfect fables of desire. Daphne in flight, still out of reach, represents an emblem of the condition that subsists on the basis that possession eludes it; Daphne immobilized, meanwhile, putting down roots, fixed, remains the figure of unfulfilled desire, precisely because she is no longer Daphne. What Apollo now holds is not the nymph he wanted, though he loves the laurel and takes it for his tree.

In the case of Ovid's Venus and Adonis, presence is doubly deferred, gratification doubly displaced. The mythic story is explanatory, an account of the origin of the annual Adonia. This festival, the rite of Adonis, appears to have taken place in spring or summer all over the Mediterranean region.[10] It seems that on the first day of the Adonia, the reciprocal love of Venus and Adonis was celebrated, with ripe fruit and sweet cakes, in the presence of their images as lovers, while on the second, the body of the hero was ritually consigned to the waves with bitter lamentation.[11] Love and death were thus brought into close conjunction, the intensity of desire affirmed by the emphasis on its transience.

Ovid's version of the story begins with the passing of time and the swift succession of the years; it ends with the short-lived anemone.[12] The flower that springs from the blood of Adonis is explicitly identified as a reminder of Venus's grief, her longing for lost presence; but by insisting on its ephemeral character, the text presents the flower itself as the emblem of yet another absence. Venus promises that the metamorphosis she brings about will constitute an everlasting memorial, but it is at once made clear that this is to be no more than an annually recurring image, and an image that is in

[7] Ovid, Bk. 1, ll. 450–567.

[8] Ovid, Bk. 1, ll. 687–712.

[9] T. W. Baldwin, *William Shakspere's Small Latine and Lesse Greeke*, 2 vols. (Urbana: U of Illinois P, 1944), 2:417–55. For an account of Ovid's appeal in the Renaissance, see William Keach, *Elizabethan Erotic Narratives: Irony and Pathos in the Ovidian Poetry of Shakespeare, Marlowe, and Their Contemporaries* (New Brunswick, NJ: Rutgers UP, 1977), 3–35; and Jonathan Bate, *Shakespeare and Ovid* (Oxford: Clarendon Press, 1993), 1–47.

[10] Barkan, 80.

[11] See Theocritus, "The Festival of Adonis" in *The Idylls of Theocritus and the Eclogues of Virgil*, trans. C. S. Calverley (London: G. Bell and Sons, 1913), 82–91; Bion, "Lament for Adonis" in *The Greek Bucolic Poets*, trans. A.S.F. Gow (Cambridge: Cambridge UP, 1953), 144–47; Plutarch, "Alcibiades" in *Plutarch's Lives*, trans. Bernadotte Perrin, Loeb Classical Library, 11 vols. (London: William Heinemann, 1914–26), 4:1–115, esp. 4:47–49.

[12] Ovid, Bk. 10, ll. 519–739.

turn especially fleeting, since the winds for which it is named so easily destroy it. In this way Ovid's lyrical narrative progressively withdraws the compensating presence it promises. The flower—beautiful, fragile, mutable, and all that remains of a youth who became an object of desire for the goddess of love—thus appears in its elusiveness the quintessential signifier of desire itself. Nor is it named: even the identity of the windflower is deferred for the reader, the unspecified answer to a kind of riddle constructed by the text.[13]

Shakespeare's Venus, however, unlike Ovid's we are to assume, never succeeds in eliciting the desire of Adonis. All she gets is the flower; but in Shakespeare's poem she does possess it, indeed, cradles it in her breast next to her throbbing heart, and kisses it (ll. 1173, 1185–86, and 1188). And yet its destiny there, she recognizes, is to wither, and in Shakespeare's version there is no mention even of its annual reappearance. What the Renaissance in general and this text in particular adopt from Ovid is above all the notion of erotic metamorphosis itself: the object the lover finally possesses is not the object of desire but something else, a substitute, a stand-in. At the moment when the desiring subject takes possession of the object, something slips away, eludes the lover's grasp, and is lost.

But if Ovid's tale of Venus and Adonis offers absence as the recurring figure of desire, Shakespeare's poem surpasses its source, in audacity as well as length, by setting out to explain the origin of desire in its entirety. Love, we are invited to understand, was once reciprocal, which is to say that its conquest was absolute: Mars, stern god of war, became Venus's prisoner and learned to be a lover (ll. 97–114). But Venus's new love is unrequited: now the goddess is "Sick-thoughted" and Adonis "sullen" (ll. 5 and 75). When Adonis's insistence on hunting the boar brings his death and her irretrievable loss, Venus decrees that henceforth love will always be anarchic in character:

> "It shall suspect where is no cause of fear,
> It shall not fear where it should most mistrust;
> It shall be merciful, and too severe,
> And most deceiving when it seems most just;
>   Perverse it shall be, where it shows most toward;
>   Put fear to valour, courage to the coward."
>                                        (ll. 1153–58)

Her words are necessarily authoritative. As the personification of love, Venus does no more here than proclaim her own nature. Shakespeare's myth of origins is also a definition of love.

### III

A definition, however, ought surely to be definitive, a characteristic account of a representative state of affairs. And yet this narrative is hardly a typical love story. By conventional standards the gender roles of the central figures are disconcertingly reversed; meanwhile, the genre of the

---

[13] Ovid, Bk. 10, ll. 725–39.

narrative, now lyrical, now bordering on farce, seems oddly unresolved. As a result, love itself appears at one moment grossly material and at another delicately insubstantial, no more than airy nothing. Is there, then, a definition here or only a bravura display of a range of skills on the part of a young and ambitious poet, in a text as anarchic as the emotion its central figure both demonstrates and defines?

First, gender. There can be little doubt that Elizabethan heroines, whether tragic or comic, whether Juliet or Rosalind, are permitted to be more outspoken in love than their Victorian counterparts. Even so, the voluble and unremitting pursuit of a coy young man by a relentless goddess wildly exceeds romantic convention. As is commonly noted, it is "Rose-cheek'd Adonis" (l. 3), with his white hands (ll. 362–64) and his voice like a mermaid's (l. 429), who blushes and pouts (l. 33), while Venus pulls him off his horse and tucks him under her arm (ll. 30–32). The "tender boy" (l. 32) is inert, like a bird in a net (l. 67), but Venus resembles an eagle (l. 55). And in case the reader should forget how these things are traditionally done, the poem gives us horses that behave in a much more predictable manner, Adonis's courser neighing and bounding imperiously at the sight of the jennet (l. 265) and majestically asserting control (l. 270). The text makes witty capital out of the scandal it creates when Venus draws explicit attention to the role reversal. Adonis is, she tells him, " 'more lovely than a man' " (l. 9); if only, she sighs, things were the other way round: " 'Would thou wert as I am, and I a man' " (l. 369).[14]

But palpably she is not, and the result is a good deal of slightly salacious comedy at the level of the poem's action, or rather lack of action: "Backward she push'd him, as she would be thrust, / And govern'd him in strength, though not in lust" (ll. 41–42). Venus pins Adonis to the ground as she kisses him goodnight, "And glutton-like she feeds, yet never filleth" (l. 548). The exhausted Adonis eventually ceases to struggle, "While she takes all she can, not all she listeth [i.e., wants]" (l. 564). A good joke is evidently worth repeating. Even when their physical positions are reversed, the text explains, the case of Venus remains hopeless:

> Now is she in the very lists of love,
> Her champion mounted for the hot encounter.
> All is imaginary she doth prove;
> He will not manage her, although he mount her.
> (ll. 595–98)

At the same time, however, *Venus and Adonis* is lyrical about the passion it also presents as absurd and, at Adonis's death, is unaffectedly elegiac in its lament for perfection destroyed:

---

[14] Ironically, even the boar, she complains, inadvertently achieves a kind of consummation denied her as a woman:

> " 'Tis true, 'tis true, thus was Adonis slain:
> He ran upon the boar with his sharp spear,
> Who did not whet his teeth at him again,
> But by a kiss thought to persuade him there;
>     And nuzzling in his flank, the loving swine
>     Sheath'd unaware the tusk in his soft groin."
>     (ll. 1111–16)

> "Alas, poor world, what treasure hast thou lost!
> What face remains alive that's worth the viewing?
> What tongue is music now? what canst thou boast
> Of things long since, or any thing ensuing?
>    The flowers are sweet, their colours fresh and trim,
>    But true sweet beauty liv'd and died with him."
> (ll. 1075–80)

Throughout the text one mode of address displaces another with remarkable agility. For earlier generations of critics the resulting question of genre represented the central critical problem of the poem. Was it primarily comic, or mainly tragic, or possibly satirical?[15] Or was it simply so confused in its rapid shifts from high camp to low mimetic that it was impossible to make any real sense of it at all?[16] Despite stylistic and thematic debts to the *Metamorphoses*, the text is no mere imitation of Ovid's disengaged and economical narrative; neither is it a generic copy of any existing Elizabethan text, regardless of parallels with Lodge's *Glaucus and Scilla*. In terms of poetic decorum, this tragical-comical-pastoral(-mythical) love story defies the literary classifications of its period.

Where, then, in all this indeterminacy, is any consistent definition of love to be found? Is passion no more than the crude appetite of an overheated, "love-sick queen" (or quean [l. 175])? Or is it, conversely, the effect of a delicate appeal to the finest senses?

> "Bid me discourse, I will enchant thine ear,
> Or like a fairy trip upon the green,
> Or like a nymph, with long dishevell'd hair
> Dance on the sands, and yet no footing seen.
>    Love is a spirit all compact of fire,
>    Not gross to sink, but light, and will aspire."
> (ll. 145–50)

What exactly is the significance of the personification of love as a goddess who leaves no imprint on the sand, makes no dent in a bank of primroses, and has no impact on her beloved either? Is her reiterated lightness (ll. 151–52, 155, and 1192) an indication of lyric grace or vacuous triviality? What is the character of the desire that finds its inaugural moment in this myth of origins?

## IV

At one place the poem makes what appears to be a categorical statement, and the text seems, indeed, definitive. Adonis is speaking. He insists that Venus's desire is not love at all but rather its promiscuous, irrational,

---

[15] For the range of literary classifications, see John Doebler, "The Many Faces of Love: Shakespeare's *Venus and Adonis*," *Shakespeare Studies* 16 (1983): 33–43; and John Klause, "*Venus and Adonis*: Can We Forgive Them?" *Studies in Philology* 85 (1988): 353–77, esp. 353–55. Not everyone, however, has supposed that the poem can be easily classified: New Criticism characteristically celebrates the ambiguity of the text. See, for instance, Kenneth Muir, "*Venus and Adonis*: Comedy or Tragedy?" in *Shakespearean Essays*, Alwin Thaler and Norman Sanders, eds. (Knoxville: U of Tennessee P, 1964), 1–13; Norman Rabkin, "*Venus and Adonis* and the Myth of Love" in *Pacific Coast Studies in Shakespeare*, Waldo F. McNeir and Thelma N. Greenfield, eds. (Eugene: U of Oregon Books, 1966), 20–32.

[16] Douglas Bush, *Mythology and the Renaissance Tradition in English Poetry* (Minneapolis: U of Minnesota P, 1932), 139–49, esp. 149. See also C. S. Lewis, *English Literature in the Sixteenth Century Excluding Drama* (Oxford: Clarendon Press, 1954), 498–99.

destructive simulacrum, lust (ll. 789–98). The goddess has misrepresented the true nature of her desire: " 'Call it not love, for love to heaven is fled, / Since sweating lust on earth usurp'd his name' " (ll. 793–94). And Adonis undertakes to disentangle the two, specifying each as the antithesis of the other:

> "Love comforteth like sunshine after rain,
> But lust's effect is tempest after sun;
> Love's gentle spring doth always fresh remain,
> Lust's winter comes ere summer half be done;
> Love surfeits not, lust like a glutton dies;
> Love is all truth, lust full of forged lies."
>                     (ll. 799–804)

A grateful critical tradition, eager to regulate the wayward textuality of the poem by locating within it a clear thematic statement, the expression of an *autho*ritative design, has tended to reproduce Adonis's values as the key to the moral truth of the text.

The tradition goes back at least to Coleridge, who was relaxed about the identification of Venus with lust, arguing that although the poem was about concupiscence, it was not morally dangerous because Shakespeare had directed the reader's attention beyond "the animal impulse itself" to the images and circumstances in which it is presented.[17] A century later, however, Lu Emily Pearson emphasized how much was at stake in the antithesis Adonis had affirmed:

> Venus is shown as the destructive agent of sensual love; Adonis, as reason in love. The one sullies whatever it touches; the other honors and makes it beautiful. The one is false and evil; the other is all truth, all good. Reason in love, truth, beauty—these are the weapons with which lust must be met, or the ideals of man must go down in defeat before the appetites.[18]

Pearson's moral vehemence sounds archaic now, but what surprises is the degree to which Adonis's condemnation of Venus and lust has survived the sexual revolution of the 1960s. Heather Dubrow is much kinder than Pearson, but the term *lust* reappears in her account, however softened by the attribution to Venus of motherliness: "Though lust is Venus' primary motive, it is by no means her only one and by no means an adequate label for her behavior: tender maternal love is commingled with her lust. . . . "[19] Male critics, meanwhile, are relentless: according to one writer who echoes the view of his fellows, Shakespeare "casts Venus as a frenzied older woman driven by comic lust for a very young man barely emerging from boyhood."[20] And although the poem has nothing to say about her age except

[17] Samuel Taylor Coleridge, *Biographia Literaria*, ed. J. Shawcross, 2 vols. (Oxford: Clarendon Press, 1907), 2:16.

[18] Lu Emily Pearson, *Elizabethan Love Conventions* (Berkeley: U of California P, 1933), 285.

[19] Heather Dubrow, *Captive Victors: Shakespeare's Narrative Poems and Sonnets* (Ithaca, NY, and London: Cornell UP, 1987), 46. Cf. "Venus lusts after Adonis, but she is also maternally protective of him" (Keach, 77).

[20] John Doebler, "The Reluctant Adonis: Titian and Shakespeare," *Shakespeare Quarterly* 33 (1982): 480–90, esp. 484. Doebler repeats the earlier judgment of Don Cameron Allen, who proposes that Venus is "a forty-year-old countess with a taste for Chapel Royal altos." Later in the poem Venus comes "to discourse foolishly on love like a fluttery and apprehensive Doll Tearsheet of forty"; see Allen's *Image and Meaning: Metaphoric Traditions in Renaissance Poetry* (Baltimore, MD: Johns Hopkins UP, 1968), 43 and 57.

that her beauty is perfect and annually renewed (ll. 133–44), the goddess's supposed decline has nonetheless proved explanatory for some male readers: "Her vulnerability is that of the older woman, desperate to renew her youth in the arms of a young lover."[21] Even a critic who allows that Venus represents "the drastically imperfect amalgam of lust and caring that is likely to be found in all lovers" finds it necessary to point out that "the suffocating, devouring lust of Venus is too 'vicious' (in both the antique and the modern senses) to escape censure."[22] In this way criticism provides itself with a definitive signified, a univocal thematic "message" beyond the undecidabilities of the text, beyond, that is to say, the heterogeneity of its mode of address.[23]

V

This critical reiteration of the taxonomy of desire that Adonis so confidently delivers is problematic, however, because it inevitably attributes the central affirmation of the poem to a hero who is, as the text repeatedly reminds us and the plot of the story insists, so young that he knows nothing of love (ll. 127–28, 409, and 806). It is, of course, not inconceivable that Adonis could be speaking with preternatural wisdom: Helena in *A Midsummer Night's Dream* speaks of love with an insight that her role in the story might not lead us to expect (1.1.232–39).[24] But if Helena speaks "out of character" here, her observations are confirmed, in the absence of a controlling narrative voice, by the events of the play. The narrative voice in *Venus and Adonis*, however, does not reproduce the neat antitheses the hero enunciates. On the contrary, while Adonis urges Venus to call it not love but lust, the text names desire both love and lust with apparent indifference:

> The studded bridle on a ragged bough
> Nimbly she fastens—O how quick is *love!*—
> The steed is stalled up, and even now
> To tie the rider she begins to prove:
>    Backward she push'd him, as she would be thrust,
>    And govern'd him in strength, though not in *lust*.
>           (ll. 37–42 [my emphasis])

Meanwhile, the steed in question leaps, neighs, and bounds (l. 265) in response to a jennet identified as his "love" throughout (ll. 287, 307, and 317). The animal's condition is variously "love" and "desire" (ll. 311 and 276). As for Venus, "desire doth lend her force" (l. 29); her language is "lustful" (l. 47); still, "she cannot choose but love" (l. 79). In her case "careless lust stirs up a desperate courage," but "love," too, lacks moral scruples and picks locks to get at beauty (ll. 556 and 576). Venus, of course,

---

[21] Gordon Williams, "The Coming of Age of Shakespeare's Adonis," *Modern Language Review* 78 (1983): 769–76, esp. 776.

[22] Klause, 371 and 364.

[23] The most perceptive account I have found of the poem's "tonal shifts" is Nancy Lindheim, "The Shakespearean *Venus and Adonis*," *SQ* 37 (1986): 190–203.

[24] See the Arden Shakespeare edition of *A Midsummer Night's Dream*, ed. Harold F. Brooks (London: Methuen, 1979).

calls it love, but the text calls *her* "love" the moment Adonis has completed his disquisition:

> With this, he breaketh from the sweet embrace
> Of those fair arms which bound him to her breast,
> And homeward through the dark laund runs apace;
> Leaves love upon her back deeply distress'd.
>
> (ll. 811–14)

It is not obvious that one set of terms is used ironically: indeed, irony is precisely the quality that the polyphony of the text renders elusive. The poem seems to invest with a certain indeterminacy the terms Adonis so categorically distinguishes.

In this respect the narrative voice is characteristic of its historical moment. In the early modern period *love* and *lust* are not consistently used as antitheses: on the contrary, both terms are synonyms for desire, each innocent or reprobate according to the context, and occurring interchangeably without apparent irony. The emergence of a radical distinction between the two—a process inadvertently encouraged, as it turns out, by the voice of Adonis—marks a moment in the cultural history of desire which, as modern criticism unwittingly reveals, has proved formative for our own cultural norms and values.

In the mid-sixteenth century William Baldwin published *A treatise of Morall Phylosophie*, a collection of precepts derived from a range of classical authorities, each duly named in the margins of the page. The work was exceptionally popular: twenty-four editions appeared between 1547 and about 1640. The earliest editions allow a certain overlap between the categories of love and lust: indeed, in 1550 the chapter heading "Of the worlde, the loue, and pleasures therof " appears in "The Table" as "Of the worlde, the lustes, and pleasures therof."[25] While this might be no more than a printer's error, we should note that Baldwin places "Loue, luste, and lecherye" together in a single short chapter.[26] The love in question is mainly *caritas*, which has no sexual connotations, except that in one instance he defines "Repentaunce" as "the ende of fylthy loue," where the adjective has the effect of aligning love with the sin of lechery. At the same time, "Luste is a lordlye and disobedient thynge," whereas "Dishonor, shame, euell ende and damnacion, wayte upon lecherie, and all other like vyces."[27] The implication seems to be that lust is a powerful impulse but in itself morally neutral, so that, like the will, it needs to be brought under control in the interests of virtue, while lechery is by definition wicked.

Later editions of the *Treatise* are modified by the intervention of Thomas Paulfreyman, who repeatedly edited and enlarged Baldwin's text. By 1564 *love* has been removed from the chapter heading and from the table of contents. But if this simplifies the position in respect of love, lust remains as equivocal as before. Appropriately qualified, it evidently belongs with lechery, as in "Flie lecherous lustes" or "fired to the filthy luste of lecherie."[28] On

---

[25] William Baldwin, *A treatise of Morall Phylosophie* . . . (London, 1550), sigs. I8$^r$ and R6$^r$. I owe this observation to Peter Blayney.

[26] William Baldwin, sig. O2$^{r–v}$.

[27] William Baldwin, sig. O2$^v$.

[28] William Baldwin, *A treatyce of moral philosophy* . . . (London, 1564), fols. 185$^v$ and 186$^r$.

the other hand, in a different context it might equally well be morally neutral: "Enforce thy self to refraine thine euill lustes and folow the good: For the good mortifieth and destroieth the euill."[29] Evidently at this moment *lust* is not necessarily to be condemned out of hand.

In 1594, a year or more after the publication of *Venus and Adonis*, Thomas Bowes issued an English translation of Pierre de la Primaudaye's *Academie Francoise*. There is in Bowes's translation some uncertainty about the moral implications of lust: "I will begin then with the affection of loue, which is a motion whereby the heart lusteth [*appete*] after that which is good. . . . "[30] Almost immediately, however, a tentative moral distinction begins to appear. The will is drawn to what is good and desires to embrace it, "and this loue is called *Cupiditie, Lusting*, or *Coueting* [*cupidité, ou concupiscence, ou convoitise*]." But this love is not "true love," which is the love of the good for itself and not for the sake of possession.[31] Here lust is evidently not to be endorsed since it is proprietary, but at the same time, it has no specifically sexual connotations; as in Baldwin, it is possible to lust after the good.

In the longer term, however, a change was taking place. During the course of the sixteenth century, *lust* was to lose its innocence, or at least its potential innocence, since a reprobate meaning was always available. Understood in the Middle Ages as delight, pleasure, desire, or sinful passion, according to context, by the mid-seventeenth century the term had acquired a primarily sexual and strongly pejorative meaning. Coverdale's version of Numbers 14:8, "Yf the Lorde haue lust vnto us," was evidently acceptable in 1535; but in the Authorized Version of 1611, the phrase appeared as "If the Lord delight in vs."[32] In 1533 the translator of the popular *Enchiridion* of Erasmus thought it appropriate to render *libido* as "bodyly luste," "the luste of the body," "lechery," "fylthy lust," or "unclenly lustes."[33] *Lust* alone was evidently considered not specific enough:[34] a qualifier of some sort was necessary to do justice to a condition in which human beings, God's handiwork, are reduced to "fylthy swyne / to gotes / to dogges / and of all brute beestes / unto ye most brute," and which, in Erasmus's humanist analysis, wastes time, destroys health, hastens old age, and (perhaps worst of all) obliterates the use of reason.[35] Just over 150 years later, a new translation of the *Enchiridion* was published as *A Manual for a Christian Soldier*. Here the qualifying words and phrases have disappeared, and *libido* is translated simply as "lust." Without in any way softening the value judgments inscribed in Erasmus's text, the version of 1687 leaves it to "lust" alone to do the work of defining a condition that reduces human beings to the level of

---

[29] William Baldwin, *A treatyce*, fol. 185$^{r-v}$.

[30] Pierre de la Primaudaye, *The French academie* . . . (London, 1618), 479; see also Pierre de la Primaudaye, *Academie Francoise* (Paris, 1580), fol. 166$^r$.

[31] La Primaudaye, *The French academie*, 480; *Academie Francoise*, fol. 166$^v$.

[32] *Oxford English Dictionary*, sv *lust*, sb., 1d.

[33] Erasmus, *A booke called in latyn Enchiridion militis christiani and in englysshe the manuell of the christen knyght* . . . (London, 1533), sigs. N1$^r$, Q5$^v$, Q6$^r$, R3$^r$, and R2$^v$. This English translation of the *Enchiridion* may have been made by William Tyndale; see E. J. Devereux, *Renaissance English Translations of Erasmus: A Bibliography to 1700* (Toronto: U of Toronto P, 1983), 104.

[34] There is one counter-example: the next chapter heading (an epilogue of remedies against incentives to *libido*) is translated as "A shorte recapitulacyon of remedyes agaynst the flame of lust" (sig. R3$^v$). Here I think the destructive "flame" does some of the work of the other qualifying words or phrases.

[35] Erasmus, sigs. Q5$^v$ and Q6$^{r-v}$.

beasts.[36] (Twentieth-century translators also tend to render *libido* as "lust."[37])

This handful of examples, most of them taken from repositories of popular morality, merely amplifies what the *OED* already indicates: in the course of the early modern period, with whatever advances and reversals, *lust* gradually became exclusively sexual and specifically reprobate. But the dictionary, which defines individual words in isolation, on the assumption that they are "full" of their own meanings, does not record the network of differences which constitutes a taxonomy. The shifting meaning of *lust* depends, at least in part, on the emergent difference between *lust* and *love*. Predictably, therefore, in this period of change the connotations of *love* are no less problematic. The name of a condition that may be divine, purely social, romantic, or exclusively sexual, but which is in all these cases intense, leads to semantic indeterminacies and gives rise to anxieties in the process. Sir Thomas More, for example, was deeply critical of William Tyndale because Tyndale translated the biblical "charity" as "love." The problem, from More's Christian humanist point of view, is that *love* carries the wrong connotations unless it is appropriately qualified by an adjective that distinguishes between the divine and the sexual, since sexual love is not, of course, highly valued.[38] Tyndale, however, to More's disgust, consistently repudiates the adjective:

> If he called charitie sometyme by the bare name of loue: I wold not stick therat. But now wheras charite signifieth in english mens eares, not euery common loue, but a good vertuous & wel ordred loue, he . . . wyl studiously flee fro ye name of good loue, & alway speke of loue, & alway leaue out good.[39]

The problem, as More identifies it, is that Tyndale's practice is motivated by the Lutheran project of elevating faith at the expense of charity. Because their theology makes salvation a question of faith and not good works, the Reformers deliberately conflate charity with the merely erotic love that exists between a man and his paramour:

> and therfore he chaungeth ye name of holy vertuous affeccion, into ye bare name of loue comen to the vertuous loue that man beareth to god, and to the lewde loue that is betwene flecke & his make.[40]

While poetry and romance idealize love, humanist morality holds it in contempt. Erasmus has no greater patience than does his friend More with sexual love (*amor*), and he includes it under the heading of *libido* in the *Enchiridion*. Love is just as absurd and just as reductive as all erotic desire:

---

[36] Erasmus, *A Manual for a Christian Soldier* (London, 1687), 184–92.

[37] See, for instance, the following modern editions: Erasmus, *Handbook of the Militant Christian*, trans. John P. Dolan (Notre Dame, IN: Fides Publishers, 1962), 147–59; and *The Enchiridion of Erasmus*, ed. and trans. Raymond Himelick (Bloomington: Indiana UP, 1963), 177–84.

[38] Cf. Sir Thomas More, *Utopia*, trans. Raphe Robynson, ed. Israel Gollancz (1551; London: Dent, 1898), 102–3.

[39] Sir Thomas More, *A Dialogue concernynge heresyes & matters of Religion . . .* in *The Workes of Sir Thomas More Knyght . . .* (London, 1557), 103–288, esp. 221.

[40] More, *A Dialogue concernynge heresyes*, 222.

Set before thyne eyen howe ungoodly it is / howe altogyder a mad thing to loue / to waxe pale / to be made leane / to wepe / to flatter / and shamfully to submyt thy selfe unto a stynkyng harlot most fylthy and rotten / to gape & synge all nyght at her chambre wyndowe / to be made to the lure & be obedyent at a becke / nor dare do any thing except she nod or wagge her heed / to suffre a folysshe woman to reigne ouer the / to chyde the: to lay unkyndnesse one agaynst ye other to fall out / to be made at one agayne / to gyue thy selfe wyllynge unto a queene / that she myght mocke / k[n]ocke / mangle and spoyle the. Where is I beseche the amonge all these thynges the name of a man? Where is thy berde? Where is that noble mynde created unto moste beautyfull and noble thynges?[41]

In view of our own taxonomies, it is tempting to speculate on the meaning of *love* in this instance. The emotions described are romantic, even Petrarchan. "Harlot," however, is not appropriate in the context of romantic love; nor, of course, is violence, which evokes the fabliau genre rather than romance. But the point, presumably, is that Erasmus does not distinguish among them: all passion is degrading.

The humiliating harlot reappears in the first part of *The French academie*; evidently she had entered into the European popular consciousness, along with the corresponding value judgment on love. "True" love, by contrast, is not sexual:

> For we see some men so bewitched with a harlot, that if neede bee, and shee command it, they will hazard their honour and credit, and oftentimes make themselues an example to a whole countrey vpon an open scaffold. And then they labour to couer their folly with this goodly name of *Loue*, which is better tearmed [of] *Euripides* by the name of *Fury* and madnesse in men. For true and good loue, which is the fountaine of friendship, is alwaies grounded vpon vertue, and tendeth to that end: but this slipperie and loose loue, is a desire founded vpon . . . the opinion of a *Good*, which indeede is a most pernitious euill.[42]

It is not clear that the moralists commonly recognize a radical difference between love and lust, or even between love and lechery. As late as 1616, Thomas Gainsford's commonplace book *The Rich Cabinet* demonstrates that there was still some uncertainty about whether these two categories were antithetical or synonymous. Gainsford at first sets up a contrast between the two, but this gradually gives way to similarity. His observations are divided under topics and are listed alphabetically. "Love" therefore comes immediately after "Lechery." If this is simply a trick of the alphabet, Gainsford nonetheless exploits its effect by setting up love initially as the contrary of lechery. While lechery reduces human beings to the level of beasts and generally performs much as love does in Erasmus, love in Gainsford at first uplifts and ennobles. But the simple opposition does not hold for long. Gradually there is a reversion to type, as it emerges that love is irrational, frivolous, a form of madness, like a monster, and then "libidinous and luxurious like a Goat."[43] Eventually all the old commonplaces are reaf-

[41] Erasmus, *A booke called in latyn Enchiridion*, sig. Q7ʳ⁻ᵛ.

[42] La Primaudaye, *The French academie*, 98–99.

[43] Thomas Gainsford, *The Rich Cabinet Furnished with varietie of Excellent discriptions* . . . (London, 1616), fol. 86ʳ. For the section on "lechery," see fols. 82ᵛ–84ʳ; for "love," see fols. 84ᵛ–87ᵛ.

firmed, and any clear distinction between love and lechery can no longer be detected: "Love doth trouble wit, hinder Art, hurt nature, disgrace reason, lose time, spoile substance, crosse wisedome, serue folly, weaken strength, submit to beautie, and abase honour."[44] Meanwhile, it is worth noting, lechery is a kind of love and a form of lust, the differences once again specified only by the appropriate adjectives: "Lechery is in plaine tearmes extreame lust, vnlawfull loue, brutish desires, beastlie wantonnesse, and the itch or scab of old concupiscence."[45]

## VI

Evidently, the terms *love* and *lust* were changing in relation to one another: a new system of differences, which is to say a new taxonomy, was in the process of construction. But there is no single moment of transformation: the vocabulary of the period is marked by attempts at policing the language on the one hand and by constant slippages on the other. While the sharp and unconditional antitheses of Adonis are evidently one option in the 1590s, the indeterminacies of the narrative voice in Shakespeare's poem are another and were probably a more familiar practice in the period. Critics with a strong sense of cultural history, who have nevertheless wanted to identify Adonis as the conscience of the text, have been driven to invoke Neoplatonism, somewhat incongruously, as the moral framework of this racy, salacious Ovidian narrative.[46]

As for Venus herself, she was capable of signifying a whole range of meanings. While the Neoplatonists were anxious to distinguish the heavenly from the earthly Venus, others were content to acknowledge her heterogeneity. Richard Linche's *The Fovntaine of Ancient Fiction*, an early instance of cultural history, derived from Vincenzo Cartari's mid-sixteenth-century Italian book on images of the gods of the ancients, explained to English readers why there were so many classical statues and pictures of the goddess. The reason was that she represented "several natures and conditions," from lechery to holy matrimony:

> According therfore to the opinion of the Poets, Venus was taken to be the goddesse of wantonnes & amorous delights, as that she inspired into the minds of men, libidinous desires, and lustfull appetites, & with whose power & assistance they attained the effect of their lose concupiscence: whervpon also they entermed her the mother of loue, because that without a certaine loue and simpathie of affections, those desires are sildome acomplished. And vnto hir they ascribe the care and charge of marriages and holie wedlockes. . . . [47]

Linche does not reveal how anomalous he finds this range of natures and conditions in 1599.

But history was on the side of Adonis. In 1615, more than twenty years after the poem was first printed,[48] Alexander Niccholes cites Adonis, without naming him, as a proper authority on the contrast between love and

[44] Gainsford, fol. 87[r].
[45] Gainsford, fol. 84[r].
[46] See T. W. Baldwin, *On the Literary Genetics of Shakspere's Poems & Sonnets* (Urbana: U of Illinois P, 1950), 73–93; and Heather Asals, *"Venus and Adonis:* The Education of a Goddess," *Studies in English Literature 1500–1900* 13 (1973): 31–51.
[47] Richard Linche, *The Fovntaine of Ancient Fiction* . . . (London, 1599), sig. Cc2[r-v].
[48] By this time there had been nine more editions.

lust. Niccholes quotes Shakespeare's text anonymously with two minor variations, both well within the range of likely errors in transmission. Love and lust are contraries, Niccholes declares, and in support of this position, he urges, "one thus writeth":

> Loue comforteth like sunne-shine after raine,
> But lusts effect is tempest after sunne.
> Loues golden spring doth euer fresh remaine,
> Lusts winter comes ere summer halfe be done.[49]

In the account Niccholes gives, lust is everything that love is not, so that love is defined by the exclusion of its differentiating opposite. Lust is what does not last, for example, and does not discriminate its objects. It is also impoverished, lacking. Niccholes turns Adonis's "glutton" (l. 803) into a beggar: "In Loue there is no lacke, in Lust there is the greatest penury, for though it be cloyed with too much, it pines for want. . . . " Moreover, lust destroys the domestic enclave that love creates: "the one, most commonly, burnes downe the house that the other would build up."[50] The context of this sequence of antitheses is a treatise giving advice on how to achieve the great blessing of conjugal happiness, *A Discourse, of Marriage and Wiving: and of The greatest Mystery therein contained: How to choose a good Wife from a bad.* The book represents an argument, the title page assures its readers, "Of the dearest vse, but the deepest cunning that man may erre in: which is, to cut by a Thrid [i.e., thread] betweene the greatest Good or euill in the world."

As Niccholes's text indicates, the realignment of love and lust is motivated by the newfound valorization of marriage in the course of the century following the Reformation rejection of the celibate ideal. In this context the radical distinction between love and lust is a critical issue. "Lvst," Niccholes affirms, is "the most potent match-maker in all Marriages under thirty, and the chiefe breaker of all from eighteene to eight[y]. . . . "[51] Lust makes unstable marriages. Love holds the family together; lust endangers it. In consequence, love is now endorsed by the moralists and lust repudiated. The difference between them, and not the irrationality of both, has become the concern of a prescriptive morality.

What philology records, it cannot be too strongly stressed, is not a fall from a merry Middle Ages, when sexual desire was innocent and the body and its pleasures beyond the range of moral judgment. On the contrary, in the earlier epoch lechery was a deadly sin, celibacy the way of perfection, and asceticism the privileged way of life for those capable of sustaining it. Love belonged in romances, which were held to be essentially trivial, mere entertainment. But the celebration of love as the foundation of a lifetime of concord, and the inclusion of desire within the legality of marriage, brought with it an imperative to distinguish between true love, which would lead to conjugal happiness on the one hand and, on the other, appetite, which was the worst possible basis for a stable social institution. True love was sexual, but it was also companionable; lust, by contrast, was precipitate, inconsistent, turbulent, and dangerous.

As markers of a cultural shift, the semantic changes may perhaps be

---

[49] Alexander Niccholes, *A Discourse, of Marriage and Wiving* . . . (London, 1615), 31–32.
[50] Niccholes, 32.
[51] Niccholes, 30.

indicated, however sketchily, by comparing two considerations of marriage, widely separated chronologically, both of which address the problems of love and lust. First, in 1411–12, Thomas Hoccleve discusses the question in his *Regement of Princes*, addressed to the Prince of Wales on the eve of his accession to the throne as Henry V. In Hoccleve's account, celibacy is evidently preferable to marriage, but within marriage it is best to struggle against fleshly lusts. A man should take care to choose a wife on the basis of virtue: marrying for lust is bound to lead to disaster.[52] This sounds familiar, but the problems begin, predictably, with the respective meanings of the terms. Hoccleve confesses that he finally gave up waiting for a benefice and took a wife, whom he married for love (l. 1561). His interlocutor, the Beggar who has become his moral guide, is not satisfied with this account; he suspects, rightly as it turns out, that Hoccleve does not know the difference between love and lust, that he sees them as "conuertible" (i.e., interchangeable [l. 1563]). This is a serious error: love, that is, "goode" love (l. 1628), is love of virtue, "loue of the persone" (l. 1633), and it lasts; lust, meanwhile, is sexual desire or pleasure, and though lawful lust is necessary for procreation, lust for lust's sake is against God's commandments. Nowadays, he writes, people use aphrodisiacs, but this is contrary to the will of God.

The *Regement of Princes* thus holds apart love and lust by identifying as lust everything that has to do with sex. No sooner, however, has the text established this taxonomy than the precarious system of differences it has created with such difficulty collapses in a verse that precisely treats love and lust as "conuertible." Love's heat is suddenly synonymous with lust, and both are sexual:

> Also they that for luste chesen hir make
> Only, as other while it is vsage,
> Wayte wel, that whan hir luste is ouerschake,
> And there-with wole hir loues hete asswage,
> Thanne is to hem an helle, hire mariage.
> (ll. 1653–57)[53]

The Beggar, a kind of Adonis *avant la lettre* but invested by the text with a good deal more authority, cannot in the event hold apart the terms he sets out to define as antithetical. There is nothing here about marriage as companionship, no endorsement of nuptial love, no idealization of married pleasure. In the circumstances the only way to differentiate love from lust is to purge it of all sexual reference, and so rigorous a policing of its meaning cannot, it appears, be effectively sustained, since meaning is not at the disposal of the individual speaker.

We have reached a quite different and recognizably modern world, however, when in 1638 Robert Crofts provides a rhapsodic account of the romantic and companionable happiness of married love and family life:

---

[52] Thomas Hoccleve, *The Regement of Princes* (1405) in *Hoccleve's Works*, ed. Frederick J. Furnivall, Early English Text Society ES 72, 3 vols. (London: Kegan Paul, Trench, Trübner, 1897), Vol. 3, ll. 1555–764.

[53] Marrying for lust was still a danger in 1585. In one instance, however, lust is identified as a component of love, but the two are not interchangeable; see "The wanton wyfe, whose love is all for luste . . . " in Geoffrey Whitney, Ms. Harvard Typ. 14, fol. 48. I owe this reference to Steven W. May.

It is said, there is no pleasure in the world like that of the sweet society of Lovers, in the way of marriage, and of a loving husband and wife. Hee is her head she commands his heart, he is her Love, her joy, she is his honey, his Doue, his delight.

They may take sweet councell together, assist and comfort one another in all things, their joy is doubled and Redoubled.

By this blessed vnion, the number of Parents, friends, and kindred is increased; It may be an occasion of sweet and lovely Children, who in after times may bee a great felicity and joy to them. . . .

A multitude of felicities, a million of joyfull and blessed effects, spring from true Love.

And indeed this Nuptial Love and society sweetens, all our Actions, discourses, all other pleasures, felicities, and even in all Respects, Encreases true Joy and happinesse.[54]

Crofts sees no reason why married lovers should not have recourse to the arts of love to enhance their pleasure, and he advises husbands to talk to their wives about love and its value or to tell them love stories, both happy and sad. He even includes a selection of sample poems and songs for the purpose. Some people, he continues, would think this sort of advice profane:

But wee may know that it is good and commendable, for such as doe, or intend to liue in that honourable and blessed estate of marriage, to bee possest with conjugall Love, and consequently such honest love discourses, deuices, and pleasures, as encrease the same, are to bee esteemed good and commendable.[55]

On the other hand, Crofts is entirely explicit in his condemnation of lust. He reaffirms the dichotomy between "true," which is to say married, love and those extramarital desires for forbidden objects, which destroy the family and destabilize society: "Let us also (while wee view the excellency of Lawfull and true Loue) beware of unlawfull and Raging Lusts. There is wel nigh as much difference betweene true Love and unlawfull Lusts, as betweene heaven and hell."[56] In Crofts's text the antithesis between love and lust is clear and is beginning to be familiar from a twentieth-century point of view. We could find something of the same taxonomy of desire in any Harlequin romance, where the happy ending depends on the ability of the protagonists to distinguish between true love, on the one hand, and, on the other, an infatuation of the senses, which is no basis for marriage. And yet it is worth noting, first, that Crofts still apparently feels it necessary to invoke an adjective: the repeated phrase in this chapter is "unlawfull lusts."[57] Second, the term is not arbitrary: the text does not base the distinction between love and lust on a dualism of mind and body,[58] but on a duality of lawful and unlawful, married and unmarried: unlawful lusts lead to fornication, adultery, incest, rape, breach of promise. The fully fledged dualism of caring and sensuality in current popular romance is an effect of the Cartesian crystallization of the *cogito*, identity as mind, which

---

[54] Robert Crofts, *The Lover: or, Nvptiall Love* (London, 1638), sigs. A7ᵛ–A8ʳ.
[55] Crofts, sig. C6ᵛ.
[56] Crofts, sig. D6ᵛ.
[57] Crofts, sigs. D6ᵛ–D8ʳ.
[58] There is dualism elsewhere, but "sensual" love is not generally identified in this text as "lust" (Crofts, sigs. B1ᵛ–B2ʳ).

was evidently not yet part of Crofts's culture.[59] And third, "love," too, still benefits from a defining adjective: "true love," of course, has survived unchanged into the modern era.

## VII

The power and the durability of the cultural change brought about by Shakespeare's Adonis and Niccholes and Crofts, assisted by countless Puritan divines, is evident in the readings of *Venus and Adonis* I have already cited. A substantial proportion of twentieth-century criticism, by endorsing the opposition Adonis formulates and finding in it the thematic truth of the poem, reproduces the taxonomy he helps to cement; such criticism thereby enlists Shakespeare in support of family values, the naturalization of the nuclear family as the only legitimate location of desire. Interpretation takes place within a framework, often unacknowledged, of value judgments about true and false love, "healthy" sexual dispositions, or the proper (which is to say "natural") relations between men and women. True love is identifiable in terms of a set of norms produced in the early modern period, norms now so familiar that they pass for nature. They represent the means by which a culture subjected an anarchic passion to the legality that is marriage, the terms on which unpredictable sexual desire was conscripted as the foundation of a stable social institution. True love is, or ought to be, we are to understand, companionable and based on shared convictions; the rhetoric of lovers is properly transparent, their exchanges honest, not designed to persuade; and genuine love occurs only between equals or near-equals, who treat each other with respect.

Venus, of course, fails on all counts. The love she represents is in these terms palpably unhealthy and contrary to nature. She is altogether too passionate, too persistent, too manipulative, too old. The phrase "Sick-thoughted Venus," virtually a circumlocution for lovesickness, as the Arden editor recognizes, comes in the criticism to justify the diagnosis of a sexual pathology: critics write, for example, that "She is introduced as 'Sick-thoughted' (l. 5), the primary notion of amorous languishment being overlaid with that of sick excess";[60] "in the light of that epithet her desire for the young Adonis can only be taken as unnatural and disorderly."[61] Leonard Barkan's account of the poem finds the love it defines "passionate and excessive,"[62] and Jonathan Bate considers the desire of Venus "perverse," while noting that perversity is also a common element of love. The poem, he proposes, is about transgression as a component of passion; it is thus "a celebration of sexuality even as it is a disturbing exposure of the dark underside of desire."[63]

But what exactly is it that is transgressed in *Venus and Adonis*? Or, what is the "wholesome" arrangement that constitutes the criterion for the critical

---

[59] See Catherine Belsey, *Desire: Love Stories in Western Culture* (Oxford: Basil Blackwell, 1994), 21–41.

[60] Williams, 770. See also Keach, 66.

[61] David N. Beauregard, "*Venus and Adonis*: Shakespeare's Representation of the Passions," *ShStud* 8 (1975): 83–98, esp. 94.

[62] Barkan, 271.

[63] Bate, 48–65, esp. 65.

identification of psychosexual pathology here? Whatever Venus is propos-
ing for Adonis, it is not marriage. In the first place, she is married already.
The text does not mention Vulcan, but the invocation of Mars would surely
remind most readers of the humiliating story of the adulterous couple
caught in her husband's net and exposed to view in the very act of love.[64]
And in the second place, it was not yet obvious in the early 1590s that the
only proper destiny of lovers was to found a nuclear family. That belief, I
have suggested, was still in the process of construction. The condition the
poem records is not true love as the basis of marital concord but the tragic
passion of the classic love stories, and the narrative bears out the characterization of desire in the goddess's final curse, a definition that applies
prophetically for others and retrospectively for her.

The invocation of family values as a framework for making sense of *Venus
and Adonis* betrays, it seems to me, both the complexity of cultural history
and the polyphony of Shakespeare's text, which draws on Ovid and the
poetic and romance traditions as well as on popular morality. If the poem
is definitive for the period, it is so to the degree that it brings an emergent
taxonomy into conjunction—and conflict—with a residual indeterminacy,[65]
an understanding of sexual desire as precisely sensual, irrational, anarchic,
dangerous but also, and at the same time, delicate, fragile, and precious.

Family values represent an effort to bring desire into line with Law, in the
Lacanian sense of that term, with the taxonomies and the corresponding
disciplines inscribed in the symbolic order. The family promises gratification in exchange for submission to the rules: true love is desire that is
properly regulated; it is for an appropriate (heterosexual) object; and its
story is told in Shakespearean comedy and, in due course, in the nineteenth-
century novel. True love obeys the rules of gender and genre, and its
moment of closure is marriage, the metonym of a lifetime of happiness.

*Venus and Adonis* tells a quite different story. It is at the moment when
Venus is compelled to realize that gratification is not an option ("All is
imaginary she doth prove" [l. 597]) that the text invokes the trompe-l'oeil of
the painted grapes. Venus perceives that the fulfillment of her desire is
"imaginary" because her entreaties, arguments, threats, and promises fail to
arouse any response in Adonis. Passion is not subject to reason or entreaty,
to regulation or Law. On the contrary, desire is anarchic, and its cause is not,
in the end, the persuasive powers of another person, not even a goddess,
but the missing *objet a*, the presence that the ordering mechanisms of the
symbolic both promise and withhold. Irrational, irregular, incited by prohibition, and thus quite unable to take "no" for an answer, desire is in every
sense of the term an outlaw.

It follows that desire repudiates the rules, the classifications, and the
proprieties that historically take up their place in the symbolic order. The
queen of love has her own law, the poem affirms (l. 251), but it is a
topsy-turvy one that enslaves only the ruler. What the text proposes is that

---

[64] Ovid, Bk. 4, ll. 171–89.

[65] For another symptom of this indeterminacy, see Margaret Mikesell's astute account of an
unconscious regression to the praise of celibacy within the humanist defense of marriage in
Vives's influential conduct book for women ("Marital and Divine Love in Juan Luis Vives'
*Instruction of a Christen Woman*" in *Love and Death in the Renaissance*, Kenneth R. Bartlett, Konrad
Eisenbichler, and Janice Liedl, eds. [Ottawa: Dovehouse Editions, 1991], 113–34).

desire rejects the taxonomies of both gender and genre. Love is for a boy who looks like a girl and who is in one sense too young for the difference to matter; its modes of address are at once absurd and lyrical and tragic. Passion is contrary, contradictory; "love is," the text affirms, "wise in folly, foolish witty" (l. 838).

*Venus and Adonis*, which participates in the construction of family values, can also be read as indicating the altogether utopian character of a social project that sets out to subject desire to discipline, regulation, legality. Itself a trompe-l'oeil, moving between genres, unclosed, unfurnished with a final signified, the poem sustains the desire of the reader-critic to the degree that it refuses to yield the gratification of a secret meaning, a moral truth concealed behind the folds of its heterogeneous textuality.

# Taking Tropes Seriously: Language and Violence in Shakespeare's *Rape of Lucrece*

## KATHARINE EISAMAN MAUS

Around 1601 Gabriel Harvey, writing in the margin of his copy of Chaucer, remarked that Shakespeare's "Lucrece, and his tragedie of Hamlet, Prince of Denmark, have it in them, to please the wiser sort." His remark suggests that *The Rape of Lucrece* helped establish Shakespeare's seriousness as a poet, a suggestion borne out by the popularity of the poem in its own time and the enthusiastic praise it received from many of Shakespeare's contemporaries.[1] *The Rape of Lucrece* has fared less well at the hands of modern critics, however, who persistently object to its elaborate rhetoric. "Action in *Lucrece* is smothered in poetry," Richard Wilbur complains. Douglas Bush deplores the poem's "incessant conceits" and "endless rhetorical digressions"; Ian Donaldson the way "the poem repeatedly begins to analyse the nature of a moral predicament, only to break off abruptly, diverting us into an extended metaphor, lament, or topical digression." J. W. Lever surmises that "the opportunities for conscious eloquence tempted Shakespeare's facility and led to a piling up of tropes." Even Coppélia Kahn, who argues convincingly for the significance of some of the poem's major concerns, sees the "rhetorical setpieces" as distracting from "the poem's insistent concern with the relationship between sex and power."[2] For all five critics, the rhetoric of *The Rape of Lucrece* conceals, confuses, overwhelms. In this essay I shall explore the decorum of poetic language in *The Rape of Lucrece*. I shall argue that both protagonists construe particular metaphors as if they were literally true, drawing apparently unwarranted conclusions from them, and that the narrative voice

For helpful comments on drafts of this article I am grateful to Elizabeth Harvey and Fred Maus. For bibliographical advice and/or the loan of books, I would like to thank Lawrence Danson, Deborah Esch, Jules Law, Ronald Levao, Richard Kroll, Thomas Roche, and Scott Wayland.

[1] Gabriel Harvey's comment is reprinted in *The Reader's Encyclopedia of Shakespeare*, ed. O. J. Campbell (New York: Thomas Y. Crowell, 1966), pp. 305–6. For a complete account of the reception of *The Rape of Lucrece*, see Hyder Edward Rollins, ed., *A New Variorum Edition of Shakespeare: The Poems* (Philadelphia: Lippincott, 1938), pp. 447–57.

[2] Richard Wilbur, "The Narrative Poems: Introduction," in *William Shakespeare: The Complete Works*, gen. ed. Alfred Harbage (London: Penguin, 1969), p. 1404; Douglas Bush, *Mythology and the Renaissance Tradition in English Poetry*, rev. ed. (New York: Norton, 1963), pp. 152, 154; Ian Donaldson, *The Rapes of Lucretia* (Oxford: Clarendon, 1982), p. 40; J. W. Lever, "Shakespeare's Narrative Poems," *A New Companion to Shakespeare Studies*, eds. K. Muir and S. Schoenbaum (Cambridge: Cambridge Univ. Press, 1971), p. 125; Coppélia Kahn, "The Rape in Shakespeare's *Lucrece*," *Shakespeare Studies*, 9 (1976), 45. In *The Motives of Eloquence* (New Haven: Yale Univ. Press, 1976), pp. 94–110, Richard Lanham approaches Shakespeare's elaborate and self-conscious rhetoric more sympathetically, but eventually he merely transfers to the characters the faults other critics ascribe to the poet. I shall discuss the limitations of this line of argument later in this essay.

displays the same literalizing tendencies. I shall go on to show how and why the use and abuse of tropes should become such an important issue in *The Rape of Lucrece*.

I

As Ovid and Livy recount it, the story of Lucretia's violation by Tarquin Sextus and her subsequent suicide is full of impetuous action, sudden violence, unexpected revelations. But in Shakespeare's version the pell-mell momentum of the original Latin story becomes a marginal effect, conveyed in a prefatory "Argument." "The same night he treacherously stealeth into her chamber, violently ravished her, and early in the morning speedeth away. Lucrece, in this lamentable plight, hastily dispatcheth messengers. . . ."[3] By contrast the poem proper concentrates not upon action but upon what happens in the interstices between the "important" moments: what Tarquin thinks on his way down the hall to Lucrece's bedroom; how Lucrece occupies herself between the time she sends off her messenger and Collatine's return.

Shakespeare's poem is essentially an account, punctuated by terrible violence, of two people making important decisions. As Ian Donaldson declares, "No other version of the Lucretia story explores more minutely or with greater psychological insight the mental processes of the two major characters, their inconsistent waverings to and fro, before they bring themselves finally and reluctantly to action."[4] And the plot of *Lucrece* results from these choices. This is not a story in which factors beyond human control play a part. Nothing seems simply inevitable; the poem teases the reader with alternative possibilities. What if Collatine had kept his good fortune to himself? What if Tarquin's conscience had overcome his lust, instead of vice versa? What if the blazing beauty of the sleeping Lucrece had blinded Tarquin permanently, instead of only temporarily? "Then Collatine again, by Lucrece' side, / In his clear bed might have reposèd still" (ll. 381–82). What if Collatine had arrived to save Lucrece at the last moment? What if Lucrece had resolved to kill Tarquin rather than herself?

Neither character's choices seem to reflect his or her best interests, and Tarquin and Lucrece must constantly resist the temptation to behave logically. So their decision-making becomes not the activity of a moment but a continuously repeated process. Tarquin rides from Ardea apparently already determined upon rape, but he must re-examine and re-justify his intentions, both to himself and to Lucrece, making the same decision again and again until he finally stamps out his torch and leaps upon his victim. Lucrece likewise resolves on suicide shortly after Tarquin's departure but must continue to debate the wisdom of this course even after her mind is supposedly made up.

The difficult process of decision-making is, for both characters, inseparable from their employment of a few crucial metaphors. For Tarquin, the crucial metaphor is a military one. Faced with the competing and mutually exclusive claims of honor and desire, the intolerable conflict between "frozen conscience and hot-burning will," he imposes a version of martial order: "Affection is my captain, and he leadeth; / . . . / My heart shall never countermand mine eye" (ll. 271–76). Since, for Tarquin, "love is war," he believes that he can employ whatever tactics he must to take Lucrece's fort, offering the enemy no quarter:

---

[3] All *Rape of Lucrece* citations are quoted from *William Shakespeare: The Complete Works*, gen. ed. Alfred Harbage (London: Penguin, 1969).

[4] Donaldson, p. 44.

297

> His drumming heart cheers up his burning eye,
> His eye commends the leading to his hand;
> His hand, as proud of such a dignity,
> Smoking with pride, marched on to make his stand
> On her bare breast, the heart of all her land.
>
> (ll. 435–39)

The attraction of this metaphor is that, at least temporarily, it allows Tarquin to depict a rash and lawless act as coordinated and disciplined. The rape appeals to him because he conceives it as an integrative act, one that requires an elaborate but nonetheless ordered division of labor among the parts of the body. The irony, of course, is that the crime exacerbates rather than heals his fragmentation and self-torment, rendering him worse after the "cure" than he had been before.[5]

Tarquin's characteristic mode of self-justification does not involve arguing directly for the rightness of his action. Rather, he elaborates metaphors that allow him to establish a clear, if perverse, hierarchy of priorities, and then strenuously resists any attempts either to expand the interpretive possibilities of the tropes or to suggest ways in which the analogies might be faulty. Both forms of resistance appear most clearly in his response to Lucrece's pleas for mercy, pleas that essentially set up metaphors to rival his own. Lucrece likens her tears to an ocean beating upon Tarquin's "rocky and wrack-threatening heart"; he appropriates and reverses the image by claiming that his "uncontrollèd tide / Turns not, but swells the higher by this let" (ll. 645–46). Lucrece then attempts, unsuccessfully, to accept Tarquin's version of the metaphor but to modify its significance:

> 'Thou art,' quoth she, 'a sea, a sovereign king;
> And, lo, there falls into thy boundless flood
> Black lust, dishonor, shame, misgoverning,
> Who seek to stain the ocean of thy blood.'
>
> (ll. 652–55)

While Tarquin thinks of himself as a warrior, Lucrece tries to remind him of his responsibilities as a monarch; her account of his psychological state replaces the metaphor of military hierarchy he favors with the metaphor of a civil order temporarily disrupted:

> 'I sue for exiled majesty's repeal;
> Let him return, and flatt'ring thoughts retire.
> His true respect will prison false desire. . . .'
>
> (ll. 640–42)

Thus, on the one hand, Tarquin's literal-minded application of a trope helps him convince himself to commit a crime with full awareness of its gravity and its consequences. On the other hand, as Lucrece reminds us, his particular use of metaphor is hardly inevitable; there are alternative ways of representing his psychological upheaval and his decision.

The close relationship between tropes and moral choices is more fully elaborated after the rape, when the narrative focus shifts to Lucrece. Her dilemma

---

[5] Some critics have remarked upon the way Shakespeare presents Tarquin's rape as a self-violation; Sam Hynes, "The Rape of Tarquin," *Shakespeare Quarterly*, 10 (1959), 451–53; Donaldson, p. 52.

is more complex and more controversial than Tarquin's. Classical writers had celebrated Lucretia for her indomitability, but Christians often condemned her suicide. In *The City of God* (Bks. XVI–XX) Augustine initiates the criticism and defines its terms. In the Augustinian view, if Lucretia is indeed raped by Tarquin she cannot be guilty of inchastity. Augustine maintains that, since the virtues are properties of the will, acts one commits under duress cannot affect one's virtue. Chastity, he insists, is an attitude of the mind and not a physical accident. But Lucretia's innocence of sexual crime ironically exacerbates the sinfulness of her suicide, which for Augustine is the murder of a guiltless person. Not all Christian commentators agree with Augustine's reasoning, but the effect of the casuistical tradition as Shakespeare inherits it is to establish Lucretia's motives for suicide as an important issue for moral scrutiny.[6] And Shakespeare's Lucrece does indeed provide lengthy justification for her behavior.

What are we to think of Lucrece? Is she guilty of anything, and if so, of what? Coppélia Kahn has argued that Lucrece's suicide is the necessary consequence of her position as female chattel in a patriarchal society.[7] This thesis, however, does not seem entirely adequate either to the classical Lucretia or to the character as Shakespeare conceives her. For Ovid, Lucretia is distinguished not by her quintessential femininity but by her admirable "masculine" spirit: she is *"animi matrona virilis"* (*Fasti* II, 847.) In Shakespeare's poem, too, Lucrece's actions do not quite accord with her declarations that she is merely Collatine's property. "For me, I am the mistress of my fate," she maintains (l. 1069), and in a sense she is right. She makes her decision for suicide without consulting the men whom she supposes her owners; when her husband and father protest her innocence, insisting upon the moral difference between rape and adultery, she refuses to accept their verdict.[8] The reaction of Collatine and his followers to Lucrece's self-immolation is bewilderment: they are left "Stone-still, astonished with this deadly deed" (l. 1730). Far from being the culturally acceptable thing to do in a patriarchal society, Lucrece's suicide shocks the Roman men; its supererogatory character is precisely what makes it seem both heroic and troubling, sublime and confused, to its witnesses and to the reader.

In fact, Lucrece's suicide is the consequence of her enforced participation in the same vision that motivates Tarquin.[9] The reasons she cannot accept Augustine's reasoning, urged upon her as it is by her male relatives, are adumbrated when she explains to herself and the reader her justification for suicide:

---

[6] For accounts of the Christian response to the legend of Lucretia see Donaldson, pp. 21–39, and D. C. Allen, "Some Observations on *The Rape of Lucrece*," *Shakespeare Survey*, 15 (1962), 89–91. It is not clear that Shakespeare read Augustine on Lucretia, though most modern critics assume he was aware of the Augustinian position. D. C. Allen, Coppélia Kahn, and Ian Donaldson all discuss Shakespeare's reaction to the Augustinian critique of Lucretia, as does Roy Battenhouse in *Shakespearean Tragedy: Its Art and Christian Premises* (Bloomington: Indiana Univ. Press, 1969), pp. 3–41.

[7] Kahn, 45–72. For a more optimistic (in my opinion, over-optimistic) description of the way Lucrece is changed by the rape, see Laura G. Bromley, "Lucrece's Re-Creation," *SQ*, 34 (1983), 200–211.

[8] Shakespeare obtains his account of the male relatives' reaction from Livy: "consolantur aegram animi avertendo noxam ab coacta in auctorem delicti; mentem peccare, non corpus, et unde consilium afuerit, culpam abesse." *Ab Urbe condita* I, LVIII, 9–10. Coppélia Kahn is incorrect when she asserts that a focus upon intentions rather than consequences is a specifically Christian innovation; the pagan Livy could have gotten his moral intuitions from the Stoics or the Aristotelians.

[9] For a different account of some of the similarities and differences between Lucrece and Tarquin see Jerome Kramer and Judith Kaminsky, " 'These Contraries Such Unity Do Hold': Structure in *The Rape of Lucrece*," *Mosaic*, 10 (1977), 145–55.

'To kill myself,' quoth she, 'alack, what were it
But with my body my poor soul's pollution?
They that lose half with greater patience bear it
Than they whose whole is swallowed in confusion.
That mother tries a merciless conclusion
    Who, having two sweet babes, when death takes one,
    Will slay the other and be nurse to none.

'My body or my soul, which was the dearer
When the one, pure, the other made divine?
Whose love of either to myself was nearer
When both were kept for heaven and Collatine?
Ay me! the bark pilled from the lofty pine,
    His leaves will wither and his sap decay:
    So must my soul, her bark being pilled away.

'Her house is sacked, her quiet interrupted,
Her mansion battered by the enemy;
Her sacred temple spotted, spoiled, corrupted,
Grossly engirt with daring infamy.
Then let it not be called impiety
    If in this blemished fort I make some hole
    Through which I may convey this troubled soul.'
                                            (ll. 1156–76)

In order to find Augustine's argument plausible one must accept two axioms.
First, one must be willing to admit a conceptual distinction between the body
and the soul. Lucrece declares this separation here and elsewhere: "Though my
gross blood be stained with this abuse, / Immaculate and spotless is my mind"
(ll. 1655–56). But, in addition, one must also grant the priority of the soul
over the body, as Augustine does explicitly and as Lucrece's male relatives do
implicitly when they insist that "Her body's stain her mind untainted clears"
(l. 1710). Lucrece, however, balks at the second assumption. "My body or my
soul, which was the dearer?" (l. 1163). This is not a merely rhetorical question.
What she yearns for is her condition before the rape when there was no need
to make a choice between the body and the soul. She finds the conflict between
them impossible to endure, but refuses to privilege one element and resolve
the conflict.

Lucrece thinks about her body in terms of metaphors: house, fortress, mansion, temple, tree bark.[10] Essentially, these metaphors emphasize the protective
and enclosing function of the body—the way the body surrounds the soul and
wards off danger. Once the house is sacked and battered, the inhabitant suffers,
regardless of her guilt or innocence; this is one of the lessons of the Troy picture
before which Lucrece will stand later in the poem. The significance of these
metaphors for Lucrece's thinking becomes clear when one remembers the alternative image employed by a different female character threatened with sexual
violence:

> Fool do not boast,
> Thou canst not touch the freedom of my mind
> With all thy charms, although this corporal rind
> Thou hast immanacled, while Heaven sees good.
>                                 (*Comus*, ll. 662–65)

[10] Leonard Barkan discusses the way a number of Shakespeare's contemporaries use the metaphor
of the house for the body in *Nature's Work of Art: The Human Body as Image of the World* (New
Haven: Yale Univ. Press, 1975), pp. 134–74.

Milton's Lady thinks of the body as a "rind," an excrescence, and thus possesses an Augustinian assurance of moral invulnerability to physical outrage. Lucrece's apparently similar image of the body as the bark around a pine stresses, instead, the vital reliance of the tree upon its protective cover.

Why does Lucrece not adopt the kind of imagery available to the Lady in *Comus*? Why is she drawn to metaphors that imply the dependence of the soul upon the body? Although Coppélia Kahn's account of Lucrece's moral reasoning is partial, she is right to focus upon the significance of gender. Lucrece's virtues are feminine ones: purity, constancy, integrity. In the violent, contradictory, and changeable world of pre-republican Rome, these virtues survive only in a carefully restricted environment. The tragedy, according to Shakespeare, issues originally from the fatal rashness of Lucrece's husband Collatine, a male Pandora, who "Unlocked the treasure of his happy state" to his kinsman Tarquin (l. 16) displaying "that rich jewel he should keep unknown" (l. 34). The image implies that Lucrece, like Pandora's treasure, needs to be kept in a box. Early in the poem Lucrece's virtue is clearly linked to her lack of experience: "unstained thoughts do seldom dream on evil; / Birds never limed no secret bushes fear" (ll. 87–88). Tarquin, tearing aside the bedcurtain, also tears away the moral and intellectual veils that had sheltered her innocence. Her rape calls into question—*violates*—her faith in the existence of values she had taken for granted, values she invokes in her appeal to her implacable opponent: "knighthood, gentry, and sweet friendship's oath, / . . . / . . . holy human law and common troth" (ll. 569–71). In her apostrophe to Opportunity after Tarquin's departure, Lucrece indicates her new awareness of the way the unavoidable presence of evil complicates and adulterates virtue:

> 'Unruly blasts wait on the tender spring;
> Unwholesome weeds take root with precious flow'rs;
> The adder hisses where the sweet birds sing;
> What Virtue breeds Iniquity devours.'
>
> (ll. 869–72)

Her despair after the rape is despair for an irredeemably lost simplicity, a simplicity inconsistent with the experience of injustice, conflict, and duplicity.

Retreat from new and painful consciousness is as impossible for Lucrece as is physical retreat. When she awakens to find Tarquin in her bedroom, her first impulse is to close her eyes, but the vision within is as terrifying as the vision without:

> She dares not look; yet, winking, there appears
> Quick-shifting antics ugly in her eyes.
> Such shadows are the weak brain's forgeries,
>     Who, angry that the eyes fly from their lights,
>     In darkness daunts them with more dreadful sights.
>     (ll. 458–62)

In Shakespeare's Rome, where the men engage with the "real world" and women remain indoors, Lucrece's dilemma is a matter of the way female virtue is defined; but her problem is not necessarily an exclusively feminine one. Perhaps Gabriel Harvey thinks of *Lucrece* in connection with *Hamlet* because both play and poem feature protagonists whose innocence is destroyed when they are forced to recognize other people's wickedness.

Nonetheless, Lucrece tries to reconstruct a vision of unity by asserting interdependence and consistency whenever she can. The soul and body, appearances and realities, her interests and Collatine's, must be forced into harmony.

Even when the existence of contradiction is impossible to ignore, she tries to formulate a law to regulate the conflict. As she meditates before the picture of the attractive but duplicitous Sinon, she reaches the patently false but entirely characteristic conclusion that virtuous-looking exteriors always betoken vicious souls. What she cannot tolerate is the possibility that there are no constants, that the relationship between body and soul is simply arbitrary. Thus her suicide can be seen as a desperate attempt to resist the possibilities of contradiction and inconsistency to which Tarquin's violence has introduced her.

The suicide, however—comprehensible though it might be—is ironically fraught with the very contradictions Lucrece seeks to avoid. She "revenges" herself upon Tarquin by completing the assault he had begun, plunging the phallic knife into the "sheath" of her breast (l. 1723; in Latin, "sheath" is *vagina*). She insists upon her sacrifice for Collatine even as she ignores his wishes; she proves her innocence by exacting the penalty for guilt; she broadcasts and validates her utterance even while silencing herself more effectively than had Tarquin with the bedclothes. What Lucrece's death ultimately displays is not a willed unity but a tragic dividedness, as her blood separates into pure red and contaminated black streams, and the black stream in turn into a "congealèd-face" and a "wat'ry rigoll." Like Tarquin, then, Lucrece uses crucial metaphors to organize and integrate her moral thinking, refusing to acknowledge the subversive alternatives the poem so plentifully supplies.

## II

What is happening when Tarquin compares himself to an army scaling Lucrece's fort, or when Lucrece imagines her body as a battered mansion? The usual assumption would be that these metaphors express states of mind. Both characters prefer metaphors which render their moral choices plausible. Thus Lucrece, who initially finds attractive the metaphor of the body and soul as "two babes" because the figure suggests the equality of body and soul, soon remarks that this metaphor makes her decision for suicide seem irrational. She answers her own objections not by confronting them directly, but by shifting to other, more congenial metaphors.

Nonetheless, the characters' rhetoric often seems as much constitutive as symptomatic, creating as well as expressing their states of mind. Tarquin's *prosopopoeia*, his personification of fears and desires and of parts of the body as independent entities, is one indication of his moral disarray. But the trope also contributes to that disarray by implying that the personified impulses may take their own courses without reference to his intentions. Phrases like "my heart shall never countermand mine eye" or "affection is my captain, and he leadeth" suppress the fact of choice and allow Tarquin to avoid, at least temporarily, full recognition of his own culpability.

Lucrece's language similarly seems to determine the course of her reasoning. When Lucrece indicts Night, Opportunity, and Time after the rape, she employs both *prosopopoeia* and *metalepsis*, a rhetorical figure related to metaphor in which the remote is substituted for the obvious. Addressing "hateful, vaporous, and foggy Night," insisting that "thou art guilty of my cureless crime" (ll. 771–72), she simultaneously displaces responsibility from Tarquin and creates a plausible alternative culprit. By mystifying the fact of Tarquin's guilt, these tropes make it easier for Lucrece eventually to convict herself of a sin she has not committed.

In other ways, too, Lucrece's language persistently obscures the crucial question of agency: does the possessive pronoun in "my cureless crime" or "my life's foul deed" imply that she has committed an evil action or that an evil action has been committed against her? When she imagines that "The orator, to deck his oratory, / Will couple my reproach to Tarquin's shame" (ll. 815–16), is she using the word "reproach" to mean "complaint" or to mean "blameworthiness"? Her ambiguities have literally fatal consequences.

The problematic relationship between language and psychological state is suggested when Lucrece, after a night spent crying out against her wrong, sends a messenger to Collatine and must wait for his return. In the interval she finds herself frustrated and bored:

> The weary time she cannot entertain,
> For now 'tis stale to sigh, to weep and groan.
> So woe hath wearied woe, moan tirèd moan,
> That she her plaints a little while doth stay,
> Pausing for means to mourn some newer way.
>             (ll. 1361–65)

As Richard Lanham has noted, Lucrece's grief is not entirely spontaneous, but requires that she have something to say.[11] She turns to a representation of the Trojan war for relief, not because it offers her the possibility of consolation, but because its novelty inspires her with new ways to describe and understand, and thus to experience her despair. This is not to say that discourse creates her grief. Her language is not prior to her psychological state in any simple way. Lucrece's model is Philomela, the raped bird-woman who not only suffers sexual outrage but who also makes it the constant subject of her utterance; and Lucrece remembers that in order to sing, Philomela must lean against a thorn, inflicting and re-inflicting upon herself Tereus's unwelcome penetration. The pain demands representation, but the representation requires the experience, even the deliberate exacerbation, of pain; the relation between emotion and speech seems more a perverse reciprocity than a simple relation of cause and effect. And it is a difficult cycle, constantly subject to disruption and blockage. Lucrece stutters when she attempts to plead with Tarquin, struggles through several drafts of her letter to Collatine, and stammers again when he finally arrives, interrupting both her story and her revelation of the culprit with "many accents and delays, / Untimely breathings, sick and short assays" (ll. 1719–20). Collatine likewise is struck mute upon his homecoming and babbles incoherently after Lucrece's suicide. On the one hand, grief and fear interrupt discourse, which inevitably seems an inadequate vehicle for feeling. On the other hand, grief and fear motivate discourse; Lucrece acquires her own voice in the poem only at the moment when she is faced with violence.

### III

This intimacy between the characters' metaphors and their decisions, and between their language and their psychological states, may seem unsurprising. Shakespeare's contemporary, George Puttenham, remarks that tropes "alter and affect the mind by alteration of sense," and Francis Bacon that "men believe that their reason governs words, but it is also true that words react on the

---

[11] Lanham, p. 104.

understanding."[12] It would be wrong, however, to regard *The Rape of Lucrece* as merely an anatomy of unfortunate individuals confused by the idols of the marketplace. The crucial metaphors of the poem are not the exclusive property of the characters, but are invoked throughout the narrative.

For example, Tarquin's military trope is not his alone. It pervades *The Rape of Lucrece* from the moment Tarquin leaves the siege of Ardea to lay siege to his kinsman's wife, through Lucrece's extended meditation upon the sack of Troy, to Lucius Junius Brutus's final revolutionary vow. Nor is the conviction that body and soul are inseparable merely a whim of the protagonists; Shakespeare's rhetoric asserts it constantly. The vividness of the psychomachiae in *Lucrece* depends upon the metaphoric embodiment of mental events:

> And then with lank and lean discolored cheek,
> With heavy eye, knit brow, and strengthless pace,
> Feeble Desire, all recreant, poor, and meek,
> Like to a bankrout beggar wails his case.
> (ll. 708–11)

The very term "will" that, for Augustine, signifies detachment from and transcendence of the physical, becomes crucial in *Lucrece* precisely because of its ambiguity, the paronomastic possibility of invoking both "desire" and "genitalia" at the same time. Tarquin conflates mental and physical when he tells Lucrece that "thou with patience must my will abide" (l. 486); but so does the third-person narrative when it describes Tarquin's "disputation / 'Tween frozen conscience and hot-burning will" (ll. 246–47). The words "lust" and "pride" are similarly ambiguous. When Tarquin overcomes his initial indecision and begins to force his way toward Lucrece's bedchamber, Shakespeare writes that his "servile powers . . . stuff up his lust" (ll. 295–97), describing at the same time the physiology of erection and the psychology of resolution.

Lucrece is likewise delineated in terms that minimize the difference between body and soul; she is the "fair fair" (l. 346), the virtuous and beautiful woman whose internal and external loveliness is denoted by the same word. In a characteristic passage Shakespeare writes of Lucrece's breasts: "Save of their lord no bearing yoke they knew / And him by oath they truly honorèd" (ll. 409–10). The "bearing yoke" is, literally, Collatine's weight during sexual intercourse. But metaphorically it is the yoke of marriage, the *jugum coniugalis*,

---

[12] George Puttenham, *The Arte of English Poesie*, eds. Gladys Doidge Willcock and Alice Walker (1936; rpt. Cambridge: Cambridge Univ. Press, 1970), p. 176; Francis Bacon, *The New Organon* LIX, in *Francis Bacon: A Selection of His Works*, ed. Sidney Warhaft (New York: Odyssey, 1968), p. 341. Many modern philosophers and literary theorists discuss the truth-value of metaphor and its role in human understanding. Important formulations include: Max Black, "Metaphor," *Proceedings of the Aristotelian Society*, 55 (1954–55), 273–94; Jacques Derrida, "White Mythology: Metaphor in the Text of Philosophy," *New Literary History*, 6 (1974), 5–74; Nelson Goodman, *Languages of Art* (Indianapolis: Hackett, 1976), 50–95; Paul Ricoeur, *The Rule of Metaphor* (Toronto: Univ. of Toronto Press, 1977), pp. 216–313 and "The Metaphorical Process as Cognition, Imagination, and Feeling," *On Metaphor*, ed. Sheldon Sacks (Chicago: Univ. of Chicago Press, 1978), pp. 141–57; Donald Davidson, "What Metaphors Mean," *On Metaphor*, pp. 29–46; Paul de Man, "The Epistemology of Metaphor," *On Metaphor*, pp. 11–45; George Lakoff and Mark Johnson, *Metaphors We Live By* (Chicago: Univ. of Chicago Press, 1980). Though versions of the issues these writers address seem important in *The Rape of Lucrece*, it is impossible to align the poem with a theory of metaphoric meaning. Shakespeare is concerned not with the nature of metaphor in general, but with the way a powerfully seductive figurative language may function in particular circumstances.

the wifely obligation of loyalty to the husband. The distinction between these two meanings of "bearing yoke," one physical or literal, one spiritual or metaphoric, is difficult to maintain in this context, however, when Lucrece is represented by synecdoche: not she but her breasts have taken an oath.

Other tropes likewise help render the protagonists' convictions plausible. Synecdoche and personification are not only invoked by Tarquin, but are also applied to him:

> The curtains being close, about he walks,
> Rolling his greedy eyeballs in his head.
> By their high treason is his heart misled,
>   Which gives the watchword to his hand full soon. . . .
>                                       (ll.367–70)

Oxymorons like "modest wanton" reinforce Lucrece's paradoxical sense of herself as both guilty and innocent; so does the poem's very attempt to exculpate her:

> For men have marble, women waxen minds,
> And therefore are they formed as marble will.
> The weak oppressed, th'impression of strange kinds
> Is formed in them by force, by fraud, or skill.
> Then call them not the authors of their ill,
>   No more than wax shall be accounted evil
>   Wherein is stamped the semblance of a devil.
>
> Their smoothness, like a goodly champain plain,
> Lays open all the little worms that creep;
> In men, as in a rough-grown grove, remain
> Cave-keeping evils that obscurely sleep.
> Through crystal walls each little mote will peep.
>   Though men can cover crimes with bold stern looks,
>   Poor women's faces are their own faults' books.
>                                       (ll. 1240–53)

This passage seems to begin by denying Lucrece's guilt on Augustinian grounds; the victim of another's crime is not to blame. But the metaphor of the wax is a tricky one. It absolves Lucrece by construing her passivity as absolute. If Lucrece does not possess a will of her own, intentions and preferences of her own—if she is pure malleability—then what can Tarquin have violated? And if all male influence upon women is conceived as the irresistible pressure of hard substance upon soft, then rape is hardly outrageous; it is almost in the nature of things. This "defense" of Lucrece, in other words, by denying her the status of a moral agent, not only deprives her of her best claim to innocence but makes Tarquin's assault seem excusable.

Moreover, in the second stanza the smoothness and softness of the metaphoric wax produces an important swerve in the direction of the argument, which begins to treat of feminine openness: "Through crystal walls each little mote will peep. . . . / Poor women's faces are their own faults' books." Women's bodies are transparent; their "faults" not things stamped upon them from without but peeping from within. Blamelessness becomes blame. By the end of the second stanza the narrator, under the sway of his trope, is asserting precisely that unfortunate intimacy between body and soul which proves crucial in Lucrece's decision for suicide. When Ian Donaldson complains that *The Rape of Lucrece* does not make clear "what moral universe [the characters] inhabit,"[13] his uncertainty perhaps derives from the fact that the narrative employs, in the same dubious ways, metaphors that are rendered questionable when the protagonists use them to justify their actions. The poem seems to collude with both protagonists in their "errors."

IV

An analysis that centers upon characterization, then, cannot fully explain how and why metaphor is so problematic in *The Rape of Lucrece*. The problem is larger than the characters, and has to do with the way poetic language functions in *Lucrece*.

We have already seen that the protagonists' violence and heroism are the result of their construing tropes in their strong form; that is, not as assertions of resemblance, but of identity. Love is not merely *like* war; it is war. Lucrece's body is not merely *like* a fortress; the analogy can be extended in unlimited and surprising directions. Significantly, the tropes the protagonists take so literally are not Shakespeare's inventions, but part of the traditional vocabulary of Elizabethan love poetry, as it is inherited from Petrarch and Ovid, from canzoniere and Italian sonneteers, and developed by Wyatt, Surrey, Sidney, Spenser, and many others. The configuration of characters—warrior-lover, absent husband, chaste-but-desirable woman—is likewise conventional, as is the poem's attention not to the exigencies of plot but to the elaborate analysis of extreme and often irrational emotional reactions.

But a comparison with Spenser makes clear the way *The Rape of Lucrece* deviates from this tradition:

> Gaynst such strong castles needeth greater might
> Then those small forts which ye were wont belay:
> Such haughty minds enur'd to hardy fight
> Disdayne to yield unto the first assay.
> Bring therefore all the forces that ye may,
> And lay incessant battery to her heart,
> Playnts, prayers, vows, ruth, sorrow and desmay,
> Those engines can the proudest love convert.
>                                        (*Amoretti* xiv, 5–12)

The wit here lies in the contrast between the violent analogies Spenser invokes and the gentle means he proposes to employ; and innumerable poems by other authors feature bashful soldier-lovers thoroughly routed by a stern glance from their fair adversaries. The differences between making love and making war, and between women and fortresses, are as important to these poems as are their similarities. In *The Rape of Lucrece*, on the other hand, Tarquin and Lucrece enact the violence that in a sonnet sequence is restricted to the figurative and the imaginary. When Tarquin steals up to Lucrece's bed, this is how Shakespeare describes what he sees:

> Her hair like golden threads played with her breath—
> O modest wantons, wanton modesty!
> Showing life's triumph in the map of death,
> And death's dim look in life's mortality.
> Each in her sleep themselves so beautify

---

13 Donaldson, p. 45.

As if between them twain there were no strife,
But that life lived in death, and death in life.
(ll. 400–406)

There is nothing especially original in the ordinary sense about these images. The "hair like golden threads," the death-mimicking sleep, the exclamation upon the beloved's mysterious combination of purity and desirability, the fascination with her breath: all are commonplace in the erotic poetry of Shakespeare's contemporaries. What distinguishes Shakespeare's rhetoric is its unusual appositeness to the events narrated in the poem. Lucrece is a "modest wanton" here because while sleeping, she is simultaneously chaste and careless; but in a few stanzas the formulation will take on a new kind of appropriateness for a woman divided between untainted mind and outraged body. The play on life and death, mortality and immortality, looks forward to Lucretia's controversial insistence upon suicide and her consequent eternal fame. The situation—the lover hovering over a beautiful woman, seizing the opportunity for intimacies she would not tolerate when awake—had recommended itself to Boccaccio, Ariosto, and Sidney.[14] The difference is that in the *Decameron* the rape is a fiction invented by a male voyeur, in *Orlando Furioso* the impotence of the would-be violator renders sexual assault impossible, in *The Old Arcadia* a mob of "clownish villians" interrupts the proceedings, and in *Astrophel and Stella* rape is a momentary fantasy—Astrophel actually steals only a kiss from the virtuous Stella, and flees terrified by her anger. In *The Rape of Lucrece*, by contrast, the violent possibilities suggested in the rhetoric are inexorably realized. The facts of the narrative lend an unexpected urgency to apparently conventional rhetorical formulae and situations.

In its way of actualizing conventional imagery, *The Rape of Lucrece* resembles other early Shakespearean tragedy. Writing on synecdoche and mutilation in *Titus Andronicus*, Albert Tricomi describes "the shackling of the metaphoric imagination to the literal reality of the play's events";[15] and Leonard Forster remarks of *Romeo and Juliet*:

> the enmity of the Montagues and Capulets makes the cliché of the 'dear enemy' into a concrete predicament; the whole drama is devoted to bringing the cliché to life, and others are similarly enacted. The petrarchistic lover 'died' at his lady's kiss: Romeo in the vault actually does so.[16]

Many critics of sixteenth-century English literature have noted the way poets of the 1580s and 1590s simultaneously employ and modify the conventions of love poetry, aware on the one hand that the very wit and intensity of the inherited mode are liable to degenerate into a facile deployment of ossified paradoxes and hackneyed imagery, and on the other hand unwilling to abandon the advantages of the older style, especially its efficacy as a means of rendering complex psychological and metaphysical states in a relatively restricted number of highly charged images.[17] The early Shakespeare seems characteristically to

---

[14] Ariosto, *Orlando Furioso* Canto 8, pp. 42–43; Boccaccio, *Decameron*, 2, 9 (one of the sources for *Cymbeline*); Philip Sidney, *The Old Arcadia*, Bk. 3 and "Second Song," *Astrophel and Stella*. *The New Arcadia* deletes Musidorus's attempt to rape the sleeping Pamela.

[15] Albert H. Tricomi, "The Aesthetics of Mutilation in *Titus Andronicus*," *SS*, 27 (1974), 19.

[16] Forster, *The Icy Fire* (Cambridge: Cambridge Univ. Press, 1969), p. 51.

[17] See *inter alia* Forster; Rosemund Tuve, *Elizabethan and Metaphysical Imagery* (Chicago: Univ. of Chicago Press, 1947), pp. 221, 422; J. W. Lever, *The Elizabethan Love Sonnet* (London: Methuen, 1956), pp. 53–71, 96–100, 274–77; Louis L. Martz, "The *Amoretti*: Most Goodly Temperature," *Form and Convention in the Poetry of Edmund Spenser*, ed. William Nelson (New

rehabilitate the conventional language of desire by unleashing its violent potential. In *The Rape of Lucrece* the literalized metaphors that provide the rationale for the protagonists' choices are also the source of the poem's rhetorical energy. The interests of the characters and the interests of the poet coincide in a disconcerting way; Shakespeare like his protagonists takes tropes seriously.

In *Lucrece*, however, Shakespeare seems determined not only to exploit the benefits of this form of rhetorical rehabilitation but also to reveal its considerable moral and epistemological drawbacks. Jerome Kramer and Judith Kaminsky have remarked upon "how dense the poem is in contrast, paradox, and dichotomy."[18] This is true not only in the sense that these critics describe— i.e., in the sense that the imagery of conflict appropriately pervades a tragedy of unresolvably competing interests—but also in the sense that particular images tend to collide in ways that point up their mutual incommensurability.

For example, in the elaborate description of Lucrece's face early in the poem— red and white, beauty and virtue—the (pastoral) field of flowers and the (epic) field of war strive for predominance in time-honored Petrarchan fashion. But there is nothing natural, inevitable, or even stable about either the correspondences or the rivalries. Initially white is associated with virtue, red with beauty. Later red becomes virtue's color, white becomes beauty's. Meanwhile their relationship to one another is further complicated by the ambiguous prescription that "the red should fence the white" (l. 63); is the "fencing" a protective shielding (developing the defensive metaphor from the previous line) or is it a mutual sparring which continues the metaphors of antagonism from the earlier part of the stanza? The elements of the paradox remain tensely opposed—"oft they interchange each other's seat" (l. 70)—but meanwhile the terms of the opposition shift in a bewildering way. The colors of Lucrece's complexion seem to "stand for" her important qualities as the devices on a heraldic shield represent the traits of its owner;[19] but the relationship between symbol and substance is mutable and apparently arbitrary.

This shiftiness is characteristic of *The Rape of Lucrece*. Analogies are no sooner invoked than they begin to collapse and must be replaced by others, often with different implications. As Tarquin approaches the bed, Lucrece, still hidden behind the bedcurtains, is described as a "silver moon" (l. 371)—lovely, cool, and chaste as Cynthia—but as Tarquin draws the curtains in the next line she becomes a "fair and fiery-pointed sun / Rushing from forth a cloud" to dazzle Tarquin's gaze (ll. 373–74). The effect of the passage is to undermine any sense that a particular metaphor might be authoritative or exhaustive. Lucrece may be a moon in one sense or at one moment, a sun in another sense or at another moment. Again and again the relationship between tenor and vehicle is made to seem provisional and tenuous, sometimes even contradictory or paradoxical. As he debates his chosen course early in the poem, Tarquin "doth despise / His naked armor of still-slaughtered lust" (ll. 187–88). Since Tarquin uses his phallus as a weapon the metaphor of armor seems appropriate; but the paradoxes of the formulation simultaneously point up the metaphor's limitations. One who wears armor is not naked, one who is slaughtered has no need of armor, and while the epithet "still-slaughtered" makes sense applied to a flaccid penis it does not make sense applied to a soldier.

---

York: Columbia Univ. Press, 1961), pp. 146–68; Douglas Peterson, *The English Lyric From Wyatt to Donne* (Princeton: Princeton Univ. Press, 1967), pp. 164–284.

[18] Kramer and Kaminsky, p. 145.

[19] Muriel Bradbrook discusses heraldic imagery here and elsewhere in *Lucrece* in *Shakespeare and Elizabethan Poetry* (London: Chatto and Windus, 1951), pp. 110–16.

Even when the terms of the metaphoric correspondence seem obvious, interpretive problems arise. Tarquin, on his way to Lucrece's bedchamber, finds one of her gloves and pricks himself on a needle that has been stuck through it. This constitutes, clearly enough, a proleptic allegory of Tarquin's fate; his rape of Lucrece is also a self-wounding. He cannot handle the phallic instrument without hurting himself. But the precise significance of the episode is surprisingly difficult to define exactly. The narrator describes the needle as in effect warning Tarquin of Lucrece's refusal to tolerate outrage, "As who should say, 'This glove to wanton tricks / Is not inured'" (ll. 320–21). But insofar as the glove and the needle are tropes of the sexual organs the episode reinforces our sense not of Lucrece's resistance but of her penetrability. And Tarquin imposes yet a third construction upon his experience:

> 'So, so,' quoth he, 'these lets attend the time,
> Like little frosts that sometime threat the spring
> To add a more rejoicing to the prime
> And give the sneapèd birds more cause to sing.'
> (ll. 330–33)

In another context the leaps from trope to trope, the play of interpretive possibilities, might seem merely witty. In *The Rape of Lucrece*, the fact that the metaphors are so closely linked to the tragic action makes such leaps disconcerting and complicates the pleasure one takes in rhetorical virtuousity. Both Tarquin and Lucrece as well as the narrator, as we have seen, privilege particular tropes—they treat them as if they were unqualifiedly true, using them as guides to judgment and to action. But this valorization seems fraught with difficulties in a poem that emphasizes the limitations of its metaphors and advertises a variety of interpretive options even for tropes the significance of which might seem obvious.

## V

It seems reasonable, therefore, to try to escape the problems of figurative language by exploring alternative forms of representation. *The Rape of Lucrece* suggests two such alternatives: the summary, relatively nonfigural prose of the "Argument," and naturalistic visual depiction as exemplified by the painting of Troy that Lucrece confronts late in the poem. The advantages and shortcomings of the prose argument are fairly obvious. What it gains in clarity and brevity it loses in power and completeness; it tells more of the tale than the poem can, but it fails to convey any sense of the protagonists' motives or their inner lives. It is a way of rendering different phenomena, not a better or more reliable way of rendering the same phenomena.

The possibilities of visual art seem more promising. *Lucrece*'s concern with the relative merits of visual and verbal representation is one manifestation of its rhetorical self-consciousness. In his standard school-text, *De Copia*, Erasmus explains that *enargeia* or vividness, the primary characteristic of eloquence, is obtained

> when in order to amplify or adorn or delight we do not set forth a thing simply, but display it to view as if it were portrayed in colors in a picture, so that it would seem that we have painted, not narrated, and that the reader has seen, not read.[20]

---

[20] "[*Enargeia*] utemur quoties vel amplificandi, vel ornandi, vel delectandi gratia, rem non simpliciter exponemus, sed ceu coloribus expressam in tabula spectandam proponemus, ut nos de-

Most Renaissance rhetoricians agree with classical authorities that metaphor is the most effective way of rendering visual effects by verbal means; when Richard Sherry claims that "none sheweth the thing before our eyes more evidently" than metaphor, he is echoing Aristotle and Cicero. The "darkness" and "doubleness" of tropes, the substitutions of improper names for proper ones, paradoxically "give pleasant light," as Henry Peacham claims, "removing unprofitable and odious obscurity."[21]

Nonetheless, even a poem as charged with metaphor as *The Rape of Lucrece* inevitably lacks the visual dimension of a painting or a dramatic production. The deficiency seems important in *Lucrece* because throughout the poem vision is associated with the manifest, the immediate, the unquestionably real. "To see sad sights moves more than hear them told," the narrator informs us (1. 1324); Tarquin in the grip of passion tells Lucrece that ". . . Will is deaf and hears no heedful friends: / Only he hath an eye to gaze on Beauty" (ll. 495–96). Both characters convince themselves of the reality of their moral lapses by fantasizing that those lapses are somehow visible: Tarquin believes that his "digression . . . will live engraven in my face" (ll. 202–3); Lucrece that the decay of chastity "will show, charactered in my brow" (1. 807). After the rape she exclaims:

> 'O unseen shame, invisible disgrace!
> O unfelt sore, crest-wounding private scar!
> Reproach is stamped in Collatinus' face,
> And Tarquin's eye may read the mot afar.'
> (ll. 827–30)

Lucrece begins by acknowledging the indetectability of the crime, but after two lines she is proclaiming its conspicuousness. The outrage seems real to her only insofar as it may be *seen*—thus she arranges to advertise it, assuming that the display of her bleeding body will constitute an immediately convincing proof of her violated innocence.

However, no sooner does the poem insist upon the superior certainty and cogency of the visible than it qualifies that privilege. Perhaps "Beauty itself doth of itself persuade / The eyes of men without an orator" (ll. 29–30); but Shakespeare's Tarquin, unlike Ovid's or Livy's, is inflamed not by the sight of Lucrece but by a report of her. And the reliability of visual evidence is impugned almost as often as it is invoked. Lucrece's face reveals her nature; but Tarquin's majestic demeanor turns out to be fraudulent. The inarticulate "honest looks" of the groom who attends Lucrece are subject to misinterpretation; his mistress construes his bashful blush as a reproach.

The question of the relation between visual and verbal representation is posed especially acutely near the end of the poem, as the violated Lucrece confronts a picture of Troy, a massive and varied panorama of violation.[22] For Lucrece

---

pinxisse, non narrasse, lector spectasse, non legisse videatur" (my translation). Erasmus, *De utraque verborum ac rerum copia*, in *Opera omnia* (Basel, 1540), I, 66. For an illuminating discussion of Erasmus's rhetorical theory see Terence Cave, "*Enargeia*: Erasmus and the Rhetoric of Presence in the Sixteenth Century," *L'Esprit Createur*, 16, 4 (1976), 5–19.

[21] Richard Sherry, *A Treatise of Schemes and Tropes* (1550), ed. Herbert Hildebrand (Gainesville: Scholars' Facsimiles, 1961), p. 40. Cf. Aristotle, *Rhetoric*, III, ii, 13; Cicero, *De Oratore*, III, xl, 160–61. Henry Peacham, *The Garden of Eloquence* (1593), ed. William Crane (Gainesville: Scholars' Facsimiles, 1954), p. 13.

[22] Clark Hulse discusses this episode perceptively in *Metamorphic Verse: The Elizabethan Minor Epic* (Princeton: Princeton Univ. Press, 1981), pp. 175–94. Hulse shares my interest in the verbal representation of visual art in *Lucrece*, but his discussion takes a different course. He argues that

and for Shakespeare the sack of Troy is a culturally primal event; not only the birth of Western literature but the founding of both Rome and Britain follow, according to legend, upon the Trojan diaspora. After "sigh has wearied sigh, moan wearied moan" the painting provides Lucrece "means to mourn some newer way"—harking back to origins, and seeming at first to offer a welcome alternative to the complications of rhetoric.

For the task of the "conceited painter" initially seems to be a relatively simple one, the precise depiction of a scene that contains a wide variety of human possibility: virtue and vice, courage and timidity. Nothing about the process as it is described in the early stanzas seems difficult or surprising. The great commanders are graceful and majestic, the youths quick and dexterous, the cowards pale and trembling. Faces, often deceptive in the world of *Lucrece*, seem trustworthy here: "blunt rage and rigor" roll appropriately in Ajax's eye; Ulysses's "mild glance" shows "deep regard and smiling government."

> The face of either ciphered either's heart;
> Their face their manners most expressly told.
> (ll. 1396–97)

But visual representation soon begins to seem more problematic. It becomes obvious that the scene does not represent a transcript of anything that was ever actually before someone's eyes. The events of years crowd into the same picture. Trojan boys are shown mustering for battle and simultaneously being killed on the field; the sack of Troy occurs alongside the capture of Sinon the day before; and the picture features Hector and Achilles, long dead by the end of the war. If *The Rape of Lucrece* seems to be narrative striving for a missing visual element, the painting described in the poem seems to yearn for the missing dimension of temporality, and to usurp the privileges of narrative by displaying successive episodes in a deceptive present.[23]

In other ways as well, the "realism" of the painting seems increasingly artificial. The men listening to Nestor's speech are portrayed according to the laws of perspective:

> Here one man's hand leaned on another's head,
> His nose being shadowed by his neighbor's ear;
> Here one, being thronged, bears back, all boll'n and red;
> Another, smothered, seems to pelt and swear.
> (ll. 1415–18)

Shakespeare's apparently naïve, "literal" description of the painted crowd as a collection of grotesquely amputated shapes emphasizes the difference between

---

Lucrece acquires consciousness of herself as a tragic figure while she meditates before the painting. In my view, though Lucrece uses the painting to help herself understand her situation, the fact that both she and Tarquin constantly reaffirm choices makes it difficult to isolate critical moments of change or development in this way. Certainly Lucrece's selection of a painting is partly determined by conclusions she wishes to reach, in fact already has reached. She would have a different set of interpretive options if, for example, she chose to confront a painting of the rape of the Sabines, an event in which the sexual violation of women bears a different relation to the destruction and foundation of civilizations.

[23] The representation of successive episodes in the same painting or tapestry is common in medieval and Renaissance art. Nelson Goodman discusses the convention and some of its permutations in "Twisted Tales; or, Story, Study, and Symphony," *On Narrative*, ed. W.J.T. Mitchell (Chicago: Univ. of Chicago Press, 1980), pp. 99–115. The relevant point for *Lucrece* is not that the painter has employed unusual means but merely that the power of his realism depends upon the effective deployment of convention.

a naturalistic rendering and "things as they really are." Technical concerns may even dictate content rather than vice versa. Achilles, whom one would expect to occupy a place near the center of the painting, is artfully relegated to the margins:

> . . . for Achilles' image stood his spear,
> Griped in an armèd hand; himself behind
> Was left unseen, save to the eye of mind:
> A hand, a foot, a face, a leg, a head
> Stood for the whole to be imaginèd.
> (ll. 1424–28)

Synecdoche is as powerful a device for the painter, it seems, as for the poet. "The eye of mind," the spectator's imagination, must supply what is not or cannot be represented, most obviously perhaps for the identification of the despairing Hecuba, distorted by suffering—"Of what she was no semblance did remain"—or of the harmless-seeming Sinon. These two figures, victim and aggressor, represent the painter's ultimate achievement, which turns out to involve not the establishment of an easy correspondence between the visible and the real, but a thorough subversion of that correspondence.

For the reader, of course, this painting has always been patently a verbal rather than a visual construct, and thus cannot very well function as an "alternative" to rhetoric. It is conceivable that a character might be allowed what the reader is denied: an escape from linguistic traps to a representational mode of superior reliability. Significantly, however, Lucrece finds the painting helpful not because it provides a respite from, or a corrective to, the complexity of figurative language but because it functions much as her rhetoric functions, employing similar techniques and encouraging similar confusions.

The tragedy of *The Rape of Lucrece* is that the dangers of metaphor prove inescapable for Tarquin, for Lucrece, and for the narrative voice. Whether or not rhetoric is inevitably problematic is a different issue. At the end of the poem Lucius Junius Brutus, supposed an idiot, unexpectedly seizes the initiative. Known for linguistic irresponsibility, "for sportive words and uttering foolish things" (l. 1813), he suddenly emerges as an articulate public figure urging revenge and revolution. But it is too late to learn whether his invocations, vows, and protestations constitute an alternative, more straightforward rhetoric—a language that might reflect and affect the world in a new way—or whether Brutus merely displaces the same old problems into a new sphere.

The foregoing analysis may suggest why *The Rape of Lucrece* so often frustrates modern critics. Its rhetoric indeed seems to "get in the way," interfering with rather than facilitating a clear view of characters, events, and moral dilemmas. I would suggest, however, that the obtrusiveness and unreliability of language in *The Rape of Lucrece* is not evidence of Shakespearean incompetence, but rather of an acute and profoundly uneasy self-consciousness about poetic techniques and resources.

# "And Let Mild Women to Him Lose Their Mildness": Philomela, Female Violence, and Shakespeare's *The Rape of Lucrece*

## Jane O. Newman

I N SHAKESPEARE'S *THE RAPE OF LUCRECE*, AS ALL READERS of the poem know, the progress of the narrative is frequently interrupted by interior monologues and rhetorical set pieces that dilate Livy's and Ovid's essentially political story of Lucrece's rape and suicide into a lengthy, almost psychological investigation of the motivation for and implications of both Lucrece's and Tarquin's actions.[1] Among these rhetorical interludes, Lucrece's address to Night, Opportunity, and Time (ll. 764–1022) and her ekphrastic self-identification with the fall of Troy (ll. 1366–568) have in particular been the subject of no little scholarly debate, perhaps in some measure because they seem both to figure and to result from supposedly Shakespearean innovations that distinguish *The Rape of Lucrece* from its sources and from other early modern versions of the same material.[2] Yet the surrounding matter and circumstances of one of these "Shakespearean" sections— namely, the lengthy apostrophes to Night, Opportunity, and Time, where the figure of the bird-woman, Philomela, twice appears—demand that we look again at the question of *Lucrece*'s source texts. They do so not because they reveal something "new" or "modern" about Lucrece's "psychology" but because they reveal a great deal about Shakespeare's representation of rape and of women's political agency. Obscured in both the Shakespearean representation of Lucrece's story and in its critical reception is an image of woman's reaction to rape that differs radically from Lucrece's. This image, which is uncovered when one examines contemporary editions of Ovid's *Fasti* (one of *Lucrece*'s source texts), is well represented by the Philomela legend mentioned by Lucrece, and it offers an alternative to the ideological

---

[1] The sources for Shakespeare's *Lucrece* have been discussed by T. W. Baldwin in *On the Literary Genetics of Shakspere's Poems & Sonnets* (Urbana, IL, 1950), 97–153; and by Geoffrey Bullough in *Narrative and Dramatic Sources of Shakespeare*, 8 vols. (London and New York, 1957–75), 1:179–99. Hans Galinsky investigates the Lucretia tradition in *Der Lucretia-Stoff in der Weltliteratur* (Breslau, 1932), as does Ian Donaldson in *The Rapes of Lucretia: A Myth and its Transformations* (Oxford, 1982). The story is conventionally recognized as political in the versions by Livy and Dionysius of Halicarnassus and as sentimental in the version by Ovid. Critics rarely note the political context in Ovid, even though this context, conveyed in the description of the origins of the *Regifugium* feast, is central. See below, p. 321.

[2] On Machiavelli's use of the Lucretia story in Book 3 of the *Discourses* and in *Mandragola*, see Hanna Fenichel Pitkin, *Fortune is a Woman: Gender and Politics in the Thought of Niccolò Machiavelli* (Berkeley, Los Angeles, and London, 1984), 111–12. On Coluccio Salutati's political reading of the Lucretia story in *Declamatio Lucretiae* (c. 1496), see Stephanie H Jed, *Chaste Thinking: The Rape of Lucretia and the Birth of Humanism* (Bloomington and Indianapolis, IN, 1989). Unless otherwise noted, all quotations of Shakespeare follow the *Riverside Shakespeare*, ed. G. Blakemore Evans (Boston, 1974).

314

script played out by the Lucretia story, a script that blames the victim, allows her to internalize guilt, and defines her as an agent of political change solely in terms of a male's ability to avenge her.

Philomela belongs to and represents the countertradition of vengeful and violent women associated with Bacchic legend. This tradition is replete with images of different, more direct forms of political agency for women, images that in fact challenge the fundamental organization and distribution of power in the Western, patriarchal state. I will argue that this tradition, which materializes onstage in copies of Ovid's *Metamorphoses* in both *Titus Andronicus* and *Cymbeline*, is also pointedly invoked—but then just as pointedly excised—in and by Shakespeare's *Lucrece*.[3] It nevertheless haunts the margins (both literally and figuratively) of the sources of *Lucrece*, of the poem itself, and of its critical reception. Investigating these margins and the sources represented in and by them allows us to read *Lucrece* as figuring the ways in which criticism can permit one set of images and political options to recede when those options jostle the foundations of conventional ideological assumptions about gender, power, and the state. Claire McEachern has suggested that "traditionally the relationship between Shakespeare and his literary sources . . . has been imagined as linear and determinative, an empirical matter of subtractions and additions." She argues for a new kind of source criticism in which questions of the "transference of formal ingredients" are replaced by questions of how Shakespeare read his sources and how he intervened in the ideology inscribed in them.[4] Like McEachern, I am interested in how ideology both produces and is produced by literary and critical texts. At the same time, however, I will argue that we can discern ideology formation precisely at the level of such "empirical matters" as early modern annotational practice. Philology, source study, and ideology criticism are thus not at odds with one another but rather collaborate to reveal specific instances of ideology formation. In the case of Shakespeare's references to Philomela in *Lucrece*, "excavating" the text's margins uncovers the traces of ideologically less-familiar images of women's responses to rape; these traces can, in turn, reveal how the need to create a monolithic image

---

[3] The same mechanism of inclusion followed by refusal shapes the text of *Titus* as well. There the example of Lucrece is invoked multiple times (4.1.63–64, 90–91, for example) only to be rejected in favor of the Philomela option in 5.2. Although it is not how I proceed in the present essay, a comparative study of the two texts, *Lucrece* and *Titus*, and of their interdependence specifically in producing images of women's "legitimate" reaction to rape is a desideratum. Additionally, a historical investigation of their varying receptions might reveal which scenarios of female behavior are considered "proper" and for whom. J. C. Maxwell, editor of the Arden *Titus* (London and New York, 1987), would discourage such comparisons. He takes pains to try to separate the play from the poem in matters of dating (xxiv) and speaks of a scholar's "natural reluctance" to attribute the play to Shakespeare (xx).

[4] McEachern, "Fathering Herself: A Source Study of Shakespeare's Feminism," *Shakespeare Quarterly* 39 (1988): 269–90, esp. 269 and 272. McEachern's argument that Shakespeare challenges the patriarchal attitudes present in the sources of *Much Ado About Nothing* and *King Lear* and is thus not as complicit in the reproduction of patriarchy as some feminist critics have claimed is convincing, but it can be challenged by examining his interaction with and transformation of the sources for *Lucrece*. Of course Shakespeare is not monolithic and can himself be read, in McEachern's words, as a "document" of the "contradictions, inconsistencies, and incongruities" of Renaissance gender ideology (270–71).

of mediated political agency for women often shapes the way "textual choices" are made.[5]

The motif of excavation in relation to the identity of Rome is one favored by Freud, and I rely on Freud's understanding of Rome as a diffuse, multilayered archaeological site in my exemplification of a method of reading the textual artifact of *Lucrece*, the complex dramatic poem that arguably initiated Shakespeare's concern with the Eternal City and that takes the question of how to read (textual) foundations as its central topic.[6] When Lucrece cries "How Tarquin must be us'd, *read* it in me: / Myself thy friend will kill myself thy foe, / And for my sake serve thou false Tarquin so" (ll. 1195–97 [my emphasis]), she invokes Brutus's ability to give an activist political reading to the text of the rape and her suicide, a reading that clearly distinguishes itself from her father's and her husband's passive reactions. Given the political power invested in the raped female body, it is not by chance that Freud uses an archaeological metaphor in discussing the roots of women's identity. As he suggests in "Female Sexuality" (1931) and as Luce Irigaray has pursued in "This Sex Which is Not One" (1977), the sociopolitical and ideological self-image as well as the survival of patriarchal culture depend on the repression and exclusion of all but vague traces of an archaic and alternative female civilization.[7] Coppélia Kahn has shown that much of *Lucrece* is concerned with the definition and perpetuation of patriarchal political values and forms, including honor and fidelity, as well as with women's role as sexualized object in the reproduction of patriarchal norms.[8] Small wonder, then, that in the reception of *Lucrece* alternate forms of women's political agency not complicit in the reproduction of patriarchy have been as repressed, as silenced, as Philomela herself, since what was at stake was the construction of the ideological text of a gender hierarchy in which the virtue and moral integrity of a Lucretia must be transplanted to the biological *vir* (here Brutus) in order to produce political change.

Following Freud's, Irigaray's, and Kahn's lead, I propose to expand the notion of what it means to read early modern texts and their sources both "historically" and "politically" by addressing the complexity of the multi-layered textual foundations of *Lucrece*. My goal is to problematize the concept of source study and philology as disinterested methods, as well as to expand on their capacity to explain textual details that collude with but also point to ideology formation. Like Brutus, authors and critics often find

[5] Gillian Murray Kendall writes of the "textual choice" that Titus makes to "remember" or invoke one specific source for and version of the story of the Roman woman, Virginia, rather than any of the many others available at the time; see " 'Lend me thy hand': Metaphor and Mayhem in *Titus Andronicus*," *SQ* 40 (1989): 299–316, esp. 313.

[6] See Sigmund Freud, "Civilization and its Discontents" in *The Standard Edition of the Complete Psychological Works of Sigmund Freud*, ed. and trans. James Strachey and Anna Freud, 24 vols. (London, 1953–74), 21:57–243. On Freud's use of the image of Rome as an archaeological site, see Marjorie Garber, *Shakespeare's Ghost Writers: Literature as uncanny causality* (New York and London, 1987), 52–54; and David Damrosch, "The Politics of Ethics: Freud and Rome" in *Pragmatism's Freud: The Moral Disposition of Psychoanalysis*, Joseph H. Smith and William Kerrigan, eds. (Baltimore and London, 1986), 102–25. I am grateful to Kelley Delaney of the University of California, Irvine, for the Damrosch reference.

[7] See Freud, "Female Sexuality," 21:225–43; and Luce Irigaray, *Ce Sexe Qui n'en Est Pas Un* (Paris, 1977), 21–32.

[8] See Kahn, "The Rape in Shakespeare's *Lucrece*," *Shakespeare Studies* 9 (1976): 45–72.

and interpret a text according to local ideological and political needs; they nevertheless seek to mask, elide, and silence these needs by claiming, in discussions of Shakespeare's poem, for example, to have located or established in "objective" fashion the "historical" texts that Shakespeare "could have known and used."[9] "It is in the significant *silences* of a text, in its gaps and absences," however, as Terry Eagleton has written, "that the presence of ideology can be most positively felt."[10] My own essay is of course just as politically motivated as past source studies have been, but I will not be silent about that motivation; I seek to demonstrate that beneath the surface of Shakespeare's "hybrid" poem lies an ideology of gender that represses traditions of female political agency more threatening to patriarchy than Lucrece's.[11] "Excavating" the "lost" historical "scenario" of female violence present in the margins of *Lucrece* allows that scenario to become visible.[12]

## I

The text of Shakespeare's *Lucrece* twice calls attention to the tale of Philomela, the chaste woman raped by a tyrannical relative. Both references are brief and appear almost parenthetical, even ornamental. The first reference to Philomela occurs at the close of Lucrece's apostrophes to Night, Opportunity, and Time and seems designed to create syntactical parallels between the two violated women. The text reads:

> By this, lamenting Philomele had ended
> The well-tun'd warble of her nightly sorrow,
> And solemn night with slow gait descended
> To ugly hell, when lo the blushing morrow
> Lends light to all fair eyes that light will borrow;
>   But cloudy Lucrece shames herself to see,
>   And therefore still in night would cloist'red be.
>                                      (ll. 1079–85)

The juxtaposition of the bird with Lucrece, who has, like Philomela, just completed a "well-tun'd warble of . . . sorrow," seems to suggest similarities between the two. Yet the lines just preceding these strain to point out the ironic dissonance of the reference. Lucrece has just claimed that she will not "hide the truth of this false night's abuses. / My tongue shall utter all, mine eyes like sluices, / As from a mountain spring that feeds a dale, / Shall gush pure streams to purge my impure tale" (ll. 1075–78). Most of Shakespeare's

---

[9] See Baldwin, *Literary Genetics*, 99. See also Richard Levin's essay "The Ironic Reading of *The Rape of Lucrece* and the Problem of External Evidence" (*Shakespeare Survey* 34 [1981]: 85–92) for an attack on critics who claim to be interested in "reconstructing the historical meaning of the poem" (85). Levin's own definition of a historical approach to the text is as limited as Baldwin's, although in a different way.

[10] See Eagleton, *Marxism and Literary Criticism* (Berkeley and Los Angeles, 1976), 34–35.

[11] The notion of the hybrid text is based on my understanding of the implications of Donna Haraway's classic essay "A Manifesto for Cyborgs: Science, Technology, and Socialist Feminism in the 1980s" in *Coming to Terms: Feminism, Theory, Politics*, Elizabeth Weed, ed. (New York and London, 1989), 173–204; Haraway offers a theory of intertextuality appropriate to the insights provided by postmodern theory.

[12] On reading texts for such lost scenarios, see Julia Reinhard Lupton, "Afterlives of the Saints: Hagiography in *Measure for Measure*," *Exemplaria: A Journal of Theory in Medieval and Renaissance Studies* 2 (1990): 375–401, esp. 380.

readers would have heard echoes here of the Ovidian Philomela in Book VI of *Metamorphoses*, who threatens to take revenge for the "unspeakable act" ("*nefas*" [l. 524])[13] of rape committed by Tereus the king by publicly speaking it:

> If I should have the chance, I would go where people throng and tell it; if I am kept shut up in these woods, I will fill the woods with my story and move the very rocks to pity. The air of heaven shall hear it, and, if there is any god in heaven, she shall hear it too.
>
> (ll. 545–49)

But the horrific difference in Ovid's tale is that Philomela's "tongue" cannot "utter all," because Tereus cuts out the tongue that she means to use against him and then violates her mutilated, speechless body again and again. In contrast, Lucrece's continuing ability to speak the story of her shame and to name Tarquin as the rapist thus appears to give her access to a form of rhetorical political agency that the legendary Philomela is initially and horribly denied. And indeed, in telling her tale, the legendary Lucretia's rhetoric (re)produces rhetoric and political action in turn. Seneca writes: "to Brutus we owe liberty, to Lucretia . . . we owe Brutus." Lucretia's "first imitator," Brutus, realizes the promise of her "heroic" self-sacrifice, "tak-[ing] over from Lucretia the function of preserving chastity" in and restoring honor to a Roman world.[14] The apparent contrast of a silent Philomela, robbed of the potential for such an impact on the political moment to which she belongs, effectively casts Lucretia's suicide as the only form of political intervention available to women.

A similarly complex interaction between the two stories and figures characterizes the second reference to Philomela in *Lucrece*, where Lucrece claims that it is "Philomele" whom she seeks to "imitate":

> Come, Philomele, that sing'st of ravishment,
> Make thy sad grove in my dishevell'd hair;
> As the dank earth weeps at thy languishment,
> So I at each sad strain will strain a tear,
> And with deep groans the diapason bear;
>     For burthen-wise I'll hum on Tarquin still,
>     While thou on Tereus descants better skill.
>
> And whiles against a thorn thou bear'st thy part
> To keep thy sharp woes waking, wretched I,
> To imitate thee well, against my heart
> Will fix a sharp knife to affright mine eye,
> Who if it wink shall thereon fall and die.
>     These means, as frets upon an instrument,
>     Shall tune our heart-strings to true languishment.
>
> (ll. 1128–41)

---

[13] *Metamorphoses*, trans. Frank Justus Miller, vols. 3 and 4 of *Ovid in Six Volumes*, ed. G. P. Goold, The Loeb Classical Library (Cambridge, MA, and London, 1984–89). Unless otherwise noted, all quotations of the *Metamorphoses* will follow this edition and will be cited parenthetically in the text by book and line number.

[14] "*Bruto libertatem debemus, Lucretiae Brutum*"; see Seneca, "To Marcia: On Consolation" ("*Ad Marciam De Consolatione*"), *Moral Essays*, ed. and trans. John W. Basore, 3 vols. (Cambridge, MA, 1951), 2:1–97, esp. 48–49. For Brutus as Lucretia's "first imitator," see Judith Still, "Lucretia's Silent Rhetoric," *Oxford Literary Review* 6, 2 (1984): 70–86, esp. 84. On Brutus's visibility in the political tradition, see Jed, 11.

Here again what strikes one initially is the similarity between the women. Lucrece can be read as imitating the bird-woman in her own songs "of ravishment" that follow, in her meditation on suicide (ll. 1156–211), and in the Troy ekphrasis (ll. 1366 ff.). But the musical harmony suggested by Lucrece's "diapason" and the bird's "descant" instead signals difference, in that the songs are in different registers and in dramatically different musical forms. The reference to Philomela ultimately makes visible precisely what distinguishes Philomela's "sad strain[s]" from Lucrece's "deep groans," makes us aware, that is, that the two women represent the story of rape in different keys, so to speak, keys that have been diversely handled in their reception.[15]

Two recent feminist readings of the poem by Katharine Eisaman Maus and Laura G. Bromley, for example, in their disagreement about whether Lucrece is in the end like Philomela or not, reveal the submerged dissonance between the two legends that the poem seeks to harmonize by recalling only their formal complementarity in the reference to the "humming" and "descanting" of the victimized women.[16] But it is at the level of plot that the story of Philomela most clearly diverges from that of Lucrece. Critics have long assumed that Shakespeare knew Ovid's version of the Philomela story (in Golding's translation). And yet, while it is true that the invocation of a self-wounding Philomela explains how Lucrece could be made to serve as a model for all women subjected to the needs of male culture, the scenario of a self-wounding Philomela does not appear in Ovid's text. Considering the Ovidian intertext in its entirety allows us to understand why references to "the nightingale leaning on a thorn," whose paradoxical "muteness" represents her "mutilation," do not fully account for the significance of the Philomela story in Shakespeare's poem, especially in its contrapuntal role.[17]

Insofar as Ovid's *Metamorphoses* tells the story of an honorable woman

[15] I am grateful to J. Hillis Miller for calling my attention to how the musical imagery ironizes the relationship between Lucrece and Philomela at this point in the text. The two distinct ways in which they sing of rape nevertheless also point to how the two tales ultimately depend on one another, as do the two parts of the song.

[16] In apparent response to the critical tradition that interprets Shakespearean texts as the site of women's silencing, Maus and Bromley both take the reference to Philomela in *Lucrece* as the occasion to point to places in the text where a female protagonist does gain a voice. They disagree, however, on Lucrece's relationship to Ovid's character. For Maus, Lucrece is like Philomela, while for Bromley they are more different than alike; see Maus, "Taking Tropes Seriously: Language and Violence in Shakespeare's *Rape of Lucrece*," *SQ* 37 (1986): 66–82, esp. 73; and Bromley, "Lucrece's Re-Creation," *SQ* 34 (1983): 200–211. Nancy Vickers discusses the legend of the bird-woman briefly in her analysis of some of the sonnets but does not comment on its presence in *Lucrece*; see " 'The blazon of sweet beauty's best': Shakespeare's *Lucrece*" in *Shakespeare and the Question of Theory*, Patricia Parker and Geoffrey Hartman, eds. (New York and London, 1985), 95–115. Parker builds on Vickers's interpretation of *Lucrece* by explicating the sociopolitical and rhetorical structures of gendered "commodification" that drive the rhetorical "displays" Vickers analyzes; see Parker's "Rhetorics of Property: Exploration, Inventory, Blazon," *Literary Fat Ladies: Rhetoric, Gender, Property* (London and New York, 1987), 126–54, esp. 126–31.

[17] While Patricia Klindienst Joplin considers the truncation of the Philomela legend in Shakespeare's version to be revealing, she does not pursue this critical lacuna in her essay. Joplin's article is not really about Shakespeare's *Lucrece*, which is mentioned only in a note; see "The Voice of the Shuttle is Ours," *Stanford Literature Review* 1 (1984): 25–53, esp. 30 and 31, n. 11.

raped by a loathsome tyrant, it would of course initially seem to offer the parallel to the story of Lucretia that Shakespeare's text attempts to make. Philomela is, like Lucrece, the lamb ("*agna*") to Tereus's wolf (*Metamorphoses* VI, ll. 527–28; cf. *Lucrece*, l. 677); like Lucrece, she tears her hair and laments after the rape. But Ovid's rape victim differs radically from her Renaissance sister in that she recognizes more rapidly and with greater clarity where to place the blame for the crime. Lucrece delays, first accusing Time, Opportunity, and Night; Ovid's Philomela rails against Tereus immediately and calls down his sword upon her when she threatens to declaim the deed in public. His dismemberment of her is a kind of second rape (he draws his phallic sword from its sheath, the "*vagina*" [*Metamorphoses* VI, l. 551]); then follow a third, fourth, and still more rapes ("*repetisse*" [l. 562]), as Tereus's violence seeks to break the spirit of a rebellious woman. He then abandons her to a sequestered existence in the "hut deep hidden in the ancient woods" (l. 521).

Joplin has made clear that, although maimed and isolated, Philomela nevertheless remains true to her word. She is thus as "vocal" about Tereus's crime as Lucrece is about Tarquin's. Yet not only the parallels but also the divergences are remarkable. Philomela communicates by means of a non-verbal rhetoric that represents woman's language of gesture (as opposed to Lucrece's almost obsessive compliance with the phallogocentric logic of reading and writing[18]), weaving in nimble silence the tapestry (l. 576) on which the story of her violation is told. This is the alternative "text" (from *texere*, to weave) that she sends to her sister, Procne, Tereus's wife. The effect of Philomela's ingenious form of rhetoric is profound (and pointedly unlike Lucrece's seemingly analogous description of the tapestry or painting of Troy, which rewrites and thus silences the act of weaving, a rebellious act as undertaken by Philomela, by repeating a story of violation to no direct political end).[19] First, Philomela inspires another woman, her sister, Procne (rather than a man, Brutus), to threaten the tyrant's hold on phallocratic power by mimicking his abuse of it. Indeed, Procne usurps the (male) position as the avenger of the rape victim. Just as unsentimental as Brutus in Livy's, Ovid's, and Shakespeare's texts, who proclaims an end to weeping over Lucretia's/Lucrece's body, Ovid's Procne has "no room for tears" (l. 585; cf. also l. 611) and, like Brutus, calls for an avenging sword (l. 612). Siding with her sister against her husband, Procne promises to imitate him by cutting out *his* tongue and castrating him (ll. 616–17), thus taking aim at the symbolic source of patriarchal power and the literal offending member in the crime of rape. In contrast to Lucrece, then, Procne threatens to turn the sword against the victimizer rather than against the victim; the rape of

---

[18] Lucrece identifies herself as a text several times, as in "The light will show, character'd in my brow, / The story of sweet chastity's decay . . . " (ll. 807–8), and in her challenge that the text of her suicide be "read" by others (l. 1195).

[19] For another reading of the Troy ekphrasis as politically effective, see S. Clark Hulse, " 'A Piece of Skilful Painting' in Shakespeare's *Lucrece*," *SS* 31 (1978): 13–22. For Hulse, Lucrece is invested with agency only through her "power . . . in the realm of art" (21), an art that ultimately remains no more than art for art's sake. For a discussion of texts and images that represent women's weaving as subversive in a different way, see Georgianna Ziegler, "Penelope and the Politics of Woman's Place in the Renaissance" in *Gloriana's Face: Women, Public and Private, in the English Renaissance*, S. P. Cerasano and Marion Wynne-Davies, eds. (Detroit, 1992), 25–46.

a chaste woman will, she makes clear, cause the dissolution rather than the perpetuation of phallocratic rule.[20]

What follows in *Metamorphoses* is precisely the reverse of Lucrece's act of self-sacrifice for the sake of the state, although in both cases the tyrant is ultimately eliminated. Not by chance, it is "the time when the Thracian matrons were wont to celebrate the biennial festival of Bacchus" (*Metamorphoses* VI, ll. 587–88). Joining a female community of Bacchic celebrants, Procne attires herself as a devotee of the god:

> The queen . . . equips herself for the rites of the god and dons the array of frenzy; her head was wreathed with trailing vines, a deer-skin hung from her left side, a light spear rested on her shoulder. Swift she goes through the woods with an attendant throng of her companions, and driven on by the madness of grief, Procne, terrific in her rage, mimics thy madness, O Bacchus!
>
> (ll. 591–97)

With her women, she finds the maimed Philomela and dresses her, too, in the "trappings of a Bacchante" (ll. 598–99). Distorted elements of familiar Greek rites associated with Dionysianism— particularly the emphasis on the dismemberment of a living being, the women's access to the tools of ritual slaughter, and the confusion of distinct forms of ceremonial practice— appear in the subsequent substitution of Procne and Tereus's son, Itys, for his father and thus of a male body for Lucrece's female body in the act of bloody sacrifice:[21]

> While Procne was thus speaking Itys came into his mother's presence. His coming suggested what she could do, and regarding him with pitiless eyes, she said: "Ah, how like your father you are!" . . . And when they reached a remote part of the great house, while the boy stretched out pleading hands as he saw his fate, and screamed, "Mother! mother!" and sought to throw his arms around her neck, Procne smote him with a knife between breast and side—and with no change of face. This one stroke sufficed to slay the lad; but Philomela cut his throat also, and they cut up the body still warm and quivering with life. Part bubbles in brazen kettles, part sputters on spits; while the whole room drips with gore.
>
> (ll. 619–22, 638–46)

The murder of Itys by the women dislodges men from the position of political agency and responsibility heretofore reserved for them in a way that the Lucrece story does not. Philomela and Procne, pretending that they have prepared a "sacred feast after their ancestral fashion" ("*patrii moris sacrum mentita*" [l. 648]), feed pieces of the boy to Tereus, who goes mad when he realizes that his body has become the tomb of the heir to patriarchal rule (l. 655). Rather than reviolating herself (as Lucrece does in committing suicide and as the truncated story of Philomela as a self-

---

[20] Lucrece's suicide means the continuation of phallocratic forms of government despite the fact that it causes the shift from tyranny to a republic, since the two forms of political organization differ only externally and do not challenge the transfer of power from male to male (see pp. 317–18, below). In *Titus Andronicus* (5.2.166–205), of course, the power to avenge is once again wrested out of a woman's hand in intertextual fashion, so to speak, as Titus himself declares that he will usurp "Progne's" role (l. 195) in the act of dismemberment and cooking.

[21] On the significance of the details of these echoes of sacrificial practice, see pp. 318–20, below.

wounding nightingale would have us think is Lucrece's only option), Philomela becomes jubilantly violent, "hurl[ing] the gory head of Itys straight into his father's face; nor was there ever any time when she longed more to be able to speak, and to express her joy in fitting words" (ll. 658–60). To escape the raging Tereus's sword, both she and her sister are then transformed into birds; but the image Ovid leaves us with is that of a triumphant rather than a lamenting Philomela, who, engaging in an act of ritualized violence, acts as a jubilant witness to the end of Thracian tyranny.[22]

Scholars of *Lucrece*'s source texts have attended to the Ovidian intertext and to Shakespeare's use of the story but have not investigated the nature of the relationship between the violent Philomela and the self-sacrificing Lucrece. In neglecting to do so, they have enacted a selective process not unlike Shakespeare's own, though they have been perhaps less aware than he of the act of elision in which they have engaged. As Baldwin writes, Shakespeare's Lucrece does not "go into the story" of Philomela in any detail.[23] This brevity can now be seen to have been well motivated, for to have done so would have intervened in her (and Baldwin's) ability to reinscribe the inevitability of the role assigned to Lucrece since Livy, namely the conversion of rape into suicide, of abuse into self-sacrifice for the sake of the state. The manifest absence, even deletion, of the revenge alternative from Lucrece's options is figured in the truncation of the full Philomela story. Women's response to rape and their participation in political renewal are thereby limited, ideologically speaking, to actions that require their self-destruction.

It could be argued that Shakespeare's elision of significant details from the Philomela story (an elision reproduced by source criticism to date) was an oversight if there were not a moment in the text of *Lucrece* that invokes but then immediately dismisses the alternative of violent female reprisal. In her address to Time, Lucrece explicitly calls up the specter of a response to her violation that echoes the actions of Procne and Philomela. She begs Time to

> Devise extremes beyond extremity,
> To make [Tarquin] curse this cursed crimeful night.
>           . . .
> Let there bechance him pitiful mischances
> To make him moan, but pity not his moans;
> Stone him with hard'ned hearts harder than stones,
>     And let mild women to him lose their mildness,
>     Wilder to him than tigers in their wildness.
>                         (ll. 969–70 and 976–80)

---

[22] It is probably not by chance that the lines that follow the Philomela story tell of the subsequent early death of her and Procne's father, Pandion of Athens (*Metamorphoses* VI, ll. 675–76). Here, too, the male leader who has held his power only by engaging in the "traffic in women" meets an early end. For an analysis of Pandion's actions in marrying Procne to Tereus in the first place, see Joplin, 31–38.

[23] See Baldwin, *Literary Genetics*: "there is only a bare mention of the Tereus story in *Lucrece*. Lucrece simply calls on Philomel to sing of Tereus while she sings of Tarquin (1128–48), but does not go into the story" (132). Bullough fails to even mention the bird-woman by name: "The end of the night takes Lucrece's mind back to the nightingale (which had ended 'The well-tun'd warble of her nightly sorrow' [1080]) and the likeness between Tarquin and Tereus (1133–34)" (1:181).

Lucrece's Bacchic visions, which read as if she would have Tarquin become a character in a neo-Senecan tragedy of revenge, are almost immediately displaced by self-contempt at her own use of "idle words" in a "case" that is "past the help of law." "The remedy indeed," she decides, "Is to let forth my foul-defiled blood" (ll. 1016, 1022, and 1028–29). But the invocation of "wild women's" work of the very sort done by Procne and Philomela is uncanny in the technical sense, since it signals the return of a repressed scenario (or, perhaps, a scenario that will be displaced onto Brutus, the only man in the family whose heart is "hard'ned" enough in the end to avenge Lucrece's violation and death[24]). *Lucrece* thus both participates in and reveals the mechanism behind the closing off of the option of female violence against the rapist.

It might be objected that, unlike *Titus Andronicus*, Shakespeare's *Lucrece* contains no reference to the violent Philomela of *Metamorphoses* VI explicit enough to provide evidence for an act of repression at *Lucrece*'s textual foundations. Here the other Ovidian source pointed out by Baldwin is helpful.[25] As Baldwin notes, the Lucretia story is also told in *Fasti*; there it recalls precisely the Bacchic alternative. Ovid's story of Lucretia (*Fasti* II, ll. 685–856) concludes with a four-line allusion to the story of Philomela. The text reads:

> Do I err? or has the swallow come, the harbinger of spring, and does she not fear lest winter should turn and come again? Yet often, Procne, wilt thou complain that thou hast made too much haste, and thy husband Tereus will be glad at the cold thou feelest.[26]

The relationships among these lines, *Metamorphoses* VI, and *Lucrece* initially seem subtle. First, the reference to the sadistic pleasure that Tereus will feel when Procne, as swallow, arrives too early in the spring and feels the cruel cold of winter is dependent on the violence that marks the end of the intertext of *Metamorphoses* VI. Procne's harrowing by Tereus may thus be understood as the "reward" she receives in the four-line coda to the Lucretia story in *Fasti* for her actions in the lengthier *Metamorphoses* VI. Second, the description of Tereus's sadism in *Fasti* II can be seen as an intertext for Tarquin's masochistic musings just before his rape of Lucrece, when Tarquin "reads" the delays that the "locks," "unwilling portal," "wind," and "glove" (*Lucrece*, ll. 302–29) afford him:

> "So, so," quoth he, "these lets attend the time,
> Like little frosts that sometime threat the spring,
> To add a more rejoicing to the prime,
> And give the sneaped birds more cause to sing.
> Pain pays the income of each precious thing. . . .
> (ll. 330–34)

---

[24] On the "chastening" of Brutus, who rebukes the "effeminate" tears of Lucretius and Collatine in Livy and Shakespeare, see Jed, 10–11.

[25] Baldwin, *Literary Genetics*, 132.

[26] "[F]allimur, an veris praenuntia venit hirundo / nec metuit, ne qua versa recurrat hiems? / saepe tamen, Procne, nimium properasse quereris, / virque tuo Tereus frigore laetus erit" (*Fasti*, trans. James George Frazer, vol. 5 of *Ovid in Six Volumes* [cited in n. 13 above]). Unless otherwise noted, all quotations of *Fasti* will follow this edition and will be cited parenthetically in the text by book and line number.

The reference in these lines to the "frosts" of an impending "spring" works as a submerged citation of Tereus's delighted invocation of Procne's pain, caused in *Fasti* by the "cold" of a returning winter.

When we turn to marginal glosses by Paulus Marsus on the four lines that conclude Ovid's tale of Lucretia, the relationships among the texts are no longer hidden or subtle. That Marsus's commentary was important and available to Shakespeare has long been known. Baldwin goes to great lengths to demonstrate the impact of a contemporary edition of Ovid's *Fasti* with its lengthy marginal commentary by Marsus. Citing an edition printed in 1550, Baldwin states that Marsus's notes on Ovid were considered "the standard commentary of that day."[27] Baldwin further maintains that Shakespeare had "used a copy of Ovid with the notes of Marsus, who had correlated most of the other Latin sources, especially Livy," when composing *Lucrece*. I find it significant that Baldwin, in discussing the "variorum Ovid" that he identifies as Shakespeare's source for *Lucrece*, does not include Marsus's commentary on *Fasti*'s four lines about Procne.[28] Ovid's lines, quoted above in English, read as follows in the 1510 Latin edition:

> *Fallimur an veris praenuncia venit hirundo*
> *An metuit neque* [!] *versa recurrat hyems:*
> *Saepe tamenn progne nimium properasse quaereris*
> *virque tuo thereus frigore laetus erit.*[29]

Marsus begins his commentary on these lines (853–56) just to the right of the last line. The gloss spills over onto the following page, where we read in his annotation to the reference to "*thereus*": "*Thereus: de quo supius diximus in caristiis*" ("Tereus: about whom I said [more] above in the section on the Caristia [the family love feast held at Rome in February]").[30] When we look *supius*—above—for the prior point in the narrative where a reference to Tereus is made, we find it at line 629 in the explanations of the February feastdays. When Ovid explains who is specifically *not* invited to partake in the Caristia, he names, among others: "*et soror et Procne Tereusque duabus iniquus*" ("Procne and her sister and Tereus, who wronged them both").[31] The exclusion of Philomela, Procne, and Tereus from the feast is not surprising, since it would hardly be appropriate to include those involved in rape, incest, and infanticide in a "family love feast."

It is significant that Marsus draws our attention at line 856 to Ovid's mention at line 629 of Tereus, Procne, and Philomela's exclusion from the feast, thus reminding us of the reasons for this exclusion, namely their violent and bloody story; more significant are his additional marginal

---

[27] Baldwin, *Literary Genetics*, 99.

[28] Baldwin, *Literary Genetics*, 153. For Baldwin's discussion of the "variorum Ovid," see 106. According to Marsus himself, his glosses on the *Fasti* first appeared in 1482. Here I quote the edition printed in Milan in 1510. On the history of editions of Ovid's *Fasti*, see P. Ovidius Naso, *Die Fasten, Herausgegeben, übersetzt, und kommentiert von Franz Bömer*, 2 vols. (Heidelberg, 1957), 1:56–57. In the 1482 edition of the *Fasti* printed in Venice, Marsus comments: "*Anni. Mcccclxxxii annotamus quo quidem anno haec excripsimus & imprimenda dedimus.*" I consulted the Bodleian copy of the 1482 edition (Shelfmark Auct. O 2, 23) and the Tübingen copies of the 1510 (Shelfmark Ce 425 R) and the 1550 (Shelfmark Ce 417 R) editions.

[29] fol. 74ʳ. Abbreviations in the Latin original have been silently expanded.

[30] fol. 74ᵛ; my translation.

[31] *Fasti* II, l. 629; my translation.

glosses at line 629. In the margin to the right of that line of *Fasti* II, Marsus writes: *"Therei Prognes & philomenes fabula latius in metamorphoses libri vi"* ("The story of Tereus, Procne, and Philomela is told at greater length in Book VI of the *Metamorphoses*"). Marsus then proceeds to relate the entire story in a lengthy marginal note, with special emphasis on the Bacchic aspect of Procne's reaction to the tapestry that Philomela wove—*"orgia simulans in silvas venit"* ("imitating the wild festivals of Bacchus, she entered the woods"). His commentary underscores the horror of Itys's murder by stressing the role played by Philomela in the deed; although the boy's fate has already been described in Marsus's summary (*"Itim filium interemit pr[?]ique epulandum apposuit"* ["She killed the boy, Itys, and served him up at the banquet"]), Marsus elaborates: *"Absit et progne et soror: hoc e[?] Philo-m[?]ea: qua ambae in necem Itys conspiravere"* ("Let both Procne and her sister, Philomela, stay away [from the festival of Caristia], the Philomela who conspired with her in the death of Itys"). The marginal note in fact gives the rape victim herself a considerably greater role in the act of vengeance than does Ovid's original text.[32]

Among the several sources for *Lucrece* cited by Baldwin is Thomas Cooper's *Dictionarium Historicum & Poeticum*, published with his *Thesaurus Linguae Romanae et Britannicae* in 1565. Cooper's version of the Philomela story is just as long as his tale of Lucretia and similar to it in its indebtedness to the classical sources. Yet, interestingly, Cooper alters the Philomela story that Ovid tells to emphasize the Bacchic elements in particular:

> Philomela, . . . beinge very cunnynge in woorkyng and imbrodering, did in such sorte set out the whole matter in a garme[n]t, . . . and sent the same by a servaunt to hir sister Progne, Tereus his wyfe. Who, although she weare greatly moved with the matter, yet she did deferre the reve[n]gement, untill the sole[m]ne sacrifices of Bachhus, At which tyme, beyng accompanied, as the manner was, with a great number of other women, she taketh hir sister out of pryson, and bringeth hir into the palaice. Wheare by hir counsayle she killed hyr yonge sonne Itys, and served hir husbande with it at supper. . . .[33]

Had Cooper consulted any contemporary edition of Ovid, he would have found ample support for his emendations of the tale. Had Shakespeare used either Cooper's *Dictionarium* or an edition of the *Fasti* similar to the one edited by Marsus, as Baldwin suggests he did, he would have found information about a maenadic Philomela which calls into significant question his (and any other) Lucrece's claim to "imitate" her "well" while internalizing the blame for and consequences of the rape.[34]

[32] For Marsus's commentary on *Fasti* II, l. 629, see the 1510 Milan edition, fol. 67ʳ. English translations of his commentary are my own.

[33] See Cooper, *Dictionarium Historicum & Poeticum*, "Philomela." All Cooper citations refer to individual entries in the *Dictionarium*, reprinted as part of the *Thesaurus Linguae Romanae et Britannicae* (Menston, UK, 1969), No. 200 in *English Linguistics 1500–1800: A Collection of Facsimile Reprints*, comp. and ed. R. C. Alston. The manuscript abbreviation *ē* has been expanded to either *en* or *em* throughout. According to Alston's prefatory note to the 1969 edition, Cooper's 1565 *Thesaurus* was reprinted in 1573, 1578, 1584 (twice), and 1587.

[34] The important exception to this standard version of the story is, of course, the Philomela-Lucrece connection in John Quarles's *Tarquin Banished*, printed along with *Lucrece* in the 1655 edition, in which an angry band of nightingales swarms around Tarquin and "pickt out his eyes." Quarles's text is available in *A New Variorum Edition of Shakespeare: The Poems*, ed. Hyder Edward Rollins (Philadelphia and London, 1938), 439–46, esp. 445.

Both Cooper and, for that matter, Paulus Marsus were, like Shakespeare, men of their time, and they used the available editions in composing their glosses and commentaries on classical figures and texts. Cooper's and Marsus's common desire to emphasize the infanticidal element of the Philomela story and to associate the sisters' behavior with orgiastic Bacchic rites resulted not from an idiosyncratic reading of the sources, I would maintain, but from careful consideration of a still earlier tradition of Ovid commentary. The source for Marsus's knowledge of *Metamorphoses*, for example, was probably an edition of the work with annotations by the sixth-century Christian grammarian Luctatius Placidus (called Lactantius), whose *Argumenta in Ovidii Metamorphosin* some scholars attribute to the famous Donatus. Most sixteenth-century editions of the *Metamorphoses* also contained notes by Raffaele Regio of Bergamo (called Raphael Regius), who published his commentary on the *Metamorphoses* in 1492. Although Marsus's first version of his commentary on *Fasti*, published in 1482, clearly could not have relied on Regius (since it predated the publication of Regius's notes), it may have been via Lactantius that both scholars were led to emphasize the Bacchic elements of the legend.[35] In any case, an examination of these commentaries suggests that the mention of Philomela would have conjured up the image of women reacting with violence against those who violated them rather than against themselves, with violence sanctioned, moreover, by its inscription in a ritualistic (Bacchic) frame.

The narrative of a violent Philomela seems to have been the object of some fascination in Shakespeare's time. In a 1543 edition of the *Metamorphoses* printed in Basel, for example, an edition that contains both Lactantius's and Regius's notes, the opening lines of the Philomela story in the center of the page are dwarfed by the massive annotations that surround it. Lactantius's notes, printed first, summarize the entire story at the outset in an "Argumentum." For him the relationship of Procne's and Philomela's actions to Bacchic rites appears obvious: "*et more bacchantis ad stabula venit, sororem raptam in regiam duxit, filium Ityn interemit, et dapibus immiscuit*" ("and as was the Bacchic custom, she [Procne] came to the hut, led her violated sister to the palace, killed her son, Itys, and mixed his body in with the sacrificial meal").[36] In this edition, printed in the margins after Lactantius's notes and following them in locating the murder of the boy in the context of ritual violence, Regius's notes elaborate on the Bacchic aspect in particular:[37]

> *Progne vero furijs accensa Bacchi sacra se celebrare simulans, una cum Bacchis ad sororem venit. eamque secum pampinis tectam in urbem adduxit, in cubiculoque suo occultavit. Perfectis vero Bacchi sacrificijs Progne Ityn communem filium interemit, cujus carnes coctas patri apposuit comedendas.*

---

[35] On Lactantius, see Christian Gottlieb Jöcher, *Allgemeines Gelehrten-Lexicon*, 2 vols. (Leipzig, 1750–51; rpt. 1960), 2:2570; and on Regius, see *Contemporaries of Erasmus: A Biographical Register of the Renaissance and Reformation*, Peter G. Bietenholz and Thomas B. Deutscher, eds., 3 vols. (Toronto, 1986–87), 3:134.

[36] fol. 139; my translation. I consulted the Tübingen copy of the 1543 Basel edition of the *Metamorphoses* (Shelfmark Ce 410 fol. R). Abbreviations in the Latin original have been silently expanded.

[37] Baldwin maintains that Shakespeare was familiar with Regius's commentary; see *William Shakspere's Small Latine and Lesse Greeke*, 2 vols. (Urbana, IL, 1944), 2:439.

(But Procne, driven by the furies [and] imitating the sacred rites of Bacchus, came with the Bacchantae to her sister and, with them, draped in vines, led her to the city, hiding her there in her bedchamber. Procne, having accomplished the Bacchic sacrifices, [then] killed Itys, the son [whom she had borne to Tereus], and served his cooked flesh up for his father to eat.)[38]

In Regius's view, Itys's death and the act of cannibalism that follows it are accomplished in the context of traditional Bacchic behavior. Several pages later, in glosses on the lines that narrate the murder, he offers additional material on the intricacies of such practices, making it impossible to think of the consequences of the initial rape in anything other than the context of the cult.[39]

The historical source texts and traditions that Marsus and, in turn, Cooper and Shakespeare could have known and used in their research on both Lucretia and Philomela thus display a clear fascination with maenadic behavior. Even if Shakespeare had been a man of such "small Latine" as Anthony Brian Taylor has recently asserted, the emphasis on the Bacchic elements of the story and on Philomela's collusion with Procne in the butchering of her son would have been difficult to overlook.[40] Shakespeare's reference to Philomela represents a (perhaps deliberate) deviation from this textually widespread tradition, a turn away from the tradition of wild women not unlike the one Lucrece herself performs. And yet his very reference to women's wildness calls attention to this tradition, one explicitly not represented by his text. The failure to report the historicity of this tradition as it was associated with Philomela has made it possible for critics to tell a story about the sources of Shakespeare's *Lucrece* that bypasses the opportunity to evaluate fragmentary evidence as a clue to the text's historical origins in favor of a narrative about the inevitability of women's ongoing (self-)victimization.[41]

## II

The extent to which the tradition of a vengeful Philomela involved in infanticidal blood sacrifice has been repressed in both Shakespeare's text and scholarship about the text makes visible precisely what is at stake in the early modern version of Lucrece's story: namely, the guarantee that political renewal be conceived of in very narrow terms as a transfer of power within an essentially closed phallocratic political economy in which monar-

---

[38] fol. 140; my translation. Abbreviations in the Latin original have been silently expanded.

[39] Cf. fol. 145.

[40] See Taylor, "Golding's Ovid, Shakespeare's 'Small Latin', and the Real Object of Mockery in 'Pyramus and Thisbe,' " *SS* 42 (1989): 53–64. Even Taylor indirectly acknowledges that Shakespeare would have resorted to some versions of the *Metamorphoses* in Latin; "for *Metamorphoses* . . . he used the original or Golding. . . . In his case, however, a comparative lack of facility in reading Latin probably accentuated the use of a favoured translation like Golding" (54, n. 12).

[41] Carlo Ginzburg has suggested comparing philology (and with it the question of sources) with the other so-called "conjectural sciences" of archaeology and psychoanalysis, all of which are based on the study of fragments, traces, as symptomatic evidence of historical occurrences. Such traces can be read as "revealing clues" (11) about the nature of origins that are manifestly absent from the present of the text; see "Morelli, Freud and Sherlock Holmes: Clues and Scientific Method," *History Workshop* 9 (1980): 5–36.

chy (the transfer of power from father to son) is replaced by a republic (the transfer of power from one group of men to another group of men not necessarily related to them other than under the auspices of the state). Women clearly play a limited if crucial role in this transfer and form of renewal, which can justifiably be understood as a "traffic in women," particularly insofar as it is over their violated and dead bodies that men (again, in Lucrece's case Brutus) rise to seize power and thus effect change.[42] The countertradition of women who intervene directly in this transfer of power by killing the heir, thereby providing the conditions for more thoroughgoing political change, is represented in the story of Philomela and particularly in the distorted version of Dionysian ritual it contains. In this ritual, acts of infanticide and cannibalism were not only permissible but fundamental to the symbolic structure of the expiatory myth.

Elements of what later became sacrificial tradition in Bacchic circles are visible on the surface of the Greek myth as recounted by Marcel Detienne:

> The plot is simple. A god in the form of a child is jointly slaughtered by all the Titans, the kings of ancient times. Covered with gypsum and wearing masks of white earth, the murderers surround their victim. With careful gestures they show the child fascinating toys: a top, a rhombus, dolls with jointed limbs, knucklebones, and a mirror. And while the child Dionysus contemplates his own image captured in the circle of polished metal, the Titans strike, dismember him, and throw the pieces in a kettle. Then they roast them over a fire. Once the victim's flesh has been prepared, they undertake to devour it all. They just have time to gobble it down, all except the heart, which had been divided into equal parts, before Zeus' lightning comes to punish their crime and reduce the Titan party to smoke and ashes, out of which will be born the human species.[43]

The tradition of the Dionysia was sanctioned, indeed institutionalized by the state apparatus in Athens as part of the annual ceremonies of renewal, and only later, in its Roman form as Bacchanalia, did it become subversive. It was eventually made illegal in 186 B.C. But even in its early Greek form, Dionysianism was identified with the immorality, licentiousness, and frenzy of its female devotees.[44] The most threatening of the acts associated with its initiates, namely, the occupation by women of the place of ruling-class Titans in the myth and the subsequent unleashing upon men of latent female "wildness," quickly became those acts most readily identified as crucial to the cult. They are familiar to us from such texts as Euripides's *Bacchae*, in which another son, Pentheus, is torn limb from limb by his own mother under the influence of the god. This image is invoked by Shakespeare's Lucrece in the call for women's wildness but is immediately dismissed in favor of "heroic" self-victimization.[45]

[42] Gayle Rubin, "The Traffic in Women: Notes on the 'Political Economy' of Sex" in *Towards An Anthropology of Women*, Rayna R. Reiter, ed. (New York, 1975), 157–210.

[43] Detienne, "Culinary Practices and the Spirit of Sacrifice" in *The Cuisine of Sacrifice among the Greeks*, Marcel Detienne and Jean-Pierre Vernant, eds., trans. Paula Wissing (Chicago and London, 1989), 1–20, esp. 1. Below I also cite Detienne's essay in the same volume, "The Violence of Wellborn Ladies: Women in the Thesmophoria," 129–47.

[44] For the distinction between the Greek and Roman festivals, see the excellent entry on the Dionysia in *Harper's Dictionary of Classical Literature and Antiquities*, Harry Thurston Peck, ed. (New York, Cincinnati, and Chicago, 1963), 520–22.

[45] The buried presence of the Bacchic tradition in Renaissance texts is worth further consideration. Richard Halpern's investigation of the "Dionysian mythology" that Milton's *A*

Detienne has argued with great eloquence that the theory and practice of ritual sacrifice lay at the center of the organization of political power in classical Greece and has used as a primary example Dionysianism and its relationship to dominant politico-religious sacrificial practices, which involved ritual slaughtering, cooking, and consumption of the victim. The Greeks performed these rites as a way of guaranteeing the "harmonious functioning of society" in all areas of civic activity, relying heavily in the process on the moment of (re)generation central to the original Dionysus myth. According to Detienne, those who refused to participate in the ceremonies or who performed them in unconventional ways (as in the cults of Orphism or Dionysianism) demonstrated their refusal to subscribe to the "rules of conduct" and to the political organization represented by the dominant sacrificial code, a code designed to secure the health of the state.[46]

The terms of acceptable and successful sacrificial ceremony, for example, clearly legislated the identity of the *mageiros*—the butcher, sacrificer, and cook—and his professional duties. Significant for our discussion here, the *mageiros* was always male; "just as women [were] without the political rights reserved for male citizens, they [were] kept apart from the altars, meat, and blood." This "male monopoly in matters of blood sacrifice" kept women away from and characterized them as unqualified to handle the kettle, spit, and knife, thus pushing both them and other politically marginal groups, such as cult members, into forms of vegetarianism as a sign of their exclusion from political affairs. Stories of women wielding these instruments of blood sacrifice are rare. But when they occur, they have great significance, since they reveal the fraught nature of the relationship between the sexes and the instability of a political hierarchy based on gender distinction, particularly in terms of who was admitted to positions of privilege in the sacrificing economy and who was excluded.[47]

In this context the Greek story of Procne and Philomela and their slaughtering of Itys offers a perverse challenge to traditional politico-sacrificial behavior and resonates with the threat that the Bacchanalia must have represented to Rome. In Ovid's account Procne acts as priestess-butcher, slaying the victim in a carefully aimed blow ("with a knife between breast and side"). Philomela seems to "conspire" in the ceremony (Marsus's word) by cutting Itys's throat with a sword ("*ferro*" [*Metamorphoses* VI, l. 643]). In a shocking deformation of traditional sacrificial practice, the women then cut up the body and prepare it for consumption, simultaneously roasting part of it and boiling the rest ("*pars inde cavis exsultat aenis, / pars veribus stridunt*" [ll. 645–46]), confusing and collapsing the steps of boiling and roasting, which were strictly separated by sacrificial decorum.[48] The challenge to traditional gender roles as well as to the distribution of power within the state is thus intensified by their willful mockery of the expiatory sacrificial ceremony itself. The murder of Itys in the Procne/

---

*Mask* "half-invokes in order to suppress" offers a fine example of how to structure such an investigation; see "Puritanism and Maenadism in *A Mask*" in *Rewriting the Renaissance: The Discourses of Sexual Difference in Early Modern Europe*, Margaret W. Ferguson, Maureen Quilligan, and Nancy J. Vickers, eds. (Chicago and London, 1986), 88–105, esp. 89.

[46] Detienne, "Culinary Practices," 3 and 8.

[47] For above quotations, see Detienne, "Wellborn Ladies," 131 and 133, respectively.

[48] Detienne, "Culinary Practices," 2.

Philomela story can thus be located within the realm of traditional if contested sacrificial behavior. Itys's death and the cooking and eating of his body are represented as outlandish but also as ritually necessary to expiate Tereus's crime. The son is the substitute victim, ironically offered to and consumed by the offending father, whose crime (incest/rape) is all the worse because he is king.

The two legends being considered here, of course, come out of a Greek context, in the case of Philomela explicitly so, since her father was Pandion of Athens and the rapist was Tereus of Thrace. In the case of Lucretia, the Greek tradition is present at a latent level. The story originally belonged not to Rome but to Ardea and thus to "the most ancient religious legends of the Latin stock," legends whose origins rested in "imported Greek myths" and cults "transplanted to Rome in the second half of the fourth century," as Ettore Pais has pointed out.[49] Recalling the less well-known but nevertheless traditional method of state purification associated with Bacchic women's usurpation of the expiatory apparatus is not as strange as it might initially seem, given the Hellenized context of both stories. Ovid's close association of a vengeful and violent Philomela with the story of a self-sacrificing Lucretia in *Fasti* can in part be explained by the common Greek provenance of both legends. Both legends also address a similar need for displacing the tyrant, and both find ways to do so that involve cleansing rituals of blood sacrifice.

The association that underlies Ovid's juxtaposition of the Lucretia and Philomela stories in *Fasti* is also present in Shakespeare's text. *Lucrece* depicts a politically explosive moment not unlike the one presented to us in the Philomela story, a moment that is nevertheless resolved in an act of blood sacrifice pointedly unlike the one chosen by the sisters. Against the background of the similarity of the two situations, a similarity that the text strains to reinforce, the magnitude of the gap between the two solutions becomes legible as a distension of the connection between two permissible poles of political behavior by women. The reader is meant to consider but then to dismiss the Philomela option in her/his reading of *Lucrece*.

### III

Reading the (margins of the) story of Lucrece through the lens of the traditions that shaped Shakespeare's fragmentary references to the Philomela myth in the late sixteenth century allows us to read other parts of the text historically, that is, as historically produced (and ideologically driven) in response to the potentially dangerous message of legitimate female violence as part of a mechanism of political renewal. Repressed in both Lucrece's

---

[49] See Pais, *Ancient Legends of Roman History* (1905), trans. Mario E. Cosenza (Freeport, NY, 1971), 189–97: "In the earliest history of the Roman Republic we frequently meet with legends whose origins were due to imported Greek myths. From such legends there are later developed events that are historical in appearance. . . . The stories of Lucretia and of Virginia are thus but later elaborations of legends related to the cults of Ardea which were transplanted to Rome in the second half of the fourth century. The cults of all the neighboring Latin cities were, at different times, similarly transferred to the capital of Latium. Therefore, it is fully intelligible how, in adapting itself to new soil, the myth should have been enriched with new elements of local color, and how various touches, historical in character, were added by the annalists of the second and first centuries B.C." (193 and 197).

response to her rape and in criticism of *Lucrece* but reappearing, as I noted above, with emphasis in the poem itself are, in turn, precisely those elements that would seem to make expiatory blood sacrifice necessary, elements that derive from the "origin" of Shakespeare's text in contemporary editions of Ovid. In *Fasti* the story of Lucretia appears in the entry for 24 February, the day on which the *Regifugium*, a celebration of the ejection of a polluted king from the city, was traditionally reenacted.[50] Ovid's reference, at the end of the Lucretia narrative, to the tale of a violent Philomela, with its representation of an incestuous rape committed by a tyrant and of the rituals of banishment and political cleansing by blood sacrifice in expiation of the king's sin, is, then, structurally related to the *Regifugium*. When seen in the context of *Lucrece*'s historical textual origins, Shakespeare's Lucrece's/*Lucrece*'s rejection of the tale of Philomela and its Bacchic afterlife in the Renaissance begins to seem even more clearly motivated by the need to remove the possibility of female revenge. That the repressed story of the rituals associated with the *Regifugium* does reemerge elsewhere in the poem helps to explain, in a way that scholarship has so far been unable to do, the text's "innovative" emphasis on the rape as a political crime (rather than as an opportunity for sentimentalized images of female purity and devotion), as well as on the need for expelling the king who is the source of pollution. Politicizing rather than sentimentalizing rape allows us to read *Lucrece* anew.

The special emphasis that Shakespeare places on Tarquin's rape as a crime of incest, and thus an instance of sexual pollution that violates the bonds of familial trust, may be understood as the most obvious indication of Shakespeare's awareness of the tale's original political context in Ovid.[51] That Sextus Tarquinius has raped the wife of his cousin, Lucius Tarquinius Collatinus, is obvious, although not emphasized, in Livy's narrative of the Lucretia story; Collatine's full name appears twice, first in the initial scene of boasting and again at the end of the story, where Collatine is made consul.[52] That the rape is also a sexual act between relatives by marriage is only slightly more visible in Ovid's rendering of the tale in *Fasti*. He alludes briefly to the fact that Lucretia and Sextus Tarquinius are related when he explains that she received him "courteously" ("*comiter*") because he was a relative by blood ("*sanguine iunctus erat*" [*Fasti* II, l. 788]), but he does not explore the implications of the fact that rapist and victim are related.

Annotations of Ovid's *Fasti* do, however, stress the family connections. In the 1510 edition of the *Fasti*, for example, line 788 is glossed by Antonius Constantius, whose commentary on the *Fasti* was first published in Venice in 1502.[53] They are relatives by blood, Constantius notes, "*quia Tarquinius collatinus vir lucretiae sorore tarquinii superbi genitus fuerat: ut diximus supra*" ("because Collatinus Tarquinius, the husband of Lucretia, was the son of

---

[50] See Frazer's illuminating notes on the *Regifugium* in his appendix to *Fasti*, 2:394–97.

[51] See the entries on *incesto* and *incestum* in the *Oxford Latin Dictionary*, where the scope of incest is represented as having been understood widely as any form of "improper sexual relations." Kahn devotes considerable attention to the infringement on Collatine's and Tarquin's "friendship" (52–55) but does not note that they are related, both in Ovid and in *Lucrece*.

[52] Livy, I, 57, and I, 60.

[53] On Constantius, see Jöcher, 1:2070. Antonius Constantius's commentary on the *Fasti* was first published in Venice in 1502; his notes appear alongside Marsus's in most sixteenth-century editions. Abbreviations in the Latin original have been silently expanded.

Tarquinius Superbus's sister, as we say above").[54] Paulus Marsus's glosses repeat the same information in briefer form. When we look *supra* to the commentary on lines 725–26, where the two men are mentioned together in the context of the initial dinner conversation, we find a lengthier note by Constantius that addresses the obscure reference to *"Tarquinius juvenis."* (Various commentators up through the twentieth century have debated whether this term refers to Tarquin or Collatine.) The gloss includes information about the Tarquin family tree which reappears later in an abbreviated form. Marsus's notes also underscore the Tarquin lineage, again in a somewhat more concise note. William Painter probably knew these notes, as well as the references to Livy that they contain, since his Lucretia novella in *The Palace of Pleasure* (1575) also gives Collatinus's full name at the outset, thus drawing attention to the family tie. Cooper's *Dictionarium* also underlines themes of kinship: his Lucretia is a "noble woman of Rome, wyfe to Tarquinius Collatinus," who "enterteyned" Sextus Tarquinius "for kinreds sake in hir house."[55]

In light of the marginalia, then, it is not surprising that Shakespeare should have paid extra attention to the incestuous aspect of the rape. He has Tarquin himself mention the kinship:

"Had Collatinus kill'd my son or sire,
Or lain in ambush to betray my life,
Or were he not my dear friend, this desire
Might have excuse to work upon his wife,
As in revenge or quittal of such strife;
But as he is my kinsman, my dear friend,
The shame and fault finds no excuse nor end."
(ll. 232–38)

Lucrece herself describes incest as "that abomination; / An accessary . . . / To all sins past and all that are to come, / From the creation to the general doom" (ll. 921–24). The pollution of the state represented by the incestuous, immoral behavior of the king's son is intensified by association with a crime against the family, " 'gainst law" and "duty" (l. 497). The crime is all the worse in Rome, moreover, where the family was the model of a patriarchal political structure.

Shakespeare's poem also raises the specter of illegitimacy. There is no mention of Lucrece's childbearing capacities, of other children, or of a possible pregnancy in either Livy or Ovid. In *Lucrece*, Tarquin first mentions Lucrece's children, threatening, if she refuses him, to kill her and to put her in bed with a dead slave, thus bringing shame on her issue:

"So thy surviving husband shall remain
The scornful mark of every open eye;
Thy kinsmen hang their heads at this disdain,
Thy issue blurr'd with nameless bastardy."
(ll. 519–22)

The horror of pregnancy as a result of the rape is very real for Lucrece, for whom the solution of suicide seems all the more promising because it will

[54] fol. 72ʳ.
[55] Cooper, *Dictionarium*, "Lucretia."

eliminate such visible testimony to her violation and, as Kahn points out, will avoid confusing the patrilineal line as well.[56] Through her suicide, Lucrece says, "This bastard graff shall never come to growth. / He shall not boast who did thy [i.e., Collatine's] stock pollute, / That thou art doting father of his fruit" (ll. 1062–64). Tarquin's claim that it is for her "children's sake" (l. 533) that she should yield to him nuances Kahn's reading, which emphasizes Lucrece's complicity in patriarchal structures but overlooks Tarquin's exploitation of her concern. Lucrece's reference to the possibility of impregnation works to suggest that she ultimately kills herself for the sake of her progeny—unlike Procne, who rejects maternal instinct and kills her offspring for her sister's sake (l. 633). Yet Lucrece's is a mother love more concerned with the reputation of the "princely name" (l. 599) of the house of Collatine and thus more with its status within the Roman sociopolitical hierarchy than with the intimacy of the nursery.

The "innovative" emphasis in Shakespeare's *Lucrece* on the rape as a crime against the family and the state, one exacerbated by the possibility of illegitimate offspring, testifies to the political crisis just below the text's surface. It is an emphasis that explains the peculiar and yet consistent characterization of Tarquin as a "Roman lord" and as a potentially legitimate authority figure whose primary sin is compromising his political reputation by raping his cousin's wife. The granting to Tarquin of a Roman identity and thus the exaggeration of the impact of his crime on the state can again be understood as the displaced emergence of the latent Philomela option, with its ultimate emphasis on another traditional, albeit oppositional form of political cleansing. The dimensions of the crime become visible, in turn, only against the background of the elided alternative. On the one hand, the sources and the historical record make clear that the Tarquins came to Rome from Etruria, were thus "alien[s] by blood," and could thus be considered illegitimate usurpers of power in the Latin political landscape.[57] Shakespeare's Tarquin, although "fault-full," is nevertheless clearly and consistently identified as a "lord of Rome." It is all the worse, then, that he perverts Roman values by committing the rape. Nowhere in the sources is there evidence of anything other than a morally corrupt Sextus Tarquinius ("*vir iniustis*," Ovid calls him [*Fasti* II, l. 688]). In Shakespeare's version, however, even Lucrece posits an originally and essentially moral Tarquin, to whom she openly appeals in her self-defense:

> In Tarquin's likeness I did entertain thee;
> Hast thou put on his shape to do him shame?
> To all the host of heaven I complain me:
> Thou wrong'st his honor, wound'st his princely name.
> Thou art not what thou seem'st, and if the same,
>     Thou seem'st not what thou art, a god, a king;
>     Kings like gods should govern every thing.
>                                     (ll. 596–602)

While there is an earlier suggestion that Tarquin may have feigned this godlike, kingly identity (he is a "false lord" [l. 50], who hides "base sin in pleats of majesty" [l. 93]), there emerges repeatedly a sense of loss or

---

[56] Kahn, 60–61.
[57] Livy I, 33.

privation, a sense that Tarquin was noble, a good leader and worthy scion of his (Roman) family, who loses this identity in the act of rape: "His honor, his affairs, his friends, his state, / Neglected all, with swift intent he goes / To quench the coal which in his liver glows" (ll. 45–47). Shakespeare's deliberate (mis)identification of Tarquin as a Roman thus exaggerates the impact of his actions on the state; the rape threatens the very definition of Roman civic identity and leadership. The "foul dishonor" to his "household's grave" (l. 198) that the violation represents clearly signifies the collapse of the integrity of a Roman political system organized by familial metaphors. To restore order, Tarquin must be made to "flee the city" (as in the ceremony of the *Regifugium*) in "everlasting banishment" (l. 1855).

It is because Tarquin's personal actions are construed within this political framework that it is "high treason," even "mutiny," for his eyes to betray the sense of values located in his "Roman" heart (ll. 369 and 426). The politico-military organization of the rapist's faculties, in which the "veins" are "[o]bdurate vassals" and his own "beating heart, alarum striking, / Gives the hot charge, and bids them do their liking" (ll. 427–34), emphasizes the fact that Tarquin's very body is inscribed in a public discourse. His crime appears all the worse, then, because it was directed against the political unit of the family and committed by the individual whom Shakespeare identifies with the profile of a king. Ovid suggests the connection in a terse comment: "[*Haec*] *te victoria perdet. / heu quanto regnis nox stetit una tuis*" ("This victory will ruin thee. Alack, how dear a single night did cost thy kingdom!" [*Fasti* II, ll. 811–12]). But Shakespeare's text makes this insight central to the message of Tarquin's *psychomachia* (ll. 127–280), where the choice to remain regal is clearly offered but just as clearly rejected. As a result Shakespeare's Tarquin falls further than his classical predecessors:

> The baser is he, coming from a king,
> To shame his hope with deeds degenerate;
> The mightier man, the mightier is the thing
> That makes him honor'd, or begets him hate;
> For greatest scandal waits on greatest state.
>> The moon being clouded presently is miss'd,
>> But little stars may hide them when they list.
>>> (ll. 1002–8)

In a context in which, as Kahn writes, "the rape of Lucrece . . . parallels the abuse of kingship in Rome,"[58] the sin against the state must be promptly and thoroughly expunged.

Shakespeare's Brutus articulates the solution to the king's pollution of the body politic by gendering the city of Rome as female:

> But kneel with me and help to bear thy part,
> To rouse our Roman gods with invocations,
> That they will suffer these abominations
>> (Since Rome herself in them doth stand disgraced)
>> By our strong arms from forth her fair streets chased.
> (ll. 1830–34)

---

[58] Kahn, 55.

He then interprets the text of Lucrece's suicide as a blood sacrifice, invoking its power to cleanse a feminized city of the offending member:

> Now by the Capitol that we adore,
> And by this chaste blood so unjustly stained,
> By heaven's fair sun that breeds the fat earth's store,
> By all our country rights in Rome maintained,
> And by chaste Lucrece' soul that late complained
> Her wrongs to us, and by this bloody knife,
> We will revenge the death of this true wife.
>
> (ll. 1835–41)[59]

Since Rome cannot "bleed," it is the "bleeding body" of another female that seals the covenant.

The ritualized nature of Brutus's vow, complete with choreographed gestures and imitation of the priest's actions by the representative citizenry surrounding him (ll. 1842–48), reminds us quite clearly, as does the emphasis on the rape as a crime with devastating implications for the stability of the state, of the original context for one of Shakespeare's sources, namely, the calendar of feastdays represented by Ovid's *Fasti* and specifically of the *Regifugium* rites of late February. The Lucretia legend appears in direct connection with the ceremony in *Fasti*, the Philomela story indirectly but still closely associated with it, and for good reason, since both fulfill the formal requirements for atoning for the sin of the king and thus cleansing the city. The choice that Shakespeare's text about female self-sacrifice stages—with its invocation and then rejection of a Renaissance commentary tradition fascinated by the particulars of Bacchic-Dionysian expiatory rituals that depend on and permit women's violence—becomes glaringly obvious behind the heightening of the princely crime in *Lucrece*.

## IV

Other legends survive of women who use well-motivated and politically recognizable forms of violence against corrupt rulers, as in Hecuba's blinding of Polymnestor and her slaughter of his sons. Such tales suggest that a complex tradition of women participating in sacrificial rites of revenge and expiation existed in antiquity and continued to be transmitted in the Renaissance.[60] In this tradition the corruption of the (phallocratic) state

---

[59] Brutus's oath is similar to the one sworn over Caesar's corpse in *Julius Caesar*, 3.2.105–10.

[60] The absence of Hecuba's story from the Troy ekphrasis and from critical treatments of that portion of the poem seems to parallel the pattern of elision of the full Philomela tale in *Lucrece* and in *Lucrece* criticism. A similar story could be told of the "historical" presence of an angry and vengeful Hecuba in the margins of *Lucrece*. Cooper wrote of Hecuba in his entry on Polydorus: "queene Hecuba scratched out the eies of Polymnestor." Euripides's *Hekabe*, in which the vengeance scene is described at length, had been available in multiple editions since 1503, among them Erasmus's Latin translation, published by Froben in 1524. See Kjeld Matthiessen, *Studien zur Textüberlieferung der Hekabe des Euripides* (Heidelberg, 1974), 19–22. Ovid also retells Hecuba's tale in *Metamorphoses* XIII, the text Baldwin explicitly refers to as the "source" for the Troy scene. But Baldwin neglects to address the differences between the silent, victimized Hecuba of Shakespeare's text and the violent Hecuba who appears in the source (*Literary Genetics*, 142–46).

could be expunged at its origin through the murder of the unjust king or his sons, rather than indirectly via the symbolic sacrifice of a woman. The rejection of the Philomela/Procne option in Shakespeare's text and by its critics demonstrates how a text can become implicated in the crafting of an ideological script that excludes women from the work of political renewal if that work is identified with the actions of women like the violent sisters, actions derived from and representative of a tradition of state ritual that empowered the underclass.

The repression of the full story of Philomela can be explained as the result of the ideological pressure of a postclassical gender code organized around preserving political agency for the male. The manifest absence, indeed even dismissal, of this story and of the Bacchic-Dionysian alternative for Lucrece has been reproduced in the invisibility of any alternative to the doubled act of violence against the female body (rape and suicide) in the critical reception of *Lucrece*. This invisibility makes possible feminist readings of the poem that, while quite correctly pointing out that both Roman and early modern women were trapped in positions of victimization by historical and cultural circumstance, at the same time fail to locate an alternative to that position either for earlier women or for modern readers. It also underlies interpretations of the text such as those by Sam Hynes or Richard Levin. Hynes's 1959 article "The Rape of Tarquin" sees the rape of Lucrece as symbolic of "the spiritual quality in Tarquin which his deed violates"; the scene of violence to women is read as a metaphor of the importance for men of preserving their "own moral sense."[61] Levin's reading of *Lucrece* in his 1981 essay similarly elides (perhaps unwittingly) the brutality of rape by excluding any readings of the poem that do not understand the heroine and others like her as "models of [and for] their sex."[62]

Caught in the scholarly crossfire between readings that see no escape from the position of victim and readings that represent victimization as noble, both beginning and advanced readers of *Lucrece* may be forced into a position of critical identification with and reproduction of the Roman matron's suicidal politics as long as the fragments of the Philomela scenario in the poem are left unexamined. The tradition of violent women, present in *Lucrece*'s sources but only partially visible in the text, deserves to be unearthed. Historical readings of these sources such as the present one make it possible to excavate their foundations in order to uncover an image of woman that is "not one"—that is, neither exclusively, naturally, or necessarily victimized nor the unwilling accomplice in the reproduction of patriarchy's political forms.

[61] See Hynes, "The Rape of Tarquin," *SQ* 10 (1959): 451–53, esp. 453.
[62] Levin, 89.

# THE POLITICS OF *LUCRECE**

RICHARD A. LANHAM

*The Rape of Lucrece* has long been considered, when considered at all, only as a warm-up for future dramatic greatness. Tarquin contemplating rape reminds us of Macbeth contemplating murder. Tarquin rape completed reminds us of Othello with "his reputation gone." Lucrece *before* reminds us of Desdemona; *after*, of Isabella. The Troy painting which Lucrece makes into a high-class soap opera introduces moods from *Troilus and Cressida*. Likeness to the Roman plays     setting, flamingly faithful wife, macho warrior-statesmen     occurs everywhere. Lucrece's suicide lets in a whiff of Ophelia, and of Romeo and Juliet, too. The dense cosmic imagery reminds us of *Antony and Cleopatra*. And so on.

I don't want to argue *against* such prolepsis     obviously the poem invites it. But it also invites a *backward* glance, sums up as well as prophesies. If it is a warm-up, it is an *Ovidian* warm-up, complete with compulsive isocolon, chiasmus, polyptoton, and pun. If it provides an alliterative dream land, it does so in a way that recalls earlier alliterative poetry. If it creates a world of allegorical personification run wild, it does so in traditional medieval ways. These layers of imitation lead us directly to the kind of poem *Lucrece* is, a "masterpiece" in the old and literal sense of the word, a declaration of poetic mastery. Shakespeare shows us that he has mastered the traditions, Latin and English, which he fell heir to, and what he can do with them. If we allow such a self-conscious display of poetic power, such a show-off advertisment of oneself, as a legitimate poetic genre     and why not?     *Lucrece* may be both prophecy and recollection and still a poem in its own right, perhaps a masterpiece in

* This paper was delivered at the Shakespeare Association of America Meeting in San Francisco, April, 1979.

338

the usual sense. But whether it is simply a sketchbook of rhetorical and dramatic motifs, or something more than this, an obvious way into the poem starts with its referentiality. On its success as imitation, poetic commentary, art-on-art, will depend both its own poetic status and its value as sketchbook for the plays. I've considered elsewhere the poem as an *Ovidian* imitation. I want now to consider another aspect of its backward and forward gaze, the commentary on Livy and the nature of politics.

Shakespeare takes from Livy two elements, a famous story — Lucrece's rape and suicide — and the historical moment which follows it — the Roman change, in 509 B.C., from a monarchical to a consular form of government. The masterpiece gesture which transforms Livy, changes ′′follows it′′ to ′′follows from it,′′ argues that these two elements are *causally* related, that the rape changes Lucrece in a way which fundamentally changes political reality, allegorizes, as we shall see, the birth of politics. The poem in this sense amounts to an extended *commentary* on Livy. But it is a commentary meant to serve Elizabethan England, a political lesson for England's governing class, more especially perhaps for aristocrats like the poem's dedicatee, the Earl of Southampton. For as one stratum of his multi-generic layering in *Lucrece*, along with the *Ovidian* epyllion, the medieval allegory and alliteration games, and the final top layer of poetic masterpiece, Shakespeare offers a political lesson for princes, a *speculum principis*. How does Shakespeare transform this backward-glancing commentary on Livy into forward-looking political advice? And what kind of advice? The answer lies, obviously, in the poem's two great case-studies of motive, Tarquin and Lucrece.

Lucrece was already, when Shakespeare became involved with her, a well-handled piece of rhetorical baggage. As early as the fifth century, the rhetorian Emporius, under ′′Praeceptum Deliberativae,′′ discusses for two pages how illustrative she was for what today we might call ′′the

decision-making process." (If you've never heard of Em
porius, don't worry. Nobody else has either, apparently. He
exists now simply as a few chapters in Hahn's *Rhetores
Latini Minores* [pp. 572 ff.].) But Tarquin was much less a
common road and Shakespeare develops him into an allegory
of chivalric, rather than *Roman*, political power. He thus
renders the rape an exemplum of chivalric power, a current
political lesson. The exemplum is pointed by a flood of
chivalric images, especially personifications, which attach
military coloration to virtually every act and perception in
the poem. This continuous imagery comes to represent the
way Tarquin sees the world, his physiology of vision.

Let me give you just one example. When Tarquin, trying
to get his courage up, is making an interminable speech to
his torch, he reproaches himself in this way:

O shame to knighthood and to shining arms!
O foul dishonour to my houschold's grave!
O impious act including all foul harms!
A martial man to be soft fancy's slave!
True valour still a true respect should have;
   Then my digression is so vile, so base,
   That it will live engraven in my face.

Yea, though I die, the scandal will survive
And be an eyesore in my golden coat;
Some loathsome dash the herald will contrive
To cipher me how fondly I did dote;
That my posterity, sham'd with the note,
   Shall curse my bones and hold it for no sin
   To wish that I their father had not been.

                     (11. 197-210)

His heraldic coat of arms constitutes both his clothing
and his face    makes his self isomorphic with his social role.
The warrior role ensures that he sees everything in terms of

The wind does not blow out his torch, it "wars" with it (l. 311). Lucrece seems not a woman but a castle to which he lays siege (1. 221). When he first looks at her face (ll. 50 ff.), he sees a battlefield where Virtue and Beauty fight, in three stanzas of preposterous Clevelandism, a "silent war of lilies and of roses." The journey to Lucrece's chamber becomes a military expedition in which, he tells us, "Affection is my captain," and "Desire my pilot is," and the go/no-go decision presents itself as a choice between "a league" and "invasion." The minor delays and mishaps of his midnight journey "he takes for accidental things of trial," the trial being, of course, the Knight's perpetual trial of his own fortitude. When he sees Lucrece, she is like a "map of death." And to describe the final assault, the poem allegorically subdivides Tarquin's limbs and internal organs into the table of organization and equipment standard for a chivalric army. It goes like this:

> Anon his beating heart, alarum striking
> Gives the hot charge and bids them do their liking.
>
> His drumming heart chears up his burning eye,
> His eye commends the leading to his hand,
> His hand, as proud of such a dignity,
> Smoking with pride, march'd on to make his stand
> On her bare breast, the heart of all her land;
>     Whose ranks of blue veins, as his hand did scale,
>     Left their round turrets destitute and pale;
>
> They, must'ring to the quiet cabinet
> Where their dear governess and lady lies,
> Do tell her she is dreadfully best. . .
>
> (ll. 433-444)

(If I had time to discuss how Shakespeare expands Livy, I might cite here Livy's somewhat briefer discussion of this episode: "sinistraque manu mulieris pectore oppresso.") And it goes on this way, his hand a "rude ram," her breast an "ivory wall," her heart "a poor citizen," her body a "sweet city," and a "never-conquered fort." Shakespeare makes here not simply the Ovidian point that *Militiae species amor est*, but that this imagery holds Tarquin prisoner. It constitutes, in fact, his motive for the rape, answers the question the narrator poses when he first introduces Tarquin, but never answers. Why does he do it? In Livy, he falls for her when he sees her. Shakespeare deliberately denies him that glimpse and then after suggesting several possible emulous motives, laconically remarks "But some untimely thought did instigate/His all too timeless speed" (11. 43-44). The "Untimely thought" comes from the imagery and the world view that it stands for. This view permits only a dominance relationship. Politics, war, love, they all amount to the same thing in this world —attack. Tarquin does what he does because that is all anyone in such a world can do, and this includes every allegorical personification in the poem— fight.

Tarquin is not, of course, supposed to direct this aggression toward Lucrece, and in doing so he destroys himself, commits suicide as effectively, and as dramatically, as Lucrece does later. And chivalry with him. Surely this is Shakespeare's point. Such a code will *inevitably* be misapplied, turn against itself. It is all over for Tarquin after the rape because when he besmirches his chivalric escutcheon he besmirches all there is to him. Shakespeare is less editorializing here than simply explaining a fundamental power calculus. Tarquin allegorizes a world in which all human relationships are power relationships and in which the self resides entirely in the social role. The two, Shakespeare argues, make an intrinsically unstable combination. As soon as power is misapplied -as it inevitably will be— the social self, and hence the basis of society, will be destroyed. Such a system of political power contains no cybernetic circuitry, no program to correct actions like the rape. Things can only get worse, the positive feedback grow greater and greater, one misapplication of power call forth another in revenge. The chivalric ideal was a military ideal but not, finally, a governing ideal. Within its world, politics, in our sense of the word —that is, behavior with self-correcting circuits built in— was not possible. What else did the Wars of the Roses teach, or the Hundred Years' War?

That rape in this poem means *power relationship* not *sex* Shakespeare wants so much to point out that he pointedly *evaporates* the rape itself, leaving it to float somewhere between lines 686 and 687. And no sexuality lurks anywhere else in the poem either. Just remember Venus trying to seduce Adonis to convince yourself how completely rape here becomes a metaphor for unlawful power and its effect on our sense of self. Lucrece, although she makes much of being a perfect *wife*, can thus think herself a sexual virgin. In terms of power, that's just what she was.

The poem, after Tarquin leaves, belongs to Lucrece. She undergoes what we must call a comic Fall of Man, or Fall of Person rather, and our attitude toward her falls in the same way. Before Tarquin, Lucrece has been a perfect chivalric woman: her husband's priceless treasure, complacent prize in a Virtuous-Wife contest, Saint of wifely virtue. She may not light our fire so fiercely as Tarquin's, but still our ethical judgment coincides with hers, and with the narrator's dependable moralizing. But immediately after Tarquin drags his post-coital depression off-stage, Lucrece starts to metamorphose from virtuous monument to an hysterical sentimentalist who makes love to grief for the sake of grief. "She wakes her heart by beating on her breast," we're told, and she keeps beating until it ceases to beat back. She does so for an odd reason, though. She assumes from the beginning that she is guilty of what she calls "my cureless crime." But *we* see no guilt. She is, as both her father and her husband hasten to tell her when they make the scene, entirely guiltless. Since we too see no reason for her guilt-feelings, our point of view increasingly diverges from hers until we end up laughing at her.

Just as the poem offers no overt explanation for Tarquin's rape, it offers no explanation for Lucrece's sudden assumption of guilt. In moral terms, her behavior makes no sense, and we have to seek an explanation elsewhere. We begin to find it, I think, in her sense of self. She needs guilt to play her new role. She has played the virtuous wife until now with total satisfaction. Role and self have been isomorphic. The rape undeniably does sully that role. Lucrece then has to go out and find herself a new role, go shopping for a new self. When she does so, she shows herself as imprisoned by chivalric imagery as Tarquin is. The motival structure created by the repertoire of chivalric imagery, allows Tarquin to be only a sacker of cities. And poor Lucrece, what can she be, inevitably, but the city that has been sacked? Despoiler and Despoiled are the only two roles chivalric politics permits. She does not find the way to her new role directly, to be sure, but routes herself through apostrophes to "comfort-killing Night," to the "tell tale Day" that will "quote my loathsome trespass in my looks," to "opportunity," whose "guilt is great," and to "Misshappen Time," each outburst more absurdly irrelevant than the last. She finally gets close to her new role when she concludes that since "her house is sacked," "her mansion batter'd," "her sacred temple spotted," and her "fort blemished" (all this in one stanza, 11. 1170 ff.), the logical thing would be to kill herself. Again, the poem offers no explanation for this absurd *non-sequitur* and we must figure it out for ourselves. Again, too, no *moral* explanation comes forth, only a *dramatic* one. If she kills herself that will somehow authenticate her new role, confirm that she really *is* her new part in the story. But she can't do that without the proper audience, her husband and father, and while waiting for them she finally bethinks herself of the perfect objective correlative for her new role, the Troy painting. She won't be

Helen, of course. She's going to play Troy. Logical enough. If you're going to be *a* sacked city, you might as well be *the* Sacked City.

After a little preliminary sympathizing with Hecuba, she comes to reflect on the duplicity of Sinon. "As Priam him did cherish,/So did I Tarquin; so my Troy did perish." (11. 1546-7). What really *was* her Troy? Obviously the last stage of hysterical sentimentality, to be sure, but beyond that, too, something genuinely epic in scale. Tarquin despoiled her name and unself-conscious sense of self, the role that was not a role. By coming to see herself as Sacked Troy, she has come to be not only a different self but a different *kind* of self, one whose role constantly needs authentication, finaly, as she sees, the authentication of dying. What happens to Lucrece, then, is what happens when self-consciousness enters the human world. We begin to feel guilty about playing a part that we do not feel to be entirely us. The poem's action really is epic enough to justify the allusion of Troy. After the rape the world has changed.

Human motive, no longer entirely ethical, becomes radically colored by drama. Role-playing becomes a motive in itself; often, as with Lucrece, *the* motive. People act the way they do just to *create* reality, not to do anything with it. And they will always get sidetracked from purposive endeavor by this radical need for dramatic imposture, this perpetual temptation to sentimentalize, feel for the fun of feeling. Lest we miss the point, Shakespeare introduces the ludicrous grief-contest between Lucrece's father and her husband:

Then son and father weep with equal strife
Who should weep most, for daughter or for wife.

(11. 1790-91)

Shakespeare does not represent their grief as false, any more than Lucrece's is. He makes a more radical statement.

*All* deep feeling partakes of dramatic pleasure. We can bear it because we enjoy it. Shakespeare's *Lucrece*, like Sterne's *Tristram Shandy*, counsels that you learn how to *bear* grief by learning how to *enjoy* it.

This constitutes our lesson in *Lucrece*, and the explanation for the poem's extraordinarily self-conscious artifice. For is not this what Shakespeare himself is doing? Maybe (it's not crucial to my argument) what all poetry does? Teach us how to banquet off feeling? The poem's self-conscious artifice, its sustained verbal "excess," finds its explanation just here. It intervenes between us and the action of *Lucrece* just as dramatic motive always intervenes between our intended purposes and our actual behavior. In *Lucrece*, style allegorizes behavior. Thus learning to read the poem means coming to terms with this kind of self-conscious dramatic display and seeing its central place in human motivation. And this literary lesson is of course the political lesson of *The Rape of Lucrece*. To learn to enjoy the poem is to learn to enjoy politics. The poem's continued critical depreciation is, I think, no accident. It reflects the intellectual's characteristic hatred of politics. Intellectuals hate politicians instinctively, the way academics hated Lyndon Johnson, even before Vietnam. They crave an issue-dominated politics; they want, that is, no politics at all. Politics teaches that motive is largely dramatic, that posturing is as important as purpose, and that if you fail to see this — and to *enjoy* it — you cannot rule in human affairs. Again, lest we miss the point, Shakespeare brings in Brutus, the Brutus who, having survived the Etruscan kings by posing as an imbecile, after Lucrece has sacked her own city, "throws that shallow habit by/Wherein deep policy did him disguise" (11. 1814-15) and takes command. Brutus seizes the Time and Opportunity which Lucrece can only talk about, and uses her body as a stage prop to set into motion a political revolution and the change from Kings to Consuls.

Thus Shakespeare makes the rape of Lucrece represent the change from a naive sense of self, role and society to a different *kind* of self and society, a radically dramatic one. The change is exactly reflected in the Anglo-Saxon conception of jurisprudence, and I might use jurisprudence as an example of what I mean. In our system of justice, a lawyer can argue for his client, however unsavory, in good conscience because the system defines the truth not, finally, as something that just exists out there in life but as something *finally decided on* in the courtroom. In the Anglo-Saxon conception of justice, what *really happened* is decided by the processes of debate, processes every bit as full of dramatic motive as *The Rape of Lucrece*. Reality comes through histrionic re-enactment, not around it. The whole system of case-law depends on thinking social reality to be something decided by the court. That decision then becomes a referential reality for the next decision about reality, and so on up the ladder.

Shakespeare's allegory, in *The Rape of Lucrece*, argues that the same reality prevails in politics. The change from Kings to Consuls changed not only the form of government but the definition of self and of social reality. This change is an epic subject indeed and Shakespeare clearly recognized it as such. But the old epic form depended on the old monarchic kind of political reality. The Troy story could fit in the new Consular, political reality, only in the oblique, indirect, ironic, infinitely self-conscious form which Shakespeare contrived for it in *The Rape of Lucrece*. And Shakespeare's perception seems to have been borne out. Henceforth, old Epic was possible only, as Milton saw, by reinstating the monarchic definition of social reality. But Shakespeare was moving in the opposite direction, writing an allegorical poem to teach a didactic lesson, if an infinitely tactful one. The monarchic reality, what in this poem appears as the Chivalric reality, was — when you played out its power equations to the end – suicidal. Tarquin is the sacker, Lucrece the sackee and they both kill themselves. Once self-consciousness enters the world, social reality is agreed upon, not inherited forever. And once this is true and you see it, there is no substitute for politics, for hammering out a reality in which issues and dogma often play only a small part and where hypocrisy provides the very instrument through which the self exists. And provides too the cybernetic circuit that any genuinely political power needs, for in a dramatic reality roles can be reconstituted when power abuses them. Hypocrisy can either check such abuse or reconstitute our social reality to fit it, as the case requires. Politics offers a less pure and wholehearted kind of power than chivalry but one which at least can regulate itself. And one which, so rich is our hypocritical resource, can generate a wider range of roles than master and servant.

Shakespeare has reached back to Livy to construct a political lesson for his own time and beyond. Learning how to read *Lucrece* thus constitutes an essential political education. The poem provides a speculum for all of us who come after princes, for a time when political power is finally an agreed-upon theatrical effect rather than a divinely-certified external reality. It is questionable whether Southampton and his friends got the message. And it's questionable, too, whether even we've gotten it yet.

University of California, Los Angeles.

# "THIS HERALDRY IN LUCRECE' FACE"

NANCY J. VICKERS
*French and Italian, Dartmouth*

"But, good lieutenant, is your general wiv'd?"

"Most fortunately: he hath achiev'd a maid
That paragons description and wild fame;
One that excels the quirks of blazoning pens,
And in th' essential vesture of creation
Does tire the ingener." *Othello*, II.i.60—65

The brief exchange between a governor and a lieutenant that figures as epigraph to this essay is curiously about the limits of description. As they stand in the stormy port of the "warlike isle" of Cyprus (1.43) awaiting the "warlike Moor Othello" (1.27), Montano and Cassio digress from appropriately warlike concerns to evoke Othello's exquisite and doomed bride, Desdemona. Cassio comments that she is so beautiful as to be beyond description: her charms surpass all praise that the rhetorician can muster; they cannot effectively be listed ("blazoned") or captured in rhetorical conceits ("quirks"); indeed, even the most ingenious of poets ("the ingener") would exhaust himself in attempting to do them justice.[1] Cassio thus recites not only the strengths of Desdemona but also the weaknesses of a poetic tradition that, from the classics to the Renaissance moderns, had celebrated the beauties of woman's body.

Like Shakespeare's warlike exchange, that tradition was, in large part, the product of men talking to men about women. The canonical legacy of description is a legacy shaped predominantly by the male imagination for the male imagination. This is not, of course, to deny the possibility of the flattery poem; praising a woman to her face might well be intended as a preamble to seduction, as a maneuver for advantage. But in this essay, I will focus on those occasions in which men praise beautiful women among men, on the rhetorical strategies such occasions generate, and finally on some

---

1. The text from *Othello* is cited as in *The Riverside Shakespeare* (1974). Shakespeare's text is here characteristically unstable: for a variant on 1.65, see the Arden edition (1958); for an alternate interpretation of the verb "tire" (as from "attire"), see the Variorum edition (1886).

*Poetics Today*, Vol. 6:1—2 (1985) 171—184

logical consequences of being matter for male oratory. Indeed, I will argue that occasion, rhetoric, and result are all informed by, and thus inscribe, a battle between men that is figuratively fought out on the fields of woman's "celebrated" body.

When, in "The Laugh of the Medusa," Hélène Cixous maintains "that there is such a thing as *marked* writing" she alludes to those literary codes that reinforce "a libidinal and cultural — hence political, typically masculine — economy" and thus constitute "a locus where the repression of women has been perpetuated" (1980:249). "By writing her self," Cixous continues, "woman will return to the body which has been more than confiscated from her, which has been turned into the uncanny stranger on display" (p. 250). This essay scrutinizes one manifestation of that "uncanny stranger" in an attempt to define both the motives for and the strategies of "display"; it examines a telling example of description through comparison — a fundamental tactic of rhetorical invention — by pressuring a single, canonical metaphor as it appears in Shakespeare's narrative poem *Lucrece* (1594).[2] For here the poet transforms the repetition of convention into its subversion; he simultaneously masters and undermines the descriptive mode he employs.

The warlike metaphor in question — the beautiful woman's face is (is like) a shield — informs descriptions of Shakespeare's heroine throughout the poem. By the late sixteenth century, gunpowder had, of course, seriously diminished the defensive usefulness of shields. Less and less the practical gear of the warrior, they remained, however, his emblem; they were used in nostalgically chivalric court entertainments; in pageants, tilts, and tourneys; and in a variety of decorative contexts where they displayed symbolic figurations of gentlemanly pedigree. Aristocratic Elizabethans were fascinated by the "colorful paraphernalia of heraldry" which "tended to proliferate as the practical function of knighthood disappeared" (Ferguson 1960:17; see also Stone 1965:23—27). That interest was related, Lawrence Stone has argued, to the "extreme development" of patriarchal family structure that characterized the period: ". . . it was the male line whose ancestry was traced so diligently by the genealogists and heralds, and in almost all cases via the male line that titles were inherited" (p. 591; cited by Kahn 1976:46). *Lucrece* both reflects and reinforces that fascination; from beginnning to end,

---

2. All quotations from *Lucrece* are as in the Arden edition of *The Poems* (1960) and will be indicated by line number in the text. The criticism on *Lucrece* is too abundant to be outlined. here, but four discussions of the poem have particularly influenced this study: Clark Hulse (1978) on the iconic nature of *Lucrece*; Richard Lanham (1976) on the centrality of rhetoric as motive; Coppélia Kahn (1976) and Catharine R. Stimpson (1980) on the relationship of rape and the politics of patriarchy. I am also indebted to four Dartmouth colleagues whose suggestions have, as always, been invaluable: Kevin Brownlee, Carla Freccero, Marianne Hirsch, and Peter Saccio.

Shakespeare expands his imagistic network by exploiting the highly codified vocabulary of heraldic convention.

The images here at issue are those that constitute the evolving portrait of Lucrece. Since, in this essay, descriptive passages will be discussed in the order in which they appear, a brief synopsis of the poem's action might usefully situate them. *Lucrece* opens as Tarquin, the son of a usurper king, leaves the Roman military encampment outside the city of Ardea. His hasty departure was inspired, the narrator hypothesizes, by Collatine's laudatory description of his wife, Lucrece. A relative, friend, and fellow soldier of Collatine, Tarquin has determined that he must possess his comrade's chaste and beautiful wife. When he arrives at Collatia, Lucrece welcomes him and provides him with lodging. During the night he rapes her and leaves. Lucrece's grief takes the form of a series of laments and a lengthy meditation on a "skilful painting" (l.1367) of the fall of Troy in which she seeks an image sufficient to mirror her suffering. She sends for Collatine, and, when he and his men arrive, she tells them about the rape, swears them to revenge, names the rapist, and commits suicide. Brutus seizes the moment to call for the banishment of Tarquin, and, inspired by the display of Lucrece's body, the Romans consent. Indeed, Roman history recounts their reaction as a revolt: they overthrow the government of Tarquin's father and replace a monarchy with a republic. Collatine and Brutus are its first consuls. Shakespeare's poem is clearly divided by the rape at its center: in its first half, where the extensive descriptions of Lucrece appear, the motives and meditations of the rapist dominate; in the second, the lamentations of the victim.

\*

*Lucrece* opens with a contest. Its initial focus is on "lust-breathed Tarquin" (1.3) as he speeds away from the Roman camp, but within the space of one stanza that focus shifts to present a flashback revealing the origins of his uncontrollable desire:

> Haply that name of "chaste" unhapp'ly set
> This bateless edge on his keen appetite,
> When Collatine unwisely did not let
> To praise the clear unmatched red and white
> Which triumph'd in that sky of his delight;
> > Where mortal stars as bright as heaven's beauties,
> > With pure aspects did him peculiar duties.
>
> For he the night before, in Tarquin's tent
> Unlock'd the treasure of his happy state:
> What priceless wealth the heavens had him lent,
> In the possession of his beauteous mate;
> Reck'ning his fortune at such high proud rate
> > That kings might be espoused to more fame,
> > But king nor peer to such a peerless dame.

\*

> Beauty itself doth of itself persuade
> The eyes of men without an orator;
> What needeth then apologies be made,
> To set forth that which is so singular?
> Or why is Collatine the publisher
>     Of that rich jewel he should keep unknown
>     From thievish ears, because it is his own?
>
> Perchance his boast of Lucrece' sov'reignty
> Suggested this proud issue of a king;
> For by our ears our hearts oft tainted be.
> Perchance that envy of so rich a thing,
> Braving compare, disdainfully did sting
>     His high-pitch'd thoughts, that meaner men should vaunt
>     That golden hap which their superiors want. (11.8—21; 29—42)

Shakespeare locates the ultimate cause of Tarquin's crime, and Lucrece's subsequent suicide, in an evening's entertainment. The prose argument that precedes the poem adds further clarification:[3] "In their discourses after supper everyone commended the virtues of his own wife; among them Collatinus extolled the incomparable chastity of his wife Lucretia." The prose next narrates an event that Shakespeare significantly writes out of the poetry: the competitors ride from Ardea to Rome to test their wives and, with the exception of Lucrece, all are "found dancing and revelling, or in several disports." It is for this reason that "the noblemen yielded Collatinus the victory, and his wife the fame." The argument, in contrast to the poem, then, remains faithful to Shakespeare's two principal sources, Ovid and Livy.

> Young Tarquin entertained his comrades with feast and wine: . . . Each praised his wife: in their eagerness dispute ran high, and every tongue and heart grew hot with deep draughts of wine. Then up and spake the man who from Collatia took his famous name: No need of words! Trust deeds!
>                                    (Ovid, *Fasti*, II.725—726; 731—734)
>
> The young princes for their part passed their idle hours together at dinners and drinking bouts. It chanced, as they were drinking . . . that the subject of wives came up. Every man fell to praising his own wife with enthusiasm, and, as their rivalry grew hot, Collatinus said that there was no need to talk about it, for it was in their power to know . . . how far the rest were excelled by his own Lucretia. (Livy, *From the Founding of the City*, I.lvii.5—7)

Rereading Shakespeare's classical models reveals the radical nature of his transformation of them.[4] The descriptive occasion remains the

3. It should be noted that the authorship of the "Argument" has been questioned. Michael Platt usefully compares the frame provided by the "Argument" to "an action whose beginning is 'kings' and whose end is 'consuls' " (1975:64).
4. Numerous critics have pointed out the discrepancy between the "Argument," in line with the sources, and the poem. For a particularly persuasive description, followed by an interpretation very different from my own, see Battenhouse (1969:7—8); see also Lanham (1976:96) and Bullough (1957:180). On the folly of Collatine's boast see Battenhouse

same — the lighthearted boasting contest — but the all important test, ironically proposed by Collatine in both Ovid and Livy, has been eliminated. In *Lucrece* Collatine becomes a foolish orator, not an enemy of words but their champion. He who stops the descriptive speeches is now blamed for not knowing when to stop: "When Collatine unwisely did not let / To praise. . ." (11.10—11). Moreover, in both Latin subtexts the sight of Lucrece inflames Tarquin's passion; in *Lucrece* he sets off for Collatia without having seen her. The result, then, of this rewriting is a heightened insistence on the power of description, on the dangers inherent in descriptive occasions. Here, Collatine's rhetoric, not Lucrece's behavior, wins over his companions; Collatine's rhetoric, not Lucrece's beauty, prompts Tarquin's departure.

What transpires in Tarquin's tent, then, is an after-dinner conversation during which, in a "pleasant humor" ("Argument"), his warlike guests amuse each other through a contest of epideictic oratory — oratory intended to persuade, in this case, through hyperbolic praise of its female subject.[5] Shakespeare's soldiers present "discourses" ("Argument"), and his narrator characterizes them as orators (1.30). Collatine is labeled a "publisher" of his possession (1.33), his descriptive speech is called a "boast" (1.36), and his rhetoric, thus, is specifically in the mode of "blazon." The verb "to blazon," "to describe in proper heraldic language, to paint or depict in colors, to inscribe with arms . . . in some ornamental way, to describe fitly, to publish vauntingly or boastfully, to proclaim," first appears in English in the sixteenth century.[6] Although French in origin, from *blasonner*, it is related to and reacts upon the earlier English verb "to blaze," "to proclaim as with a trumpet, to publish, to divulge, to make known; and, by extension, to defame or celebrate, to depict, to portray." In France, *blasonner* was so commonly used that it signified little more than "to describe," but its usage was rooted in two specific descriptive traditions, one heraldic and the other poetic. A *blason* was, first, a codified heraldic description of a shield, and, second, a codified poetic description of an object praised or blamed by a rhetorician-poet. The most celebrated examples of French poetic blazon were the *Blasons anatomiques du corps fémenin* (1543), a collective work in which each poem praised a separate part of the female body. The metaphor, "woman's face (or

---

(1969:10—12); Bullough (1957:180); Donaldson (1982:50—51); Kahn (1976:53); Lanham (1976:96); Platt (1975:66); and Stimpson (1980:58—61).

5. Numerous sixteenth-century texts evoke similar descriptive occasions. Frederico Luigini's *Il Libro della bella donna*, for example, concludes a day of hunting and a hearty meal with an after-dinner game in which each hunter forms in words an ideal woman.

6. All references in this essay to sixteenth-century definitions of terms cite the Oxford English Dictionary.

body) is a shield," literalizes this double extension of the term "blazon" — text describing a shield and text describing a body. Collatine's boastful publication of Lucrece's virtue and beauty, then, inscribes itself within a specific mode of rhetorical praise, a mode grounded in and thus generative of metaphors of heraldic display.

A question of purpose imposes itself: to what end does Collatine blazon Lucrece? Why is he not content to enjoy his "treasure" (1.16), his "priceless wealth" (1.17), his "fortune" (1.19), in silence? Within the economy of competition, of course, wealth is not wealth unless flaunted, unless inspiring envy, unless affirming superiority. Tarquin's family has recently assumed power and is thus "espoused to more fame" (1.20), but it is Collatine who owns the "peerless dame" (1.21). In the play of power between Tarquin and Collatine, at least for the privileged duration of this after-dinner sport, Collatine has carried the day — or rather, the evening. Description within a like context clearly serves the describer and not the described. Praise of Lucrece is more precisely praise of Collatine, be it as proud possessor or as proud rhetorician. But more important, Collatine's descriptive gesture entails a risk inherent in the gesture itself: he generates description, he opens Lucrece up for display, *in order to* inspire jealousy; and jealousy, once inspired, may be carried to its logical conclusion — theft. The cause of the rape ("the act of taking anything by force, violent seizure (of goods), robbery, and, after 1481, violation of a woman") is precisely that Collatine's self-serving oratory has fallen on "thievish" rather than passive, but none the less envious, ears. As Catharine Stimpson points out, "men rape what other men possess" (1980:58; see also Kahn 1976:71, n. 19). The rapist is indeed the villain of the piece, but the instigation of this particular villainy is more correctly located along the fine line walked by the boaster. Rape is the price Lucrece pays for having been described.

The matter for Collatine's rhetoric, the argument suggests, is Lucrece's chastity; the poem, however, progressively shifts its reader's perspective. Although virtue is always at issue, it soon competes with beauty for the distinction of being Lucrece's most appreciable quality. Beauty, the narrative voice insists, does not need the embellishments of an orator: "Beauty itself doth of itself persuade" (1.29). It "excels the quirks of blazoning pens," and is sufficiently persuasive "in th' essential vesture of creation" (*Othello*, II.i.63—64). And still, in Tarquin's tent it seems that Collatine called upon all of the conceits of descriptive convention to outdo his comrades at arms. Shakespeare's narrator succinctly re-presents Collatine's speech:

> When Collatine unwisely did not let
> To praise the clear unmatched red and white
> Which triumph'd in that sky of his delight;

> Where mortal stars as bright as heaven's beauties,
> With pure aspects did him peculiar duties. (11.10—14)

Less important than the conventional nature of the language — red and white complexion; face like a clear sky; eyes bright as stars — is the choice of detail that figures in the narrator's description of Collatine's description. The body Collatine praised, we are told, is a partial body, a face; its distinctive features are the colors of its flesh and the brightness of its eyes. Color and brightness define Lucrece. By the time the reader, like Tarquin, first "sees" Lucrece, the stage has been set for a repeat performance of a now familiar rhetorical portrait:

> When at Collatium this false lord [Tarquin] arrived,
> Well was he welcom'd by the Roman dame [Lucrece],
> Within whose face beauty and virtue strived
> Which of them both should underprop her fame.
> When virtue bragg'd, beauty would blush for shame;
>     When beauty boasted blushes, in despite
>     Virtue would stain that o'er with silver white.
>
> But beauty in that white entituled
> From Venus' doves, doth challenge that fair field;
> Then virtue claims from beauty beauty's red,
> Which virtue gave the golden age to gild
> Their silver cheeks, and call'd it then their shield
>     Teaching them thus to use it in the fight,
>     When shame assail'd, the red should fence the white.
>
> This heraldry in Lucrece' face was seen,
> Argu'd by beauty's red and virtue's white;
> Of either colour was the other queen,
> Proving the world's minority their right.
> Yet their ambition makes them still to fight;
>     The sov'reignty of either being so great,
>     That oft they interchange each other's seat.

*

> Now thinks he that her husband's shallow tongue, —
> That niggard prodigal that prais'd her so, —
> In that high task hath done her beauty wrong,
> Which far exceeds his barren skill to show.
> Therefore that praise which Collatine doth owe
>     Enchanted Tarquin answers with surmise,
>     In silent wonder of still-gazing eyes. (11.50—70; 78—84)

In the presence of the "silent war of lilies and of roses" (1.71), in Lucrece's "fair face's field" (1.72), Tarquin stands awestruck, frozen. And yet, his mind is filled with Collatine's evening oratory; before a real, as opposed to a rhetorical, beauty his thoughts tellingly return to an assessment of the paradoxes inherent in Collatine's speech. Tarquin mentally characterizes the previous blazon of Lucrece as an expression of both a prideful need to possess and a foolish propensity to squander. But more important, when the reader "sees" what Tarquin sees, that spectacle proves to be little more than a heraldic amplification of one element of Collatine's description, an amplification operated through the introduction of a conceit that literalizes the rivalry already prefigured in the narrator's synopsis — her "unmatched red and white . . . triumph'd" (11.11—12). Lucrece's face becomes an animated shield colored in alternating red and white. Collatine's original praise was "unwise" to dilate or expand upon that coloration, and yet here her milky complexion and rosy blush fill four stanzas. Shakespeare's narrator, it appears, would outdo Collatine in rhetorical *copia*.

The form the expansion assumes, moreover, makes plain the implications of the heraldic metaphor upon which it depends: here metaphor re-enacts the descriptive scene the narrative has just recounted. What we read in Lucrece's face is the story of a competition that, although between allegorical queens, is entirely cast in the vocabulary of gentlemanly combat: first, beauty and virtue strive for predominance, "virtue bragg'd" (1.54), and "beauty boasted" (1.55); then, moving to territorially figured counterclaims for the right to display the other's colors, they shift ground to a field where the "red should fence the white" (1.63); and, finally, skirmish becomes serious as two ambitious warriors confront each other, "The sov'reignty of either being so great, / That oft they interchange each other's seat" (11.69—70). The warlike tale inscribed in Lucrece's face is, then, the tale of *Lucrece*: it proceeds from a boasting match — as in Tarquin's tent; to a claim for the opponent's "field" and "colors" — as we will see in the rape; to an exchange of sovereignty — as will follow the action of the poem.

Lucrece is fully blazoned only when Tarquin approaches her bed. He draws back the curtain, and his eyes begin "to wink, being blinded with a greater light" (1.375): the beauty of Lucrece "dazzleth" (1.377) her spectator into a state of suspended contemplation. The narrator describes Lucrece's body part by part, metaphorically identifying it with a city or country to be conquered (Kahn 1976:56—57). Although his description introduces new colors, it opens and closes with variations on Collatine's "red and white." Tarquin's initial assault, in the form of a touch, awakens Lucrece, and he tellingly explains his presence by evoking not what he has just seen with his eyes (her hands, her hair, her breasts) but rather what he had previously "seen" with his ears:

> First like a trumpet doth his tongue begin
> To sound a parley to his heartless foe,

> *

> But she with vehement prayers urgeth still
> Under what colour he commits this ill.

> Thus he replies: "The colour in thy face,
> That even for anger makes the lily pale
> And the red rose blush at her own disgrace,
> Shall plead for me and tell my loving tale.
> Under that colour am I come to scale
>   Thy never-conquer'd fort: the fault is thine,
>   For those thine eyes betray thee unto mine.
>
> (11.470–471; 475–483)

Tarquin would persuade Lucrece with flattery. Indeed, taken out of the context of a rape, his language is that conventional to "loving tales": he celebrates her complexion; he represents her as a virtuously unassailable fortress; he praises the irresistible beauty of her eyes.

Tarquin goes on to define two moments in which Lucrece's beauty has acted upon him: first, the moment in which her described beauty destined her to be raped; and second, the moment, after his period of self-examination, in which her perceived beauty reinforced his conviction. It is clear, however, that the determining moment is the first: in *Lucrece* vision is shaped by description. The rapist returns obsessively to the narrator's five-line synopsis of Collatine's winning blazon; he locates motive in that initial fragmentary portrait; he speaks to his victim only of the bright eyes that "charge" and of the red and white that "color" her shield. Although Tarquin assigns responsibility to Lucrece, "the fault is thine" (1.482), his rhetoric of praise reveals its agonistic subtext. Indeed, his descriptive strategies literally repeat those of Collatine: he moves from Lucrece's complexion to her eyes; his final line, "For those thine eyes betray thee unto mine" (1.483), usurps the "peculiar duties" (1.14) of Collatine's conclusion.

In addition, Tarquin's pun on the word "color" — a word that appears more often in *Lucrece* than in any other Shakespearean text — signals the rhetorical origins of the crime. Lucrece asks under what "colour" [pretext] he "commits this ill" (1.476), and he responds that the color in her face will serve as orator to justify his action, that under that color he rapes her. This word play is not new to Tarquin; he has already used it in his self-vindicating soliloquy:

> O how her fear did make her colour rise!
>   First red as roses that on lawn we lay,
>   Then white as lawn, the roses took away.
>
> *
>
> Why hunt I then for colour or excuses?
> All orators are dumb when beauty pleadeth.
>
> (11.257–259; 267–268)

Semantic play here depends upon the sixteenth-century possibilities of the term "color": the "colors" of Lucrece's flesh — the red and white of her face — are indistinguishable from the "colors" of heraldry — the symbolic colors on the shield that is her face — which, in turn, are indistinguishable from the "colors" of Collatine's rhetoric — the embellishing figures that fatally represent that face. Here body, shield, and rhetoric become one.

After the rape, the "heraldry in Lucrece' face" is transformed: she perceives herself as marked or tainted (Kahn 1976:46—47); her face wears "sorrow's livery" (1.1222). When Collatine arrives, he stares "amazedly" at "her sad face" (1.1591), at "her lively colour kill'd with deadly cares" (1.1593), and asks "what spite hath [her] fair colour spent" (1.1600). As the color pours out of Lucrece's body (Price 1945:282), her father and her husband compete for possession of the corpse: "Then one doth call her his, the other his, / Yet neither may possess the claim they lay" (11.1793—1794). Her father laments the loss of that "fair fresh mirror" that revealed in its complexion — its red and white — the blush of his youth: "O from thy cheeks my image thou hast torn" (1.1762). Her husband "bathes the pale fear in his face" — white — (1.1775), in Lucrece's "bleeding stream" — red, now tainted with black — (1.1774), and then, significantly, fails to make rhetoric of his experience:

> The deep vexation of his inward soul
> Hath serv'd a dumb arrest upon his tongue;
> Who, mad that sorrow should his use control
> Or keep him from heart-easing words so long,
> Begins to talk; but through his lips do throng
>     Weak words, so thick come in his poor heart's aid
>     That no man could distinguish what he said. (11.1779—1785)

Shakespeare's poem closes as it opened, as men rhetorically compete with each other over Lucrece's body. Now that the victorious orator has been rendered incomprehensible, another takes over with a call to revenge. The events that begin in a playful rhetoric of praise end in a serious rhetoric of blame. *Lucrece*, then, is clearly "about the rhetoric of display, about the motives of eloquence" (Lanham 1976:82), but what is "displayed" at each privileged moment is the woman's body raped at the poem's center.

*

*Lucrece* is rare among Shakespeare's texts in that it is dedicated: "*Lucrece*: To the Right Honourable Henry Wriothesley, Earl of Southampton and Baron of Titchfield." Its dedicatory epistle predictably expresses devotion to its young dedicatee; it suggests that the poet's "untutored lines" are hardly worthy of their noble patron. Shakespeare's lines, of course, are anything but "untutored"; for *Lucrece* is a masterpiece, that is, a piece "made by an artist to prove he is a master" (Lanham 1976:82). The closing of the London theaters in the early 1590s compelled young playwrights to impose themselves as masters of alternate genres; patrons, like Southampton, had to be courted and rival poets conquered. The glossy rhetorical surface of *Lucrece* — the insistent foregrounding of "display pieces" that has prompted so much critical praise and blame (Bradbook 1952:115) — serves, above all, to demonstrate the prowess of the poet. The representation of the warrior's shield — the shield of Achilles, the shield of Aeneas — figures, of course, among the most canonically valorized tests of any descriptive poet who, in outdoing the painter, would outdo other poets also (Hulse 1978:13).[7] Entered in a contest of skill, Shakespeare's encomium of Lucrece, like Collatine's, stands as a shield, as an artfully constructed sign of identity, as a proof of excellence.

Shakespeare, it must be noted, is not the first to enter such a contest armed with such a metaphor. The rivalry among the original *blasonneurs*, each one displaying *his* part of woman's body, was quite literally fought out: Maurice Scève triumphed by virtue of the superiority of his "Eyebrow." In *Astrophil and Stella* XIII, Astrophil (Sidney) praised Stella (Penelope Rich) by inventing a competition among male gods as to "whose armes the fairest were" (1.2): Cupid won, "for on his crest there lies / *Stella*'s faire haire, her face he makes his shield" (1.10).[8] Combattants offer up blazons — poems or/as shields — for aesthetic judgment: they seek the status of best among poets or best among gentlemen. Far from being simply an "invention fine" (*Astrophil and Stella* I.6), a clever conceit that lavishes old praise in a new way, the heraldic metaphor "woman's face is a shield" emblematizes the conflict that motivates it. Here celebratory conceit inscribes woman's body between rivals: she deflects blows, prevents direct hits, and constitutes the field upon which the battle may be fought. For to describe is, in some senses — as *Lucrece* so eloquently reminds us — to control, to possess, and ultimately, to use to one's own ends.

There is something troubling about the "heraldry in Lucrece' face" — be that the face of Lucrece or of *Lucrece*. As a shining and resistant rhetorical surface,[9] the metaphor "woman's face is a

---

7. Hulse is correct in showing that at one point the face of Tarquin is briefly related to a shield (1978:14). I read that hypothesized image, "Yea, though I die the scandal will survive/And be an eye-sore in my golden coat" (11.204–205) not as a counterpoint to, but rather as determined by the earlier explicit, lengthy identification of Lucrece's face with a shield.

8. Bradbrook states that "the heraldry of Lucrece's face is set forth in a manner derived from" this sonnet (1952:110–111).

9. In an observation that disturbingly underlines the problem, Michael Platt notes that "the reader must penetrate the brilliant, artificial, and enchanting surface of *Lucrece*" (1975:61).

shield" operates a stylized fragmentation and reification of the female body that both transcends the familiar clichés of the battle of the sexes and stops the reader short. The fourteenth-century Italian humanist Coluccio Salutati suggestively associated such dazzling rhetoric with another image of a face on a shield: "Medusa," he wrote, "is artifice, is eloquence" (1951:417; translation mine).[10] He made this identification through the elaboration of a false etymology, through an interpretation of the name of Medusa's father, Forcus, as derived from the Latin *for* ("to speak"). Medusa figures in two contexts as a face on a shield: first, Perseus uses a shield to reflect her image and thus avoid looking at her directly, her mediated image permiting her decapitation; and second, when the battles of Perseus are done, he gives the head of Medusa to Athena who bears it on her aegis, an aegis copied by later warriors. As the face that one carries into battle, that turns men to stone, that curiously converts life into art, the power of the head of the Medusa resides in its ability to stupefy. "Whatever the horror the Medusa represents to the male imagination," writes John Freccero, "it is in some sense a female horror. In mythology, the Medusa is said to be powerless against women, for it was her feminine *beauty* that constituted the mortal threat to her admirers" (1972:7). That threat is, moreover, a threat of forgetting: "Medusa signifies oblivion, which is without doubt rhetoric, which changes the state of mind of a man making him forget previous thoughts" (Salutati 1951:417; translation mine). In the single stanza between the description of Collatine's boast and the vision of Lucrece's face as shield, we return to a Tarquin speeding to Collatia, "His honour, his affairs, his friends, his state, / Neglected all. . ." (11.45—46). Collatine's rhetoric has indeed stupefied the opposition, has functioned as did perfect shields "in such glorious and glittering manner, that they dazzled the eyes of the beholders" (Guillim 1660:6). Here, rhetorical display and heraldic display are of a single purpose; and here, both depend upon the figuration of a woman's face.

The association with the image of the Medusa, a beautiful woman punished with monstrousness for a forbidden sexual encounter — some traditions define it as a rape — introduces a deep ambivalence into the "heraldry in Lucrece' face." The monstrous becomes the other side of the beautiful; the obsessively spoken part — the face — the other side of the obsessively unspoken but violated part — the genitalia (Ferenczi 1927:360; and Freud 1963:105—106 and 174); and fear of the female body is mastered through polarized figurations that can only denigrate or idealize. As the display of an image

10.   I am indebted to Albert Ascoli for bringing Salutati's text to my attention.

becomes so powerful that it triggers a revolution,[11] the motives, strategies, and consequences of description assume alarming proportions. In the "world of harms" (1.28) that is the warlike context of *Lucrece*, the secret of survival is clearly neither to be a shield, nor to see a shield, but to know how to use one.

## REFERENCES

Battenhouse, Roy W., 1969. *Shakespearean Tragedy: Its Art and Its Christian Premises* (Bloomington: Indiana UP).

*Les Blasons anatomiques du corps féminin*, 1543 (Paris: Charles Langelier).

Bradbrook, M.C., 1952. *Shakespeare and Elizabethan Poetry: A Study of His Earlier Work in Relation to the Poetry of the Time* (New York: Oxford UP).

Bullough, Geoffrey, ed., 1957. *Narrative and Dramatic Sources of Shakespeare*, vol. 1 (London: Routledge and Kegan Paul).

Cixous, Hélène, 1980. "The Laugh of the Medusa," trans. Keith Cohen and Paula Cohen, in: Elaine Marks and Isabelle de Courtivron, eds., *New French Feminisms* (Amherst: Univ. of Massachusetts).

Donaldson, Ian, 1982. *The Rapes of Lucretia: A Myth and Its Transformations* (Oxford: Clarendon).

Ferenczi, Sandor, 1927. *Further Contributions to the Theory and Technique of Psychoanalysis*, ed. John Rickman (New York: Boni and Liveright).

Ferguson, Arthur B., 1960. *The Indian Summer of English Chivalry: Studies in the Decline and Transformation of Chivalric Idealism* (Durham: Duke UP).

Freccero, John, 1972. "Medusa: The Letter and the Spirit," *Yearbook of Italian Studies*, 1–18.

Freud, Sigmund, 1963. *Sexuality and the Psychology of Love*, ed. Philip Rieff (New York: Crowell-Collier).

Guillim, John, 1660. *A Display of Heraldrie*, 4th ed. (London: Blome).

Hertz, Neil, 1983. "Medusa's Head: Male Hysteria under Political Pressure," *Representations* 4, 27–54.

Hulse, Clark, 1978, " 'A Piece of Skilful Painting' in Shakespeare's 'Lucrece'," *Shakespeare Survey* 31, 13–22; reprinted in 1981, *Metamorphic Verse: The Elizabethan Minor Epic* (Princeton: Princeton UP).

Kahn, Coppélia, 1976. "The Rape in Shakespeare's *Lucrece*," *Shakespeare Studies* 9, 45–72.

Lanham, Richard A., 1976. *The Motives of Eloquence: Literary Rhetoric in the Renaissance* (New Haven and London: Yale UP).

Livy, 1939. *From the Founding of the City*, trans. B.O. Foster, vol. 1 (London: Heinemann).

Luigini, Frederico, 1554. *Il Libro della bella donna* (Venice: Plinio Pietrasanta).

Ovid, 1931. *Fasti*, trans. James George Frazer (London: Heinemann).

Platt, Michael, 1975. "*The Rape of Lucrece* and the Republic for Which It Stands," *Centennial Review* 19, 59–79.

Price, Hereward T., 1945. "Function of Imagery in *Venus and Adonis*," *Papers of the Michigan Academy of Science, Arts, and Letters* 31, 275–297.

Salutati, Coluccio, 1951. *De Laboribus Herculis*, ed. B.L. Ullman, 2 vols. (Zurich: Thesaurus Mundi).

Shakespeare, William, 1886. *Othello*, ed. Howard Furness (Philadelphia: J.B. Lippincott).

1958 *Othello*, ed. M.R. Ridley (London: Methuen).

1960 *The Poems*, ed. F.T. Prince (London: Methuen).

11. Neil Hertz, turning to a sequence of nineteenth-century texts that use the head of the Medusa as an emblem of revolution, suggestively analyzes "the representation of what would seem to be a political threat as if it were a sexual threat" (Hertz 1983:27).

1974 *Othello*, in: G. Blakemore Evans, ed., *The Riverside Shakespeare* (Boston: Houghton Mifflin) 1198—1248.

Sidney, Sir Philip, 1962. *The Poems of Sir Philip Sidney*, ed. William A. Ringler, Jr. (Oxford: Oxford UP).

Stimpson, Catharine R., 1980. "Shakespeare and the Soil of Rape," in: Carolyn Ruth Swift Lenz, Gayle Greene, and Carol Thomas Neely, eds., *The Woman's Part: Feminist Criticism of Shakespeare* (Urbana, Chicago, London: University of Illinois Press), 56—64.

Stone, Lawrence, 1965. *The Crisis of the Aristocracy 1558—1641* (Oxford: Clarendon).

# Acknowledgments

Burrow, Colin. "Life and Work in Shakespeare's Poems." *Proceedings of the British Academy* 97 (1998): 15–50. Reprinted with the permission of The British Academy.

Bate, Jonathan. "Ovid and the Sonnets; or, Did Shakespeare Feel the Anxiety of Influence?" *Shakespeare Survey* 42 (1989): 65–76. Reprinted with the permission of Cambridge University Press.

Greene, Thomas M. "Pitiful Thrivers: Failed Husbandry in the Sonnets." *Shakespeare and the Question of Theory*, edited by Patricia Parker and Geoffrey Hartman (New York: Methuen, Inc. 1985): 230–44. Reprinted with the permission of Random House UK.

de Grazia, Margreta. "The Scandal of Shakespeare's Sonnets." In *Shakespeare's Sonnets: Critical Essays*, edited by James Schiffer (New York: Garland Publishing, Inc., 1998): 89–112.

McLeod, Randall. "Unemending Shakespeare's Sonnet 111." *Studies in English Literature* 21 (1981): 75–96. Reprinted with the permission of Rice University.

Duncan-Jones, Katherine. "Was the 1609 *Shake-speares Sonnets* Really Unauthorized?" *Review of English Studies*, 2nd Series, 34 (1983): 151–71. Reprinted with the permission of Oxford University Press.

Stallybrass, Peter. "Editing as Cultural Formation: The Sexing of Shakespeare's Sonnets." *Modern Language Quarterly* 54 (1993): 91–103. Reprinted with the permission of *Modern Language Quarterly*.

Fineman, Joel. "Shakespeare's 'Perjur'd Eye.'" *Representations* 7 (1984): 59–86. Reprinted with the permission of the University of California Press.

Dubrow, Heather. "'Incertainties now crown themselves assur'd': The Politics of Plotting Shakespeare's Sonnets." *Shakespeare Quarterly* 47 (1996): 291–305. Reprinted with the permission of the Folger Shakespeare Library.

Dubrow, Heather. "Shakespeare's Undramatic Monologues: Toward a Reading of the Sonnets." *Shakespeare Quarterly* 32 (1981): 55–68. Reprinted with the permission of the Folger Shakespeare Library.

Greene, Thomas M. "Anti-hermeneutics: The Case of Shakespeare's Sonnett 129." In *Poetic Traditions of the English Renaissance*, edited by Maynard Mack and

George deForest Lord (New Haven: Yale University Press, 1982): 143–61. Reprinted with the permission of Yale University Press.

Snow, Edward A. "Loves of Comfort and Despair: A Reading of Shakespeare's Sonnet 138." *English Literary History* 47 (1980): 462–83. Reprintd with the permission of Johns Hopkins University Press.

Empson, William. "The Narrative Poems." In Essays on Shakespeare, edited by David B. Pirie (Cambridge: Cambridge University Press, 1986): 1–28. Reprinted with the permission of Cambridge University Press.

Belsey, Catherine. "Love as Trompe-l'oeil: Taxonomies of Desire in *Venus and Adonis.*" *Shakespeare Quarterly* 46 (1995): 257–76. Reprinted with the permission of the Folger Shakespeare Library.

Maus, Katharine Eisaman. "Taking Tropes Seriously: Language and Violence in Shakespeare's *Rape of Lucrece.*" *Shakespeare Quarterly* 37 (1986): 66–82. Reprinted with the permission of the Folger Shakespeare Library.

Newman, Jane O. "'And Let Mild Women to Him Lose Their Mildness': Philomela, Female Violence, and Shakespeare's *The Rape of Lucrece.*" *Shakespeare Quarterly* 45 (1994): 304–26. Reprinted with the permission of the Folger Shakespeare Library.

Lanham, Richard A. "The Politics of *Lucrece.*" *Hebrew University Studies in Literature* 8 (1980): 66–76. Reprinted with the permission of Magnes Press.

Vickers, Nancy. "'This Heraldry in Lucrece' Face.'" *Poetics Today* 6 (1985): 171–84. Reprinted with the permission of Duke Unviersity Press.